The Glannon Guide to Constitutional Law: Individual Rights and Liberties

The Glannon Guide to Constitutional Law: Individual Rights and Liberties

Learning Constitutional Law Through Multiple-Choice Questions and Analysis

Second Edition

Brannon Padgett Denning
Associate Dean and Professor of Law
Cumberland School of Law
Samford University

Wolters Kluwer
Law & Business

Published by Wolters Kluwer Law & Business in New York.

Wolters Kluwer Law & Business serves customers worldwide with CCH, Aspen Publishers, and Kluwer Law International products. (www.wolterskluwerlb.com)

To contact Customer Service, e-mail customer.service@wolterskluwer.com, call 1-800-234-1660, fax 1-800-901-9075, or mail correspondence to:

Wolters Kluwer Law & Business
Attn: Order Department
PO Box 990
Frederick, MD 21705

Printed in the United States of America.

3 4 5 6 7 8 9 0

ISBN 978-1-4548-4687-1

Library of Congress Cataloging-in-Publication Data

Denning, Brannon P., author.
The Glannon guide to constitutional law : individual rights and liberties : learning constitutional law through multiple-choice questions and analysis / Brannon Padgett Denning, Associate Dean and Professor of Law, Cumberland School of Law, Samford University. — Second edition.
pages cm
Includes bibliographical references and index.
ISBN 978-1-4548-4687-1 (alk. paper)
1. Civil rights—United States—Problems, exercises, etc. I. Title.
KF4750.D46 2015
342.7308′5076—dc23

2014030606

MIX
From responsible sources
FSC® C099992
FSC www.fsc.org

About Wolters Kluwer Law & Business

Wolters Kluwer Law & Business is a leading global provider of intelligent information and digital solutions for legal and business professionals in key specialty areas, and respected educational resources for professors and law students. Wolters Kluwer Law & Business connects legal and business professionals as well as those in the education market with timely, specialized authoritative content and information-enabled solutions to support success through productivity, accuracy and mobility.

Serving customers worldwide, Wolters Kluwer Law & Business products include those under the Aspen Publishers, CCH, Kluwer Law International, Loislaw, ftwilliam.com and MediRegs family of products.

CCH products have been a trusted resource since 1913, and are highly regarded resources for legal, securities, antitrust and trade regulation, government contracting, banking, pension, payroll, employment and labor, and healthcare reimbursement and compliance professionals.

Aspen Publishers products provide essential information to attorneys, business professionals and law students. Written by preeminent authorities, the product line offers analytical and practical information in a range of specialty practice areas from securities law and intellectual property to mergers and acquisitions and pension/benefits. Aspen's trusted legal education resources provide professors and students with high-quality, up-to-date and effective resources for successful instruction and study in all areas of the law.

Kluwer Law International products provide the global business community with reliable international legal information in English. Legal practitioners, corporate counsel and business executives around the world rely on Kluwer Law journals, looseleafs, books, and electronic products for comprehensive information in many areas of international legal practice.

Loislaw is a comprehensive online legal research product providing legal content to law firm practitioners of various specializations. Loislaw provides attorneys with the ability to quickly and efficiently find the necessary legal information they need, when and where they need it, by facilitating access to primary law as well as state-specific law, records, forms and treatises.

ftwilliam.com offers employee benefits professionals the highest quality plan documents (retirement, welfare and non-qualified) and government forms (5500/PBGC, 1099 and IRS) software at highly competitive prices.

MediRegs products provide integrated health care compliance content and software solutions for professionals in healthcare, higher education and life sciences, including professionals in accounting, law and consulting.

Wolters Kluwer Law & Business, a division of Wolters Kluwer, is headquartered in New York. Wolters Kluwer is a market-leading global information services company focused on professionals.

For my parents, Lyn and Wayne

Contents

Acknowledgments

Thanks again to Lynn Churchill for giving me the opportunity to tackle this project, and to Joe Glannon for overcoming his initial skepticism about the feasibility of a Glannon Guide for constitutional law and supporting it enthusiastically. A good deal of this volume — although not nearly enough, as it turned out — was written during a sabbatical taken in the spring of 2010. Thanks to the Cumberland School of Law and to Dean John L. Carroll for making that possible. My students Charlie Nelson, Elizabeth Barclay, and Katie Terry contributed outstanding research assistance. I also appreciate the members of my Spring 2011 Constitutional Law II class who read the work in draft form and made helpful comments and suggestions. Christine Hannan, my editor, was imperturbable in the face of my missed deadlines and pleas for additional time. Thank you, Christine, for your encouragement and unflappability! Rich Fillmore of the Class of 2014 provided invaluable assistance for this second edition.

I owe a particular debt of gratitude to my colleagues who reviewed the manuscript along the way: Randall S. Abate, Florida A & M University College of Law; Joanne C. Brant, Claude W. Pettit College of Law, Ohio Northern University; Aaron H. Caplan, Loyola Law School, Los Angeles; Lyn Entzeroth, the University of Tulsa College of Law; Edward A. Fallone, Marquette University Law School; Doni Gewirtzman, New York Law School; Cheryl Hanna, Vermont Law School; and three anonymous reviewers. Their efforts not only saved me from embarrassing errors, they also provided suggestions that greatly improved the final product. Mike Kent of Atlanta's John Marshall Law School and Marcia McCormick of the St. Louis University School of Law went above and beyond the call of duty reviewing sections of the work. Thanks to you all.

Alli and Gram again deserve my thanks for putting up with me while I wrote this. Both provided immeasurable comfort when I despaired of ever finishing this volume and quelled the rising panic that accompanied missed deadlines. Their support and the kind remarks of students — at Cumberland and elsewhere — about how helpful they found the first edition kept me going. I hope this edition is a worthy sequel.

The second edition includes discussion of all the notable cases from the Court's 2013–2014 term.

The Glannon Guide to Constitutional Law: Individual Rights and Liberties

1

A Very Short Introduction

The purpose of this book is to familiarize the reader with the doctrines that the U.S. Supreme Court uses to enforce provisions of the U.S. Constitution, with study limited to the doctrines most commonly covered in a one- or two-semester law school course in constitutional law. It is not a book about constitutional interpretation or the role of other branches (or, indeed, the role of other parts of the judiciary) in creating and enforcing constitutional law; nor is it a work of constitutional history. It is none of these things because such topics are rarely covered in the typical law school constitutional law class. Such topics are certainly not covered by the Multistate Bar Exam's constitutional law questions. For better or worse, the typical law school course equates "constitutional law" with "the work product of the U.S. Supreme Court," and so does this book.

Because "constitutional law" encompasses so much material, this is the second of two volumes. The first volume, like the first-semester constitutional law class, covers the scope of and limits on the powers of the three branches, as well as other structural topics such as constitutional limits on state power to regulate interstate commerce and separation of powers controversies. This volume covers civil rights and civil liberties, including the First and Fourteenth Amendments; related doctrines, including state action and the scope of congressional enforcement of civil liberties; and judicial protection of private property through the Contracts and Takings Clauses. Both volumes emphasize current doctrine and its application by the Court, though some description of doctrinal evolution will be included where necessary to provide context.

Each volume is meant to function as an "interactive treatise." There will be narrative portions covering particular doctrinal areas and discussing the major cases making up that doctrine. But unlike ordinary hornbooks and treatises, the Glannon Guides—this one included—provide opportunities throughout the narrative to test your comprehension of what you just read through the use of multiple-choice questions and detailed answers that explain not only why one answer is the best one, but also why the other choices are inadequate.

This volume includes different kinds of questions, and the intent is that they get more difficult as you progress through a chapter. Some questions will simply test *comprehension*—did you understand what you just read, and can you correctly identify the black-letter law? Others involve *application*, testing whether you can apply the black-letter law to facts very similar to the situation in the narrative. Still others involve advanced application, and ask you to apply the black-letter law to facts *different* than those discussed in the section. Finally, there are *capstone* questions, which force you to grapple with open questions, new facts, multiple related doctrinal areas, or some combination of these. These capstone questions appear in the final chapter, "Closing Closers." In addition, this volume includes tables and flowcharts explaining doctrines that many students find particularly confusing.

Before discussing how best to use the book, let me preempt any skepticism about the effectiveness of multiple-choice questions in testing comprehension of constitutional law. The skepticism isn't unwarranted; Joe Glannon himself was skeptical about the feasibility of creating a Glannon Guide for constitutional law. If you've had a few constitutional law classes, you might have come away convinced that the subject is too malleable, too indefinite to be tested "objectively." Not to be overly instrumental, but the drafters of the Multistate Bar Exam certainly don't think that constitutional law defies objective assessment! Rank instrumentalism aside, even if constitutional law—with all its open-textured-ness—is "best" assessed using essay exams, I firmly believe that the multiple-choice questions in these two volumes will provide useful, prompt feedback on basic concepts in constitutional law. They furnish a means, not always available in law school, to track your progress and test your comprehension. Multiple-choice questions make it hard to fool yourself: If you choose A and the answer is B, you can't pretend that you *really* chose B.

It should go without saying that this volume is not intended to be a substitute for conscientious class preparation, faithful class attendance, and diligent study. I think that the best use of this Glannon Guide would be as both a periodic self-test and as a pre-exam review. As to the former, you might use it after covering material that you found particularly difficult or confusing (e.g., the power of Congress to enforce the provisions of the Fourteenth Amendment) to test basic comprehension and application. Alternatively, you might use it at the conclusion of a major segment of the course (e.g., freedom of expression). For periodic reviews, I urge you to turn to the Glannon Guide last. Read your casebook, aided perhaps by a hornbook such as Erwin Chemerinsky's *Constitutional Law: Principles and Policies.* Use this volume to review the major points, then test your comprehension with the questions. Reading the same material in several different forms, at different levels of detail, will make it more likely to stick in your mind. The questions can then identify gaps in your understanding and allow you to study more efficiently.

As for end-of-semester review, my intent is for the narrative material to be presented succinctly enough that it could be read through to reinforce important concepts and aid in outlining. In addition, the Closing Closers pose more detailed and difficult questions that will help you identify where your comprehension is weakest.

However you use this Glannon Guide, I sincerely hope that you find it helpful. If you have comments, criticisms, or suggestions, please e-mail me at bpdennin@samford.edu.

2

Judicial Protection of Economic Liberties

A. Overview

The Constitution and the Bill of Rights contain several provisions aimed at protecting what might be described as "economic liberty." This chapter will discuss two important textual provisions: the Contracts Clause of Article I, section 10, and the Takings Clause of the Fifth Amendment. The next chapter will discuss the once and future use of the Due Process Clause of the Fourteenth Amendment as a means of protecting the economic decisions of individuals from being unreasonably regulated by the state. As we shall see in both chapters, however, the Court has generally moved from rather robust enforcement of protections for economic liberty to a regime of relatively deferential review—at least when compared with the Court's enforcement of the First Amendment's guarantee of freedom of speech, for example.

B. The Contracts Clause

1. *Introduction*

Article I, section 10, clause 1 states, "No State shall . . . pass any . . . Law impairing the Obligation of Contracts. . . ." Spurred by the Framers' experiences with Confederation-era state legislatures, which often passed laws favoring debtors over creditors, the so-called Contracts Clause was, prior to the ratification of the Fourteenth Amendment, the primary textual anchor for judicial restrictions on state interference with economic relationships. The Marshall Court invoked the Clause in a number of celebrated cases that established that Court as a guardian of economic liberty.

In *Fletcher v. Peck*, 10 U.S. 87 (1810), the Court invalidated state legislation attempting to undo the infamous sale of the Yazoo lands (comprising present-day Alabama and Mississippi) effected by a notoriously corrupt Georgia legislature. Much of the land had been resold to third parties who were innocent of the underlying fraud; the Court protected those subsequent purchasers' vested rights against the legislative attempt to get the land back. The Court then applied the Clause to *public* contracts in *Dartmouth College v. Woodward*, 17 U.S. 518 (1819), preventing New Hampshire's attempted revocation of the royal charter creating Dartmouth College and conversion of the college into a public institution. And in *Sturges v. Crowninshield*, 17 U.S. 122 (1819), the Court invalidated New York bankruptcy legislation that extinguished debts of bankrupts incurred prior to the passage of the law. (*Ogden v. Saunders*, 25 U.S. 213 (1827), however, upheld new legislation that applied to debts contracted *after* its passage.)

Because nearly every state action potentially disrupts existing contractual relationships, the Court limited the Contracts Clause's scope beginning in the mid-nineteenth century. In *Charles River Bridge v. Warren Bridge*, 36 U.S. 420 (1837), the Court held that the building of a competing free bridge did not violate the rights of a preexisting toll bridge's owners, who were granted a charter first. The Court refused to infer monopoly rights from the original grant. By 1880, the Court was writing that states cannot "bargain away the police power" in its holding that a state could ban lotteries even after previously authorizing a private company to operate one. Stone v. Mississippi, 101 U.S. 814 (1880).

Despite the Court's drawing back some protection, the Clause enjoyed robust enforcement until the New Deal, when the Court upheld state debtor relief legislation of the sort dissenters argued was responsible for the Contracts Clause's inclusion in the Constitution in the first place. Home Building and Loan Association v. Blaisdell, 290 U.S. 398 (1934).

Blaisdell involved a Minnesota mortgage moratorium law that, among other things, lengthened the statutory period in which debtors with mortgages could redeem property that had been foreclosed upon and postponed foreclosure sales. Nothing in the law impaired the amount of indebtedness itself, and the suspension of the other remedies was only temporary. State courts had upheld the law on the ground that desperate times called for desperate measures.

Chief Justice Charles Evans Hughes, however, vociferously denied that the presence or absence of an emergency had any effect whatever on the scope or operation of constitutional rights or powers. While acknowledging that legislation bearing a superficial resemblance to that passed by Minnesota had prompted the Contracts Clause's inclusion in the Constitution, he wrote that the Clause secured obligations of contract that are "impaired by a law which renders them invalid, or releases and extinguishes them" or by "derogat[ing] from substantial contractual rights." *Blaisdell*, 290 U.S. at 431. However, states have control over contractual remedies and "continu[ed] to possess authority to safeguard the vital interest of its people." *Id.* at 434. In other words, states could impair contracts somewhat, but not too much. It could not "destroy the limitation," but neither could "the limitation . . . be construed to destroy" the state's power to aid its citizens. *Id.* at 439.

Noting that the indebtedness was preserved, and that even the remedial modifications were temporary, the Court did not find the restrictions here unreasonable in light of the state's need to "protect the vital interest of the community." The "Contracts Clause," the Court concluded, was "not an absolute and utterly unqualified restriction of the State's protective power." *Id.* at 447.

Since the mid-1930s, the Court has reviewed state regulations that interfere with preexisting private contracts deferentially. Where the *state itself* attempts to wriggle out of its obligations, however, the Court has seemingly announced a more stringent standard of review.

2. *Private contracts*

Recent Supreme Court decisions regarding private contracts have offered the following synthesis of its Contracts Clause jurisprudence since *Blaisdell.* In deciding whether the Clause has been violated, the Court asks whether (1) a law substantially impairs contractual obligations; (2) is motivated by a "significant and legitimate" public purpose "such as the remedying of a broad and general social or economic problem"; and (3) the law or regulation is reasonable and appropriate to the public purpose. *See, e.g.,* Energy Reserves Group, Inc. v. Kansas Power and Light Co., 459 U.S. 400, 411-413 (1983). One commentator observed that "[t]he test is very similar to traditional rational basis review," whereby regulations are constitutional if they pursue a legitimate governmental interest and are rationally related to that interest. Erwin Chemerinsky, Constitutional Law: Principles and Policies 652 (4th ed. 2011).[1]

Energy Reserves Group offers a fairly good example of this test in operation. Kansas Power and Light had agreed to buy gas from Energy Reserves Group (ERG) at the highest price permitted by the government. (At the time, the federal government controlled the price at which natural gas could be sold.) When the sale of gas was deregulated, sellers were permitted to index the price of gas for inflation, which meant that the price that Kansas Power and Light—and in turn its consumers—would have to pay for gas would rise. Kansas responded with an emergency act prohibiting precisely what federal law permitted. ERG sued, alleging a violation of the Contracts Clause.

The Court upheld the state act, applying the three-part test described above. First, it doubted that there was a substantial impairment in ERG's contract. Specifically, the Court noted that the contract was formed against the backdrop of federal and state price regulation and that ERG's expectations had not been substantially impaired by the Kansas law. But assuming they had been to some degree, the Court noted for good measure that "the elimination of unforeseen windfall profits" was a valid public purpose, and that Kansas had "exercised its police power to protect consumers from the escalation of natural gas prices caused by deregulation." *Energy Reserves Group*, 459 U.S. at

---

1. Rational basis review of economic regulations under the Due Process Clause of the Fourteenth Amendment is discussed in Chapter 3.

412, 417. "The State reasonably could find that higher gas prices have caused and will cause hardship among those who use gas heat but must exist on limited fixed incomes." *Id.* at 417. *See also* Exxon Corp. v. Eagerton, 462 U.S. 176 (1983) (upholding state law prohibiting the passing of costs of severance tax increase imposed on oil and gas companies on to purchasers; contractual obligations were only "incidentally" impaired because law was generally applicable and not aimed specifically at contractual obligations).

Only once since *Blaisdell* has the Court invalidated a state law on Contracts Clause grounds. Minnesota passed a law requiring businesses having established pension plans and employees located in the state to make lump-sum payments to those employed for at least ten years if the company either left the state or closed the pension plan. Allied Structural Steel Co. v. Spannaus, 438 U.S. 234 (1978). Under its terms, Allied's pension plan could be terminated for any reason; rights vested and beneficiaries were paid only if the plan was still in place. In the words of the Court, Allied "relied heavily, and reasonably, on [its] legitimate contractual expectation in calculating its annual contributions to the pension fund." *Allied Structural Steel*, 438 U.S. at 246. The law substantially altered that pension contract by imposing additional obligations Allied had not foreseen or planned for. Because the state had not shown that the alteration was necessary to "meet an important general social problem," no presumption in favor of the law was warranted. *Id.* at 247. In dissent, Justice Brennan argued that the Act did not "abrogate or dilute any obligation due a party to a private contract; rather, like all positive social legislation, the Act impose[d] new, additional obligations on a particular class of persons." *Id.* at 251 (Brennan, J., dissenting). He would have upheld the law after analyzing it under the Due Process Clause of the Fourteenth Amendment.

Allied appears to be an anomaly. The more deferential approach of *Energy Reserves Group* seems to be the test. The Court has not expanded *Allied*, and has managed to distinguish it in subsequent cases.

QUESTION 1. **Grin and impair it?** Of the following, which would be most likely to be found a violation of the Contracts Clause?

A. A state law prohibiting coal mining that would cause damage to structures on the surface, as applied to preexisting mineral rights owned by a coal company.

B. A state law requiring mortgage holders to reduce the amount of indebtedness on mortgages whose collateral property has become worth less than the balance of the loan.

C. A state law fixing the price of wholesale gasoline, as applied to a supply contract between fuel wholesalers and gasoline retailers.

D. A state law imposing additional procedural requirements on mortgage holders seeking to foreclose on homes whose owners are in default.

ANALYSIS. *Blaisdell* makes clear that merely adjusting the remedies available to those entering into private contracts will not constitute the sort of "substantial impairment" that the Contracts Clause will police. Therefore, merely imposing additional procedural requirements without affecting the underlying indebtedness will not likely run afoul of the Clause's protections. You can, therefore, eliminate **D**. Imposing limits on the price of gasoline, presumably to benefit consumers and businesses in the state, and to prevent the accumulation of "windfall" profits on the part of sellers, would, after *Energy Reserves Group*, satisfy the current standard of review. As the Court said in that case, protecting consumers from high prices and eliminating unreasonable profits count as valid public purposes. Further, the imposition of price controls impairs contracts only *indirectly*, the Court held, and is not primarily aimed at contracts. Therefore, **C** can be eliminated as well. Between the remaining choices, **A** is reminiscent of the facts in *Keystone Bituminous Coal Association v. DeBenedictis*, 480 U.S. 470 (1987). There the Court concluded that the regulation, which prevented coal companies from doing precisely what they had contracted to do (mine coal), did impair contracts but was a reasonable means to advancing a legitimate public purpose. That leaves **B**, which is the best answer of the four: *Blaisdell* itself specifically distinguished debtor-friendly provisions of its moratorium from a situation in which the state attempted to reduce the amount of indebtedness unilaterally. Of the four, this is the provision likely to face the roughest time in court.

QUESTION 2. Bonus bungle. To express its anger over the bonuses paid out by firms receiving federal aid to stave off collapse, Congress passes a law prohibiting the payment of nonsalary compensation to employees of banks and investment houses for five years, and prohibiting those bonuses from accruing during that five-year period. If challenged in federal court as a violation of the Contracts Clause, the federal law would

A. Be invalidated, because it represents a total abrogation of private contracts.
B. Be upheld, unless the challengers can prove that the law is not reasonably related to a legitimate public purpose.
C. Be invalidated, because it does not benefit the public as a whole.
D. Be upheld, because it is a federal law.

ANALYSIS. Trick question! (Don't you hate those?) The Contracts Clause is a restriction on *states*. There is no federal counterpart, though at one time the Due Process Clause of the Fifth Amendment would have served a similar purpose—to permit courts to inquire into the reasonableness of federal intervention in economic matters. The answer, then, is **D. A** and **B** might be correct on another set of facts. *Blaisdell* did suggest that total abrogation of contractual obligations was beyond state power, even in extreme circumstances, and

B recites the contemporary formulation of the standard of review. *Allied* mentioned something about ensuring that interference with contractual obligations benefited all citizens and not just a select few, but the Court has generally deferred to legislative judgments on those questions.

3. *Public contracts*

When states attempt to abrogate their own contracts, the Court takes a much tougher line, as shown in *United States Trust Co. v. New Jersey*, 431 U.S. 1 (1977), the leading Contracts Clause case involving public contracts. New York and New Jersey issued bonds through the Port Authority and passed a statute in the early 1960s promising *not* to use the bond proceeds to subsidize rail traffic. That statute was later repealed, and bondholders sued. The Court first declared that the statute indeed constituted a contract between the bondholders and the states because "the language and the circumstances evince[d] a legislative intent to create private rights of a contractual nature enforceable against the state. . . ." *United States Trust Co.*, 431 at 17 n. 14. The purpose of the statute was to invoke the security of the Contracts Clause, and as a result, the state was able to receive a benefit—the marketability of the Port Authority bonds. *Id.* at 18. While the Court conceded that states had "broad powers to adopt general regulatory measures" that altered private contracts without having to worry about violating the Contracts Clause, it held that a different situation obtained when states abrogated their *own* obligations. "Impairment may be constitutional," the Court held, but only "if it is reasonable and necessary to serve an important public purpose." *Id.* at 25. Although the extent of impairment is a factor, the impairment need not be total. *Id.* at 26-27.

Applying its test, the Court found that the purposes for repeal—conservation and environmental protection—were important, but the plan to shift drivers to trains to relieve congestion and reduce pollution could have been accomplished by other means than total repeal of the statute. Further, the problems that repeal was aimed at addressing were present when the state made its obligations in the early 1960s. As one commentator noted, "although the Court did not articulate a level of scrutiny, its use of least restrictive alternative analysis and the word 'necessary' seems indicative of strict scrutiny." Chemerinsky, *supra*, at 655.

Contracts Clause Standards of Review at a Glance

Type of Contract	*Standard of Review*
Private	Impairment must (1) be substantial and not incidental, and must serve a (2) significant and legitimate public purpose and (3) be reasonable and appropriate to that public purpose
Public	Impairment must be (1) reasonable and necessary to achieve and (2) important public purposes

QUESTION 3. Green with envy. The State of Ames offered a refundable state tax credit to businesses that retrofitted their buildings and vehicles with green technology designed to reduce emissions, conserve energy, and generally lessen the business's "carbon footprint." Budget shortfalls, however, caused the legislature to repeal the tax credit after many businesses had begun to incur costs, but before they were able to claim the tax credit. Several businesses filed suit, alleging that that the repeal violated the Contracts Clause. Which of the following would be the state's best argument in defense of the repeal?

A. The statute creating the tax credit specified that the legislation created no private contractual rights.
B. A state can unilaterally revoke its promises as a sovereign.
C. The repeal was undertaken for the legitimate purpose of remedying a severe budget shortfall.
D. The repeal was reasonable under the circumstances.

ANALYSIS. One major difference between private and public contracts lies in the Court's articulated standard of review. When impairing *private* contracts, the Court has prescribed a standard of review that is more deferential than when the state is trying to avoid its own contractual obligations. Neither **C** nor **D** is correct, because each recites the wrong standard of review. Where public contracts are impaired, the state must demonstrate that impairment was reasonable and necessary to achieve important public purposes—a standard of review that sounds less deferential. For private contracts, by contrast, the state need only demonstrate that the impairment was substantial and that it was reasonable and appropriate to some significant and legitimate public purpose. (**B**, then, is incorrect, because a state may *not* unilaterally revoke its promises for any reason.) That leaves a threshold question, though: *Did* the state intend to create contractual obligations? In *United States Trust Co.* the Court said that the answer was to be found in "the language and circumstances" of the legislation. If there is evidence disclaiming any intent to create contractual obligations, then the Contracts Clause would not apply. Of the proffered answers, then, **A** is the one that would be most helpful to the state.

C. The Takings Clause of the Fifth Amendment

1. Introduction

Among the guarantees of the Fifth Amendment to the Constitution is that "private property [shall not] be taken for public use, without just compensation."

While the paradigm case the Takings Clause was intended to cover was an exercise of eminent domain by the federal (or state[2]) government, you will see in this section that the Clause covers considerably more than actual physical seizure of real estate by legislative or executive action.

To give a recent example, a plurality of the U.S. Supreme Court recently held that *judicial* action could give rise to a Takings Clause claim. Stop the Beach Renourishment, Inc. v. Florida Department of Environmental Conservation, 560 U.S. 702 (2010). According to the plurality, "States effect a taking if they recharacterize as public property what was previously private property, whether the actor accomplishing the recharacterization is the legislature, executive, or judiciary. . . . If a legislature *or a court* declares that what was once an established right of private property no longer exists, it has taken that property, no less than if the State had physically appropriated it or destroyed its value by regulation." *Stop the Beach Renourishment*, 560 U.S. at 713, 715 (plurality op.). The judicial action in question was a state supreme court ruling holding that a state statute curtailing common law rights of owners whose property fronted the beach did not constitute a taking. The Court agreed that no taking had occurred. *Id.* at 2613.

Other questions include: What "property" is covered by the Clause? What does "for public use" mean? What is "just compensation"? In addition, this section devotes considerable space to the question when governmental actions short of physical occupation—regulation, for example—can constitute a taking.

2. *Property*

The Takings Clause protects more than real estate; it covers personal and even intangible property. *See, e.g.,* Ruckelshaus v. Monsanto Co., 467 U.S. 986 (1984) (holding that trade secrets are property under the Takings Clause); Webb's Fabulous Pharmacies, Inc. v. Beckwith, 449 U.S. 155 (1980) (holding that "property" included interest on money deposited in an interpleader account pending resolution of claims regarding its disposal); Andrus v. Allard, 444 U.S. 51 (1979) (bald and golden eagle feathers and parts); *but see* Bowen v. Gilliard, 483 U.S. 587 (1987) (holding that welfare benefits were not "property" for purposes of the Takings Clause).

3. *The public use requirement*

The Takings Clause requires the payment of just compensation for a taking "for public use." Implicit in the public use requirement is a prohibition on takings for *private* use, even if just compensation *is* paid. As the Supreme Court

2. Though the Bill of Rights originally applied only to the federal government, various provisions—including the Takings Clause—have been "incorporated" through the Due Process Clause of the Fourteenth Amendment and applied to the states. The Takings Clause was actually the first provision of the Bill of Rights to be incorporated. *See* Chicago, Burlington & Quincy R.R. v. Chicago, 166 U.S. 266 (1895). Incorporation is discussed in detail in Chapter 3.

made clear, most recently in *Kelo v. City of New London*, 545 U.S. 469 (2005), however, judicial scrutiny of legislative determinations that a taking is for "public use" is minimal.

Despite the hullabaloo following the *Kelo* decision, the Court has long been deferential to legislatures in this area. It has never insisted that "public use" literally means that the seized land must be used for a road, public park, or railroad that is open to the public. Most disputes over public use involve condemnation of land that is then turned over to private parties for development or redistribution to other private parties. For example, in *Berman v. Parker*, 348 U.S. 26 (1954), the issue was whether, consistent with the public use requirement, so-called blighted areas in Washington, D.C., could be condemned and sold or leased to private interests. The Court held that they could. Redevelopment was a valid public purpose, it stated, adding that "[t]he means of executing the project are for Congress and Congress alone to determine, once the public purpose has been established." *Berman*, 348 U.S. at 33. The political process would curb any abuses, according to the Court.

Public "purpose" emerged as the main inquiry, replacing the textual requirement of public "use." *Hawaii Housing Authority v. Midkiff*, 467 U.S. 229 (1984), for example, involved Hawaii's plan to break up what it deemed a concentration of land ownership by condemning land and offering it in fee simple to Hawaii residents who were leasing that land "in order to reduce the concentration of ownership of fees simple in the State." *Midkiff*, 467 U.S. at 232. Relying on *Berman*, the Court held that "where the exercise of the eminent domain power is rationally related to a conceivable public purpose, the Court has never held a compensable taking to be proscribed by the Public Use Clause." *Id.* at 241. The Court then found that remedying failures in land markets caused by concentrations of land ownership was a legitimate public purpose and that condemnation and redistribution "is a comprehensive and rational approach to identifying and correcting market failure." *Id.* at 247.

Given *Midkiff*, the result in *Kelo* was not surprising. New London, Connecticut, wished to exercise eminent domain on behalf of private developers hoping to redevelop a waterfront area to accompany a Pfizer research facility. The neighborhood that was the target of New London's efforts was to be converted into a mixed-use district that would include hotels, shopping, and restaurants. Homeowners sued, claiming that taking land for private redevelopment was not "public use." *Kelo*, 545 U.S. at 469.

In upholding the condemnation of the land, the Court conceded that New London could neither "take petitioners' land for the purpose of conferring a benefit on a particular private party" nor "take property under the mere pretext of a public purpose, when its actual purpose was to bestow a private benefit." *Id.* at 477-478. But the Court refused to adopt a bright-line rule that "development takings," that is, taking land and then turning it over to private developers, could never satisfy the Takings Clause's public use requirement.

The City's "determination that the area was sufficiently distressed to justify a program of economic rejuvenation," the Court wrote, was "entitled to its deference." *Id.* at 469. It found the comprehensive redevelopment plan "unquestionably serves a public purpose." *Id.* at 470.[3]

QUESTION 4. Can't forget the Motor City. Eager to accommodate CarCo, a large employer that plans to build an enormous assembly plant, Motor City condemns an entire neighborhood, displacing its residents, and turns the property over to CarCo to build its facility. In its decision to condemn the neighborhood, Motor City found that it is "blighted" and that redevelopment will bring jobs and other economic benefits—not only to the soon-to-be former residents of the neighborhood, but to all residents of Motor City. David, a resident, sues to stop the condemnation, claiming that it is not for public use. After *Kelo*, a federal district court would likely:

A. Rule for David, because the condemnation is for the benefit of the developers.
B. Rule for David, because the benefits of the plant will not be shared by the public.
C. Rule for Motor City, because questions of public use are nonjusticiable.
D. Rule for Motor City, because economic redevelopment is a permissible public purpose.

ANALYSIS. *Kelo* declined to adopt a bright-line rule excluding development takings from the definition of public use. Therefore, **A** is incorrect. But even though the review of public use is deferential, it is not nonexistent; therefore, **C** is not correct. The *Kelo* Court also refused to consider the likelihood of the promised benefits ever materializing or whether they would be shared broadly. That rules out **B**. Therefore, **D** is the best choice, and it mirrors the Court's deferential treatment. Economic redevelopment is an accepted public purpose, and redeveloping a neighborhood to facilitate that redevelopment is a rational means of achieving it. According to the Court, that is all that need be proven.

QUESTION 5. Executive privilege.[4] Assume that as part of CarCo's agreement to build the new assembly plant in Question 4, Motor City agrees to condemn a house in another neighborhood and transfer it to the new CEO of CarCo, who is moving to Motor City from overseas. Motor City justifies the condemnation on the grounds that, but for the condemnation of the house, which the CarCo CEO found particularly

3. One of the dissenters in *Kelo* was Justice Sandra Day O'Connor, who wrote the majority opinion in *Midkiff.*
4. This question is based on a hypothetical in Calvin Massey, American Constitutional Law: Powers and Liberties 612 (4th ed. 2013).

desirable, the CEO might have located the assembly plant elsewhere. Is the condemnation and transfer of the house to the CarCo CEO permissible?

A. Yes, because of the expected economic benefit to Motor City.
B. No, because it is a taking for the benefit of CarCo's CEO.
C. No, unless the house was blighted.
D. Yes, because the condemnation was a rational means of achieving economic development.

ANALYSIS. Justice Stevens's opinion in *Kelo* stated that public use would not be satisfied in the case of a seizure of property for private benefit or a seizure of property on the pretext of public benefit when the actual purpose was to benefit a private party. Despite the veneer of public purpose—the plant might not be built if the CEO didn't get the house he wanted—this looks like a seizure on the mere pretext of public purpose in order to benefit a private party. On the facts given, therefore, **B** is the best answer. **D** is the correct standard of review, but only if you've established that there is nothing fishy going on regarding the transfer. Property does not have to be blighted to be the subject of eminent domain, so **C** is beside the point. Additionally, **C** is highly unlikely as a factual matter, given the home's desirability to the CEO. Few CEOs would find truly "blighted" property to be "particularly desirable." Although courts will defer to legislative determinations of blight, these facts suggest that any such determination would also be mere pretext for benefiting a private party. **A** is not the best answer, because even though there *might* be some benefit—Motor City gets the new assembly plant—that does not mean that Motor City can simply take property from one person and give it to another when the transfer really benefits only CarCo's CEO. The connection between the possible economic benefits, in other words, and the transfer of the property is even more attenuated than, say, the benefits that would have accrued from the condemnation of the neighborhood for the plant in Question 4.

QUESTION 6. Pharma karma. Pharma, a pharmaceutical company, has produced a vaccine, which it patented, for a wide variety of virulent flu strains. An epidemic, however, overwhelms its manufacturing capacity and it cannot keep up with demand. Alarmed by the rising number of deaths, the federal government encourages Pharma to license manufacture of the drug to rival RxA. When Pharma refuses, the federal government orders Pharma to turn over samples of the vaccine, along with instructions for its production. The federal government plans to give Pharma's rivals access in order to speed production. The federal government also plans to use fees it collects from other pharmaceutical companies to compensate Pharma. Pharma alleges that the government has not taken its vaccine for public use and files suit in federal district court. A judge would likely rule:

A. For the government, because the Takings Clause applies only to real property.
B. For Pharma, unless the government produces the vaccine itself.
C. For Pharma, unless the vaccine is distributed to everyone for free.
D. For the government, because its taking is rationally related to a legitimate public purpose.

ANALYSIS. "Property" includes intangible intellectual property, trade secrets, and the like. **A** is therefore incorrect. Further, as *Berman*, *Midkiff*, and *Kelo* demonstrate, the government itself need not retain control over the property taken, nor need the property be distributed to the public broadly or for free (the leaseholds in *Midkiff*, for example, weren't *given* to the lessees). So neither **B** nor **C** is right. That leaves **D**, the correct statement of the standard of review, which the program meets.

4. *Physical takings*

Any actual, permanent physical occupation of land by the government is deemed a taking, no matter how slight the intrusion. New York, for example, required landlords to permit cable television companies access to install cable facilities. Despite the fact that the cable box occupied one cubic foot of space, the Court held there to have been a compensable taking. Loretto v. Teleprompter Manhattan CATV Corp., 458 U.S. 419 (1982). The same rule applies to personal property as well. *See* Webb's Fabulous Pharmacies v. Beckwith, 449 U.S. 155 (1980) (interest on interpleader accounts). A unanimous Court, moreover, recently held that even temporary takings, in the form of periodic, government-induced flooding, can also be a compensable taking. Arkansas Game & Fish Comm'n v. United States, 133 S. Ct. 511, 519 (2012).

The Court has also recognized what could be termed "constructive physical occupation" in which government action is tantamount to physical occupation. In *United States v. Causby*, 328 U.S. 256 (1946), for example, the frequency and altitude of overflights from a nearby air base rendered the plaintiff's land useless for any purpose and, the Court held, was tantamount to physical occupation. It was, therefore, a compensable taking.

5. *Regulatory takings*

Causby provides a nice segue into a rather confusing area of takings law: the extent to which a law or regulation will be deemed to constitute a compensable taking. There are numerous governmental actions that "take" property but are not Fifth Amendment takings—taxes, for example, or regulations that prevent one from, say, using one's backyard as a hazardous waste dump. As in *Causby*, however, the limitations on the use of one's property can, at some point, become functionally indistinguishable from confiscation or physical occupation. It has been the Court's task to locate that point where the costs of those limitations shift and must be borne by the government.

The Court's regulatory takings doctrine began with an opinion by Justice Holmes in *Pennsylvania Coal Co. v. Mahon*, 260 U.S. 393 (1922), in which the Court held that a Pennsylvania law, requiring holders of mineral rights to mine coal to leave enough coal in the ground to provide support to structures located on the surface, constituted a compensable taking. While admitting that "[g]overnment hardly could go on if to some extent values incident to property could not be diminished without paying for every such change in the general law," when diminution "reach[es] a certain magnitude, in most if not in all cases there must be an exercise of eminent domain and compensation to sustain the act." *Mahon*, 260 U.S. at 413. The act here went "too far," in the Court's opinion, because the right to mine coal meant the right to extract it and sell it, and if one could not do that because of a regulation, it was tantamount to the government's depriving the company of ownership.

By contrast, in *Miller v. Schoene*, 276 U.S. 272 (1928), the Court held that an order to cut down cedar trees infected with a fungus that threatened nearby apple orchards was *not* a taking. The Court held that the state had a choice to make between the aesthetic and commercial value of the cedar and the economic value of the apple orchards. It chose the orchards. "When forced to such a choice the state does not exceed its constitutional powers," the Court wrote, "by deciding upon the destruction of one class of property in order to save another which, in the judgment of the legislature, is of greater value to the public." *Miller*, 276 U.S. at 279.

Neither *Mahon* nor *Miller* was helpful in predicting when a regulation would be upheld as merely an exercise of the police power or would, in Justice Holmes's words, go "too far" and become a compensable taking. In fact, the entire police power/takings dichotomy is unhelpful, because regulatory takings typically arise in the context of state and local governments exercising their police powers; the question is whether those powers have been exercised in a way that constitutes a taking. With one exception, the Court has eschewed bright lines, favoring an ad hoc approach that balances a number of factors. The rest of the section will discuss both the Court's "per se" rules and the balancing approach. It concludes with a discussion of "conditional takings," in which the government seeks to regulate property as a condition for granting permission to the owner to use her other property in some way.

(a) The "per se" approach The easiest regulatory takings cases involve laws or regulations that result in total destruction of the value of property. These, like actual or constructive physical occupation, are deemed *per se* takings; the only question remaining is how much the owner should be compensated. Lucas v. South Carolina Coastal Commission, 505 U.S. 1003 (1992). In *Lucas* the plaintiff had paid nearly one million dollars for two lots on the Isle of Palms in South Carolina. The state then passed a law prohibiting Lucas from putting any habitable structures on either lot, in an effort to preserve barrier islands and prevent erosion. Where "the State seeks to sustain regulation that deprives land of all economically beneficial use, we think it may resist compensation only if the logically antecedent inquiry into the nature of the owner's estate shows that the proscribed use interests were not part of his title to begin with." 505 U.S. at 1027 (footnote omitted). This limitation could exist either as part of the original conveyance or in "background principles of nuisance and property law that prohibit the uses he now intends in the circumstances in which the property is presently found." *Id.* at 1031.

QUESTION 7. Take or fake? Which of the following would most likely be found to be a compensable taking?

A. Changes in zoning ordinances that permit only single-family dwellings to be built on property originally purchased to develop multifamily structures.
B. An order that a nuclear power plant remove buildings built on a previously unknown fault.
C. Passage of a law making gambling illegal in a state where it was once permitted, as applied to an owner of numerous now-unlawful casinos.
D. An order requiring owners to allow workers access to property to install wireless routers for a new citywide wi-fi service.

ANALYSIS. Nearly all governmental regulations interfere with property rights to some degree. While Professor Richard Epstein's 1985 book *Takings* recommended treating *all* such regulations as potentially compensable under the Takings Clause, the Court has not followed suit. The Court has, however, chosen to treat those regulations that call for *actual occupation of land*, or that are tantamount to physical occupation, as presumptive takings. If the government completely deprives you of the value of your property (*Lucas*) or makes it impossible for you to use your property because of the government's actions (*Causby*), then you will have a better case than if the government simply limits or regulates particular uses of your property. In the four examples here, most of the regulations simply limit particular uses without depriving the owners of all economically beneficial uses of their land. The landowner in **A**, for example, can still develop single-family homes and sell them. *See, e.g.*, Dolan v. City of Tigard, 512 U.S. 374, 384-385 (1994). The nuclear power plant owner in **B** is subject to a police powers regulation designed to prevent a catastrophic accident; the owner has to incur costs in order to comply, but that does not convert the regulation into a taking. Similarly, although the owner of the now-illegal casinos in **C** can't use his property for gambling, that property wasn't confiscated and presumably still has some economic use. Only in the case of

D, in which the government has actually physically invaded the owner's property, would there be a taking. *Any* permanent physical invasion, no matter how small, is compensable.

(b) The balancing approach For other alleged regulatory takings, the Court has employed what it terms a "balancing approach" that considers a number of factors and is sometimes referred to as "*Penn Central* balancing," after *Penn Central Transportation Co. v. New York City*, 438 U.S. 104 (1978), in which it was first set forth. At issue in *Penn Central* was the refusal of New York's landmark preservation committee to allow the owners of Penn Central Station to build a 44-story building on top of the station, which had been designated a landmark. The owners filed suit, claiming that the regulation had taken their property and that the city ought to compensate them as a result. The Court held that such claims ought to be decided through the use of "ad hoc, factual inquiries" that considered, among other things,

> [t]he economic impact of the regulation on the claimant and, particularly, the extent to which the regulation has interfered with district investment-backed expectations. . . . [Also important] is the character of the governmental action. A "taking" may be more readily found when the interference with property can be characterized as a physical invasion by government than when interference arises from some public program adjusting the benefits and burdens of economic life to promote the common good.

Penn Central Transportation Co., 438 U.S. at 124.

Declining to find a compensable taking, the Court noted that the shareholders still had the use of Penn Station as a railway terminal. It also noted that the owners had transferable development rights that could be applied to other property it owned contiguous to the station. These factors worked to mitigate the financial burden imposed on the company by the landmark committee. Although the landmark preservation ordinance deprived the owners of all use of their air rights, the Court concluded that the ordinance's economic impact must be measured against the parcel as a whole, and not just against the property rights most directly affected. With the use of such measurement, the foregoing factors worked to mitigate the financial burden imposed on the company by the landmark committee.

The question facing the Court in *Tahoe-Sierra Preservation Council, Inc. v. Tahoe Regional Planning Agency*, 535 U.S. 302 (2002), was which of the two tests—the per se approach or balancing—applied to a temporary development moratorium. The moratorium was declared, according to the Court, while a comprehensive land use plan was being developed to address pollution in Lake Tahoe itself. Invoking the "parcel as a whole" doctrine, the Court declined to equate "a permanent deprivation of the owner's use of the entire area" with "a temporary prohibition on economic use, because the property will recover value as soon as the prohibition is lifted." *Tahoe-Sierra Preservation Council*, 535 U.S. at 332. Because a fee simple estate potentially lasts forever, the Court indicated that the "parcel as a whole" doctrine prevented it from focusing only on the rights temporarily affected by the moratorium. While the Court was careful to say that, under certain circumstances, temporary restrictions *might* be takings, it declined to apply the per se rule of *Lucas* as opposed to *Penn Central*'s ad hoc balancing test.

(c) Conditional takings One regulatory takings question has given the Court particular difficulty: To what extent can government condition development on what might otherwise be considered a taking? For example, while requiring private landowners to grant a public easement across beach property would be a taking, can government condition the grant of a permit to build a new structure on the owner's agreeing to open the property to public access? These quid pro quo regulations are known as "conditional takings."

In general, the Court has been relatively hostile to conditional takings, though it has not been able to articulate precisely why, or how conditional takings should be analyzed. In *Nollan v. California Coastal Commission*, 483 U.S. 825 (1987), the Court held that California could not condition approval to build a new structure on beachfront property on the owner's grant of an easement across his beach (basically, the hypothetical in the preceding paragraph). Starting with the assumption that the government possessed an important interest that would allow it to deny the new structure altogether, the Court found that the requirement of an easement "[u]tterly fail[ed] to further the end advanced as the justification for the [building] prohibition." *Nollan*, 483 U.S. at 837. The lack of what the Court deemed an "essential nexus" between "the condition and the original purpose of the building restriction converts that purpose to something other than it was. The purpose then, becomes . . . the obtaining of an easement to serve some valid governmental purpose, but without payment of compensation." *Id.* Unless, the Court concluded, "the permit condition serves the same governmental purpose as the development ban, the building restriction is not a valid regulation of land use. . . ." *Id.*

Even where the essential nexus is present, the Court has required that the condition be *roughly proportional* to the purpose of the restriction. The City of Tigard, Oregon, wished to condition a building permit on donation of 10 percent of the owner's property to enhance flood control—the property the owner wished to expand was in a floodplain—and for the construction of a public pathway for pedestrians and bicyclists. Dolan v. City of Tigard, 512 U.S. 374 (1994). As the Court put it, where the state attempts to condition development on the dedication of private land to some public purpose, it must demonstrate (1) the essential nexus between the "legitimate state interest" and the condition and (2) that the "degree of connection between the exactions and the projected impact of the proposed development" is proportional. *Dolan*, 512 U.S. at 386.

Applying its test, the Court concluded that the city satisfied the nexus requirement. The city wished to prevent flooding along a creek and limit development within the creek's 100-year floodplain. It also wished to reduce automobile congestion by providing greenways for bikes and pedestrians. The owner wanted to expand the store and pave a gravel parking lot, which would have increased runoff and vehicular traffic to the area. The Court found, first, that the city's interests were legitimate and that there was a nexus between its conditions and those interests.

As to the second requirement, rough proportionality, the Court wrote, "No precise mathematical calculation is required, but the city must make some sort of individualized determination that the required dedication is related both in nature and extent to the impact of the proposed development." *Id.* at 391. Here, the city had not indicated why a *public* greenway was necessary and didn't demonstrate that the additional trips generated by the expansion would justify the city's request. *Id.* at 395.

In *Koontz v. St. Johns River Water Management District*, 133 S. Ct. 2586 (2013), a divided Court extended *Nollan* and *Dolan* to situations in which a government has rejected a property owner's permit because of a refusal to accede to proposed conditions. *Id.* at 2595 ("The principles that undergird our decisions in *Nollan* and *Dolan* do not change depending on whether the government *approves* a permit on the condition that the applicant turn over property or *denies* a permit because the applicant refuses to do so."). It cautioned though that where "the permit is denied and the condition is never imposed, nothing has been taken." *Id.* at 2597. The Court also held that monetary exactions—conditioning permits on the payment of money, in this case on other government-owned land—"must satisfy the nexus and rough proportionality requirements of *Nollan* and *Dolan*." *Id.* at 2599. The Court stressed that the petitioner was not asking for a ruling that *any* requirement that someone expend money trigger a regulatory taking, requiring an application of the *Penn Central* balancing test. *Id.* at 2600. Rather, "petitioner's claim rests on the more limited proposition that when the government commands the relinquishment of funds linked to a specific, identifiable property interest such as a bank account or parcel of real property, a '*per se* [takings] approach' is the proper mode of analysis." *Id.* The dissent argued that extending *Nollan* and *Dolan* to monetary exactions would ensnare the Court in difficult line-drawing exercises and risked invalidating regular taxes not understood to constitute compensable takings. *Id.* at 2607 (Kagan, J., dissenting).

QUESTION 8. **Get back.** A developer wishes to build a neighborhood of single-family dwellings on land that she owns. Prior to groundbreaking, however, the city passes an ordinance requiring that houses built on the developer's property be set back from the street by an amount that will result in the developer being able to put only half as many houses on her land as previously planned. Of the following, which would be the best reason for a court to hold that the ordinance is not a compensable taking, if it were challenged in court?

A. It is a valid exercise of the police power.
B. The ordinance is rationally related to a legitimate governmental interest.
C. It hasn't deprived the developer of all value.
D. Zoning laws can never be compensable takings.

ANALYSIS. The government has not actually seized the developer's property, but has restricted its use with an ordinance. According to *Lucas*, all economically viable use must be destroyed by a regulation before it will be considered a per se taking; moreover, there must exist no background rules of nuisance or property law to which her ownership was subject. The ordinance is an exercise of the police power, which is, like the power of eminent domain, an aspect of sovereignty. But the fact that the government regulates land through the police power or seizes land through eminent domain does not insulate it from a Takings Clause challenge. Therefore, **A** is not correct. Nor is **D**. Zoning laws often represent significant restrictions on land use and, if they satisfy the criteria set forth in *Lucas*, could certainly effect a taking. **B** simply states the wrong standard of review; the so-called rational basis test, as you will see in Chapter 3, would apply to a *due process* challenge to the zoning ordinance. That leaves **C**, which is the correct answer. As long as the land retains some economically beneficial use, there will not be a per se taking. The more deferential balancing of *Penn Central* will apply.

QUESTION 9. How dry I am. The State of Ames passes a statute prohibiting the manufacture and sale of alcohol in the state. The law forces a brewer to shut down his brewery. Must Ames pay the brewer for the value of his now-idle property?

A. Yes, because the regulation is tantamount to a physical invasion of the brewer's property.
B. No, if the value of prohibition to the state is greater, in the state's judgment, than the value of the brewery.
C. Yes, because Ames has destroyed the value of the brewer's property.
D. A and C.

ANALYSIS. The brewer can no longer use his property as a brewery as a result of the law. But note that nothing prevents his property from being used at all, nor has the entire value of his property been destroyed by Ames's actions. Therefore, **A** is incorrect because the law is *not* tantamount to a physical invasion. Nor is **C** the correct answer; again, although his property can't be used as a brewery, the law hasn't destroyed all of its economically viable use. And if neither **A** nor **C** is correct, then **D** is incorrect as well. That leaves **B**, which is the best answer. As in *Penn Central*, the state has made a judgment between two competing (and conflicting) aims by valuing the prohibition over the ability of the brewer to use his property to produce alcohol. Accordingly, the brewer is not entitled to compensation.

QUESTION 10. School's in. Assume that in exchange for permission to build her single-family-residence neighborhood, the developer from Question 8 is asked by the city to deed to the city a percentage of the total acreage for construction of a new elementary school. The city found that the houses are marketed to young families with children and that the existing schools in the area are currently near capacity. A new school will be needed to educate the number of children the new subdivision is expected to attract. Which of the following statements would be true about the city's condition?

A. The city must demonstrate a legitimate governmental interest.
B. There must be an essential nexus between the condition and the interest.
C. There must be some individualized determination by the city that the dedication of the land to the school is roughly proportional to the impact of the neighborhood.
D. All of the above.

ANALYSIS. Under *Nollan* and *Dolan*, the government's imposition of a land use condition requiring the dedication of private land to public use must be supported by the demonstration of an "essential nexus" between the condition and a legitimate state interest *and* a rough proportionality between the exaction and the projected impact of the development. Further, to support the rough proportionality, the Court requires some kind of individualized determination about the connection and the proposed impact. In other words, the Court would not simply take the government's word for it. The correct answer, then, is **D**. Given the facts in the question, moreover, the city would likely prevail. Easing overcrowding in schools is a legitimate interest. There is a clear nexus between the condition (that land be given for a school) and the interest (easing overcrowding). Further, there is a rough proportionality here, supported by individualized assessments. The city has determined that the houses will likely go to families that have small children who will attend elementary school, which will cause overcrowding in the near-capacity schools currently in the area.

QUESTION 11. Sudden impact. In exchange for a special-use permit required by a local ordinance to construct a retail store in excess of 100,000 square feet, a city requires a large retailer to offset the impact it will have on traffic and the environment by donating land owned by the retailer elsewhere in the town for a series of parks in neighborhoods near, but not adjacent to, the proposed location of the store. The city terms this an "impact mitigation condition." The city notes in its proposal that large retail stores increase traffic, that their parking lots increase water pollution due to runoff, and that the added traffic increases air pollution. If it decides to challenge, what would the retailer's strongest argument be?

A. There is an insufficient nexus between the condition and the requirement of the special-use permit.
B. The city has physically taken the land for use as public parks.
C. The condition amounts to a forced redistribution of property to another group.
D. The condition serves no legitimate governmental interest.

ANALYSIS. Again we have an alleged conditional taking. The retailer is being asked to give over land it owns in town for a series of parks in exchange for being issued a special-use permit. The government must (1) demonstrate an essential nexus between the condition and some legitimate interest, plus (2) establish a rough proportionality between the condition and the impact of the planned development, including some sort of individualized assessment of the connection between the condition and that impact. Environmental protection is certainly a legitimate governmental interest—and a common reason for land use restrictions. Therefore, **D** is incorrect. Because the transfer is conditional, and ostensibly voluntary, neither **B** nor **C** is correct. The city hasn't yet taken the land, and won't; it will be transferred by the retailer in exchange for the special-use permit. Moreover, it isn't "forced," in the way that a sale as a result of a condemnation proceeding would be. That leaves **A**, which is the best answer, and the retailer's strongest argument. Note that the condition (donate land for parks for neighborhoods elsewhere in the city) has little connection with any of the environmental impacts allegedly associated with the large retail establishment—air pollution and traffic from increased traffic, and runoff from the large parking lot. Moreover, according to the facts given, the city has done little more than simply recite the expected impact of the large retailer. No evidence exists of any individualized assessment of the sort required by the Court's conditional takings cases.

6. *Just compensation*

The Takings Clause requires that when government takes property for public use, it must pay the owner "just compensation." But what does this mean? A century ago Justice Holmes expressed it this way: "[T]he question is what has the owner lost, not what has the taker gained." Boston Chamber of Commerce v. Boston, 217 U.S. 189, 195 (1910). Later the Court held that the owner "is entitled to be put in as good a position pecuniarily as if his property had not been taken. He must be made whole but is not entitled to more." Olson v. United States, 292 U.S. 246, 255 (1934). In other words, an owner is entitled to fair market value of the property taken from her.

There are a lot of moving parts to Takings Clause doctrine, so before we leave it, I have summarized the main points in the following flowchart.

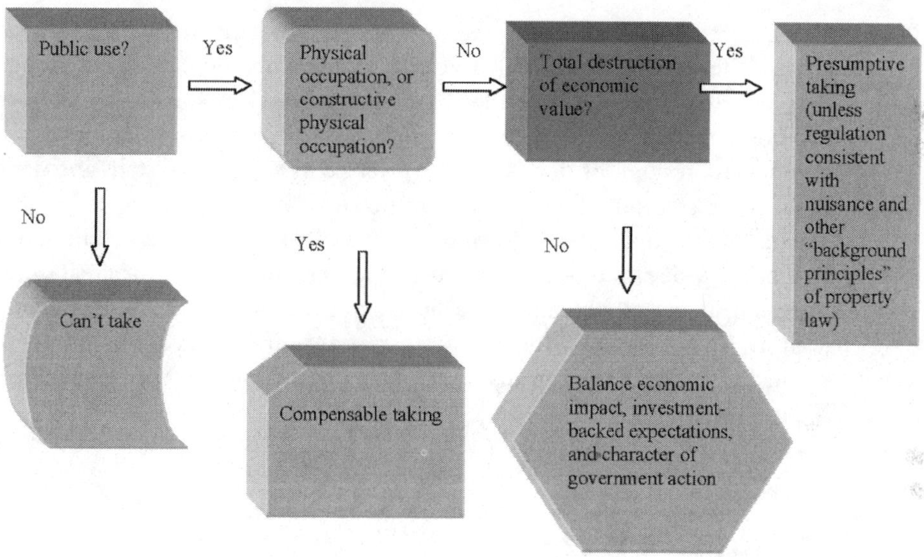

Takings Flowchart

D. Closer

QUESTION 12. Permit me? Landowner applies for permission to develop several plots she acquired decades ago. Given recent development patterns, the property would now be valuable for commercial development. The state had designated certain property adjacent to the Landowner's to be environmentally sensitive. When Landowner sought the required permits from the state, she was told that she needed either (1) to create a conservation easement to the state for certain portions of her property or (2) to agree to pay for improvements to state-owned land located elsewhere in the county. She declined and her permit was denied. If Landowner sues the state in federal court, challenging the constitutionality of its action, which of the following statements is true?

A. The judge would refuse to hear the case because there is no taking.
B. The judge would order the state to grant the permit.
C. The judge would require the state to demonstrate its conditions for the permit had a nexus and rough proportionality to the development's impact.
D. The judge would refuse to hear the case because the requirement of a payment of money cannot be a regulatory taking.

ANALYSIS. Just checking to see whether you remembered what you read earlier! The fact pattern roughly tracks that in *Koontz*. You don't have enough facts to determine whether, in fact, a taking has occurred, so **A** is incorrect. **B** is not correct, either. A state isn't required to grant a permit under constitutional law, though its denial may be reversed as a matter of state or federal law if some statutory procedures were not followed. **D** is incorrect because *Koontz* held the opposite: Requiring the payment of money as a condition for development approval—as opposed to the donation of land or creation of an easement—*does not* automatically exempt the state from Takings Clause scrutiny. That leaves **C**, which is the correct answer. The state's requirement would be subject to the nexus and rough proportionality requirements of *Nollan* and *Dolan*.

Denning's Picks

1. **B**
2. **D**
3. **A**
4. **D**
5. **B**
6. **D**
7. **D**
8. **C**
9. **B**
10. **D**
11. **A**
12. **C**

3

The Due Process Clause of the Fourteenth Amendment

A. Overview

Section 1 of the Fourteenth Amendment, proposed and ratified in the wake of the Civil War, altered the Framing-era relationship between the federal and state governments. Among other things, it says that states shall not "deprive any person of life, liberty, or property, without due process of law. . . ." U.S. Const. amend. XIV, § 1.[1] Read literally, it seems to require procedural regularity in lawmaking—that is, if due process *is* observed, then states *may* deprive persons of life, liberty, or property. As we shall see in this chapter, however, the Due Process Clause has come to stand for much more than that. Not only does it regulate the *means* by which state governments act, it limits the *ends* of state regulation as well, through the doctrine of "substantive due process." The Supreme Court accomplished this by, among other things, applying the Bill of Rights—which the Court earlier held to apply only to the federal government—to the states, following the ratification of the Fourteenth Amendment.

Under substantive due process, some governmental infringements on individual liberty—no matter how scrupulously enacted—cannot be effected without the government providing compelling reasons for doing so. Because the Court has never consistently applied one method for distinguishing these "fundamental" rights that garner searching review from other liberty interests that receive only perfunctory review, substantive due process can be a particularly confusing area of constitutional law. To confuse matters further, the Court's concern with these fundamental rights shifted in the twentieth century; whereas the late-nineteenth- and early-twentieth-century courts had been concerned with protecting individual economic liberty from unreasonable

1. Note that these requirements—and the requirement of equal protection discussed in the next chapter—apply only to actions by state and local governments. Private denials of rights are not addressed by the Fourteenth Amendment, though private action will occasionally be imputed to the state. The Court's so-called state action doctrine is discussed later in Chapter 9.

state interference, beginning in the mid-1940s the Court became concerned with interference with a panoply of non-economic individual liberties.

This section begins with procedural due process, which sets forth the minimum procedural requirements a state government must satisfy before it acts. The bulk of the chapter is devoted to describing the origins and development of substantive due process, and an analysis of the major doctrinal areas in which the Court has protected fundamental constitutional rights against unwarranted state interference, although these rights are not mentioned explicitly in the Constitution itself.

B. Procedural Due Process

1. *Introduction*

At a minimum, procedural due process guarantees that before government can deprive them of life, liberty, or property, individuals must be furnished with both notice and some kind of hearing. But this simple statement masks a couple of important questions. First, even if "life" is fairly self-explanatory, which "liberty" and "property" interests trigger due process requirements? Second, how much process is "due" before deprivation can be effected? An opportunity to be heard can mean anything from an informal meeting with a public school assistant principal to a full-fledged criminal trial. A related question is whether the opportunity to be heard must occur before or after the deprivation. However, we begin with an explanation of why state governments are not required to contact you personally and offer you an opportunity to testify before the legislature prior to, for example, raising your taxes.

2. *Legislative versus adjudicative determinations*

Very little business could get done were legislatures constitutionally required to notify all individuals affected by legislation and give them an opportunity to voice their opinions. Not surprisingly, then, the Court has held that when legislatures engage in lawmaking at what might be described as the wholesale level, due process protections do not attach. As Justice Holmes put it in *Bi-Metallic Investment Co. v. State Board of Equalization*, 239 U.S. 441, 445 (1915), "[w]here a rule of conduct applies to more than a few people, it is impracticable that everyone should have a direct voice in its adoption. The Constitution," he continued, "does not require all public acts to be done in town meeting or an assembly of the whole. General statutes within the state power are passed that affect the person or property of individuals, sometimes to the point of ruin, without giving them the chance to be heard." The "legislative determination," as it is known, is the only process that is due.

However, once the results are applied to individuals at the retail level, then those affected must be afforded notice and an opportunity to be heard. For example, if a state or local government decides to impose a property tax on its citizens, or to raise the rate of an existing tax, that is a legislative determination; individuals potentially affected are not entitled to notice and an opportunity to be heard. However, if an individual's property is assessed for purposes of levying that same tax, and the individual disputes the government's valuation, that is an "adjudicative determination," to which due process guarantees *do* apply.

3. *Which liberty and property interests are protected?*

But even where government engages in an adjudicative determination, due process applies only to recognized property rights and liberty interests. It is obvious that if the government tries to seize land you own or throw you in jail, then it is depriving you of property and liberty, respectively. But what if the government cuts off welfare benefits or revokes your license to operate a business—neither of which it was constitutionally obligated to grant or issue in the first place? Does either of those constitute "property"? If you are incarcerated and the government transfers you from a minimum- to a medium-security prison, does that transfer infringe on your "liberty"? These are the questions this section will take up.

(a) Property The Supreme Court's attitude toward property interests—particularly to government entitlements—has evolved over the years. Initially, the Court regarded welfare payments and the like as "privileges" the government could revoke at will because it was not required to issue them in the first place. With the growth of the welfare state came calls to treat those benefits as matters not of legislative grace, but of individual right. Yale law professor Charles Reich famously described these entitlements as "The New Property" and urged the Court to require governments to observe due process before depriving recipients of them. For a while, the Court agreed, holding in *Goldberg v. Kelly*, 397 U.S. 254, 264 (1970), that any government benefit that was "important" to its recipient is entitled to a pre-termination hearing. Although *Goldberg* concerned people receiving welfare payments, it was soon extended to the revocation of uninsured motorists' driver's licenses. Bell v. Burson, 402 U.S. 535 (1971). The Court then abandoned the importance-to-the-recipient test, in an effort to cabin *Goldberg*.

Today property is defined by reference to state law. As the Court put it in *Board of Regents v. Roth*, 408 U.S. 564, 577 (1972), "[t]o have a property interest in a benefit, a person clearly must have more than an abstract need or desire for it. He must have more than a unilateral expectation of it. He must, instead, have a legitimate claim of entitlement to it." Property interests, the Court went on to explain, "are not created by the Constitution" but rather "are created and their dimensions . . . defined by existing rules or understandings that stem from an independent source such as state law. . . ." *See also* Perry v. Sindermann, 408 U.S. 593 (1972) (holding that alleged promise of continued employment upon satisfactory teaching could, if established at trial, constitute property interest to which due process attached); *but see* Castle Rock v. Gonzales, 545 U.S. 748, 748 (2005) (stating that "a benefit is not a protected entitlement if government officials may grant or deny it in their discretion"; *held*, no due process violation for failure of police department to enforce restraining order against estranged husband who subsequently kidnapped and murdered daughters because police had discretion in how and whether to enforce such orders).

In *Cleveland Board of Education v. Loudermill*, 470 U.S. 532 (1984), however, the Court made clear that while property interests were established with reference to state law, procedural requirements were constitutional in nature and *not* defined by state law. The issue in *Loudermill* was whether a public employee who was discharged for cause was entitled to a pre-termination hearing prior to his firing. State law provided that he could be discharged only for cause, but that challenges to dismissal were allowed post-termination only. The board argued that his property right was not continued employment barring discharge for cause, as Loudermill argued, but continued employment barring discharge for cause with the post-termination provisions provided for in the code. The Court held for Loudermill, rejecting the state's "bitter with the sweet" approach. Due process, the Court held, "provides that certain substantive rights—life, liberty, and property—cannot be deprived except pursuant to constitutionally adequate procedures. The categories of substance and procedure are distinct." 470 U.S. at 541. "'While the legislature may elect not to confer a property interest . . . it may not constitutionally authorize the deprivation of such an interest, without appropriate procedural safeguards.'" *Id.*

(b) Liberty It is clear that governmental deprivation of liberty—through either incarceration or confinement to a mental hospital—triggers due process protections. *See, e.g.*, Hamdi v. Rumsfeld, 542 U.S. 507 (2004) (describing as "the most elemental of liberty interests" the "interest in being free from physical detention by one's own government"); O'Connor v. Donaldson, 422 U.S. 563 (1975) (due process protections apply to involuntary civil commitment proceedings); *see also* Zadvydas v. Davis, 533 U.S. 678 (2001) (interpreting federal law not to permit indefinite detention of nondeportable aliens, in part to avoid constitutional concerns).

Short of actual incarceration, the Court's cases have distinguished between government actions that alter one's legal status and those that do not. For example, the Court held in *Paul v. Davis*, 424 U.S. 693 (1976), that having one's picture circulated to merchants as an "active shoplifter" even after charges were dropped did not implicate a constitutionally protected liberty interest. Davis had suffered only a reputational injury, the Court held. On the other hand, in *Wisconsin v. Constantineau*, 400 U.S. 433 (1971), the Court held that placement on a list of "excessive drinkers" who were barred for one year from purchasing liquor or having it given to them was a protected interest. But for the placement of her name on the list, Constantineau was permitted by state law to purchase liquor; her placement on the list altered her legal status, causing her to suffer more than simply the ignominy of being known as a problem drinker.

Other liberty interests the Court has recognized include the right to an education, Goss v. Lopez, 419 U.S. 565 (1975); the right to parental custody, Stanley v. Illinois, 405 U.S. 645 (1972); the right not to be transferred from prison to a mental hospital, Vitek v. Jones, 445 U.S. 480 (1980); and the right of a prisoner to challenge his assignment to a "Supermax" prison, in which the conditions of incarceration are much more onerous than in ordinary prisons, Wilkinson v. Austin, 545 U.S. 209 (2005). However, the Court held in *Greenholtz v. Inmates*, 442 U.S. 1 (1979), that mere denial of parole did not trigger due process requirements, because the prisoner's legal status had not changed. *Revocation* of parole, however, implicates a liberty interest. Morrisey v. Brewer, 408 U.S. 471 (1972).

QUESTION 1. **Liquor is quicker.** City ordinances allow bars and taverns to serve liquor by the drink, but require them to possess a liquor license that is revocable if the establishment is cited more than five times in a single month for, among other things, serving minors. Billy, the owner of Billy's Bar, is notified that the city has cited it six times in a single month for serving underage drinkers and that its liquor license has been revoked. City law makes no provision for contesting the revocation. Has the city acted constitutionally?

A. Yes, because the city's action does not implicate a cognizable property interest.
B. Yes, because the city provided notice.
C. No, because it did not hold a trial that permitted Billy to contest the citations he allegedly received.
D. No, because it did not afford him a pre- or post-deprivation hearing on the revocation.

ANALYSIS. If you remembered from the reading that, at a minimum, procedural due process requires notice and an opportunity to be heard, then you are ahead of the game. **B** is not correct because notice *and* some kind of hearing is required. **A** is incorrect because Billy had been issued a license, and the law said that it could not be revoked unless certain conditions obtained. That means that he had more than a "unilateral expectation" of retaining it, and indeed had a property interest under state law. **C** is not correct because, as noted above and explained in more detail below, the process that is due does not always have to take the form of a full-blown civil or criminal trial. That leaves **D**, which is the correct answer: The city is obligated to provide Billy with *some* sort of opportunity to appear and contest the revocation.

QUESTION 2. Taxing conditions. In a last-minute effort to close a yawning budget deficit, the State of Ames doubles the tax on cigarettes sold in the state. Convenience store and gas station owners sue, protesting the lack of both notification and hearing prior to the enactment of the tax. The state, they allege, violated the Due Process Clause. A reviewing court should:

A. Dismiss the suit, because there is no property interest in money derived from sales of cigarettes.
B. Dismiss the suit, because the imposition of the tax was not an adjudicative determination.
C. Invalidate the tax, because due process requires notice and an opportunity to be heard.
D. Invalidate the tax, because Ames is depriving the owners of property through the tax.

ANALYSIS. Recall that due process protections operate at the retail, not the wholesale, level. As the Court has put it, *legislative determinations* of policy do not trigger procedural due process restrictions; *adjudicative determinations* do. Decisions to impose or raise taxes on a large group of people by legislatures must be controlled at the ballot box. Therefore, **B** is the correct answer. **A** is not correct because the taxpayers do, of course, have property interests in their money, but they must protect them in this instance by voting. **C** is correct about the core requirements of due process, but incorrect insofar as it suggests they apply to these facts. **D** suggests that property is inviolate, and this is contrary to the Due Process Clause, which anticipates governmental deprivation of life, liberty, or property if due process is observed.

QUESTION 3. Give me liberty or give me due process! Which of the following would likely be a cognizable liberty interest to which due process requirements attach?

A. Suspension of the driver's license of an elderly individual deemed an "unsafe driver," pursuant to a state statute permitting revocation following that determination.
B. Classification as an "enemy combatant," which subjects one to trial before a military commission as opposed to a civilian court.
C. Subjecting a public school student to corporal punishment for various serious school offenses.
D. Any of the above.

ANALYSIS. The key to a liberty interest, according to the Court, is the alteration of one's legal status. In each case above, the individual is subject to an alteration of his or her status that would likely trigger due process protections. Thus, **D** is the correct answer. The subject in **A** was permitted to drive prior to an official determination that he was "unsafe," after which he could no longer drive. That is not unlike the drinker in *Constantineau.* The Court in *Hamdi* held that due process required that American citizens classified as enemy combatants be able to challenge their classification so that they might escape confinement. Thus, **B** also describes a recognized liberty interest. And finally, like the student subject to school discipline in *Goss v. Lopez,* in **C** the student's being subject to corporal punishment involves a loss of liberty that would require some kind of notice and opportunity to be heard.

4. *What process is due?*

As we've noted, the process due someone deprived of liberty or property is, at a minimum, notice and an opportunity to be heard. *See, e.g.,* Joint Anti-Fascist Commission v. McGrath, 341 U.S. 171-172 (1951) (Frankfurter, J., concurring) ("The essence of due process is the requirement that 'a person put in jeopardy of serious loss [has] notice of the case against him and opportunity to meet it.'"). But does the government need to hold a trial-like hearing prior to every potential deprivation? In *Goldberg v. Kelly,* 397 U.S. 254 (1970), the Court seemed to hold up the pre-termination hearing as the due process gold standard, at least for any government entitlement deemed important to the recipient.

Six years later, however, the Court retreated from *Goldberg*'s rigid presumption that pre-termination hearings were the floor in favor of a balancing of factors, without explicitly overruling *Goldberg* itself. *Matthews v. Eldridge,* 424 U.S. 319 (1976), looked on its face to be quite similar to *Goldberg.* Eldridge had been receiving Social Security benefits[2] for a disability, and those benefits were discontinued after the agency determined that Eldridge was no longer disabled. Eldridge sued, claiming that he was entitled to a pre-termination hearing, not the post-termination procedures provided for by the statute. Writing for the Court, Justice Powell held:

> [W]hether the administrative procedures provided here are constitutionally sufficient requires analysis of the governmental and private interests that are affected. More precisely, our prior decisions indicate that identification of the specific dictates of due process generally requires consideration of three distinct factors: [f]irst, the private interest that will be affected by the official action; second, the risk of an erroneous deprivation of such interest through the procedures used, and the probable value, if any, of additional or procedural safeguards; and finally, the Government's interest, including the function involved and the fiscal and administrative burdens that the additional or substitute procedural requirements would entail.

Matthews, 424 U.S. at 335.

2. The agency here was the federal government, which is bound not by the Fourteenth Amendment's Due Process Clause, but by the Fifth Amendment's Clause. The requirements under the two Clauses are, however, identical.

Applying these factors, the Court held that the procedures afforded Eldridge were sufficient. The Justices noted that under those provisions, "a recipient whose benefits are terminated is awarded full retroactive relief if he ultimately prevails. . . ." It distinguished *Goldberg* on the grounds that receipt of disability was not contingent on income, that the disability recipient disadvantaged by having his benefits cut off could, if necessary, apply for public assistance. *Id.* at 340. The "sharply focused and easily documented" assessment of the recipient, the Court felt, reduced the chance of erroneous deprivation, as did "the policy of allowing the disability recipient's representative full access to the information relied upon by the state agency." *Id.* at 343-346. The Court was also persuaded that "the incremental cost resulting from the increased number of hearings and the expense of providing benefits to ineligible recipients pending decision" would be substantial. *Id.* at 347. While acknowledging that it was hard to predict how large that burden would be, it speculated that it "would not be insubstantial." *Id.* The opinion concluded with an admonition that the constitutional requirement of due process need not be satisfied only by a hearing with "judicial-type procedures" and could be satisfied by much less formal hearing mechanisms that took place after termination. *Id.* at 348.

Matthews, like other balancing tests, can be celebrated for its frank balancing of costs and benefits; it may also be criticized for failing to indicate the weight to be assigned each factor, or for asking the Court to weigh factors that are not readily comparable, or for usurping the legislature's role by the very act of balancing. It could also be said to undervalue individual dignity by balancing it off against bureaucratic convenience and bottom-line savings. But whatever else one may say about it, it is difficult to apply predictably. Nevertheless, a few generalizations are possible.

First, where the public safety requires it, government is permitted to take action as long as timely post-deprivation relief is available. *See, e.g.*, Mackey v. Montrym, 443 U.S. 1 (1979) (upholding law suspending driver's license of person refusing to submit to field sobriety tests). Second, post-deprivation relief is also constitutionally adequate "when the liberty or property interest at stake is relatively minor, and either the risk of erroneous deprivation is low or provision of pre-deprivation hearings is impractical." Calvin Massey, American Constitutional Law: Powers and Liberties 487 (4th ed. 2013). *See, e.g.*, Ingraham v. Wright, 430 U.S. 651 (1977) (possibility of tort suits for damages is sufficient remedy for erroneous administration of corporal punishment to public school student; pre-deprivation hearing not required); *see also* Connecticut Dep't Pub. Safety v. Doe, 538 U.S. 1 (2003) (upholding law requiring sex offenders to register with state upon release from prison and to disclose whereabouts; *held*, hearing unnecessary because obligation to register and disclose imposed as a result of original conviction). Third, prisoners have fared poorly in suits against prison officials for intentional or negligent destruction of property, with the Court holding that the availability of tort suits satisfied due process. *See, e.g.*, Hudson v. Palmer, 468 U.S. 517 (1984) (intentional destruction); Parratt v. Taylor, 451 U.S. 527 (1981) (negligent destruction).

QUESTION 4. Flew process. John, who shares the name of a known terrorist, finds that he is on the federal no-fly list, which complicates his efforts to travel by air. The no-fly list, which is maintained by the Federal Aviation Administration pursuant to a provision in a congressional statute, contains the names of people who are suspected of terrorism and therefore are not permitted to board flights in the United States. John sues, arguing that because he flies for business purposes, his ability to travel is very important to him; thus, he should have received notice and been granted a hearing prior to being placed on the no-fly list by the federal government. His placement on the list, he maintains, violates the Due Process Clause. A reviewing court should:

A. Dismiss the suit, because the no-fly list was a legislative determination.
B. Find for John, because pre-deprivation hearings are required where the interest at stake is very important to the individual.
C. Find for John if, in addition to the importance to him of traveling by air, he can prove that hundreds of people are erroneously placed on the list, and that those errors could be prevented by notice and a hearing.
D. Dismiss his suit if, despite the importance of flying to John and a chance that additional procedures could keep some people from being erroneously placed on the list, it would be expensive and administratively burdensome for the government to provide a pre-deprivation hearing.

ANALYSIS. While the creation of the list was a legislative adjudication, John's inclusion on that list would be characterized as the result of an adjudicative determination that he belonged on it. So **A** would not be correct. Also, it is not true that pre-deprivation hearings are required merely where a particular interest is subjectively important to an individual; that was the old *Goldberg v. Kelly* rule abandoned in *Matthews v. Eldridge.* Therefore, **B** is an incorrect statement of the law. **C** is not correct because cost and administrative burden are considered along with the importance of the interest, the risk of erroneous deprivation, and the probable value of additional safeguards in preventing errors, after *Matthews v. Eldridge.* If the government could show that it was very costly and administratively burdensome to provide hearings to everyone, it would likely win, despite the hardship and inconvenience to John caused by the lack of pre-deprivation hearings. Thus, of the four, **D** is the best answer.

C. Substantive Due Process

1. *Introduction*

Substantive due process is the infelicitous term given to judicial limits on governmental power to interfere with certain (often unenumerated or non-textual) individual rights. In *Democracy and Distrust* Professor John Hart Ely described substantive due process as an oxymoron, akin to describing a color as "green pastel redness." John Hart Ely, Democracy and Distrust 18 (1980). Law students often find it among the most confusing and frustrating areas of Supreme Court doctrine. Many suspect the Court of making it up out of whole cloth. In this section, I hope to show that even if the Court has not been a model of consistency or transparency, there is something of a method to its madness. The section attempts to sketch the origin and evolution of the doctrine—in particular the Court's mid-twentieth-century switch from the protection of economic to non-economic rights—and then look at particular applications of the doctrine in representative areas, particularly those involving personal autonomy in matters of conception and sexuality.

At the outset, though, it's helpful to keep a couple of things in mind. First, for all the controversy substantive due process generates in particular applications, the use of judicial power to protect unenumerated rights has been a part of constitutional law almost since the beginning of the Republic. In early Supreme Court cases like *Calder v. Bull*, 3 U.S. 386 (1798) (Chase, J.) and *Fletcher v. Peck*, 10 U.S. 87 (1810), members of the Supreme Court appeared willing to go beyond explicit constitutional provisions and draw on "natural law" or principles of "natural justice" to limit government. In 1856, the New York high court in *Wynehamer v. New York*, 13 N.Y. 387 (1856), invalidated a prohibition law as an "unreasonable" interference with individual liberty. Substantive due process, then, is not a recent phenomenon in either federal or state constitutional law.

Second, you should keep in mind that the debate over substantive due process can be conducted at two levels: (1) at the "retail" level of individual cases in particular doctrinal areas and (2) at the "wholesale" level of theory—how these "fundamental" rights are to be identified and using what criteria. Though the rights protected by substantive due process have changed over the years, the terms of the debate have not. Liberals in the 1920s and 1930s excoriated the Court for "inventing" economic rights and wielding judicial review to strike down state and federal legislation that interfered with them. As the focus of the Court shifted to protecting non-economic rights, particularly those dealing with personal autonomy or sexual privacy, it was conservatives' turn to criticize "judicial activism." (To be fair, some early critics of economic substantive due process, like then-Professor Felix Frankfurter and Judge Learned Hand, were equally critical of the Court's use of substantive due process to protect civil liberties.) In this section, I'll discuss both the theory and practice of substantive due process. Because the Court itself has not definitively settled the debate, this section can only raise, and not resolve, a number of questions in this important area.

2. *The Fourteenth Amendment and federal protection for civil liberties*

In 1868, the Fourteenth Amendment was added to the Constitution as part of a constitutional reconstruction that altered the balance of power between the federal and state governments. In 1833, the Supreme Court, per Chief Justice John Marshall, held that the Bill of Rights applied only to the federal government, and was not intended to apply to states. Barron v. Baltimore, 32 U.S. 243 (1833). That decision corresponded with Framing-era expectations that constitutional protections were needed against a distant and remote federal government—that state governments, being closer and more responsive to their citizens, would not be as liable to violate their civil liberties. These expectations provided cold comfort to various minority groups immediately before and after the Civil War—abolitionists, freed slaves, Unionists living in the South—who found their rights routinely violated.

Section 1 of the Fourteenth Amendment sought to redress this imbalance through constitutional guarantees against state deprivations of civil liberties. In addition to the Due Process Clause, modeled on the corresponding clause in the Fifth Amendment, Section 1 introduced the "Privileges or Immunities Clause" and an "Equal Protection Clause." The Privileges or Immunities Clause reads: "No state shall make or enforce any law which shall abridge the privileges or immunities of citizens of the United States. . . ." U.S. Const. amend. XIV, § 1.[3] During the debates over the amendments, there is substantial evidence that "privileges or immunities" was used as shorthand for a number of the provisions of the Bill of Rights. So why are courts forced to rely on the Due Process Clause?

The answer is that in the first case in which the Court was called upon to interpret the Fourteenth Amendment, it interpreted the Privileges or Immunities Clause so narrowly as to lead many to conclude that it was a dead letter. The Slaughter-house Cases, 83 U.S. 36 (1873). Interestingly, *The Slaughter-house Cases* also saw the Court reject what was, in essence, a substantive due process claim brought on behalf of New Orleans butchers who challenged Louisiana's grant of a monopoly to one slaughterhouse for slaughtering done in the New Orleans area. The butchers claimed that the monopoly unconstitutionally deprived them of the right to earn their living and further violated each of the three provisions of Section 1, including the Privileges

---

3. Don't confuse the Privileges *or* Immunities Clause of the Fourteenth Amendment with the Privileges *and* Immunities Clause of Article IV, § 2. The latter is discussed in volume 1, Chapter 5.

or Immunities Clause. The Court disagreed, stating that the "privileges or immunities" referred to included things like the ability to travel to the seat of government to make claims on it, the ability to transact business with the government, the right to free access to seaports and to courts of law, the right to petition, and the right to writs of habeas corpus, among others. 83 U.S. at 79. The Court did not interpret it as broadly as did the plaintiffs or, indeed, as broadly as did some of the Fourteenth Amendment's framers.

Despite the consensus among scholars that *The Slaughter-house Cases* were wrongly decided and the Court's interpretation of the Privileges or Immunities Clause too restrictive, the case has never been overruled. That meant that those seeking judicial protection for civil liberties had to find another vehicle. For better or worse, that vehicle was the Due Process Clause.

The Due Process Clause has been employed to guarantee individual liberties against state infringement in two ways. One, discussed below, is to interpret the "liberty" in the Due Process Clause to include a host of important but unenumerated individual rights. The second, and equally important, way is to use the Due Process Clause to "incorporate" provisions of the Bill of Rights and apply them to states. This process began in 1897, when the Supreme Court held that because of the Due Process Clause, the Takings Clause of the Fifth Amendment applied to the states.[4] Chicago, Burlington & Quincy R.R. v. Chicago, 166 U.S. 226 (1897). The process accelerated in the first half of the twentieth century when the Court incorporated the First Amendment in its entirety, and it reached a fever pitch in the 1960s when the Supreme Court under Earl Warren incorporated most of the Bill of Rights' criminal procedure amendments and applied them to the states. The accompanying chart lists the cases in which various provisions of the Bill of Rights were (or were not) incorporated.

As one can see from the list, not every provision of the Bill of Rights has been incorporated. Despite Justice Hugo Black's arguments for total incorporation, the Court adopted a theory of partial incorporation and proceeded on a case-by-case basis to inquire of particular provisions whether they were fundamental or essential to ordered liberty. The verbal formulae varied over the years, as the Court acknowledged in *Duncan v. Louisiana.* "Earlier," wrote Justice White, "the Court can be seen as having asked, when inquiring into whether some particular procedural safeguard was required of a State, if a civilized system could be imagined that would not accord the particular protection. . . . The recent cases, on the other hand, have [asked] whether . . . a particular procedure is fundamental—whether, that is, a procedure is necessary to an Anglo-American regime of ordered liberty." *Duncan*, 391 U.S. at 149 n. 14. One commentator mischievously noted that among partial incorporation's benefits is that it enabled the Justices to avoid incorporating parts of the Bill of Rights "that the justices probably did not like." Lucas A. Powe, Jr., The Warren Court and American Politics 415 (2000).

4. The Takings Clause provides that "private property shall [not] be taken for public use, without just compensation." U.S. Const. amend. V. It is discussed in Chapter 2.

For all the controversy generated by incorporation at mid-century, it is by far now the *least* controversial aspect of substantive due process. After all, the restrictions enforced against the states are at least textual, and the scope of those rights is limited to some degree by the plain language of the Bill of Rights. Moreover, whatever the expectations of the Framing era, it would now strike most people as odd that the federal government would be obliged to observe the provisions of the Bill of Rights while the states could violate them with impunity.

Provisions of the Bill of Rights and Cases Incorporating Them

Amendment	*Incorporated?*	*Case(s)*
First	Yes	Gitlow v. New York, 268 U.S. 652 (1925) (free speech); Near v. Minnesota, 283 U.S. 697 (1930) (freedom of the press); DeJonge v. Oregon, 299 U.S. 353 (1937) (freedom of assembly); Cantwell v. Connecticut, 310 U.S. 296 (1940) (free exercise); Everson v. Board of Education, 330 U.S. 1 (1947) (Establishment Clause)
Second	Yes	McDonald v. Chicago, 561 U.S. 742 (2010)
Third	Not yet decided	
Fourth	Yes	Mapp v. Ohio, 367 U.S. 643 (1961) (unreasonable search and seizure); Aguilar v. Texas, 378 U.S. 108 (1964) (warrant requirements)
Fifth	Partial	Chicago, Burlington & Quincy R.R. v. Chicago, 166 U.S. 226 (1895) (Takings Clause); Malloy v. Hogan, 378 U.S. 1 (1964) (self-incrimination); Benton v. Maryland, 395 U.S. 784 (1969) (double jeopardy)
Sixth	Yes	In re Oliver, 333 U.S. 257 (1948) (public trial and notice of accusations); Gideon v. Wainwright, 372 U.S. 335 (1963) (right to counsel if indigent); Pointer v. Texas, 380 U.S. 400 (1965) (Confrontation Clause); Klopfer v. North Carolina, 386 U.S. 213 (1967) (speedy trial); Washington v. Texas, 388 U.S. 14 (1967) (compulsory process for witnesses); Duncan v. Louisiana, 391 U.S. 145 (1968) (impartial jury)
Seventh	No	Minneapolis & St. Louis R. R. Co. v. Bombolis, 241 U.S. 211 (1916) (right to jury trial in civil cases held *not* incorporated)
Eighth	Partial	Robinson v. California, 370 U.S. 660 (1962) (cruel and unusual punishment); Murphy v. Hunt, 455 U.S. 478 (1982) (holding excessive bail and excessive fines provision *not* incorporated)

Identification and defense of nontextual rights by courts—what "substantive due process" calls to mind now—is another matter. Despite the Court's penchant for doing just that since its inception, the exercise has always been regarded as suspect, whether the Court was defending "liberty of contract" or the "right to privacy." It is to this more troublesome aspect of substantive due process that we now turn.

3. *The rise and decline of economic substantive due process*

During the late nineteenth and early twentieth centuries the Court used the Due Process Clause to invalidate what it deemed unreasonable legislative interference with economic liberties, including the so-called liberty of contract—the right of individuals to contract freely for wages and hours. This marked a reversal from *The Slaughter-house Cases* Court's refusal to entertain the claims of the New Orleans butchers. But even during the high-water mark of economic substantive due process, the Court relaxed its heightened scrutiny of legislative regulation of private property if that property was "affected with the public interest." *See, e.g.*, Munn v. Illinois, 94 U.S. 113 (1877) (upholding regulation of grain elevators); *see also* Mugler v. Kansas, 123 U.S. 623 (1887) (upholding prohibition law against suit brought by brewery owner who claimed law deprived him of his property without due process).

Regardless, history remembers this period as "the *Lochner* era," named for *Lochner v. New York*, 198 U.S. 45 (1905), the case in which the Court invalidated a law prescribing maximum working hours for bakers. By the late nineteenth century, *Munn* notwithstanding, the Court was broadly defining the rights encompassed by the word "liberty" in the Due Process Clause of the Fourteenth Amendment. One famous (and capacious) definition was given in *Allgeyer v. Louisiana*, 165 U.S. 578 (1897), in which Justice Peckham defined liberty as the

> right of the citizen to be free in the enjoyment of all his faculties; to be free to use them in all lawful ways; to live and work where he will; to earn his livelihood by any lawful calling; to pursue any livelihood or avocation; and for that purpose to enter into all contracts which may be proper, necessary, and essential to his carrying out to a successful conclusion the purposes above mentioned.

Allgeyer, 165 U.S. at 589. Less than ten years later the Court invalidated the New York law in the eponymous case by which the entire age is remembered.

The New York law challenged in *Lochner* limited bakers to working no more than 10 hours a day or 60 hours a week. The legislature justified it as a valid "police powers" measure.[5] In an earlier case, *Holden v. Hardy*, 169 U.S.

5. Unlike the federal government, whose powers are limited by the enumeration in Article I, § 8, states are not so limited. They are deemed to have the police power, which is shorthand for the power to legislate for the health, safety, welfare, and morals of their citizens. This power is inherent and need not trace its authority to an enumeration of powers in state constitutions. State legislative power is limited only by the restrictions present in the state constitution and, of course, in the U.S. Constitution.

366 (1898), the Court had upheld a state statute limiting miners and smelters to an 8-hour workday. But the Court found that *Holden* had no application here because, in its opinion, baking was not a hazardous occupation requiring state intervention. "Clean and wholesome bread," the Court wrote, "does not depend upon whether the baker works but ten hours per day or only sixty hours per week." *Lochner,* 198 U.S. at 57. As for safety, the Court was equally dismissive: "To the common understanding, the trade of a baker has never been regarded as an unhealthy one." *Id.* at 59. If the legislature could regulate bakers, the Court worried, then it could regulate the working hours of "doctors, lawyers, scientists, all professional men, as well as athletes and artisans" who "could be forbidden to fatigue their brains and bodies by prolonged hours of exercise. . . ." *Id.* at 60. New York's law was not "a fair, reasonable and appropriate exercise of the police power of the State," in the Court's eyes; rather, it was "an unreasonable, unnecessary and arbitrary interference with the right of the individual to his personal liberty. . . ." *Id.* at 56.

As Justice Harlan pointed out in his dissent, the healthiness or unhealthiness of the baking profession was a subject on which reasonable people could disagree. What, he asked, gave the Court the power to trump the legislature's not irrational conclusion that it was unhealthy and should be subject to the police power? *Id.* at 71-74 (Harlan, J., dissenting). For his part, Justice Holmes noted that the law interfered with liberty of contract in myriad uncontroversial ways. In his opinion, *Lochner* was "decided upon an economic theory [] which a large part of the country does not entertain." *Id.* at 75 (Holmes, J., dissenting).

The battle lines were drawn for the next three decades between those who saw the Court as the bulwark against unreasonable legislative interference with private property and those who thought the Court should defer to popularly elected officials on matters of economic and social policy. But despite popular caricatures of the *Lochner* Court, quite a bit of economic regulation was upheld. The key point, though, is that it was the *Court* that decided which exercises of the police powers were upheld, and which were struck down. Thus in the same term it could invalidate a federal law prohibiting employment contracts whereby the employee promised not to join a union, Adair v. United States, 208 U.S. 161 (1908), while upholding a law limiting women to a ten-hour workday, Muller v. Oregon, 208 U.S. 412 (1908). Less than a decade later, the Court upheld a statute mandating overtime pay for any employee working more than a ten-hour workday. Bunting v. Oregon, 243 U.S. 426 (1917). Reports of *Lochner*'s demise following *Bunting,* however, proved to be premature. In *Adkins v. Children's Hospital,* 261 U.S. 525 (1923), the Court invalidated a D.C. minimum-wage ordinance for women.

In the wake of the Great Depression, however, the Court retreated from economic substantive due process, as it did from its restrictive interpretations of the taxing, spending, and commerce powers. This shift away from the "hard look" judicial review of *Lochner* to a more deferential standard of review began in the mid-1930s with the Court's reinterpretation of *Munn*'s "affected with the public interest" doctrine.

New York passed a law establishing a minimum price for milk in order to stabilize prices and ensure an adequate supply. When a grocer convicted of selling milk for less than the minimum price sued, claiming that the law violated the Due Process Clause, the Court upheld the statute. Nebbia v. New York, 291 U.S. 502 (1934). Justice Roberts, noting all the ways in which business was regulated by the state, concluded that *Munn*'s "affected with the public interest" language meant no more than "subject to the police power," *id.* at 533, and that even price controls were part of a state's police power. Furthermore, he wrote that there is "no closed class or category of businesses affected with the public interest. . . ." *Id.* at 536. The Court concluded:

> So far as the requirement of due process is concerned . . . a state is free to adopt whatever economic policy may reasonably be deemed to promote public welfare, and to enforce that policy by legislation adapted to its purpose. The courts are without authority either to declare such policy, or, when it is declared by the legislature, to override it. If the laws passed are seen to have a reasonable relation to a proper legislative purpose, and are neither arbitrary nor discriminatory, the requirements of due process are satisfied. . . .

Id. at 537. Shortly thereafter, *Adkins* was overruled in *West Coast Hotel Co. v. Parrish*, 300 U.S. 379 (1937), as were earlier cases such as *Adair. See* Phelps Dodge v. NLRB, 313 U.S. 177 (1941).

The Court has never looked back. State regulation of the economy and of businesses that operate within the state is subject to *Nebbia*'s rational basis standard. Under that standard, (1) the legislature must have a legitimate end and (2) its regulation has to bear a rational relationship to that end. After the New Deal, regulation of business and economic matters is unquestionably legitimate; under the Court's deferential standard of review; moreover, a rational connection between means and ends is presumed. Even a hypothetical relationship—i.e., one that was not actually relied upon by the legislature—will suffice. Under such a standard, even foolish laws or laws that inure to the economic benefit of some particular group will not be invalidated under the Due Process Clause. The Court's deferential standard presumes that if laws embody bad policies or are harmful enough, voters will demand changes.

In later cases, the Court made its interment of *Lochner* quite explicit. Declining to strike down a Kansas law that limited the practice of debt adjusting to lawyers, Justice Hugo Black wrote:

> The doctrine that prevailed in *Lochner*, . . . and like cases—that due process authorizes courts to hold laws unconstitutional when they believe the legislature has acted unwisely—has long since been discarded. We have returned to the original constitutional proposition that courts do not substitute their social and economic beliefs for the judgment of legislative bodies, who are elected to pass laws.

Ferguson v. Skrupa, 372 U.S. 726, 730 (1963).

QUESTION 5. Nipping it in the bud. The State of Ames licenses florists. Under its statute, no one may "arrange flowers" without a florist's license. Moreover, no one may sell flower arrangements without employing a licensed florist. The licensing process requires one to pass a written test, which has a lower passage rate than the Ames bar exam. The Food King, Inc., is a large supermarket chain with stores in Ames. Most Food King grocery stores have an in-store "florist shop," where employees arrange flowers and sell them to customers. The Food King does not employ a licensed florist in its Ames stores and is cited for violating the licensing statute. The Food King sues, claiming that the law is unreasonable and irrational. It notes that the law insulates existing Ames florists from competition from stores like The Food King. Ames responds that its measure is intended to protect the consumer against fraud. Can The Food King prevail in its suit?

A. No, because the licensing statute is rationally related to consumer protection.
B. No, because the Court will not review economic and social legislation for constitutionality.
C. Yes, if the licensing statute was intended to insulate existing florists from competition.
D. Yes, because the statute is unreasonable.

ANALYSIS. Since the end of the *Lochner* era, the Court reviews economic regulation under a rational basis standard. Under that standard, to pass constitutional muster, a government needs to pursue a legitimate end, and its regulation must be rationally related to that end. Moreover, a rational basis for the regulation will be presumed by the court. This is a deferential standard of review, to be sure, but it is a form of judicial review. So **B** is incorrect. Rational basis review, however, is much more relaxed than that undertaken by the Court during the *Lochner* era. In those cases, the Court saw its role as determining for itself whether a particular exercise of the police power was reasonable or unreasonable. Because the Court has abjured that role, **D** is not the correct answer. Nor is **C**, which really goes to whether the licensing statute is wise public policy. Since 1937, in cases like *Ferguson v. Skrupa*, the Court has made clear that passing on the wisdom or public-spiritedness of legislation is not in its wheelhouse. That leaves **A**, which correctly applies the standard of review. Consumer protection is a legitimate end of the police power, and licensing to ensure quality and competence in service providers is certainly a rational means to achieve that end. Whether consumers really need protection from faux florists is regarded by the contemporary Court as a policy matter for the legislature.

There is one area in which economic substantive due process still shows some life: the law of punitive damages. Recent Supreme Court decisions have found that "grossly excessive" punitive damage awards violate the Due Process Clause of the Fourteenth Amendment.[6] Honda Motor Co. v. Oberg, 512 U.S. 415 (1994); TXO Production Corp. v. Alliance Resources Corp., 509 U.S. 443 (1993); Pacific Mutual Life Ins. Co. v. Haslip, 499 U.S. 1 (1991). *See also* Cooper Industries, Inc. v. Leatherman Tool Group, Inc., 532 U.S. 424 (2001) (holding that judicial review of punitive damage awards is de novo). Initially, the Court characterized these decisions as "procedural" in nature; recent decisions, however, seem to make clear that the Court is imposing substantive limits on the ability of state courts to make punitive damage awards.[7]

The first time the Court held that a punitive damage award was unconstitutional was in the case of *BMW of North America, Inc. v. Gore*, 517 U.S. 559 (1996). In that case, the Court invalidated a $2 million punitive damage award (reduced from $4 million) for allegedly fraudulent conduct arising out of failure to notify a purchaser that his new car had been repainted following damage in a hailstorm. *BMW*, 517 U.S. at 574-575. Gore was also awarded $4,000 in compensatory damages. *Id.* at 565.

In overturning the award, the Court announced "three guideposts" that informed its decision: "the degree of reprehensibility of the nondisclosure; the disparity between the harm . . . suffered by Dr. Gore and his punitive damages award; and the difference between this remedy and the civil penalties authorized or imposed in comparable cases." *Id.* at 574-575. Analyzing the facts in light of those guideposts, the Court concluded first that "[t]he harm BMW inflicted on Dr. Gore was purely economic" as opposed to "trickery and deceit," "affirmative acts of misconduct," "concealment of evidence," or other forms of "reprehensible conduct." *Id.* at 576, 579. Second, while "reject[ing] the notion that the constitutional line is marked by a simple mathematical formula," the Court found that the disparity between the punitive and actual damages—the $2 million award was 500 times the actual damages award—was "greater than those considered in" the Court's earlier cases. *Id.* at 582. Finally, the Court noted that "the $2 million economic sanction imposed on BMW is substantially greater than the statutory fines available in Alabama and elsewhere for similar malfeasance." *Id.* at 584. Considered together, the Court was "fully convinced that the grossly excessive award imposed in this case transcends the constitutional limit." *Id.* at 585-586.

In *State Farm Mutual Automobile Insurance Co. v. Campbell*, 538 U.S. 408 (2003), the Court invalidated a $145 million punitive damages award on a

---

6. The Eighth Amendment prohibits the imposition of "excessive fines" along with "[e]xcessive bail" and "cruel and unusual punishments." U.S. Const. amend. VIII. But the Court held the Eighth Amendment to be inapplicable to punitive damage awards. Browning-Ferris Industries of Vermont, Inc. v. Kelco Disposal, Inc., 492 U.S. 257 (1989).

7. *But see* Philip Morris, USA v. Williams, 549 U.S. 346 (2007) (concluding that to award punitive damages to a plaintiff in order to punish defendant for harm allegedly inflicted on others not before court would amount to a taking of property without due process of law).

$1 million actual damages claim in a refusal-to-settle case. Again, the Court found the reprehensibility of the conduct to be relatively low and the ratio between punitive and actual damages to be great. In fact, the Court, for the first time, came close to establishing a maximum permissible ratio between punitive and actual damages. "[F]ew awards exceeding a single-digit ratio between punitive and compensatory damages," Justice Kennedy wrote, "will satisfy due process." *State Farm*, 538 U.S. at 425. The Court did not suggest, however, when a larger ratio would be permissible, if ever.

4. *Substantive due process and civil liberties: back to the future*

Having ceded the field on economic rights, the Court did not give up entirely the project of identifying and protecting what it deemed important, nontextual constitutional rights. It simply shifted from protecting economic rights to protecting non-economic liberties. But even during the *Lochner* era the Court had protected some non-economic liberties.

In *Meyer v. Nebraska*, 262 U.S. 390 (1923), the Court reversed the conviction of a defendant convicted under a state law prohibiting the teaching of foreign languages to children. The Court further extended the liberty of the Due Process Clause to include "the right of the individual to contract, to engage in any of the common occupations of life, to acquire useful knowledge, to marry, establish a home and bring up children, to worship God according to the dictates of his own conscience, and generally to enjoy those privileges long recognized at common law as essential to the orderly pursuit of happiness by free men." *Meyer*, 262 U.S. at 399. The Court concluded that the law was "arbitrary and without reasonable relation to any end within the competency of the state." *Id.* at 403. Likewise, in *Pierce v. Society of Sisters*, 268 U.S. 510 (1925), the Court invalidated an Oregon law requiring all children to attend public school. Again the Court invalidated the law, finding that it "unreasonably interferes with the liberty of parents and guardians to direct the upbringing and education of children under their control." *Pierce*, 268 U.S. at 534-535.

But *Meyer* and *Pierce*, being products of the discredited and discarded *Lochner* era, could not directly serve as the foundation for a robust civil liberties jurisprudence. The Court was going to have to develop another theory. As discussed above, partial incorporation of the Bill of Rights provided one method for securing individual liberties against infringements by state governments. The other was to designate some liberty interests "fundamental" and require that the government demonstrate good reason for infringing on or curtailing those liberties.

(a) "Fundamental rights" and the Due Process Clause Justice Douglas first invoked "fundamental rights" in a case decided under the Equal Protection Clause. Oklahoma imposed the penalty of sterilization on individuals twice convicted of felonies involving "moral turpitude." Skinner, whose conviction for stealing a chicken placed him in jeopardy of that particularly draconian "two strikes" law, alleged that the penalty violated equal protection. Among other things, Justice Douglas noted that under Oklahoma law embezzlement and other white-collar crimes were not considered felonies involving moral turpitude, but grand larceny was. An embezzler could twice steal the same amount from her employer as a common thief, but not be eligible for sterilization. Skinner v. Oklahoma, 316 U.S. 535, 538-539 (1942).

While gesturing toward the deference afforded exercises of the police power, Douglas noted that "[w]e are dealing here with legislation which involves one of the basic civil rights of man. Marriage and procreation are fundamental to the very existence and survival of the race." *Skinner*, 316 U.S. at 541. Given the nature of the liberty interest involved, he continued, "our view [is] that strict scrutiny of the classification which a State makes in a sterilization law is essential, lest unwittingly or otherwise invidious discriminations are made against groups or types of individuals in violation of the constitutional guaranty of just and equal laws." *Id.* The Court held that the distinctions drawn between those crimes that made one eligible for sterilization and those that did not were not adequately justified by the state.

The die was cast: Borrowing from equal protection cases like *Skinner*, the Court held that laws infringing "fundamental" liberty interests would be subject to strict scrutiny. All other infringements of non-fundamental liberty interests would be presumed constitutional and would be required to satisfy the lenient rational basis standard. But *which* rights were fundamental? What criteria would the Court use to distinguish fundamental from non-fundamental rights—especially those that lacked a textual basis in the Constitution? The Courts in *Meyer*, *Pierce*, and *Skinner* simply proclaimed that the rights to acquire certain knowledge, to raise children according to a parent's own lights, and to procreate were fundamental. To avoid the taint of *Lochner*, the Justices realized that more than the Court's say-so was needed to justify this new non-economic substantive due process. As you will see below, however, whether the Court has succeeded where *Lochner*-era Courts failed is open to debate.

(b) Doctrinal examples *Contraception.* The first case after *Skinner* in which the Court invalidated a state law interfering with what it deemed a fundamental liberty interest was *Griswold v. Connecticut*, 381 U.S. 479 (1965). Connecticut barred the use of contraceptives by anyone, married or single. Moreover, Connecticut law imposed criminal penalties on anyone who aided or abetted the use of contraceptives, including anyone who counseled couples in their use. The Director of Planned Parenthood in Connecticut filed suit to reverse a conviction and fine for violating the Connecticut law. In an opinion by Justice Douglas, the author of *Skinner*, the Court invalidated the Connecticut law because it interfered with marital privacy.

Though privacy is not specifically mentioned in the Constitution, Douglas sought to avoid charges of *Lochner*-ism by inferring from a number of provisions in the Bill of Rights—he specifically mentioned the First, Third,

Fourth, Fifth, and Ninth Amendments—a more general concern with privacy. "[S]pecific guarantees in the Bill of Rights," he wrote, "have penumbras, formed by emanations from those guarantees that help give them life and substance. Various guarantees create zones of privacy." *Griswold*, 381 U.S. at 484. He then tied that general privacy concern to the marriage relationship, asking rhetorically whether we would "allow the police to search the sacred precincts of the marital bedroom for telltale signs of the use of contraceptives? The very idea is repulsive to the notions of privacy surrounding the marriage relationship." *Id.* at 485-486. It wasn't clear, however, whether the law was invalid because it infringed on a right that had roots in the Bill of Rights (privacy) or on a relationship that history and tradition had recognized as special (marriage). Interestingly, none of the Justices thought that seeking to control the sexual behavior of its citizens exceeded the state's power; all accepted the legitimacy of, for example, seeking to prevent fornication or adultery. The majority simply thought that the means used by Connecticut to do so in this case infringed on the rights of married couples to use contraceptives within the confines of their marriage.

Seven years later, however, the Court would sever the link between the privacy right recognized in *Griswold*—whatever its scope—and marriage in *Eisenstadt v. Baird*, 405 U.S. 438 (1972). *Eisenstadt* is a particularly important case because it served as a bridge between *Griswold*'s right to marital privacy and the broader right to privacy the Court relied on in *Roe v. Wade*, 410 U.S. 113 (1973), to hold that the right to terminate pregnancy is included within that privacy right.

Massachusetts prohibited the distribution of contraceptives to unmarried individuals, in part on the ground that it wanted to deter fornication. An unmarried couple sued, claiming the statute violated the Equal Protection Clause. The Court agreed, writing that "[i]f the right of privacy means anything, it is the right of the *individual*, married or single, to be free from unwarranted governmental intrusion into matters so fundamentally affecting a person as the decision whether to bear or beget a child." *Eisenstadt*, 405 U.S. at 453.

Abortion. The very next term, the implications of *Eisenstadt*'s "bear or beget" language became clear when the Court invalidated a Texas abortion ban, as well as the laws of many other states. Texas prohibited abortion except to save the life of the mother. Roe v. Wade, 410 U.S. 113 (1973). The Court held that the right to terminate a pregnancy was part of a larger "privacy" right recognized by *Griswold* and expanded by *Eisenstadt.* Those cases, wrote Justice Blackmun, "guarantee . . . certain areas or zones of privacy . . . under the Constitution." *Roe*, 410 U.S. at 152. The cases "also make it clear that the right has some extension to activities relating to marriage, procreation, contraception, family relationships, and child rearing and education." *Id.* at 152-153. Whatever its source, continued the Court, "[t]his right of privacy . . . is broad enough to encompass a woman's decision whether or not to terminate her pregnancy." *Id.*

at 153. The Court concluded that abortion was a fundamental right, and that state regulations of it were subject to strict scrutiny—that is, the state had to prove that its regulations were necessary or narrowly tailored to some compelling governmental interest.

In place of the near-total ban Texas had imposed, the Court held that the state's ability to regulate the procedure increased the closer the pregnancy got to term. Thus, during the first trimester of pregnancy the state could not regulate the procedure at all. Beginning in the second trimester, however, the Court held that the state's interest in the health of the mother became compelling and it "may regulate the abortion procedure to the extent that the regulation reasonably relates to the preservation and protection of maternal health." *Id.* at 163. The state's interest in protecting potential life, on the other hand, became compelling only at the point of "viability"—the point at which the fetus could live outside the womb—which the Court pegged at the beginning of the third trimester. "If the State is interested in protecting fetal life after viability," the Court concluded, "it may go so far as to proscribe abortion during that period, except when it is necessary to preserve the life or health of the mother." *Id.* at 164-165. Interestingly, there were only two dissenters in *Roe*, Justices Byron White and William Rehnquist. Justice Potter Stewart, who had dissented in *Griswold*, bowed to the new substantive due process and concurred.

So began two decades of litigation over the abortion issue, with anti-abortion activists, state legislatures, and two presidential administrations seeking to overturn *Roe v. Wade.* The following chart summarizes some of the major cases prior to the Court's 1992 decision in *Planned Parenthood of Southeastern Pennsylvania v. Casey*, 505 U.S. 833 (1992).

Major Post-*Roe* Court Decisions

Case	*Regulation*	*Constitutional?*
Planned Parenthood v. Danforth, 428 U.S. 52 (1976)	State requirement that married woman receive written spousal consent except where necessary to save her life	No
Maher v. Roe, 432 U.S. 464 (1977)	State Medicaid regulation funding childbirth but not nontherapeutic abortion	Yes
Bellotti v. Baird, 443 U.S. 622 (1979)	State requirement that minor receive consent of both parents or a court order permitting abortion without parental consent	No; consent can be required of one parent, as long as judicial bypass is included

Harris v. McRae, 448 U.S. 297 (1980)	Federal ban on use of Medicaid funds for abortion except in cases of rape or incest, or where necessary to save the life of the mother	Yes
Akron v. Akron Center for Reproductive Health, 462 U.S. 416 (1983) ("*Akron I*")	Ordinance requiring all abortions after first trimester to be performed in a hospital, requiring informed consent, and specifying a waiting period	No
Planned Parenthood v. Ashcroft, 462 U.S. 476 (1983)	Parental consent requirement with judicial bypass	Yes
Thornburgh v. American College of Obstetricians and Gynecologists, 476 U.S. 747 (1986)	"Informed consent" law requiring that printed material be given to woman prior to an abortion and that she give her informed consent to the procedure	No
Hodgson v. Minnesota, 497 U.S. 417 (1990)	State law requiring two-parent notification with judicial bypass	Yes
Ohio v. Akron Center for Reproductive Health, 497 U.S. 502 (1990) ("*Akron II*")	State law requiring one-parent notification with judicial bypass	Yes

In *Casey*, Pennsylvania had passed an abortion regulation statute that had five main components. First, it required a woman seeking an abortion to give her informed consent after reviewing specific information provided to her by a doctor. Second, it imposed a 24-hour waiting period on women seeking abortion. Third, minors seeking abortions had to receive the informed consent of one parent, but the law provided for a judicial bypass. Fourth, a married woman had to certify that she had notified her husband of the intended abortion. These requirements were subject to a "medical emergency" exception. Finally, the Pennsylvania act imposed reporting requirements on facilities that performed abortions. 505 U.S. at 840-842. Note that the first two requirements were seemingly forestalled by the Court's prior decisions in *Akron I* and in *Thornburgh*. As it had been numerous times before, the Court in *Casey* was asked to overrule *Roe v. Wade*.

The Court declined to do so, although the plurality opinion, co-authored by Justices O'Connor, Kennedy, and Souter, made significant changes to *Roe*'s analytical framework. While reaffirming *Roe*, the joint opinion discarded the trimester framework, replacing it with "viability." After viability a state could prohibit abortions altogether, as long as exceptions were made for the life and health of the mother. Prior to viability, however, a state could regulate abortion as long as it did not impose an "undue burden" on a woman seeking an abortion. As the join opinion explained, "a finding of an undue burden is a shorthand for the conclusion that a state regulation has the purpose or effect of placing a substantial obstacle in the path of a women seeking an abortion of a nonviable fetus." *Casey*, 505 U.S. at 877. The joint opinion stated that not every burdensome regulation would necessarily be an undue, and thus unconstitutional, burden. In particular, the joint opinion stated that the state may create "structural mechanism[s]" by which it "express[es] profound respect for the life of the unborn. . . ." *Id.* It may not "prohibit any woman from making the ultimate decision to terminate her pregnancy before viability." *Id.* at 879.

Applying the new undue burden standard, the joint opinion found that the informed consent provision, including the 24-hour waiting period, was constitutional. In so doing the joint opinion overruled *Akron I* and *Thornburgh*. "The idea that important decisions will be more informed and deliberate if they follow some period of reflection does not strike us as unreasonable." *Id.* at 885. While acknowledging that the 24-hour waiting period would make it more expensive for some women to obtain an abortion, merely increasing the expense, the Justices concluded, did not make the burden an undue one. A plurality also upheld the parental consent provision and the record keeping requirements. The joint opinion, however, did not uphold the spousal notification provision, finding that it imposed an undue burden on a woman seeking an abortion. The Justices were convinced by the facts on record that married women who do not inform their husbands of their having had an abortion usually have good reasons not to—the threat of violence chief among them. "The spousal notification requirement is thus likely to prevent a significant number of women from obtaining an abortion." *Id.* at 893.

Though *Casey* has not ended the controversy over abortion, it did reduce its prominence on the Supreme Court's docket. State and federal legislative efforts then shifted to outlawing so-called partial-birth or late-term abortions, which opponents argued were tantamount to infanticide. The first of these, a Nebraska statute outlawing pre-viability late-term abortions, was invalidated by the Court because the Court found that (1) it was drafted so that it potentially banned a generally accepted method for aborting a late-term fetus and (2) the statute lacked an exception for the health of the mother. Stenberg v. Carhart, 530 U.S. 914 (2000). *Stenberg* was also significant because a majority of the Court explicitly adopted the *Casey* joint opinion's "undue burden" standard as the test for the regulation of abortions.

Despite *Stenberg*, Congress passed and the President signed a federal partial-birth abortion ban in 2003. In 2007, a closely divided Court *upheld* that ban in *Gonzales v. Carhart*, 550 U.S. 124 (2007), even though the federal ban too lacked an exception for the health of the mother. In contrast to the ban in *Stenberg*, the congressional ban recited at length an alleged medical consensus that late-term abortions where the fetus was partially delivered into the birth canal before being aborted were *never* necessary to preserve the health of the mother. In addition, congressional drafters were careful not to conflate the partial-delivery method they were trying to ban with dilation and evacuation, a common, if gruesome, means of late-term abortion. A lengthy definition section in the congressional ban made clear that the former, not the latter, procedure was the one prohibited. 550 U.S. at 141-143.

The majority thought that Congress was entitled to "express[] respect for the dignity of human life" and act to protect the medical community by banning the procedure. *Casey*, the majority held, permitted both. Further, Congress was permitted to clearly demarcate the line between infanticide and abortion. Justice Kennedy, writing for the majority, also speculated that the ban was necessary to ensure informed consent to abortion procedures. His fear was that doctors would spare women the details of the partial-birth procedure, which would mean that the state could not "ensur[e] so grave a choice [was] well informed." *Id.* at 159. As for the claim that the ban was an undue burden because it lacked an exception for the health of the woman, Justice Kennedy wrote that because medical uncertainty existed regarding the need for such an exception, Congress had discretion to act, and that the act was not unconstitutional on its face. The Court held out the possibility that in a particular case, the ban would be unconstitutional because of the need to preserve a specific woman's health. *Id.* at 129-130.

QUESTION 6. Informed consent? The State of Ames General Assembly recently passed an abortion statute. Among other provisions, the statute contains an informed consent provision requiring a woman seeking a pre-viability abortion to receive information regarding the procedure 24 hours in advance of the procedure. The literature describes the procedure, fetal growth, and mentions alternatives to abortion, including adoption. A nurse or doctor distributes the material and then answers questions. No abortion can be performed—except in an emergency—for 24 hours after distribution of the material. In addition, a woman seeking an abortion, in addition to receiving literature, must submit to an ultrasound. The age and development of the fetus are recorded by the doctor (with the mother's personal identifying information omitted) and the ultrasound is shown to the mother. Presenting the statute to the Assembly, its chief sponsor said, "This will reduce the number of abortions performed in this state. What mother would knowingly kill her baby once she sees its picture there on the ultrasound machine sucking its thumb and moving around in her womb?" Would a court likely uphold the Ames statute if it is challenged in a lawsuit?

A. Yes, because not every burden is an unconstitutional "undue burden."
B. No, because the purpose was to place an obstacle in the path of someone seeking a pre-viability abortion.
C. No, because it is not narrowly tailored.
D. Yes, because the state is permitted to express a preference for birth over abortion.

ANALYSIS. Recall that after *Casey*, the standard of review changed to the undue burden test. Because **C** describes part of the strict scrutiny standard of review, it is incorrect. The new standard of review asks whether the regulation is a permissible means of achieving a legitimate interest, one of which is preserving the state's interest in potential life. While **D** restates this part of the *Casey* opinion, it does not go on to ask whether the means used here to express that preference are permissible. To be a permissible means of achieving a legitimate end, the regulation may not be an undue burden, defined by the *Casey* joint opinion as having the purpose or effect of placing a substantial obstacle in the path of a woman seeking a pre-viability abortion. While **A** is correct—not all burdens will be "undue"—it does not address the question whether the ultrasound requirement is such a burden. Therefore, it is not the best answer. That leaves **B**, which, on these facts, is the best answer. *Casey* says that undue burdens can result from either purposes or effects. The facts strongly suggest that the purpose in proposing the ultrasound requirement was to pressure a woman not to have an abortion by showing her pictures of the fetus. The sponsor says nothing about wanting the woman to make an informed choice; his remarks seem aimed only at preventing her from going through with the procedure.

QUESTION 7. **Undue burdens?** Which of the following restrictions on abortion would be *least* likely to pass constitutional muster if challenged?

A. A five-day period of reflection before an abortion could be performed.
B. A ban on abortions performed in clinics receiving public funds.
C. A requirement that facilities performing abortions maintain records of all abortions performed and report any complications resulting from abortions to the state.
D. A law requiring unemancipated minors to have the consent of at least one parent prior to receiving an abortion, unless a judge permits the minor to bypass the consent requirement.

ANALYSIS. Rephrased in terms of *Casey*'s standard of review, the question is which of the choices would likely be found to be an "undue burden." If you read the foregoing material carefully, you will recall that two of the choices actually passed muster under *Roe*'s strict scrutiny regime. *Maher* and *Harris* upheld funding restrictions on abortion, making clear that infringement of the right and refusal to subsidize it were conceptually distinct. *Casey* itself said that simply making abortions more expensive did not, ipso facto, impose an undue burden on the right. Therefore, **B** would likely be upheld. The same goes for **D**; a number of pre-*Casey* decisions made clear that as long as a judicial bypass was available, the requirement of parental consent for minors was constitutionally permissible. The record keeping requirements described in **C** are similar to those upheld in *Casey*, so they are also unobjectionable. That leaves **A**, which is the best answer. Although the 24-hour waiting period was upheld in *Casey*, the Court hinted that it might not be as solicitous toward waiting periods in excess of 24 hours. Certainly the state would have a considerable burden to bear explaining why a period of five days was necessary to promote "reflection." Further, because *Casey* held that any regulation with the purpose *or effect* of placing a substantial obstacle in the path of a woman seeking to terminate a nonviable fetus, even if the legislature's heart was pure in believing that five days was necessary to promote reflection, the effect of such a lengthy waiting period would likely be found to be a substantial obstacle.

Familial relationships. *Meyer, Pierce*, and *Griswold* all recognized the family as a special unit and limited the state's ability to interfere with family decisions about education, child rearing, and childbearing. Subsequent cases have reinforced the privileged position of the family, affirming the earlier view of the *Meyer* and *Pierce* Courts that aspects of family ordering are "fundamental."

The City of East Cleveland, Ohio, passed an ordinance prohibiting all but single families from occupying housing units, and then defining "family" to exclude a group consisting of a mother, son, and grandchildren, one of whom was a cousin to the other grandchildren. The Moore family sued. Moore v. City of East Cleveland, 431 U.S. 494 (1977). A plurality of the Court concluded that freedom of choice in matters of marriage and family was a fundamental one, and that interference with those rights had to be "examine[d] carefully," scrutinizing "the importance of the governmental interests advanced and the extent to which they are served by the challenged regulation." *Moore*, 431 U.S. at 499. The City claimed that the ordinance was intended to alleviate "overcrowding, minimiz[e] traffic and parking congestion, and avoid[] an undue financial burden on East Cleveland's school system." *Id.* at 499-500. While terming the goals "legitimate," the plurality concluded that "the ordinance . . . serves them marginally, at best." *Id.* at 500. For example, the Court noted that the ordinance would permit "any family consisting only of husband, wife, and unmarried children to live together, even if the family contained a half dozen licensed drivers, each with his or her own car. At the same time it forbids an adult brother and sister to share a household, even if both faithfully use public transportation." *Id.* The Court rejected suggestions that the liberty associated with family "extends only to the nuclear family" and paid homage to the tradition of extended family members all living under one roof. It concluded that the Constitution "prevents East Cleveland from standardizing its children—and its adults—by forcing all to live in certain narrowly defined family patterns." *Id.* at 506.

But as the Court made clear in an earlier case, on which East Cleveland had relied, family liberty extends only to individuals who are truly related to one another. In *Village of Belle Terre v. Boraas*, 416 U.S. 1 (1974), the Court refused to invalidate an ordinance prohibiting unrelated persons from occupying the same house. Analyzing the ordinance under the deferential rational basis standard, the Court concluded that the ordinance was rationally related to legitimate state interests such as preserving property values, reducing noise and crowding, and alleviating traffic congestion. The lack of any fundamental interest involvement in *Village of Belle Terre* is what made the ordinance permissible, whereas the East Cleveland ordinance was invalidated.

Even within a family, the Court has tended to privilege the rights of otherwise fit parents to raise their children free from the interference of others or the state. Washington State permitted any person to petition for visitation rights with children if such visitation was in the child's best interest. Grandparents of a deceased father petitioned for visitation rights over the objections of the children's mother (their daughter-in-law). Troxel v. Granville, 530 U.S. 57 (2000). A plurality of the Court held that the law violated the liberty interests of a fit, custodial parent to decide how her children were to be raised. Under the law, the wishes of the custodial parent were not given any weight at all. *Troxel*, 530 U.S. at 72-73.

QUESTION 8. Child's work. The State of Ames has banned all employment of children under 17 years of age. "Employment" is defined broadly as any job, task, service, or undertaking for which the child receives compensation in cash or in kind. Which of the following parties would have the greatest chance of successfully challenging the statute?

A. A 16-year-old who alleges that the law infringes on her liberty to offer her services as a lifeguard.

B. Parents of a 15-year-old who require their son to do housework and yard work in exchange for a weekly cash allowance.

C. The owner of a local ice cream shop whose entire workforce consists of 15- and 16-year-olds.

D. None of the above. The law is rationally related to legitimate governmental interests.

ANALYSIS. Review time! This question pulls together a few threads of this chapter. We know that, after *Lochner*, economic regulations, like the Ames law here, will not generally be subject to strict scrutiny, but will receive the more deferential rational basis review. The law does indeed infringe on the "liberty of contract" of employers and employees, but that fact alone is not enough to warrant judicial intervention. Therefore, **A** and **C** are incorrect. But if you then concluded **D** must be the correct answer, you were a little hasty. There is one potential plaintiff among the choices who might have a good chance of winning—the parents! If, as *Meyer*, *Pierce*, and *Troxel* maintain, parents have a fundamental right to raise their children relatively free from governmental interference, then a law that is broad enough to forbid you from requiring your children to work in exchange for an allowance (or simply as part of the family responsibilities) would seem to infringe upon that freedom. At the very least, the government would have to justify its sweeping definition of employment, or its lack of an exception for entities such as family businesses. The case wouldn't necessarily be a slam-dunk, but of the available choices, **B** is the best answer.

QUESTION 9. It's a family affair. Following a scandal that received substantial attention in the press, Ames revised its probate code to prohibit inheritance by adult adoptees if the testator had disinherited his natural children. Julius, a wealthy Ames citizen, had a natural son from whom he had been estranged for many years; he had no other heirs. To prevent his substantial estate from passing to his son, Julius adopted Octavius, an adult with whom Julius was quite close. Julius then made a will naming Octavius as his heir and disinheriting his natural son. After the will was executed, Ames's law was passed. What is Julius's strongest argument against the constitutionality of the Ames inheritance law?

A. The law interferes with Julius's liberty to dispose of his property as he sees fit.
B. The law is unreasonable.
C. The law is not narrowly tailored to any compelling governmental interest.
D. The law unreasonably interferes with Julius's liberty of contract.

ANALYSIS. This question also serves as a mini-review. If you'll recall, economic and social matters that don't rise to the level of fundamental rights are deemed legitimate objects of regulation, and are subject to a rational basis test. Regulation often interferes with one's ability to dispose of property at will, so **A** is incorrect. Moreover, the Court no longer, as in the days of economic substantive due process, passes on the reasonableness or unreasonableness of economic regulation, meaning that **B** is not a good choice. **D** too is incorrect; numerous laws interfering with liberty of contract exist and are regularly upheld by courts. That leaves **C**, which is the best answer. Note that this law does not simply regulate the disposition of property, but also has the effect of interfering with the effects of an adoption and the disposal of property among family members. In essence, the state is relegating adopted children, in some situations, to a second-class position. The law permits the disinheritance of some natural children for the benefit of other natural children, but forbids it where the beneficiary is adopted. Such interference would likely trigger strict scrutiny.

A third aspect of family life that the Court has singled out for special treatment is marriage. As we saw in *Griswold*, the Court's original recognition of a right of privacy was closely connected to the marriage relationship. In subsequent cases, the Court has protected the decision to marry from interference by the state, even among those who are, in the old English euphemism, currently "guests of Her Majesty's government"—prisoners, in other words.

In a long-overdue decision, the Court invalidated Virginia's ban on interracial marriage in *Loving v. Virginia*, 388 U.S. 1 (1968), stating that the Constitution guarantees an individual "the freedom to marry, or not marry, a person of another race" free from state interference. Later, in *Zablocki v. Redhail*, 434 U.S. 374 (1978), the Court invalidated a Wisconsin law prohibiting marriage by one whose child support obligations were in arrears. Though the case was decided under the Equal Protection Clause, the law received strict scrutiny because the Court held that marriage was a fundamental right. *Zablocki* in turn furnished the basis for the Court's holding in *Turner v. Safley*, 482 U.S. 78 (1987), that the state could not condition a prisoner's ability to marry on the warden's permission. Though the Court accepted the state's reasons for wanting to restrict marriage among inmates, it found the regulation was too intrusive.

Note, however, that the Court's right-to-marry decisions are all premised on traditional conceptions of marriage as being between a man and a woman. As we shall see in the section below on sexual autonomy, cases like *Loving* and *Zablocki* have not, heretofore, furnished the basis for the right of same-sex couples to marry.

The "right" to die. The title of this section is something of a misnomer. The Court has never, in so many words, recognized a fundamental right to "die." It has, however, decided several cases dealing with the conditions under which persons—or their surrogates—can refuse unwanted medical care. Later the Court took up challenges to state laws banning assisted suicide, as plaintiffs sought the Court's recognition of a fundamental right of certain patients to control the circumstances of their own death.

In *Cruzan v. Missouri Dep't of Health*, 497 U.S. 261 (1990), the Court was asked to invalidate Missouri's requirement that clear and convincing evidence be presented of an incompetent patient's wishes before surrogate decision-makers (here, parents) can withdraw hydration and nutrition. Nancy Cruzan had been in a "persistent vegetative state" for seven years. Her parents wished the feeding tubes to be removed, and presented testimonial evidence—Nancy

Cruzan had not left a living will, durable power of attorney, or the like—at the trial court that Nancy had not wished for extraordinary life-prolonging measures be used. The Missouri Supreme Court, however, reversed the trial court, holding that the standard had not been satisfied. The parents sued, claiming that the standard violated her due process rights.

In its opinion, the Court was careful to distinguish between two situations—the right of an otherwise competent person to refuse unwanted medical care, including hydration and nutrition, and that of an *incompetent* person to do so through surrogate decisionmakers. As to the first, the Court assumed arguendo that "the United States Constitution would grant a competent person a constitutionally protected right to refuse life-saving hydration and nutrition." *Cruzan*, 497 U.S. at 279. The Court noted that the doctrine of informed consent had deep roots in Anglo-American law; it developed in response to the law's view of medical treatment without consent as a battery. To assume that the rights of a competent person are the same as those of an incompetent patient, the Court continued, "begs the question" because the latter "is not able to make an informed and voluntary choice to exercise a hypothetical right to refuse treatment. . . ." *Id.* at 280. The Court then reframed the question, asking whether Missouri's clear-and-convincing evidence standard for withdrawal of treatment by surrogates violated the Constitution. The Court concluded it did not.

The Court held that the state's interests—protection and preservation of human life—were permissible ones to pursue. The state's heightened evidentiary requirements, moreover, were "legitimate" given the irrevocability of an erroneous determination that the patient would have wanted life-sustaining treatment to be withdrawn. "We believe," the Court concluded, "that Missouri may permissibly place an increased risk of an erroneous decision on those seeking to terminate an incompetent individual's life-sustaining treatment." *Id.* at 283. Justice O'Connor concurred, but wrote separately to express her opinion that the state might be constitutionally required to recognize delegation of decisionmaking authority to surrogates. *Id.* at 289-292 (O'Connor, J., concurring). The dissenters agreed that the right to refuse unwanted medical care was a fundamental right, but, unlike the majority, they would extend it to incompetent persons and permit the right's exercise free of the state's heightened evidentiary requirement for withdrawal of treatment. *Id.* at 301-302 (Brennan, J., dissenting).

By the end of the decade, competent but terminally ill patients were challenging state laws that prohibited the assistance of another to commit suicide. Two lawsuits reached the Court in 1997. One, *Washington v. Glucksberg*, 521 U.S. 702 (1997), presented the question whether the ban on assisted suicide violated the due process rights of competent, terminally ill patients to receive medical assistance to end their own lives. The other, *Vacco v. Quill*, 521 U.S. 793 (1997), asked the Court to decide whether the distinction between a ban on assisted suicide and the right of a patient to refuse life-saving medical treatment enshrined in New York law violated the Equal Protection Clause. The Court upheld both, refusing to find in either the Due Process or Equal Protection Clause a fundamental right to end one's life with assistance.

Chief Justice Rehnquist's majority opinion first took up the question whether there was a fundamental right to assisted suicide. He rejected any analogies to the right recognized in *Cruzan*, noting that unlike the doctrine of informed consent that was recognized at common law, suicide and assisted suicide had long been illegal. *Glucksberg*, 521 U.S. at 702-703, 710-711. Further, he noted that "States' assisted suicide bans ha[d] in recent years been reexamined and, generally, reaffirmed." *Id.* at 716. "To hold for respondents," the Court wrote, "we would have to reverse centuries of legal doctrine and practice, and strike down the considered policy choice of almost every State." *Id.* at 723. This the Court was unwilling to do.

Because it concluded that the liberty interest here—committing suicide with the assistance of a medical professional—was *not* a fundamental one, the Court applied the rational basis standard. The Court found that each of the state's asserted interests—preserving human life, safeguarding the ethics and integrity of the medical profession, protecting vulnerable groups from coercion and undue influence, and preventing a possible slide from assisted suicide to involuntary euthanasia—were legitimate ones. *Id.* at 703-704. The ban, moreover, was "at least reasonably related to the . . . promotion and protection" of the interests. *Id.* at 735. Although the decision was unanimous, Justices O'Connor and Breyer expressed some concern that laws against assisted suicide could be applied to physicians who, in an effort to alleviate pain and suffering, administer drugs in doses sufficient to hasten the end of life, though that would not be the primary intent. Both expressed the opinion that, were a state to apply assisted suicide statutes in such a way, serious constitutional questions would be raised. *Id.* at 736-738 (O'Connor, J., concurring); *id.* at 792 (Breyer, J., concurring).[8]

QUESTION 10. DPA, DOA? Citing a study alleging that a high percentage of durable powers of attorney (DPAs) are either forged or obtained through fraud or undue influence, the Ames General Assembly has prohibited the delegation of medical decisionmaking authority to surrogates. Wendy, the wife and designated surrogate of Bill, who is in a persistent vegetative state, would like to exercise her authority and remove her husband's ventilator. Wendy sues, claiming that the law violates the Due Process Clause. A reviewing court would likely:

A. Strike down the law because it infringes Bill's right to die.
B. Uphold the law as a rational means of achieving a legitimate state interest.
C. Strike down the law because it is not narrowly tailored.
D. Uphold the law because it is an exercise of the state's police power.

8. In *Vacco*, the companion case to *Glucksberg*, the Court concluded that New York's distinction between assisted suicide and the withdrawal of life-sustaining medical care was not an arbitrary or irrational one and thus did not violate the Equal Protection Clause.

ANALYSIS. We know from *Cruzan* and *Glucksberg* that the Court seems to regard the right of a competent individual to refuse unwanted medical treatment as fundamental. The Court stressed in *Glucksberg* and *Vacco,* however, that there was no right to commit suicide, assisted or not. Therefore, **A** is not the correct answer—there is no fundamental right to "die." State infringements of fundamental rights, moreover, are not deferentially reviewed under a rational basis standard, but rather are subject to strict scrutiny. **B**, therefore, is not the correct answer because it states the wrong standard of review. **D** is not the right answer either, because though the statute *is* an exercise of the state's police power, that says nothing about whether it is a *constitutional* exercise of that power. That leaves **C**, which is the best answer. The right to refuse unwanted medical care is a fundamental right, according to the Court. Delegating that decisionmaking power to a surrogate guarantees that one's wishes will be respected if one becomes incapacitated. While the prevention of fraud and preservation of life are no doubt compelling state interests, those interests could be achieved short of barring *all* durable powers of attorney; additional witness requirements, for example, could help ensure that the document was genuine and that no undue influence was applied. Depriving otherwise competent individuals of all means to ensure their wishes will be carried out in the future would sweep too broadly to survive strict scrutiny.

QUESTION 11. **Can't I get a witness?** Assume that, after *Cruzan,* Missouri passed a statute stating that the clear-and-convincing evidence standard could be satisfied *only* by some writing—such as a living will or health care directive—expressing the wishes of an incompetent patient. Oral testimony will no longer be admissible. Which of the following would be the best argument for such a statute's constitutionality?

A. The state is entitled to act to preserve life; excluding oral testimony is a reasonable means to ensure that care is not mistakenly withdrawn.
B. Preservation of life is a compelling governmental interest.
C. There is no fundamental right to delegate decisionmaking authority other than to the patient.
D. A and C.

ANALYSIS. According to *Cruzan,* the state is entitled to enact rules that preserve the status quo for incompetent patients in furtherance of its choice to protect life against mistaken deprivation. So while **B** may be true, it does not address whether the state may try to preserve life in this manner. Moreover **C** is incorrect, if one reads between the lines of *Cruzan*: Justice O'Connor seemed to suggest that the state *was* obligated to provide some method for the delegation of decisionmaking authority so that the patient's wishes, whatever they were, are respected when the patient is no longer able to express them. That means **D** is incorrect as well, leaving **A**, which is the best answer. Under the logic in *Cruzan*, if the state can impose a heightened evidentiary standard, it can also specify what sorts of evidence would (and would not) be admitted to satisfy that standard. It wouldn't be unreasonable or arbitrary to conclude that what amounts to hearsay testimony about the wishes of someone who cannot testify is not as reliable as some document written and witnessed ahead of time.

QUESTION 12. **Perpetrating palliation?** Ames's assisted suicide statute prohibits a physician from knowingly administering drugs to patients in quantities that would hasten the patient's death. A doctor who works with hospice patients is charged with assisting suicide, because he administers high doses of morphine to terminally ill patients to alleviate their pain. The state alleges that what he does is tantamount to assisted suicide. A terminally ill patient sues, claiming that the Ames statute is unconstitutional if applied in this manner. What would be the strongest argument supporting the patient's position?

A. The law deprives the patient of the fundamental right to control end-of-life decisions.
B. The state has no legitimate interest in regulating medical care.
C. The law forces terminally ill patients to endure pain and deprives them of the ability to receive medical care to alleviate that pain.
D. The law does not take into account the patient's quality of life.

ANALYSIS. Neither *Cruzan* nor *Glucksberg* recognized a fundamental right to control end-of-life decisions. Therefore, **A** is not the correct answer. **B** is incorrect because the state *does* have a legitimate interest in both regulating medical care and preserving life. States regulate medical care in numerous ways—through physician licensing and medical malpractice statutes, to name two. According to *Cruzan*, a state is not required to take into account any diminution of a patient's quality of life when regulating end-of-life matters, so **D** isn't the answer. That leaves **C**, which is the strongest argument of the lot. Recall that both Justice O'Connor and Justice Breyer assumed that assisted suicide laws were not, and would not be, applied to palliative care of terminally ill patients, even though to alleviate pain, drugs may be administered in such quantities that death would result. Those Justices assumed that a person could not constitutionally be forced to endure pain at the end of life simply because the administration of drugs would hasten death. This is the flip side of the right to refuse unwanted medical treatment.

Sexual autonomy and same-sex marriage. The final area of non-economic substantive due process in which the Court has been active of late is the area of what, for lack of a better term, might be called "sexual autonomy" or "intimate associations." More bluntly, to what extent may the state constitutionally regulate the sex lives of its citizens? Recall that the Court in *Griswold* assumed that preventing fornication and adultery was a legitimate aim of the state. Traditional definitions of the police power, moreover, included "morality" among the list of things that power safeguarded (in addition to health, safety, and welfare).

By the 1970s, these assumptions were being called into question. And by the 1980s, many read into the Court's *Griswold-Eisenstadt-Roe* line of cases a right to be free from state regulation of non-commercial sexual behavior between consenting adults. If recognized, this right would be of considerable help to homosexual couples, who could face prosecution for "sodomy" under laws still on the books in many states.

Initially, though, the Court was unwilling to go along. In *Bowers v. Hardwick*, 478 U.S. 186 (1986), the Court refused to recognize what it termed a fundamental right to engage in homosexual sodomy, and upheld Georgia's criminalization of sodomy (which, despite the Court's characterization, applied to heterosexual conduct as well). Justice Byron White's majority opinion noted that sodomy laws had been around for many years, and that any argument that a right to engage in such activity was part of the nation's history and tradition was "at best, facetious." 478 U.S. at 194. The Court went on to hold that the ban was rationally related to Georgia's legitimate interest in expressing moral disapproval of sodomy, even though the Attorney General of Georgia conceded at oral argument that no heterosexuals had been charged under the law.

Ten years passed before the Court signaled it was ready to revisit *Bowers.* In *Romer v. Evans*, 517 U.S. 620 (1996), an equal protection case,[9] the Court invalidated a Colorado constitutional amendment that disqualified sexual orientation for protection under state and local antidiscrimination laws.[10] The Court's opinion did not even mention *Bowers.* Almost a decade after *Romer*, the other shoe dropped, and the Court overruled *Bowers.* Lawrence v. Texas, 539 U.S. 558 (2003). Curiously, though, the Court did *not* recognize a new fundamental right; but neither did it review the Texas statute with the deferential rational basis test used in the Court's other cases.

Unlike Georgia's statute, the Texas law banned homosexual sodomy only. Responding to an erroneous report of a disturbance involving a gun, the police observed John Lawrence engaged in anal sex with another man. He was charged with and convicted of violating Texas's sodomy statute.

Before the Supreme Court, Texas asserted its right to express, through the ban, its citizens' moral disapproval of homosexual sodomy. The Court disagreed. "The statutes," the Court wrote, "seek to control a personal relationship that . . . is within the liberty of persons to choose without being punished as criminals." *Lawrence*, 539 U.S. at 567. At least where consenting adults were

---

9. *Bowers* did not address the question whether bans on homosexual, but not heterosexual, sodomy would violate the Equal Protection Clause.

10. *Romer* is discussed in Chapter 4.

concerned, the "liberty protected by the Constitution allows homosexual persons the right to" express their sexuality "in intimate conduct with another person," especially when that conduct is "but one element in a personal bond that is more enduring." *Id.*

Texas's interest in expressing majoritarian moral disapproval of homosexual sodomy was not, in the Court's view, a legitimate governmental interest. "The State cannot demean [petitioners'] existence or control their destiny by making their private sexual conduct a crime," the Court concluded. *Id.* at 578. But the opinion was careful to note that

> [t]he present case does not involve minors. It does not involve persons who might be injured or coerced or who are situated in relationships where consent might not easily be refused. It does not involve public conduct or prostitution. It does not involve whether the government must give formal recognition to any relationship that homosexual persons seek to enter.

Id.

The inspiring rhetoric of the majority opinion, however, masked some uncertainty. First, although the Court overruled *Bowers*, it did not hold that there was a fundamental right of consenting adults to engage in sexual activity. Its holding that the expression of majoritarian moral disapproval of homosexual conduct wasn't "legitimate" suggests that the Court applied some form of the rational basis standard. This more rigorous form of rational basis—which will be seen again equal protection cases—was described as having "bite" by Professor Gerald Gunther. Gerald Gunther, *The Supreme Court, 1971 Term—Foreword: In Search of Evolving Doctrine on a Changing Court: A Model for a Newer Equal Protection*, 86 Harv. L. Rev. 1 (1972).

But it was clear that the standard applied was not the rational basis standard of *Ferguson v. Skrupa*. Specifically, the Court did not presume that the Texas law was constitutional, nor did it hypothesize other, acceptable reasons Texas might have had for passing the law. Second, it was unclear whether, after *Lawrence*, morality is *never* a legitimate basis for lawmaking. Finally, it was curious that, as in *Griswold*, the majority's opinion emphasized the effect of the law on homosexuals in a relationship. As it happens, Lawrence and Garner, the man he was with, were not in a relationship at the time of Lawrence's arrest.

Though the majority opinion in *Lawrence* took pains to forestall attempts to invoke its decision in the ongoing controversy over gay marriage, it found itself revisiting the issue in *United States v. Windsor*, 133 S. Ct. 2675 (2013), and in *Hollingsworth v. Perry*, 133 S. Ct. 2652 (2013). In the latter, the Court declined to rule on the merits of California's Proposition 8, which had amended the California Constitution to eliminate recognition of same-sex marriages. The Court held that no party had standing to appeal a district court's judgment that the amendment violated the Equal Protection and Due Process Clauses since the state itself had declined to defend Prop 8 in Court. *Hollingsworth*, 133 S. Ct. at 2668.

In *Windsor*, however, the Court did reach the merits of a legal challenge to the portion of the federal Defense of Marriage Act defining marriage as being between a man and a woman. This federal definition of marriage affected over one thousand federal laws and regulations. While the Court suggested that its opinion was grounded in principles of federalism—state law, after all, usually governed domestic relations—the core of the opinion invoked the due process and equal protection principles. *Windsor*, 133 S. Ct. at 2692 (noting that it was "unnecessary to decide whether this federal intrusion on state power is a violation of the Constitution because it disrupts the federal balance"). New York, the Court noted, had undertaken to confer "protection and dignity" to same-sex marriages. *Id.* The federal law, in the Court's view, sought to strip this protection out of "animus"; in so doing, it violated the Due Process and Equal Protection Clauses. *Id.* at 2693. "The avowed purpose and practical effect of the law here in question," the Court concluded, "are to impose a disadvantage, a separate status, and so a stigma upon all who enter into same-sex marriages made lawful by the unquestioned authority of the States." *Id.* Aside from the Court's mention of *Lawrence* and its protection of certain aspects of the personal bond that develops between two people, it was vague about both (1) what the nature of the liberty interest violated by DOMA was and (2) what standard of review applied. It's possible that the Court could draw upon the *Loving-Zablocki-Turner* line of cases and hold that the right to marry is fundamental without regard to the sexuality of the couples seeking marriage. For an example of a court recently taking this tack, see Kitchen v. Herbert, 2014 WL 2868044, at *22 (10th Cir. 2014) (striking down Utah's same-sex marriage ban as a violation of plaintiffs' fundamental right to marry).

Despite the Court's studied ambiguity, and in contrast to its cautious tone in *Lawrence*, the Court's reasoning seemed to invite scrutiny of same-sex marriage bans in the states. *See id.* at 2709 (Scalia, J., dissenting) ("In my opinion, however, the view that *this* Court will take of state prohibition of same-sex marriage is indicated beyond mistaking by today's opinion."). Lower federal courts seem to have taken the hint, with a number of them striking down same-sex marriage bans, relying in part on language from the *Windsor* decision. *See, e.g.*, DeBoer v. Snyder, 973 F. Supp. 2d 757 (E.D. Mich. 2014) (holding Michigan constitutional amendment mandating heterosexual marriage violated the Equal Protection Clause; declining to rule on due process challenge); Tanco v. Haslam, 2014 WL 997525 (M.D. Tenn. 2014) (preliminarily enjoining Tennessee's anti-recognition laws on equal protection grounds, as applied to six named plaintiffs); Lee v. Orr, 2014 WL 683680 (N.D. Ill. 2014) (Illinois ban on same-sex marriage unconstitutional as applied to a particular county); Bostic v. Rainey, 970 F. Supp. 2d 456 (E.D. Va. 2014) (Virginia ban on same-sex marriage unconstitutional); Bourke v. Beshear, 2014 WL 556729 (W.D. Ky. 2014) (finding that Kentucky anti-recognition law was unconstitutional); Obergefell v. Wymyslo, 962 F. Supp. 2d 968 (S.D. Ohio 2013) (Ohio anti-recognition law unconstitutional).

QUESTION 13. Marry Mary? In response to the threat of judicial recognition of same-sex marriage under the Ames State Constitution, the Ames General Assembly proposed, and the voters of the State properly ratified, an amendment to the state constitution prohibiting the recognition of same-sex marriage. Supporters argued that traditional marriage was "under attack" and that the amendment was needed to "protect" marriage against "the homosexual lobby" and its "gay" agenda. Recognition of same-sex marriage, they argued, would undermine the traditional family and erode morals. Mary and Maggie are a same-sex couple that resides in Ames and wishes to challenge the ban under the Due Process Clause of the Fourteenth Amendment in federal district court. Which of the following would be the strongest argument available to the judge for striking down the ban?

A. Ames's ban violates Mary and Maggie's fundamental right to marry.
B. Ames cannot show that its ban sweeps too broadly and is not narrowly tailored.
C. Ames's ban does not further a legitimate governmental interest.
D. Ames's ban infringes upon Mary and Maggie's liberty interest.

ANALYSIS. Remember that the question asks you to choose the *strongest* argument among those listed. Even if you think each is weak, one is clearly better than the others, based on the current state of case law. While it is true that *Loving* et al. have recognized a fundamental right of marriage for heterosexual couples, the Supreme Court has not—as of this writing—suggested that those cases apply to same-sex couples. Therefore, **A** is not a particularly strong argument based on the current state of doctrine. If the right to same-sex marriage is not yet a fundamental right, then any other answer implying that strict scrutiny is the proper standard of review is also not very strong. That eliminates **B.** If you were tempted by **D**, remember that many state laws infringe upon individuals' liberty interests to, e.g., take drugs or engage in other activities the law disallows. The issue usually is whether the liberty interest in question is fundamental or not. Only if it can be defined as fundamental do we require the government to bear a heavy burden before permitting it to infringe. That leaves **C**, which is the best answer. From both *Lawrence* and *Windsor*, we know that the Court considers statements like those in the facts to exhibit "animus" of the sort condemned first in United States Dep't. of Agric. v. Moreno, then later in *Lawrence* and *Windsor*. As the Court has held, the desire to single out and disadvantage some identifiable group just because you don't like them or because you consider them "immoral" is not a legitimate governmental interest.

(c) Substantive due process recap As you can see, substantive due process can be a particularly confusing area of constitutional doctrine. Therefore, it might be helpful to summarize some of the main features of contemporary doctrine. To oversimplify, if a state infringes upon a liberty interest deemed by the Court to be fundamental, then it must satisfy strict scrutiny. That is, the law or regulation must further a compelling governmental interest and it must be narrowly tailored to that interest. Infringements of all other liberty interests need satisfy only the rational basis test, meaning that they must further a legitimate governmental interest and be rationally related to that interest. Laws infringing non-fundamental liberty interests are, by and large, presumed constitutional; and courts will often hypothesize legitimate ends or rational reasons for pursuing them through the means chosen, even if there is no evidence the legislature *actually* pursued those ends or relied on the reasons why the means were rationally related. This is all summarized in the supplied chart.

Contemporary Due Process Framework (Simple)

Nature of Liberty Interest	*Examples*	*Standard of Review*	*Representative Cases*
Fundamental	Procreation, family arrangements, child rearing, heterosexual marriage	Strict scrutiny: (a) compelling governmental interest; (b) regulation is "necessary" or "narrowly tailored" to meet that interest	*Zablocki v. Redhail*; *Moore v. City of East Cleveland*
Non-fundamental	Economic liberty, all other liberty interests not recognized by the Court as "fundamental"	Rational basis: (a) legitimate governmental interest; (b) regulation must be rationally related to that interest	*Ferguson v. Skrupa*; *Washington v. Glucksberg*

But the Court's doctrine does not always conform to the simple framework described above. In neither *Casey* nor *Lawrence* did the Court confine itself to the strict scrutiny/rational basis dichotomy, either creating a new standard of review (undue burden in *Casey*) or applying the rational basis standard in a much less deferential manner (in *Lawrence*). The next chart illustrates the more complicated due process framework.

Contemporary Due Process Framework (Complicated)

Nature of Liberty Interest	*Examples*	*Standard of Review*	*Representative Cases*
Fundamental	Procreation, family arrangements, child rearing, heterosexual marriage	Strict scrutiny: (a) compelling governmental interest; (b) regulation is "necessary" or "narrowly tailored" to meet that interest	*Zablocki v. Redhail*; *Moore v. City of East Cleveland*
?	Termination of pregnancy	Undue burden	*Planned Parenthood of Southeastern Pa. v. Casey*
?	Private, noncommercial, consensual sexual activity; same-sex marriage	Rational basis with "bite"	*Lawrence v. Texas*; *United States v. Windsor*
Non-fundamental	Economic liberty, all other liberty interests not recognized by the Court as "fundamental"	Rational basis: (a) legitimate governmental interest; (b) regulation must be rationally related to that interest	*Ferguson v. Skrupa*; *Washington v. Glucksberg*

Recall that at the beginning of this chapter I said that the debate over substantive due process can be conducted at the retail, doctrinal level or at the wholesale level. That is, it is all well and good to say that "fundamental" rights are given extra protection, but how does one determine whether a liberty interest will be deemed fundamental? Unfortunately, the Court has never settled on a single test for identifying fundamental rights ex ante, but individual members have employed a variety of tests that overlap and some that even conflict. This section will discuss the main ones, with examples.

Fundamental rights as natural rights. Early cases (*Lochner, Meyer, Pierce*) often made general claims about liberties that could be presumed to exist or to be inherent in one's personhood, and that government was not free to arbitrarily or unreasonably infringe upon. The Court held that certain rights are fundamental because the Court said they were. This confidence, in turn, stemmed from a belief, alluded to above, that there are some rights that—even if not God-given—are somehow inherent.

The classic statement, repeated often in these old substantive due process cases, is from *Allgeyer*, in which the Court defined "liberty" in the Fourteenth Amendment to

> embrace the right of the citizen to be free in the enjoyment of all his faculties; to be free to use them in all lawful ways; to live and work where he will; to earn his livelihood by any lawful calling; to pursue any livelihood or avocation, and for that purpose to enter into all contracts which may be proper, necessary, and essential to his carrying out to a successful conclusion the purposes above mentioned.

Meyer v. Nebraska added to the list certain non-economic rights, including the right "to acquire useful knowledge, to marry, to establish a home and bring up children, [and] generally to enjoy those privileges long recognized at common law as essential to the orderly pursuit of happiness by free men." Both cases simply assume the existence of such rights—most of which are not explicitly enumerated in the Constitution—and that no government is free to abridge them without good reason.

The Bill of Rights as a source of fundamental rights. Beginning in the early twentieth century, the Court began to "incorporate" specific provisions of the Bill of Rights through the Fourteenth Amendment and apply them to the states. Despite the urging of Justices including Hugo Black, the Court never incorporated the Bill of Rights in toto. Rather, the Court adopted the theory of "selective incorporation," whereby only those provisions "implicit in the concept of ordered liberty" would be applied to the states. Some have suggested that the Privileges or Immunities Clause of the Fourteenth Amendment was the provision originally intended to secure rights against the states—a reading that, whatever its historical merits, was foreclosed by the Court in *The Slaughter-house Cases.*

The Bill of Rights as a source of penumbral emanations. As the Court shed the mantle of guardian of economic rights in the 1930s, it simultaneously took up that of protector of individual liberties. However, the Court was just as anxious to signal a total retreat from the old regime of economic substantive due process. This left it with a problem: how to continue the protection of non-economic liberties begun in cases like *Meyer* and *Pierce* without seeming to endorse the economic substantive due process component of them. One way was through incorporation.

Other early cases, such as *Skinner v. Oklahoma* (which was decided under equal protection doctrine), simply announced the fundamental-ness of rights like that of procreation. Justice Douglas, who wrote both *Griswold* and *Skinner*, then attempted in *Griswold* to tie earlier cases to specific provisions of the Bill of Rights. *Meyer* and *Pierce* were disingenuously characterized as First Amendment decisions; and the right to privacy recognized in *Griswold* was rooted in those earlier cases and in the "penumbras" said to "emanate" from specific provisions of the Bill of Rights.

Common law interpretation. Another technique is for the Court to build on prior cases, with subsequent cases reinterpreting and perhaps broadening the holdings of past decisions. For example, *Eisenstadt* severed the connection between the privacy right created in *Griswold* and the marriage context in which the Court made its decision. The right, according to the *Eisenstadt* Court, had to be an individual one, and it had to apply to married and unmarried persons. Subsequently, *Roe* relied on both cases for the proposition that the privacy right encompassed an array of decisions, including the decision to terminate a pregnancy. By contrast, the *Bowers* Court refused to read the prior cases as standing for a broad autonomy right, restricting the cases instead to their particular contexts—childbearing, marital privacy, and contraception. None gave any warrant for regarding as "fundamental" the right "to engage in homosexual sodomy," according to the Court.

History and tradition. Perhaps the most "conservative" theory of substantive due process—conservative in the sense that it rather limits the judicial creation or recognition of substantive due process rights—is that urged by the late Chief Justice Rehnquist. According to Rehnquist, only those rights that have ascertainable roots in history or in our traditions (such as those protected at common law) should qualify for protection against state interference. For example, in *Cruzan*, his majority opinion assumed that a competent individual has a liberty interest in refusing unwanted medical care, including care that would hasten death, but felt comfortable doing so because the right to refuse care was implicit in the concept of informed consent necessary at common law, lest the medical care become battery. Both Rehnquist and Justice Antonin Scalia have separately urged that any right that the Court is asked to recognize be stated specifically, in order that the Court can ascertain whether that right was, in fact, recognized historically. The criticism of this position is that it freezes rights and takes no account of developments in the law.

The only certainty is that these debates will likely persist even as Court personnel, and the rights for which plaintiffs seek protection, change. As you can see in the substantive due process timeline below, the Court's concern has shifted over the years away from economic rights to those involving personal liberty and autonomy. Even within the due process doctrine questions remain that the Court will have to address, and that will likely flesh out many of the rights that the Court has recognized. Could a state require people to meet a stricter standard for exercising medical decisions on behalf of an incompetent person than that required by Missouri in *Cruzan*? Is *Lawrence* the end of all morals-based legislation? What (if anything) does it portend for the gay marriage debate? The Court's decisions in these areas often leave as many questions open as they answer. These unanswered questions form the basis for the future work of the Court and for future doctrine.

A Substantive Due Process Timeline

1856	*Wynehamer v. New York* (striking down state prohibition statute)
1868	Ratification of the Fourteenth Amendment
1873	*The Slaughter-house Cases* (rejecting substantive due process arguments brought by New Orleans butchers)
1877	*Munn v. Illinois* (permitting state regulation of property "affected with the public interest," such as grain elevators)
1887	*Mugler v. Kansas* (rejecting substantive due process claim brought by brewer that state prohibition statute was unconstitutional deprivation of property without due process of law)
1897	*Allgeyer v. Louisiana* (upholding Due Process Clause claim challenging constitutionality of Louisiana insurance regulation law)
1898	*Holden v. Hardy* (upholding regulation of miners' working hours)
1905	*Lochner v. New York* (invalidating state regulation of bakers' hours)
1908	*Adair v. United States* (striking down federal law prohibiting interstate railroads from enforcement of "yellow-dog" contracts); *Muller v. Oregon* (upholding regulation of hours of working women)
1913	*Coppage v. Kansas* (striking down state prohibition on use of yellow-dog contracts)
1923	*Adkins v. Children's Hospital* (invalidating D.C. ordinance mandating minimum wage for women); *Meyer v. Nebraska* (invalidating state law prohibiting teaching of foreign languages); *Pierce v. Society of Sisters* (invalidating state law mandating attendance at public schools only) *Meyer* and *Pierce* among first examples of non-economic substantive due process enforced by the Court
1934	*Nebbia v. New York* (rejecting substantive due process challenge to price controls for milk)
1937	*West Coast Hotel v. Parrish* (overruling *Adkins*, upholding minimum-wage law)
1938	*Carolene Prods. Co. v. United States* (articulating presumption of constitutionality and rational basis review for "economic and social legislation"; possible exceptions to presumption discussed in footnote 4)
1942	*Skinner v. Oklahoma* (invalidating, under Equal Protection Clause, forced sterilization for certain repeat offenders; *held*, procreation is a "fundamental" right, the infringement of which by state requires more than rational basis)
1963	*Ferguson v. Skrupa* (contemporary articulation of extremely deferential standard of review for state legislation regulating aspects of economy)

1965 *Griswold v. Connecticut* (invalidating Connecticut birth control statute; law infringed upon "fundamental right" of privacy of married couples, derived from "emanations" of provisions of the Bill of Rights)

1972 *Eisenstadt v. Baird* (invalidating Massachusetts law prohibiting unmarried persons from buying contraceptives)

1973 *Roe v. Wade* (striking down state abortion law)

1986 *Bowers v. Hardwick* (rejecting Due Process Clause challenge to Georgia law prohibiting "sodomy" as applied to same-sex couple)

1990 *Cruzan v. Missouri Dep't of Health* (upholding state law requiring clear and convincing evidence of incompetent person's wishes before termination of life support)

1992 *Planned Parenthood v. Casey* (upholding in part, striking down in part provisions of Pennsylvania law regulating abortion; holding that regulations imposing an "undue burden" on ability to procure abortion unconstitutional)

1997 *Washington v. Glucksberg* (upholding state ban on assisted suicide; rejecting Due Process Clause challenge)

2000 *Stenberg v. Carhart* (striking down Nebraska statute barring late-term, partial-birth abortions because statute lacked exception for the health of the mother; *held,* statute placed an "undue burden" on women needing late-term abortions)

2003 *Lawrence v. Texas* (overruling *Bowers,* striking down state law outlawing same-sex sodomy)

2007 *Gonzales v. Carhart* (upholding federal partial-birth abortion statute, distinguishing *Stenberg*)

2013 *United States v. Windsor* (striking down federal Defense of Marriage Act's definition of marriage that excluded same-sex couples)

D. Closer

QUESTION 14. Toy story. The Ames General Assembly recently passed a law prohibiting the sale or use of "sex toys," defined as "devices designed primarily for the stimulation of human genitals." The only reason given by the General Assembly is that the sale of sex toys promotes the "commercialization" of sex and exposes the public to advertisements for those devices they might find objectionable. Which of the following potential plaintiffs would have the best chance of successfully challenging the Ames sex toy law?

A. Amy, the owner of Luv Stuff, an adult-oriented store that sells sex toys, who claims that the law barring sale is a violation of her due process rights.
B. Barbara and Steve, a married couple, who claim that the ban on use violates their due process rights.
C. Jim, whose sexual dysfunction requires him to use sex toys to satisfy himself and his partner.
D. Kim and Laura, a lesbian couple in a committed relationship who regularly use sex toys when together.

ANALYSIS. I hope you thought this one was a little tough. Let's begin by reviewing the law itself: it prohibits "sale or use" of a sex toy. So you have two potential liberty interests that are infringed. The first is "sex toy sale"; the second (and certainly more personal) is "sex toy use." Look at the choices and think about the potential plaintiff who can be most easily eliminated. The ban on sex toy sales looks like a kind of economic and social regulation. We know that since the mid-1930s, states are permitted to regulate economic and social issues subject to the minimum rational basis test. Preventing the "commercialization of sex" by prohibiting the sale of sex toys would probably qualify as a legitimate interest, and the bar on their sale would at least not be irrational, whether one agreed with it or not. Therefore, **A** is not the right answer, because Amy as the owner of a business subject to regulation by the ban would not be the best plaintiff to bring suit challenging it. The other three potential plaintiffs, however, would be challenging the *use* provision. These present a more promising group of challengers. So, is there a fundamental *right* to use a sex toy? Certainly not one that the Court has recognized for individuals in general. That would mean, for example, that **C** is not the right answer. However useful sex toys might be to Jim's condition, the Court has, heretofore, not recognized a fundamental right to conduct consensual sexual relations free from state interference. You might think that, after *Lawrence*, **D** is a promising choice. It might be, but only if a reviewing court applies the "rational basis with teeth" standard employed in *Lawrence*; otherwise, the plaintiffs might find themselves in the same position as Amy and Jim. Note, too, that Ames did not offer majoritarian moral disapproval as a basis for enacting its ban on sex toy use. In the absence of any reason, and in the absence of Supreme Court authority for the proposition that there is a fundamental right to use sex toys, a reviewing court employing the rational basis test might hypothesize that the use ban was intended to reinforce the ban on sale, and vice versa. The best candidate for plaintiff to challenge the use ban is the married couple in **B**. As far back as *Griswold*, the Court has recognized a limitation on the ability of the state to monitor consensual sexual relations among married couples. Even the State of Georgia admitted at oral argument in *Bowers v. Hardwick* that it would be unconstitutional to enforce its sodomy ban (which prohibited heterosexual as well as homosexual sodomy) against married persons because of *Griswold.* If it was abhorrent to the Court to contemplate police violating the "sacred precincts of the marital bedroom" for signs of contraceptive use, the same revulsion would likely attach to a police search of a married couple's bedroom for signs of sex toy use. At the very least, the broad ban on all use of sex toys—even among married persons—would sweep more broadly than necessary to effectuate the purpose of preventing the commercialization of sex, even assuming that interest qualified as "compelling."

Denning's Picks

1. **D**
2. **B**
3. **D**
4. **D**
5. **A**
6. **B**
7. **A**
8. **B**
9. **C**
10. **C**
11. **A**
12. **C**
13. **C**
14. **B**

4

The Equal Protection Clause of the Fourteenth Amendment, Part I: Suspect, Non-suspect, and Quasi-suspect Classifications

A. Overview

The Fourteenth Amendment to the Constitution contains a provision prohibiting a state from "deny[ing] any person within its jurisdiction the equal protection of the laws." U.S. Const. amend. XIV, § 1. Once derided as "the usual last resort of constitutional arguments," Buck v. Bell, 274 U.S. 200, 208 (1927), the guarantee of equal protection assumed a prominent position in the Supreme Court's jurisprudence beginning in the mid-twentieth century. Indeed, it was on equal protection grounds that the Court invalidated de jure racial segregation; in the aftermath of *Brown*, it was tempting to see the Equal Protection Clause as a means to eradicate all manner of societal inequality. While the Court had success employing the Clause to combat race and sex discrimination, as well as discrimination involving the exercise of "fundamental" rights, it never was successful employing the Clause to secure a wide variety of what are deemed "positive" or "social" rights, such as the right to employment or a minimum standard of living.

This chapter will examine the Court's use of the Equal Protection Clause to invalidate legislative classifications based on "suspect" or "semi-suspect" criteria, such as race. Chapter 5 will examine the Court's use of the Clause to protect classifications that impinge on or penalize the exercise of certain fundamental rights.

Because all laws classify and, to some extent, treat those covered and those excluded unequally, the Court has employed standards of review similar to those used in Due Process Clause cases, in which the Court is more or less deferential to the governmental classification depending on the interest at stake. For example, whatever else the framers of the Fourteenth Amendment intended, they wanted to prohibit laws that would keep recently freed slaves in a state of permanent peonage tantamount to slavery, which had been outlawed by the Thirteenth Amendment. Therefore, laws that classify according to race have drawn the strictest scrutiny. By contrast, laws whose classifications aren't drawn according to "suspect" criteria are examined under the deferential rational basis test. There is even a version of rational basis with "bite," similar to that employed in due process cases like *Lawrence v. Texas*, employed for certain classifications but not formally acknowledged by the Court as a standard of review. In contrast to due process cases, however, equal protection doctrine has a third, formal standard of review—intermediate scrutiny—that the Court employs for gender classifications.

The remainder of this chapter will take us through the various standards of review and, within those standards, examine how the Court has applied them in common types of cases. We begin with rational basis review, the default rule for equal protection cases. The following section will discuss not only the traditional rational basis review, but also its less deferential version employed by the Court from time to time. Next, we move to the other side of the spectrum, examining the classifications that are deemed "suspect," and that garner strict scrutiny from the Court. While race is the paradigmatic suspect classification, we will examine alienage classifications as well. We conclude with an examination of gender classifications and the application of intermediate scrutiny in those cases, as well as in those classifying on the basis of illegitimacy.

Below is a chart summarizing the standards of review employed by the Court in equal protection cases:

Equal Protection Standards of Review at a Glance

Standard of Review	*Strength of Government Interest*	*Required Fit between Classification and Interest*	*Party Bearing Burden of Proof*
Rational basis	Legitimate	Rational relationship	Challenger
Intermediate scrutiny	Important	Substantial relationship	Government
Strict scrutiny	Compelling	Necessary or narrowly tailored	Government

Two final notes: The Fourteenth Amendment, by its terms, applies to the states, not to the federal government. While the Due Process Clause of the

Fourteenth Amendment tracks the same clause in the Fifth Amendment, which *does* apply to the federal government, there is no textual Fifth Amendment analogue to the Equal Protection Clause. However, in *Bolling v. Sharpe*, 347 U.S. 497 (1954), the Court held that the Fifth Amendment's Due Process Clause contains an "equal protection component" that imposes identical equal protection obligations on the federal government. However unsatisfying it may be as a textual matter,[1] it is now accepted at least as a matter of stare decisis—and of symmetry as well. It would be jarring, to say the least, to hold that state governments may not discriminate on the basis of race while the federal government could do so with impunity. Moreover, the equal protection provisions of the Fifth and Fourteenth Amendments apply to "state action" undertaken by either the federal or state governments, as opposed to that undertaken by private parties. State action is discussed further in Chapter 9.

B. Rational Basis Review

1. *Introduction*

Traditional rational basis review requires that the *challenger* establish that the classification (1) does not further a legitimate governmental interest and (2) bears no rational relationship to that interest. Further, the Court will hypothesize a purpose that would sustain the classification, *even if there is no evidence the legislature relied on that purpose in enacting the classification.*

As we'll see, however, the Court has, on occasion, claimed to apply rational basis while in fact applying a less deferential standard of review. This more searching review, in which both the ends of regulation and the fit between those ends and the classification are scrutinized by the Court, was dubbed rational basis with "bite" by one influential law review article. Gerald Gunther, *The Supreme Court, 1971 Term—Foreword: In Search of Evolving Doctrine on a Changing Court: A Model for a Newer Equal Protection*, 86 Harv. L. Rev. 1, 12 (1972). This less deferential rational basis test is a puzzle, in part because the Court never acknowledges that it is doing anything different than applying the traditional rational basis test.

2. *Traditional rational basis*

Two famous cases illustrate the classic rational basis review. In *Railway Express Agency, Inc. v. New York*, 336 U.S. 106 (1949), the Court upheld a city ban on the use of advertising vehicles, but permitted firms that owned their own trucks to advertise their business on those trucks. The reason given for the ban

---

1. One obvious objection is that if equal protection is always a "component" of due process, then the Equal Protection Clause in the Fourteenth Amendment is a meaningless redundancy.

was traffic safety—the advertising vehicles were alleged to pose a distracting hazard to drivers in the city. Owners of advertising vehicles sued, arguing that if advertising on vehicles posed that much of a hazard, then the ban should cover businesses advertising on their own delivery trucks as well as vehicles used solely as mobile billboards. The Court rejected this argument, noting that "local authorities may well have concluded that those who advertise their own wares on their trucks do not present the same traffic problem in view of the nature or extent of the advertising which they use." *Railway Express*, 336 U.S. at 110. The Court preferred to defer to the city's judgment:

> [T]he fact that New York City sees fit to eliminate from traffic this kind of distraction but does not touch what may be even greater ones in a different category, such as the vivid displays on Times Square, is immaterial. It is no requirement of equal protection that all evils of the same genus be eradicated or none at all.

Id. In other words, legislatures are entitled to regulate piecemeal, instead of comprehensively, and may attack problems according to their perceived severity without interference from the Court. That a classification is underinclusive (by not regulating each source of the perceived evil) or overinclusive (by including in the classification items that are *not* a source of the perceived evil) will not be, by itself, reason to invalidate it under the Equal Protection Clause. Note too that the *Railway Express* Court speculated why the city may have drawn the line it did, and upheld the law on that basis, without proof that the city relied on the Court's hypothesized justification.

Consider *United States Railroad Retirement Board v. Fritz*, 449 U.S. 166 (1980), in which the Court upheld a scheme to deprive certain former railroad workers of their vested pensions. Until the early 1970s, former railroad workers who went to work for non-railroad employers were entitled to collect both a pension from the railroad retirement plan and Social Security. *Fritz*, 449 U.S. at 177. To ensure the solvency of that railroad plan, however, the government divested pensions from non-retired workers who no longer worked for railroads and who, as of 1974, had less than 25 years of service in the railroad industry. The workers stripped of their dual benefits sued, claiming that the classification violated the Equal Protection Clause. *Id.* at 178.

Congress was entitled to "eliminate[] windfall benefits for all classes of employees, [so] it is not constitutionally impermissible for Congress to have drawn lines between groups of employees for the purpose of phasing out those benefits," the Court wrote. *Id.* at 177. The only question was whether the line it drew was "patently arbitrary or irrational. . . ." *Id.* The majority concluded it was not: "Congress could properly conclude that persons who had actually acquired statutory entitlement to windfall benefits while still employed in the railroad industry had a greater equitable claim to those benefits than the members of the appellee's class who were no longer in the railroad employment when they became eligible for dual benefits." *Id.* at 178. As long as there are "plausible reasons" for congressional action, it must be sustained; whether

Congress actually relied on those reasons was irrelevant for the Court because it "has never insisted that a legislative body articulate its reasons for enacting a statute." *Id.* at 179.

For a recent example of the Court's application of rational basis, see *Armour v. Indianapolis*, 132 S. Ct. 2073 (2012), in which the Court upheld a city's refusal to refund assessments paid before an old system of funding sewer improvement projects was replaced and unpaid amounts assessed under the old system were forgiven. Taxpayers who had prepaid the amounts due under the old funding system argued that the refusal to refund violated the Equal Protection Clause. *Armour*, 132 S. Ct. at 2079. Applying the rational basis test, the Court argued that not forgiving the amounts due after replacing the funding system could have proven administratively burdensome and expensive. *Id.* at 2081. The Court noted that, likewise, computing and processing refund checks could have proven as burdensome and expensive, the latter expense compounded by the difficulty of finding money in the city's budget with which to make the refunds. *Id.* at 2081-2082. "Finally," the Court concluded, "the rationality of the distinction draws support from the fact that the line that the City drew—distinguishing past payments from future obligations—is a line well known to the law," citing lower court cases involving other amnesty programs. *Id.* at 2082.

QUESTION 1. Optical oligarchy. The State of Ames bars opticians from the manufacture of eyeglasses unless pursuant to a prescription from either an optometrist (who has a doctor of optometry degree) or an ophthalmologist (who has a medical degree). McGoo, an optician (who has neither degree), sues, claiming that the law simply places low-cost providers at a disadvantage relative to the other eye doctors. A reviewing court would likely:

A. Uphold the law, because the legislature could have rationally believed that citizens' health and safety were better served by having licensed eye professionals prescribe eyeglasses.
B. Invalidate the law, because opticians are as qualified as ophthalmologists or optometrists to ascertain the correct prescriptions for lenses.
C. Uphold the law, unless the plaintiff can prove that enriching ophthalmologists and optometrists at opticians' expense was the real purpose of the law.
D. Invalidate the law, because it is unreasonable.

ANALYSIS. The facts here are similar to those in *Williamson v. Lee Optical of Okla., Inc.* 348 U.S. 483 (1955), in which the Court upheld a law similar to that in the question. As in due process cases, we know that states may exercise their police power to regulate the health, safety, and welfare of their citizens. The regulation of the manufacture of eyeglasses does not, as far as we know, constitute a "suspect" classification. The rational basis test applies, therefore. The aims—consumer protection and protection of citizens' health and welfare—are undoubtedly legitimate. We also know that the Court no longer reviews legislation for its wisdom or reasonableness. Therefore, **D** is not correct. We also know that the Court will uphold a classification if there is any conceivable purpose that the classification serves. Therefore, **C** is not correct. (In fact, it is not clear that even if that were the purpose, it would be illegitimate.) Because the Court will not second-guess legislative judgments implicit in its classifications, **B** isn't correct either. Obviously, the legislature thought that ophthalmologists and optometrists were better qualified than opticians to prescribe eyeglasses. That leaves **A**, which is the correct answer: The legislature could have rationally believed that licensed professionals, including ophthalmologists and optometrists, are better suited than opticians to accurately prescribe eyeglasses for their patients.

QUESTION 2. Drop the cop. The State of Ames requires that all uniformed police officers retire at age 50 in an effort to ensure their physical fitness and mental. The law does not apply to detectives or other plainclothes police officers. Phil sues, claiming that the law violates equal protection. He notes that many officers under 50 are neither physically fit nor mentally alert. He also argues that it is a violation to single out uniformed cops for this treatment while allowing detectives 50 years old and older to remain on the force. A reviewing court should:

A. Invalidate the requirement because it is overinclusive, presuming as it does that all officers 50 and over are unfit, not alert, or both.
B. Invalidate the requirement because it singles out uniformed police while leaving detectives untouched, and is thus underinclusive.
C. Uphold the requirement, unless Phil can prove it was motivated by discrimination.
D. Uphold the requirement, because the fit between the means and ends need not be especially precise, as long as it is not completely without foundation.

ANALYSIS. These facts are taken from another case, *Massachusetts Board of Retirement v. Murgia*, 427 U.S. 307 (1976). Again the Court upheld the law. Remember that while there needs to be a rational relationship between means and ends, that fit does not have to be precise. Simply because a classification tends to cover too much or too little relative to the purpose does not mean that the classification is invalid—at least, not if the classification is a non-suspect one. Therefore, neither **A** nor **B** is correct. The Court has said repeatedly that states may regulate piecemeal. Further, classifications necessarily discriminate between classes; therefore, **C** is incorrect because it is irrelevant. Only discrimination against members of protected classes garners strict scrutiny. That leaves **D**, the correct answer. It is not completely unreasonable to think that, on the whole, physical prowess and even mental acuity decline in late middle age; even if individual counterexamples are available, the state is not required to make allowances for those and may instead draw a bright line.

3. *Rational basis with "bite"*

Before we discuss the cases in which the Court has applied what one commentator called rational basis with "bite," it bears repeating that this is not an official standard of review. The Court employs it without any acknowledgment that it is doing anything other than applying the classic rational basis test. In the cases described in this section, however, it is clear that the Court is more closely scrutinizing governmental aims or classifications than it did in cases like *Railway Express* or *Fritz.*

In *United States Department of Agriculture v. Moreno*, 413 U.S. 528 (1973), for example, the Court invalidated a congressional amendment[2] rendering households composed of unrelated persons ineligible for food stamps. Legislative history suggested that at least one member of Congress supported the amendment because it would eliminate "hippies" from participation in the food stamp program. *Moreno*, 413 U.S. at 534. The Court concluded that the exclusion did not further the stated purpose of the act (to alleviate hunger and benefit the agricultural economy) and that the real purpose was to target hippies. This the Court held to be illegitimate: "[I]f the constitutional conception of 'equal protection of the laws' means anything, it must at the very least mean that a bare congressional desire to harm a politically unpopular group cannot constitute a legitimate governmental interest." *Id.* The Court also rejected the government's claim that the exclusion of unrelated persons from the definition of "household" was permissible as an anti-fraud measure, calling it "wholly without any rational basis." *Id.* at 538.

Moreno lay fallow until the Court employed it again in *Romer v. Evans*, 517 U.S. 620 (1996), to invalidate a Colorado constitutional amendment ("Amendment 2") that repealed all state and local laws protecting homosexuals from discrimination and prohibiting the passage of any such laws in the future. Recall that *Bowers v. Hardwick*, 478 U.S. 186 (1986), had rejected a due process challenge to criminal penalties for sodomy, but had not addressed an equal protection challenge. The language of Amendment 2 was so sweeping that the Court concluded that it was "a fair . . . inference from the broad language of the amendment that it deprives gays and lesbians even of the protection of general laws and policies that prohibit arbitrary discrimination in governmental and private settings." *Romer*, 517 U.S. at 630. This, the Court felt, was quite literally a denial of equal protection of the laws for gays and lesbians on the basis of a single trait, homosexuality. *Id.* at 633.

---

2. Recall that the Court has interpreted the Due Process Clause of the Fifth Amendment to have an "equal protection component," which binds the federal government as the Equal Protection Clause of the Fourteenth Amendment binds the states.

Because the Court regarded Amendment 2's "sheer breadth" as "so discontinuous with the reasons offered for it that the amendment seems inexplicable by anything other than animus toward the class that it affects; it lacks a rational relationship to legitimate state interests." *Id.* at 632. The state said it was needed to protect landlords, employers, and other citizens' freedom of association. But the Court noted that these interests could have been advanced using something much less broad than the language of Amendment 2. *Id.* at 634-635. Quoting *Moreno*, the Court noted that animus against a particular group, such as homosexuals, was not a legitimate state interest. *Id.* at 635.

QUESTION 3. Failure to lunch. With numerous websites urging college students to apply for food stamps as a means of dealing with the high cost of tuition and books, Congress amended the program to disqualify any person enrolled as a full-time student. Members of Congress overwhelmingly support the amendment and used the floor to criticize the abuse of the program by middle-class young people whose parents probably still claim them as dependents. Congress notes that such persons were never meant to benefit from the plan and that scarce resources must be conserved for the truly needy, whose numbers have risen during the recent economic downturn.

If a federal court upholds the amendment, it is probably because:

A. The law is rationally related to the legitimate interest of conserving scarce resources in a governmental relief program.
B. The law is substantially related to an important governmental purpose.
C. The Equal Protection Clause applies only to states, not to the federal government.
D. There is no fundamental right to food stamps.

ANALYSIS. Remember we're looking for reasons that a court might *not* invalidate the amendment. Ordinarily, unless a law classifies on the basis of a suspect characteristic, such as race, courts will apply a deferential version of rational basis review, cases like *Moreno* notwithstanding. That means that **B** is not the correct answer, because it does not recite the appropriate standard of review here. Nor is **C** correct. While the Fourteenth Amendment does apply only to states, the Court has found an equal protection component in the Fifth Amendment's Due Process Clause, which does bind the federal government. While true, **D** is not the best answer; as the text above indicates, sometimes courts will invalidate laws even where no fundamental right or suspect classification is involved. **A** furnishes the best reason a court would uphold the law: Conserving scarce resources for their intended purpose is a legitimate interest, and barring from eligibility those who Congress believes are abusing aid programs is a rational means of effecting that interest. Note too, on the facts present, that that belief appears to be a sincere one. It does not appear that Congress is out to "get" college students the way that, in *Moreno*, some members of Congress allegedly targeted "hippies" for exclusion. In other words, something more than the bare desire to target the politically unpopular is at work here.

In *Moreno* and *Romer*, the Court focused on governmental ends; in other cases, the Court focuses on the fit between the means and the classification employed to achieve these ends. As in *Romer*, a sense that the end is illegitimate can be reinforced by a gulf between the stated ends and the means used to achieve it. In other cases, the discontinuity between means and ends can produce a sense that perhaps the motive is something other than what the legislature has specified. Ends and means, thus, produce a feedback loop of sorts.

Consider the case of *City of Cleburne v. Cleburne Living Center, Inc.*, 473 U.S. 432 (1985). Cleburne, Texas, required a special-use permit for the operation of a group home for the mentally retarded. Cleburne Living Center applied for and was denied that permit. Declining to find mental retardation a "quasi-suspect" class, the Supreme Court nevertheless invalidated the ordinance on rational basis grounds.

Not all group homes were required to obtain a special-use permit. Specifically, "apartment houses, multiple dwellings, boarding and lodging houses, fraternity or sorority houses, dormitories, apartment hotels, hospitals, sanitariums, nursing homes for convalescents or the aged[,] private clubs or fraternal orders, and other specified uses" were entitled to build in the zone where the Cleburne Living Center sought to locate. *Cleburne Living Center*, 473 U.S. at 447.

The city offered several reasons for requiring the special-use permit: (1) opposition from existing property owners, (2) fear that students from the junior high across the street would harass the occupants of the home, (3) the site's location on a 500-year floodplain, and (4) concern about the size of the home and the eventual number of occupants. The Court dismissed each in turn. First, it held that "mere negative attitudes . . . are not permissible bases" for treating the home differently. *Id.* at 448. Second, "denying a permit based on . . . vague, undifferentiated fears [of student harassment] is again permitting some portion of the community to validate what would otherwise be an equal protection violation. . . ." *Id.* at 449. Third, the Court found the floodplain argument weak, as the site was available for group homes for the elderly and hospitals, any of which could locate without a special-use permit. Finally, it noted again that there were no limits "on the number of people that could occupy this home as a boarding house, nursing home, family dwelling, fraternity house, or dormitory. The question is whether it is rational to threat the mentally retarded differently." *Id.*

Because of the poor fit between the reasons given for requiring homes for the mentally retarded, but no others, to get a special-use permit, the Court concluded that the requirement "appears to us to rest on an irrational prejudice against the mentally retarded." *Id.* at 450. It invalidated the requirement.

Yet another example of rational basis with bite is found in *Plyler v. Doe*, 457 U.S. 202 (1982), in which the Court invalidated a Texas law denying free public education to the children brought to the United States illegally by their parents. Though the Court had previously held that education was *not* a fundamental right, San Antonio Independent School District v. Rodriguez, 411 U.S. 1 (1973), and that illegal aliens are not a "suspect class," the Court nevertheless claimed it had a "fundamental role in maintaining the fabric of our society" and invalidated the Texas law. Curiously, Justice Brennan's majority opinion held that the law could not be said to be "rational unless it furthers some substantial goal of the State." *Id.* at 224. By substituting "substantial" for "rational" in the standard of review, the Court seemed to be raising the bar.

The Court closely examined, and rejected, the proffered justifications for the law. First, the mere illegality of the children's presence in the United States did not justify the law. Federal law certainly didn't authorize Texas to impose additional disabilities on those here illegally. *Plyler*, 457 U.S. at 225-226. Nor was the Court impressed by the argument that Texas ought to be able to conserve its resources for lawful residents. The Court doubted that immigrants flooded Texas to take advantage of its public school system. *Id.* at 228. The Court was also skeptical of claims that the children of illegal immigrants imposed special burdens on the school system. "In terms of educational cost and need, however, undocumented children are 'basically indistinguishable' from legally resident alien children." *Id.* at 229. Finally, the majority rejected the notion that the children could be excluded because they were less likely to stay in Texas. Neither, the majority pointed out, was there any guarantee that Texas citizens educated in the public school system would stay in Texas. *Id.* at 229-230. In sum, the Court concluded, "whatever savings might be achieved by denying these children an education, they are wholly insubstantial in light of the costs involved to these children, the State, and the Nation." *Id.* at 230.

QUESTION 4. Adoption angst. The State of Ames permits same-sex couples to serve as foster parents. Recently, however, the State prohibited homosexual couples from permanently adopting children, even those for whom they have been longtime foster parents. During floor debates, several members pointed out that data suggest that married, heterosexual households furnish a more stable home environment for children, and that they opposed adoption by gay couples on that ground. Others expressed hostility toward homosexuals and homosexuality in general. Rob and Steve, longtime foster parents to Amy, wished to adopt her and sued the state, claiming that the ban on adoption was unconstitutional. Which of the following would be helpful to them in overturning the ban?

A. Evidence that many foster parent relationships continued many years with no apparent ill effect on the children.
B. Evidence that the state permitted adoption by unmarried heterosexual couples.
C. Evidence that the ban was the product of animus toward gays and lesbians.
D. Any of the above.

ANALYSIS. While in most cases, courts applying a rational basis test will assume facts sufficient to create a rational relationship between means and ends, cases like *Cleburne* have seen the Court apply a less deferential version in which it looks closely at the fit between the end of a law and the means used to achieve it. If there is a particularly poor fit, the Court, as in *Cleburne*, may question whether the purpose given is a pretext for some less legitimate purpose for the legislation. In *Cleburne* the Court felt the fit was so poor that only an irrational fear of the disabled could be behind the special-use permit requirement. Here the reason given for Ames's law is to promote the interest of children, which allegedly is best furthered by adoption into heterosexual, married families. If evidence existed undermining that premise, one could argue that there was a poor fit between the purpose and the ban. Therefore, **A** would be very helpful: If you could show that long-term foster parent relationships (including those involving gay men and women) were no less stable than adoptive ones, that would call the ban into question. Similarly, **B** would be helpful in showing that the state, in practice, did not necessarily believe that *only* married couples were fit to adopt. In addition, if you could demonstrate **C**—that animus was really behind the ban—that would enable you to invoke *Moreno* and its claim that legislating disabilities against identifiable groups because of animus was not a legitimate governmental interest. Because each selection would be useful in overturning the ban, the correct answer is **D**.

A final example can be found in *United States v. Windsor*, 133 S. Ct. 2675 (2013), in which the Court invalidated a portion of the federal Defense of Marriage Act, which defined marriage as being between a man and a woman. This federal definition of marriage affected over one thousand federal laws and regulations. While the Court suggested that its opinion was grounded in principles of federalism—state law, after all, usually governed domestic relations—the core of the opinion invoked the due process and equal protection principles. *Windsor*, 133 S. Ct. at 2692 (noting that it was "unnecessary to decide whether this federal intrusion on state power is a violation of the Constitution because it disrupts the federal balance"). New York, the Court noted, had undertaken to confer "protection and dignity" to same-sex marriages. *Id.* The federal law, in the Court's view, sought to strip this protection out of "animus"; in so doing, it violated the Due Process and Equal Protection Clauses. *Id.* at 2693. "The avowed purpose and practical effect of the law here in question," the Court concluded, "are to impose a disadvantage, a separate status, and so a stigma upon all who enter into same-sex marriages made lawful by the unquestioned authority of the States." *Id.* Aside from the Court's mention of *Lawrence* and its protection of certain aspects of the personal bond that develops between two people, it was vague about both (1) whether sexual preference was now a suspect or quasi-suspect class and (2) what standard of review applied.

The difficulty with the *Moreno-Cleburne-Romer-Windsor* line of cases is that the Court won't acknowledge that it is applying a different standard of review. This means that it is nearly impossible to predict when the Court will employ "rational basis with bite" as opposed to the classic rational basis test applied in cases like *Railway Express.* Generalizations are, therefore, hazardous. Taken as a whole, however, the cases seem to reflect the Court's willingness to intervene and invalidate laws that appear to be motivated by some invidious purpose, even if the law infringes on no officially recognized fundamental right or is aimed at members of a non-suspect class. In addition, the Supreme Court can do justice in individual cases while continuing to restrain lower courts by not officially creating an additional standard of review whose contours are not clearly defined.

C. Suspect Classes and Strict Scrutiny

1. *Introduction*

Suspect classifications must satisfy strict scrutiny, which places the burden on government to prove (1) a compelling governmental interest and (2) that the classification is necessary or narrowly tailored to that interest. Though strict scrutiny is often said to be "strict in theory but fatal in fact," Gunther, *supra*, at 8, we shall see that is not always the case. In this section, we'll examine the suspect classifications — racial classifications in particular — that receive strict scrutiny.

2. *Race*

Classifications by race are the quintessential "suspect classifications." In the infamous case of *Korematsu v. United States*, 323 U.S. 214, 216 (1944), the Court wrote that "all legal restrictions which curtail the civil rights of a single racial group are immediately suspect," even as the Court went on to uphold the exclusion of American citizens of Japanese descent from areas of the West

Coast. Later cases have approved the use of race for much more benign purposes in the area of university admissions. In both cases, however, the Court engaged in deference to government, which seems to be in tension with strict scrutiny's "strict in theory but fatal in fact" reputation.

(a) Requirement of discriminatory intent To be cognizable under the Fourteenth Amendment, discriminatory intent needs to be proven. Evidence of intent can come from a number of sources. A law may be discriminatory on its face, as were laws prohibiting blacks and whites from attending school together. In the case of facial discrimination, intent will be presumed. *See, e.g.,* Strauder v. West Virginia, 100 U.S. 303 (1880) (invalidating law expressly prohibiting jury service by African Americans). A law may also be facially neutral but be applied in a discriminatory manner. The classic case in this regard is *Yick Wo v. Hopkins,* 118 U.S. 356 (1886), in which a facially neutral requirement that all laundries be constructed of brick was enforced in a racially discriminatory manner: Only wooden laundries owned by Chinese immigrants were cited for violating the law. White-owned wooden laundries were left alone. Again, intent is presumed if no other explanation can be found.

But disparate impact alone is insufficient to prove discriminatory intent. The Court rejected a claim that giving qualifying tests to applicants for jobs as police officers in the District of Columbia constituted racial discrimination in *Washington v. Davis,* 426 U.S. 229 (1976), even though four times as many African American candidates as white candidates failed the test. The Court rejected the argument that these numbers established racial discrimination, writing that "the basic equal protection principle [is] that the invidious quality of a law claimed to be racially discriminatory must ultimately be traced to a racially discriminatory purpose." 426 U.S. at 240. The Court went on to say, though, that the discrimination need not be facial: "[A]n invidious discriminatory purpose may often be inferred from the totality of relevant facts, including the fact . . . that the law bears more heavily on one race than another." *Id.* at 242. It declined, however, to infer discriminatory purpose solely from that disproportionate impact. The Court further concluded that the mere fact the test was being used was not sufficient evidence of discriminatory intent, especially in light of the extraordinary efforts the police department was making to recruit minority candidates into its ranks. *Id.* at 246.

The following year the Court further explained how discriminatory purpose may be inferred from a facially neutral statute. Arlington Heights v. Metropolitan Housing Development Corp., 429 U.S. 252 (1977). "[W]ithout purporting to be exhaustive," the Court listed the following as "subjects of proper inquiry in determining whether racially discriminatory intent existed":

> The historical background of the decision . . . particularly if it reveals a series of official actions taken for invidious purposes. . . . The specific sequence of events leading up to the challenged decision also may shed some light on the decisionmaker's purposes. . . . Departures from the normal procedural

> sequence also might afford evidence that improper purposes are playing a role. Substantive departures too may be relevant, particularly if the factors usually considered important by the decisionmaker strongly favor a decision contrary to the one reached.
>
> The legislative or administrative history may be highly relevant, especially where there are contemporary statements by members of the decisionmaking body, minutes of its meetings, or reports. In some extraordinary instances the members might be called to the stand at trial to testify concerning the purpose of the official action, although even then such testimony frequently will be barred by privilege.

Arlington Heights, 429 U.S. at 267-268. In a later case, though, the Court permitted defendants to rebut the presumption of discriminatory intent by demonstrating by a preponderance of the evidence that—despite any discriminatory motive—the defendant would have reached the same decision anyway. Mt. Healthy City School District Board of Educ. v. Doyle, 429 U.S. 274 (1977).

(b) Racial discrimination Whatever hopes for racial reconciliation existed in the minds of the framers of the Reconstruction Amendments, by the end of the nineteenth century racial equality had been subordinated to sectional reconciliation between the North and the South. The promise of cases like *Strauder* was replaced with the not-so-benign neglect of *Plessy v. Ferguson*, 163 U.S. 537 (1896), in which the Court gave its imprimatur to the rule of "separate but equal," by which the races could be legally separated as long as all races were affected and separate facilities were equal in quality. The Court dismissed the argument that separation implied inferiority, condescendingly suggesting that if that was true, it was "solely because the colored race chooses to put that construction upon it." *Plessy*, 163 U.S. at 551. Justice John Marshall Harlan was the lone dissenter; he wrote that "[o]ur Constitution is color-bind, and neither knows nor tolerates classes among citizens." *Id.* at 559 (Harlan, J., dissenting). *Plessy* ratified what was, by the early twentieth century, the prevailing social practice of racial segregation in schools, residences, and social interaction. In the South, this separation was often de jure and enforced by a combination of public and private sanctions, including violence and terror.

The National Association for the Advancement of Colored People (NAACP) and its Legal Defense Fund (LDF) decided, in the early decades of the twentieth century, to make the best of a bad situation and began litigating to force states to provide educational opportunities for African Americans that were, in fact, equal to those provided for whites. In effect, the LDF sought to make it prohibitively expensive for cash-strapped Southern states to maintain Jim Crow. The LDF began with graduate education, concluding that it would be less controversial. Their lawyers, including future Supreme Court Justice Thurgood Marshall, scored some important victories. In *Missouri ex rel. Gaines v. Canada*, 305 U.S. 337 (1938), the Court invalidated Missouri's attempt to keep its law school all white by paying the out-of-state tuition for black students to attend law school elsewhere. In *Sweatt v. Painter*, 339 U.S.

629 (1950), the Court ordered the University of Texas law school to admit black students after concluding that the Jim Crow law school provided by the state was equal neither in facilities nor in reputation to the university's law school. And in *McLauren v. Oklahoma State Regents*, 339 U.S. 637 (1950), the Court struck down efforts by Oklahoma to physically segregate black students admitted to graduate school from the other, white students in the program.

The LDF's campaign culminated in *Brown v. Board of Education*, 347 U.S. 483 (1954), in which the Court held that separate could never be equal in elementary and secondary education. "We conclude," the Court wrote, "that in the field of public education the doctrine of 'separate but equal' has no place."[3] *Brown*, 347 U.S. at 495. The Court deferred the question of remedy until the next term. Brown v. Board of Education, 349 U.S. 294 (1955) (*Brown II*). In *Brown II*, the Court gave the South some leeway to implement desegregation, which it wrote must occur "with all deliberate speed," and left district court judges in the South with the responsibility of overseeing those efforts. *Brown II*, 349 U.S. at 301. It would be a number of years before the Court again took up the question of desegregation in schools.

Though *Brown* spoke of segregation in *schools*, it quickly became evident that the principle underlying *Brown* was the broadly applicable one of racial equality. Following *Brown*, the Court issued a number of short per curiam (unsigned) decisions desegregating all types of public facilities, including parks, golf courses, and pools. Despite *Brown*'s limiting language, the Court inevitably cited it as authority for the Court's actions.

When, in the late 1960s, it returned to school desegregation, the Court quickly found itself up against the limits of its power. Persistent racial disparities in some areas were caused by the fact that blacks and whites tended to live apart from one another—a tendency reinforced by racially restrictive covenants prohibiting sales to blacks. These factors complicated efforts to integrate schools in or near all-white or all-black neighborhoods. Some local governments took advantage of this fact and approved so-called freedom of choice plans that allowed families to choose the school their children would attend. Not surprisingly, parents chose the school nearest their houses, and schools remained segregated, though no longer by law. The Court invalidated such a plan in *Green v. County School Board*, 391 U.S. 430 (1968), signaling an end to the era of "all deliberate speed," in which state and local governments moved with much more deliberation than speed.

Three years later, the Court approved a plan in Charlotte, North Carolina, that bused students of one race to schools in other areas to achieve integration. Swann v. Charlotte-Mecklenburg Board of Education, 402 U.S. 1 (1971). The Court approved the busing plan because of Charlotte's history of maintaining segregated schools. "Absent a constitutional violation," the Court wrote,

3. Recall that the Court also invalidated segregation in District of Columbia schools, finding an "equal protection component" in the Fifth Amendment, which lacked an explicit Equal Protection Clause binding the federal government. Bolling v. Sharpe, 347 U.S. 497 (1954).

"there would be no basis for judicially ordering assignment of students on a racial basis." *Swann*, 402 U.S. at 28. The Court took pains to point out that "[t]he constitutional command to desegregate schools does not mean that every school in every community must always reflect the racial composition of the school system as a whole." *Id.* at 24. *See also* Keyes v. School District No. 1, 413 U.S. 189 (1973) (holding that dual school system requiring desegregation efforts existed, despite lack of de jure segregation, where city had intentionally gerrymandered school district boundaries to maintain segregated schools).

Busing became a popular remedy for persistent racial imbalances, but the remedy itself engendered serious backlash from parents, many of whom fled larger cities for suburbs or abandoned the public school system altogether in favor of private education. When a Detroit district judge ordered suburban school districts to be included in a plan to desegregate Detroit's schools, the Supreme Court reversed him, holding that for such a remedy to be supported "it must be shown that racially discriminatory acts of the state or local school districts, or of a single school district have been a substantial cause of interdistrict segregation." Milliken v. Bradley, 418 U.S. 717, 744-745 (1974).

Court supervision of school desegregation ends when governments have achieved "unitary" status: when all vestiges of the "dual" or segregated school systems have been eradicated. Board of Education v. Dowell, 498 U.S. 237 (1991). Judicial supervision of schools cannot "extend beyond the time required to remedy the effects of past intentional discrimination." *Dowell*, 498 U.S. at 248.

QUESTION 5. Sudden impact. The University of Ames, the flagship state university in Ames, in an effort to become the preeminent state university in the region, has tightened admissions standards. It now requires that applicants score in the eightieth percentile in one of two standardized college admissions tests, and that they have a high school GPA in the ninetieth percentile. As a result of the changes in admissions standards, the number of eligible African American and Latino applicants fell dramatically relative to the number of eligible Asian American and Caucasian applicants. Studies show that the latter classes of candidates are three times as likely to be eligible for admission as the African American or Latino applicants. An ineligible African American candidate sues, claiming that the new standards violate her right to equal protection under the law. A reviewing court would:

A. Dismiss the suit because there is no state action.
B. Permit the suit to go forward because of the otherwise inexplicable impact on students of certain races.
C. Dismiss the suit because there is no proof of discriminatory intent on the facts.
D. Require the state to prove that its use of the higher test scores was narrowly tailored to some compelling governmental interest.

ANALYSIS. The facts indicate that the University of Ames is a flagship state university. It would therefore be an arm of the state and subject to the Fourteenth Amendment. Therefore, **A** is not correct. Moreover, after *Washington v. Davis*, it is clear that mere disparate impact will not be sufficient to maintain a claim for discrimination under the Equal Protection Clause; therefore, **B** is incorrect. Because a prima facie case of racial discrimination cannot be made out on these facts, a reviewing court would not apply strict scrutiny, rendering **D** incorrect. That leaves **C**, which is the correct answer. While disparate impact can be probative of discriminatory intent, it is not sufficient.

QUESTION 6. Shallow pool. Ames City, a city in the State of Ames, historically compiled jury pools using the state's list of registered drivers. Recently, however, it began to use voter registration records as a basis for selecting jurors. As a result, the number of African American jurors fell by over 80 percent. Which of the following would allow for an inference of racial discrimination?

A. The disparate impact of the switch on African American participation in juries.
B. The fact that the clerk of court, who approved the switch, complained prior to the switch that black jurors were less likely to convict black drug defendants.
C. The fact that Ames City had made it difficult for African Americans to register to vote in the past.
D. Any of the above.

ANALYSIS. While discriminatory intent is required to make out a prima facie case of racial discrimination under the Fourteenth Amendment, plaintiffs may compile evidence that would allow a fact finder to infer discriminatory intent even where it does not appear on the face of a law or other official action. Among the factors mentioned in *Davis* and *Arlington Heights* were disparate impact (probative of intent, but not sufficient on its own); the historical background of decisions, including evidence of past discrimination; and legislative history. Those factors are present in **A**, **B**, and **C**, which means that the best answer is **D**. The presence of those conditions could allow a fact finder to infer discriminatory intent from the switch.

(c) Race-based preferences In the wake of judicial decisions like *Brown*, and even in the face of legislative efforts like the 1964 Civil Rights Act, which prohibited private discriminate in places of public accommodation, simply outlawing discrimination was not sufficient to overcome the legacy of institutionalized racism in the United States. The federal government, as well as many state and local governments, began to enact race-based preferences in university admissions and in government contracting.

What are popularly known as "affirmative action" programs are controversial, in part because they violate the anti-discrimination norm that many feel the Fourteenth Amendment embodies. The state, this argument runs, should not be classifying people on the basis of race, regardless of whether the intent is to help racial groups or harm them. Others, however, see the Fourteenth Amendment as embodying an "anti-subordination" norm; that is, the government should not classify on the basis of race if that classification has the intent or effect of subordinating or denigrating members of that race. However, government may—and in some cases must—act in positive ways to remedy the effects of past discrimination. Race-based preferences would be one such way to aid members of historically disadvantaged minorities to make up ground lost during the time of their subordination.

Whether one adopts the anti-discrimination or anti-subordination view of the Fourteenth Amendment is not simply an academic or philosophical question. It has important implications for the standard of review employed to assess the constitutionality of things such as race-based preferences. Those favoring the anti-discrimination view, for example, will be suspicious of *any* government-sponsored racial classification and would likely review all classifications using strict scrutiny. Anti-subordination advocates, by contrast, would first ask whether the purpose of the classification was to harm or aid a racial group; if the latter, then something less than strict scrutiny—intermediate scrutiny, for example—will be recommended as the proper standard of review.

Understanding the different interpretations of the Fourteenth Amendment is essential for navigating the judicial debates surrounding race-based preferences, where parties seem to be talking past one another. If you don't believe that there can be a "benign" racial classification, then you will not be inclined to favor race-based preferences. In the sections that follow, we trace the Court's approach to race-based preferences in the two main areas in which cases have arisen: (1) education and (2) public contracting and employment.

Affirmative action and education: Bakke. The first challenge to a race-based admissions program came to the Court in *DeFunis v. Odegaard*, 416 U.S. 312 (1974), in which a white law school applicant challenged the University of Washington for failure to admit him while admitting minority candidates with lower grades and test scores. A lower court ordered him to be admitted, and when the law school noted that it would not kick him out if it won (DeFunis was in his third year by this time), the Court dismissed the case as moot.

Four years later, a new case involving the University of California-Davis medical school made its way to the Court. Regents of the Univ. of Calif. v. Bakke, 438 U.S. 265 (1978). The medical school had a program that reserved 16 of the 100 slots in each year's entering class for members of four minority groups. Alan Bakke, who was white, sued, arguing that the program deprived him of the ability to apply for those reserved slots based on his race. In defense of its program, the state offered several justifications: (1) the need to increase the number of minorities in medical schools and the medical profession; (2) remedying the effects of societal discrimination; (3) increasing the number of doctors who will practice in underserved communities; and (4) obtaining the educational benefits that accrue to student bodies that are ethnically diverse. *Bakke*, 438 U.S. at 305-306.

There was an interesting split on the Court. Four members of the Court would have avoided the constitutional question and invalidated the program as a violation of Title VI of the Civil Rights Act of 1964, which prohibits the exclusion of individuals from participation in a federal program on the basis of their race. (The university was a recipient of federal funds.) *Id.* at 325 (Stevens, J., concurring in judgment in part and dissenting in part).

Four other Justices (Brennan, White, Marshall, and Blackmun) would have reached the constitutional question, evaluated the program under intermediate scrutiny, and upheld it. The state, Justice Brennan wrote, "may take race into account when it acts not to demean or insult any racial group, but to remedy disadvantages cast on minorities by past racial prejudice, at least when appropriate findings have been made by judicial, legislative, or administrative bodies. . . ." *Id.* at 325 (Brennan, J., concurring in the judgment in part and dissenting in part).

Justice Lewis Powell's vote was the deciding one; and though in his opinion he spoke only for himself, he delivered the judgment in *Bakke* and charted the course for future Courts to follow in this area. First, he rejected the call to relax the standard of review based on the intentions motivating the classifications. He termed the problems attending such a distinction to be "intractable" and wrote that there "is no principled basis for deciding which groups would merit 'heightened judicial solicitude' and which would not." *Id.* at 296. To be upheld, all racial classifications had to satisfy strict scrutiny.

Looking at the proffered justifications, Justice Powell found only one—securing the educational advantages of a racially and ethnically diverse student body—to be "compelling." *Id.* at 314. Attempting simply to ensure that a certain percentage of students came from particular backgrounds "must be rejected . . . as facially invalid. Preferring members of any one group for no other reason than race or ethnic origin is discrimination for its own sake." *Id.* at 307. Nor could the state attempt to remedy societal discrimination at large, at least where the remedy was not tied to past discrimination by the state itself. "We have never approved a classification that aids persons perceived as members of relatively victimized groups at the expense of other innocent individuals in the absence of . . . findings of constitutional or statutory violations." *Id.* Finally, Powell saw "no evidence" that "members of particular ethnic groups over all other individuals . . . promote better health-care delivery to deprived citizens." *Id.* at 311.

However, achieving a diverse student body, Powell wrote, was "a constitutionally permissible goal for an institution of higher education." *Id.* at 311-312. An "otherwise qualified medical student with a particular background—whether it be ethnic, geographic, culturally advantaged or disadvantaged—may bring to a professional school of medicine experiences, outlooks, and ideas that enrich the training of its student body and better equip its graduates to render . . . their vital service to humanity." *Id.* at 314.

Nevertheless, Justice Powell voted to invalidate the admissions set-asides, because they failed the second part of strict scrutiny—that the classification be necessary to the accomplishment of its goal. "Petitioner's special admission program, focused *solely* on ethnic diversity, would hinder rather than further attainment of genuine diversity." *Id.* at 315. Justice Powell went on to write that while "race or ethnic background may be deemed a 'plus' in a particular applicant's file," it could not serve as *the* factor or otherwise insulate a student from competing with all other applicants for spots in the class. *Id.* at 317. Quotas would be unconstitutional, but, he added, courts should not "assume that a university, professing to employ a facially nondiscriminatory admissions policy, would operate it as a cover for the functional equivalent of a quota system. In short, good faith must be presumed" as long as evidence shows that students were evaluated "on an individualized, case-by-case basis. . . ." *Id.* at 318-319 and n. 7.

Public contracting and employment. Because Justice Powell wrote only for himself, considerable uncertainty lingered about the constitutional status of race-based preferences. Observers worried about the fate of *Bakke* and of affirmative action in higher education generally because of cases decided after *Bakke* in which the Court seemed to ratchet up the burdens on state and local (and eventually the federal) government to prove both a compelling interest and narrow tailoring. Many of these cases involved public employment or government contracting. These cases furnished fuel for affirmative action critics who thought they heralded the end of *Bakke* and of affirmative action generally. Such predictions, as we shall see, proved premature.

Post-*Bakke* cases involving public employment were a mixed bag. On the one hand, the Court approved racial preferences to remedy past discrimination in hiring. *See, e.g.*, United States v. Paradise, 480 U.S. 149 (1987). In *Paradise,* the Court upheld a federal court order that a qualified black officer be hired or promoted whenever a white officer was hired or promoted in Alabama's Department of Public Safety. 480 U.S. at 167.

But a fractured Court invalidated a Michigan plan for teacher layoffs that overrode a contractual "last hired, first fired" provision in order to preserve the jobs of recently hired minority teachers. Wygant v. Jackson Board of Education, 476 U.S. 267 (1986). Writing for a plurality, Justice Powell found that the plan was not narrowly tailored to any compelling governmental interest. Specifically, Justice Powell rejected the notion that providing role models for minority students was compelling enough to override the collective bargaining agreement's provision that layoffs would proceed according to seniority. *Wygant*, 476 U.S. at 275-276.

As in *Bakke*, public contracting cases initially featured a debate over the proper standard of review. Early cases gave more deference to federal programs designed to benefit minorities than the Court did to state and local governments. For example, in *Fullilove v. Klutznick*, 448 U.S. 448, 472-473 (1980), and later in *Metro Broadcasting, Inc. v. FCC*, 497 U.S. 547, 566-567 (1990), the Court evaluated contracting set-asides for minority-owned businesses and broadcasting license preferences for minority-owned broadcasters, respectively, under intermediate scrutiny, not strict scrutiny. It did so in *Metro Broadcasting*, moreover, even though the year before the Court subjected a local government set-aside to a quite rigorous application of strict scrutiny. Richmond v. J.A. Croson, 488 U.S. 469 (1989). The reason given for differentiating between federal programs and state and local programs was that Congress had broad power to enforce the Fourteenth Amendment, and therefore the Court should be more deferential to remedial programs that Congress implemented.[4] No such deference should be accorded *state* classifications according to race, however.

Thus, when Richmond, Virginia, enacted a policy requiring prime contractors on city works programs to reserve 30 percent of the value of the contract to award to minority-owned subcontractors (defined as a 51 percent share being held by individuals who were African American, Asian American, Spanish-speaking, Eskimo, or Aleut), the Court was extremely skeptical. It ultimately invalidated the program. *Croson*, 488 U.S. at 507-508.

The city defended the program as necessary to remedy what it perceived as discrimination in the city's construction industry. It noted that though the city was 50 percent African American, less than 1 percent of prime contracts were awarded to minority-owned businesses during a seven-year period. The city conceded, however, that "[t]here was no direct evidence . . . that the city's prime contractors had discriminated against minority-owned subcontractors." *Id.* at 480. Despite the remedial aims asserted by Richmond, the Court found that the program was not narrowly tailored to any compelling governmental interest. *Id.* at 507-508.

As to the compelling governmental interest, while remedying past discrimination *usually* qualifies, the *Croson* Court emphasized that a "generalized assertion that there has been past discrimination in an entire industry provides no guidance for a legislative body to determine the precise scope of the injury it seeks to remedy." *Id.* at 498. The Court felt that the evidence to support Richmond's claims simply wasn't there. For the Court to completely defer to the possibly self-serving rationales for race-based set-asides would erode earlier pronouncements dating back to *Bakke* that remedying general societal discrimination was insufficiently compelling. *Id.* at 505-506. "To accept Richmond's claim that past societal discrimination alone can serve as a basis for rigid racial preferences would be to open the door to competing claims for 'remedial relief' for every disadvantaged group." *Id.* at 505.

The Court, moreover, found the scope of the remedy to be "gross[ly] over-inclusive[]," precluding any ability to assess whether or not it was narrowly tailored to a possible compelling governmental interest. *Id.* at 506. Specifically,

4. For more on Congress's power to enforce the Fourteenth and Fifteenth Amendments, see Chapter 10.

the Court wondered why groups like "Eskimos" and "Aleuts" were included in the set-aside when no evidence existed that either were present in any number in Richmond, much less subject to invidious discrimination in government contracting. *Id.* Such overbreadth "strongly impugn[ed] the city's claim of remedial motivation." *Id.*

Further, the Court noted that no race-neutral solutions for expanding minority contracting opportunities were explored. It seemed, to the Court, the set-aside "cannot be said to be narrowly tailored to any goal, except perhaps outright racial balancing." *Id.* at 507.

As noted above, however, critics of affirmative action were shocked when, in the next term, the Court decided *Metro Broadcasting*, upholding a federal broadcast licensing preference for minority-owned broadcasters, using intermediate as opposed to strict scrutiny. 497 U.S. at 569. The tension between *Fullilove/Metro Broadcasting* on the one hand, and *Croson* on the other, however, was resolved when, in *Adarand Constructors, Inc. v. Pena*, 515 U.S. 200 (1995), the Court overruled those parts of *Fullilove* and *Metro Broadcasting* that reviewed federal set-asides under intermediate scrutiny. 515 U.S. at 227. *Adarand* made clear that *all* racial classifications, federal or state, invidious or benign, were subject to strict scrutiny. Given the rigor with which that standard was applied in *Croson*, it began to look as if perhaps strict in theory *would be* fatal in fact to race-based preferences, including the admissions policies of a number of state universities and public schools.

QUESTION 7. Teacher, teacher. Ames City is a racially diverse city in the State of Ames. Recently, the new superintendent of the Ames City School District announced a hiring initiative aimed at filling the ranks of Ames City teachers, which had been depleted by recent retirements. The superintendent announces that she expects that the new cadre of teachers will "look like Ames City," will furnish role models for Ames City's students, and will be diverse enough to serve the needs of minority students in the Ames City school district. To that end, she announces a goal of 30 percent minority teachers in the new round of hiring.

Which of the following would be most helpful in defending the constitutionality of the superintendent's initiative?

A. Claiming that the set-asides will ensure that teachers can be role models for minority students.
B. Evidence that the Ames City school district had systematically refused to hire minority teachers in the past.
C. Evidence that the 30 percent hiring goal tracks the percentage of minority students in the Ames City school system generally.
D. Evidence that school systems elsewhere in the State of Ames had practiced racial discrimination in the hiring of teachers in the past.

ANALYSIS. From *Bakke* we know it is impermissible to assume that only members of minorities can serve as role models for other minorities. Therefore, **A** wouldn't be very helpful. That argument was again rejected in *Wygant*, when the Court refused to permit teacher layoffs to be made according to race, when the collective bargaining agreement specified a "last hired, first fired" rule. Moreover, **C** suggests racial balancing for race's sake, something that every Court since *Bakke* has condemned as impermissible under the Equal Protection Clause. Further, **D** smacks of an effort to remedy *societal* discrimination; again, since *Bakke*, that has been off limits to governments. That leaves **B**, which is the best answer. If it can be proven that the Ames City schools systematically denied minority teachers opportunities, remedial measures may be taken. There should be some evidence, of course, that the "hiring goal" bears some relationship to the extent, scope, and duration of the discrimination it is designed to remedy.

Affirmative action and education: reprise. Because of the Court's growing skepticism toward race-based preferences in government contracts and in public employment, as discussed above, a number of challenges were mounted to the admissions programs of state universities and professional schools following *Adarand*. In companion cases *Grutter v. Bollinger*, 539 U.S. 306 (2003) and *Gratz v. Bollinger*, 539 U.S. 244 (2003), a majority of the Court embraced both *Bakke*'s framework and its application of that framework in challenges to the admissions policies of the college of arts and sciences and the law school of the University of Michigan.

The University of Michigan Law School conducted individual assessments of students applying for admission. Among the "soft variables" considered by the law school was an applicant's race or ethnicity, if the applicant was African American, Hispanic, or Native American. *Grutter*, 539 U.S. at 306. In addition, the law school sought to enroll a "critical mass" of minorities so that members of particular minority groups would not feel isolated or forced into the role of spokesperson for their race. *Id.* at 306.

Writing for a majority of the Court, Justice O'Connor embraced Justice Powell's *Bakke* opinion, including its rejection of a relaxed standard of review for "benign" racial classifications. "[S]uch classifications are constitutional only if they are narrowly tailored to further compelling governmental interests." *Id.* at 326.

In the majority's view, Michigan had "a compelling interest in attaining a diverse student body." *Id.* at 328. Surprisingly, given that government usually bears the burden of proof on this issue, the Court further held that "[t]he Law School's educational judgment that such diversity is essential to its educational mission is one to which we defer." *Id.* The Court went on to cite studies supporting Michigan's contention that diversity promoted better learning outcomes compared with non-diverse classroom settings. *Id.* at 330-333.

The Court also found that the law school's plan was narrowly tailored and did not operate as a quota. *Id.* at 334-335. Despite evidence cited in the dissenting opinion that the law school carefully tracked the racial and ethnic composition of its class and tended to admit members of the favored minority groups in percentages that corresponded to the percentages of minorities that applied for admission, the majority concluded that "[t]he Law School's goal of attaining a critical mass of underrepresented minority students does not transform its program into a quota." *Id.* at 335-336. As long as race was used only as a "plus" in "a highly individualized, holistic review of each applicant," it was not unconstitutional. *Id.* at 337. Further, the Court refused to interpret narrow tailoring to "require exhaustion of every conceivable race-neutral alternative" or to sacrifice its "reputation for excellence" in order to "provide educational opportunities to members of all racial groups." *Id.* at 339.

The structure of the college of arts and sciences' admissions policy, however, led another majority to invalidate it. Under the undergraduate admissions plan, students were ranked according to a selection index; points were awarded to applicants for things like GPA, SAT score, difficulty of courses taken, residency, and legacy status. *Gratz*, 539 U.S. at 255. Students with 100 or more points were automatically admitted. Students of particular ethnic or racial backgrounds were awarded 20 points. As a practical matter, this meant race was decisive "for virtually every minimally qualified underrepresented minority applicant." *Id.* at 272. The Court found that this offended Justice Powell's call in *Bakke* for individualized consideration of applicants and that applicants be permitted to compete for all available slots. *Id.* An interesting feature of the two cases was Justices Ginsburg, Souter, and Breyer's call for the Court to distinguish between benign and invidious racial classifications, as Justice Brennan and others had done in *Bakke. See id.* at 302 (Ginsburg, J., dissenting).

But the Court's application of strict scrutiny in *Grutter* and its application in *Parents Involved in Community Schools v. Seattle School District No. 1*, 551 U.S. 701 (2007), could not have been more different. *Parents Involved* concerned not higher education, but student assignment policies for elementary and secondary schools in Seattle and Louisville, Kentucky. Seattle schools used race to allot space in oversubscribed high schools. Classifying students as "black," "white," and "other," schools could not exceed the racial composition of the district as a whole: 41 percent white and 59 percent nonwhite. *Parents Involved*, 551 U.S. at 710-712.

In Louisville, race was used in the assignment of students to elementary schools and in the processing of transfer requests. Students were designated "black" or "other"; schools were required to maintain a minimum black enrollment of 15 percent, but the enrollment of black students was not permitted to exceed 50 percent. Students were permitted to select a school to attend, as long as their attendance would not upset the racial balance at the school. *Id.* at 716-717. In neither case were the plans adopted to remedy past discrimination. Seattle had never run a segregated schools system; and while Louisville had in the past, its school system had not been under federal court supervision for several years. *Id.* at 712, 715-716.

Applying strict scrutiny, the Court noted that it had recognized two interests as compelling in past cases: (1) remedying effects of past discrimination and (2) an "interest in diversity in higher education," though it went on to say that neither was applicable here. *Id.* at 720-723. Neither of the schools could use the remedying-past-discrimination justification. Further, Chief Justice Roberts wrote that *Grutter* was unavailable because the schools were explicitly seeking racial balancing, as opposed to using race as one factor among many in pursuit of educational diversity. *Id.* at 724-725.

For its part, Seattle argued that its use of race was an attempt to combat the effects of segregation in housing, while Louisville argued that its use of race was an attempt to secure the benefits of a racially integrated environment. But Chief Justice Roberts pointed out for the plurality that, "[i]n design and operation, the plans are directed only to racial balance, pure and simple, an objective this Court has repeatedly condemned as illegitimate." *Id.* at 726. "Accepting racial balancing as a compelling state interest," he continued, "would justify the imposition of racial proportionality throughout American society, contrary to our repeated recognition" of the constitutional mandate to treat people as individuals, as opposed to fungible representatives of the respective racial groups. *Id.* at 730.

Justice Kennedy, however, was not willing to say that the prevention of "racial isolation" caused by housing patterns could *never* be a compelling governmental interest. "[I]t is permissible," he wrote, "to consider the racial makeup of schools and to adopt general policies to encourage a diverse student body, one aspect of which is its racial composition." *Id.* at 788 (Kennedy, J., concurring). "A compelling interest exists in avoiding racial isolation. . . ." *Id.* at 797 (Kennedy, J., concurring). With the dissenters, then, Justice Kennedy's concurrence meant that five justices accepted that preventing racial isolation can be a compelling governmental interest.

Kennedy joined the plurality, however, in its determination that the means used to avoid that isolation were not narrowly tailored here. Chief Justice Roberts wrote that "[t]he districts have . . . failed to show that they considered methods other than explicit racial classifications to achieve their stated goals." In other words, the majority was more insistent than in *Grutter* that race-neutral means be explored. *Id.* at 735. Justice Kennedy's concurrence suggested that the drawing of school attendance zones, strategic site allocation, and the like were alternatives to the reliance on race alone to avoid the problem of racial isolation. *Id.* (Kennedy, J., concurring).

Fisher v. University of Texas, 133 S. Ct. 2411 (2013), could signal a further retreat from *Grutter*'s relatively relaxed application of strict scrutiny. At issue was the use of race in undergraduate admissions at the University of Texas at Austin. An earlier program had been held to be unconstitutional by the Fifth Circuit Court of Appeals in a case that the Supreme Court declined to review. Hopwood v. Texas, 78 F.3d 932 (5th Cir. 1996), *cert. denied*, 518 U.S. 1033 (1996). Following *Hopwood*, the Texas legislature enacted a plan guaranteeing admission to certain Texas colleges for students graduating in the top 10 percent of their high school class. The University also substituted "a new holistic metric of a candidate's potential contribution to the University, to be used in conjunction with" the applicant's test scores. *Fisher*, 133 S. Ct. at 2415-2416. Following the Court's decisions in *Grutter* and *Gratz*, the University of Texas resumed its consideration of race as a factor in undergraduate admissions. *Id.* at 2416.

When a disappointed applicant sued, claiming that the use of race in admissions violated the Equal Protection Clause, the Fifth Circuit sustained the program, holding "that *Grutter* required courts to give substantial deference to the University, both in the definition of the compelling interest in diversity's benefits and in deciding whether its specific plan was narrowly tailored to achieve its stated goal." *Id.* at 2417.

Reversing the Fifth Circuit, Justice Kennedy wrote that while *Grutter* did counsel deference to a university's judgment about the benefits of a diverse student body, "there must still be a further judicial determination that the admissions process meets strict scrutiny in its implementation." *Id.* at 2419-2420. On this question, Kennedy emphasized, "the University receives no deference. [I]t is for the courts, not for university administrators, to ensure" that the means chosen are narrowly tailored to the university's compelling interests. *Id.* at 2420. This means, Kennedy added, that courts must conduct "a careful judicial inquiry into whether a university could achieve sufficient diversity without using racial classifications." *Id.* Justice Ginsburg dissented, continuing to express her support for a candid differentiation between invidious and benign uses of race in admissions. *Id.* at 2433-2434 (Ginsburg, J., dissenting).

The following charts summarize the current state of the law regarding race-based preferences—specifically, which governmental interests have been recognized as "compelling" and which classifications have been regarded as "narrowly tailored."

Race-Based Classifications: Compelling State Interests at a Glance

Interest	*Case Recognized*	*Scope*
Pursuing educational benefits of diverse student body in higher education	Regents of Univ. Calif. v. Bakke (1978); Grutter v. Bollinger (2003)	Court will defer to institutional judgment that diversity is essential to education; unclear whether it extends to primary and secondary schools
Remedying past discrimination	U.S. v. Paradise (1987)	Requires proof of discrimination; Court will not accept "generalized assertions" of remedial purpose absent proof
Avoiding racial isolation in schools caused by segregated patterns of housing	Parents Involved in Community Schools v. Seattle School Dist. No. 1 (2007)	Kennedy, J., concurring; plus Justices Breyer, Stevens, Souter, and Ginsburg provided five votes for proposition that avoiding "racial isolation" was a compelling governmental interest

Race-Based Classifications: Narrow Tailoring at a Glance

Permitted Uses of Race	*Scope*
Race as a "plus" factor in higher education admissions	Must be part of an individualized, holistic review of each applicant; no deference due to university administrators; availability of race-neutral means must be considered
Accelerated promotion or hiring requirements	To remedy past discrimination by institution or entity

(d) Race and the political process Occasionally, the Court has invalidated efforts to use the political process to further discrimination, even if the discrimination itself cannot be reached by the Fourteenth Amendment because there is no state action. For example, in *Anderson v. Martin*, 375 U.S. 399 (1964), the Court invalidated a law requiring the race of a candidate to be printed on the ballot along with the candidate's name. Other cases from the 1960s involved efforts to prevent the passage of housing discrimination statutes or prevent the expansive use of busing as a means of desegregating schools. Where extraordinary measures such as amending the state constitution were required to reverse such measures, the Court found that the Equal Protection Clause had been violated.

In *Reitman v. Mulkey*, 387 U.S. 369 (1967), for example, the Court invalidated an amendment to the California Constitution—passed by popular referendum—that enshrined an absolute right of a property owner to sell, lease, or rent property to anyone for any reason. The Court held that the intent of the amendment was to permit private racial discrimination in housing and was, for that reason, unconstitutional. *Mulkey*, 387 U.S. at 378-379. (The Court found that the amendment itself involved the state in an "invitation to discriminat[e]" to such a degree that state action was present. See Chapter 9 for a discussion.)

Two years later, in *Hunter v. Erickson*, 393 U.S. 385 (1969), the Court invalidated an amendment to a city charter in Akron, Ohio, that required housing discrimination ordinances to be approved by a majority of the voters. *Hunter*, 393 U.S. at 393. The Court held that only laws aimed at ending housing discrimination based on race, color, religion, or national origin had to be so approved. The amendment's explicit concern with laws protecting individuals from racial and religious discrimination, the Court held, violated the rights of those minorities by "plac[ing] special burden[s]" on them "within the governmental process." *Id.* at 391. Because only those minorities were affected, the Court held that the requirement violated the Equal Protection Clause.

Finally, the Court again invalidated an initiative prohibiting the use of busing to achieve integration in the schools. Washington v. Seattle School District No. 1, 458 U.S. 457 (1982). While the initiative prohibited the assignment of students to schools other than those nearest their homes, there were a number of exceptions, including the special educational needs of the student and the inadequacy of the closest school. *Seattle School District*, 458 U.S.

at 462. Moreover, the initiative excepted any constitutionally required, court-ordered busing. *Id.* at 463.

Mulkey and *Hunter* had been criticized for not clearly describing either the source or the scope of the principle the Court used to invalidate the measures. In *Seattle School District*, Justice Blackmun attempted to synthesize both cases. In his words, both cases "guarantee[ed]racial minorities the right to full participation in the political life of the community" and prohibited measures that "subtly distort[ed] governmental processes in such a way so as to place special burdens on the ability of minority groups to achieve beneficial legislation." *Id.* at 467.

While majorities may make it difficult for *everyone* to make use of the political process, they can't rig it so that particular disadvantages fall on minorities. The Washington initiative, in the Court's view, "use[d] the racial nature of an issue to define the governmental decisionmaking structure, and thus impose[d] substantial and unique burdens on racial minorities." *Id.* at 470. In its practical effect, the Court saw the Washington measure as on par with the amendment in *Hunter*. "Those favoring the elimination of de facto school segregation now must seek relief from the state legislature, or from the statewide electorate." *Id.* at 474. Moreover, "by specifically exempting from [the measure] most non-racial reasons for assigning students away from their neighborhood schools, the initiative expressly requires those championing school integration to surmount a considerably higher hurdle than persons seeking comparable legislative action." *Id.*

But not all action repealing previously granted rights or protections constitutes an equal protection violation. On the day the Court decided *Seattle School District*, it upheld a California constitutional amendment that prohibited state courts from ordering busing if the U.S. Constitution did not compel it. Crawford v. Board of Education, 458 U.S. 527 (1982). The Court found that this amendment was facially neutral and did not alter the political process to the disadvantage of racial minorities. Plaintiffs were still free to seek busing as a remedy, but the grounds on which it might be required by state courts were altered. *Crawford*, 458 U.S. at 536, 545. Presumably, part of the difference between the outcomes in the two cases is the absence in *Crawford* of numerous exceptions permitting assignment to non-neighborhood schools for non-racial reasons. Still, though, advocates of expanded busing (which would presumably benefit racial minorities) in *Crawford* are still forced to resort to extraordinary means—amending the state constitution—relative to the ones used by those seeking other sorts of remedies from the legislature.

QUESTION 8. **On the merits.** Voters in the State of Ames approved an initiative amending the state constitution to prohibit state universities from considering any factor other than high school grade point average and SAT or ACT score in making admissions decisions. Opponents of this initiative sue, claiming that the purpose is to prohibit admissions offices from taking race into account as part of an effort to secure for Ames's universities the benefits of a diverse student body. The initiative, they claim, violates the Equal Protection Clause. A reviewing court would likely:

A. Uphold the initiative, because it does not mention race and did not single out racial minorities for particular disadvantages.
B. Invalidate the initiative, because it makes it more difficult for supporters of affirmative action to secure their preferred policies in the political process.
C. Uphold the initiative, because there is no state action.
D. Invalidate the initiative because the Equal Protection Clause guarantees minorities full participation in the political process.

ANALYSIS. *Hunter* and *Mulkey* held that the state cannot permit its lawmaking processes to be employed in the service of private discrimination, that the state's involvement was sufficient to support a finding of state action. Therefore, as an initial matter **C** is not the correct answer. There is state action here, and the restrictions of the Fourteenth Amendment apply. *Seattle School District* did hold that what the Equal Protection Clause guarantees is that racial minorities be permitted to participate fully in the political life of a community, that singling them out for particular disabilities is not permitted. But **D** isn't the best answer either, because it merely states the matter in question. *Crawford* held that making it *equally* difficult for all persons to secure particular types of legislation would pass muster. According to the facts, *no* other criteria are permitted to be considered—musical ability, legacy status, athletic ability—and so race is not the only criterion excluded. While this facial neutrality is not sufficient to insulate the initiative from challenge, the lack of numerous exceptions carving out all criteria *but* race suggests that the measure does not simply target minorities. That means that **B** is not the correct answer, leaving **A**, the best answer.

The Court, in fact, recently decided a case whose facts are similar to the preceding question. When Michigan voters amended the state constitution to prohibit the use of racial preferences in university admissions, as well as in public contracting and public employment, opponents sued, arguing that the provisions violated the Equal Protection Clause, citing *Mulkey*, *Hunter*, and *Seattle School District.* Schuette v. Coalition to Defend Affirmative Action, 2014 WL 1577512 (2014). Six members of the Court rejected the challenge. In a plurality opinion, Justice Kennedy distinguished the earlier cases, writing that the question the Michigan case posed was "not how to address or prevent injury caused on account of race but whether voters may determine whether a policy of race-based preferences should be continued." *Schuette*, 2014 WL 1577512, at *15. By enacting the ban, according to the plurality, "the Michigan voters exercised their privilege to enact laws as a basic exercise of their democratic power," using "the initiative system to bypass public officials who were deemed not responsive to the concerns of a majority of voters" who preferred not to have the state grant racial preferences. *Id.* Justices Scalia and Thomas concurred, calling for *Hunter* and *Seattle School District* to be overruled because both were, in their opinion, "[p]atently atextual, unadministrable, and contrary to our traditional equal-protection jurisprudence. . . ." *Id.* at *22 (Scalia, J., concurring).

For his part, Justice Breyer also concurred, writing to express his belief that the Constitution permits, but does not require, "narrowly tailored race-conscious programs designed to bring about greater inclusion and diversity." *Id.* at *28 (Breyer, J., concurring). "But," he cautioned, "the Constitution foresees the ballot box, not the courts, as the normal instrument for resolving differences and debates about the merits of these programs." *Id.* He likewise distinguished *Hunter* and *Seattle*, noting that in the earlier cases "minorities had participated in the political process and they had won. The majority's subsequent reordering of the political process repealed the minority's successes and made it more difficult for the minority to succeed in the future." *Id.* at *29 (Breyer, J., concurring). Here, however, the voters simply moved decisionmaking authority from an unelected body (the faculty that made admissions policy) "and placed it in the hands of the voters." *Id.*

Justice Sotomayor, joined by Justice Ginsburg, dissented. In her view, the Michigan referendum was on all fours with earlier cases, like *Hunter*. "A majority of the Michigan electorate," she wrote, "changed the basic rules of the political process in that State in a manner that uniquely disadvantaged racial minorities." *Id.* at *31 (Sotomayor, J., dissenting) (footnote omitted). "Our precedents," she continued, "do not permit political restructurings that create one process for racial minorities and a separate, less burdensome process for everyone else." *Id.* at *32 (Sotomayor, J., dissenting).

3. *Alienage*

Lawful resident aliens are a protected class, and laws treating them differently than citizens are subject to strict scrutiny. However, the Court has created a number of exceptions to this general proposition. According to one commentator, "in practice . . . the only alienage classifications subject to strict scrutiny are those used by *states*, and then only with respect to matters that do not implicate a state's legitimate power 'to preserve the basic conception of a political community.'"[5] Calvin Massey, American Constitutional Law: Powers and Liberties 771 (4th ed. 2013).

In fact, many of the cases applying strict scrutiny were decided contemporaneously, at a time when the Court was using the Equal Protection Clause

5. Because Congress has broad powers over immigration, see U.S. Const. art. I, § 8, cl. 4 (authorizing a "uniform Rule of Naturalization"), the Court will usually examine *federal* alienage classifications using minimal scrutiny. *See* Matthews v. Diaz, 426 U.S. 67 (1976) (upholding a five-year residency requirement before one becomes eligible for Medicaid).

instead of the Due Process Clause to enforce substantive values. For example, in *Graham v. Richardson*, 403 U.S. 465 (1971), the Court invalidated state attempts to restrict lawful resident aliens' eligibility for public assistance. Two years later, in *Sugarman v. Dougall*, 413 U.S. 634 (1973), the Court invalidated a New York law requiring that civil servants be U.S. citizens. The Court noted that this was a "flat" ban, suggesting that laws banning "some or all aliens from closely defined and limited classes of public employment on a uniform and consistent basis. . . ." *Dougall*, 413 U.S. at 639.

The Court rejected New York's argument that its ban was "precisely drawn" in light of the state's professed desire to limit participation in the civil service to those who are part of the political community. But the Court did acknowledge that the power to "require citizenship as a qualification for office" applied not only "to the qualification of voters, but also to persons holding state elective or important nonelective executive, legislative, and judicial positions, for officers who participate directly in the formulation, execution, or review of broad public policy [or] perform functions that go to the heart of representative government." *Id.* at 647. The same year the Court voided the exclusion of resident aliens from the practice of law, In re Griffiths, 413 U.S. 717 (1973), despite the fact that one might credibly say that lawyers, though unelected, play a role in the formulation and execution of public policy.

Subsequent decisions have shed little light on where the "political function" line begins or ends. On the one hand, the Court has invalidated laws barring aliens from becoming notaries public, Bernal v. Fainter, 467 U.S. 216 (1984); from becoming engineers, Examining Board v. Flores de Otero, 426 U.S. 572 (1976); and from receiving college financial aid, Nyquist v. Mauclet, 432 U.S. 1 (1977). But it has upheld, under its political functions exception, bans on aliens becoming police officers, Foley v. Connelie, 435 U.S. 291 (1978); probation officers, Cabell v. Chavez-Salido, 454 U.S. 432 (1982); and even public school teachers, Ambach v. Norwick, 441 U.S. 68 (1979). In *Norwick*, the Court justified its decision to employ minimal scrutiny on the "critical part" that teachers play "in developing students' attitude toward government and understanding of the role of citizens in our society." 441 U.S. at 78.

QUESTION 9. **There goes the neighborhood.** Concerned over the possibility that continued economic problems in the United States could result in a transfer of American property to foreign hands, the State of Ames passes a law prohibiting aliens from owning more than 30 percent of stock in a corporation chartered in Ames. Frederick, an English investor who is a longtime resident of the United States, seeks to purchase a controlling interest in an Ames corporation. He sues, challenging the stock ownership ban. A reviewing court should:

A. Uphold the ban, because only citizens of the United States are protected under the Fourteenth Amendment.

B. Invalidate the ban, because owning stock in a private company is not a "political" function.
C. Uphold the ban, because diffusion of property could imperil the political community of Ames.
D. Invalidate the ban, because classifications based on alienage are presumptively unconstitutional.

ANALYSIS. Believe it or not, many states used to have restrictions on alien ownership of land. Moreover, an early-twentieth-century Supreme Court decision upheld this ban. Terrace v. Thompson, 263 U.S. 197 (1923) (holding that preserving land affected "the safety and power of the state itself"). That changed with pre-*Graham* cases, such as *Takahashi v. Fish and Game Commission*, 334 U.S. 410 (1948), in which the Court invalidated a California law denying aliens the ability to obtain commercial fishing licenses. The situation in the facts resembles the *Takahashi* case. With that in mind, consider the answers. **A** is incorrect; the Equal Protection Clause protects all "persons" within a state's jurisdiction, not just citizens. **C** is incorrect as well, because it does not accurately reflect the current doctrine. **D** is incorrect because some alienage classifications are *not* presumptively unconstitutional. That leaves **B**, which is the best answer: The ban on stock ownership does not implicate the "political function" exception that garners only rational basis scrutiny. Wherever the line lies between those performing important public functions and those that who are not, it is clear that a private individual's ownership of land or property in a state is *not* a public or political function; therefore, restrictions on alien ownership would garner strict scrutiny.

QUESTION 10. Alienation. The State of Ames requires public defenders to be American citizens. Robert, a Canadian citizen, is duly licensed to practice in Ames and is a longtime Ames resident, but he has never applied for U.S. citizenship. He sues, claiming that the ban is not narrowly tailored to fulfill a compelling governmental interest. A reviewing court should:

A. Invalidate the ban, unless Ames can satisfy strict scrutiny.
B. Dismiss his suit, because he has no constitutional right to be a public defender.
C. Invalidate the ban, because the practice of law may not be conditioned on citizenship.
D. Dismiss his suit, because public defenders are officers of the court who participate directly in the formation of public policy and the administration of the criminal justice system.

ANALYSIS. Questions about alienage are not easy to write because of the difficulty of discerning a clear distinction between the positions for which the Court has permitted alien exclusion and those for which it has not. Nevertheless, if you read the answers carefully, one is better than the rest. **A** isn't correct, because whether strict or minimal scrutiny applies is the matter in question. **B** is correct as far as it goes, but is beside the point: While one may not have a "right" to a public job, the Constitution does impose some limits on the reasons why one may be excluded from a position. You might have been drawn to **C** because of the *Griffiths* case, discussed above, but the exclusion here is not from the practice of law in toto, but only from becoming a public defender. That leaves **D**, which is the best answer, though it admittedly assumes that the court *would* find that public defenders' role in the judicial system is equivalent to the performance of a public function. But they seem to qualify at least as much as the probation officers in *Chavez-Salido.*

D. Intermediate Scrutiny and Gender Classifications

As noted at the beginning of the chapter, while the standards of review for equal protection cases track those used in due process cases, the special case of gender classification spawned a third level of scrutiny, intermediate scrutiny. Under this standard of review, gender-based classifications must be "substantially related" to "important" governmental interests. The standard of review was a compromise that emerged as the Court considered adopting strict scrutiny for gender classifications.

1. Toward intermediate scrutiny

Prior to the early 1970s, gender classifications received only minimal scrutiny; the Court regularly upheld disabilities imposed upon women, many of which were rooted in sexist stereotypes. *See, e.g.,* Goesaert v. Cleary, 335 U.S. 464 (1948) (upholding Michigan statute prohibiting women, other than the wife or daughter of male bar owner, to tend bar; *held,* rational basis for ban existed). Beginning in the early 1970s, however, the Court, while not explicitly replacing the traditional rational basis review, began to closely scrutinize gender classifications with an eye to invalidating those for which no good reason existed. In *Reed v. Reed,* 404 U.S. 71 (1971), for example, the Court invalidated a state law designating men as administrators of an intestate decedent's estate. Administrative convenience did not justify the automatic preference for males over females. *Reed,* 404 U.S. at 76-77.

In *Frontiero v. Richardson,* 411 U.S. 677 (1973), the Court invalidated a federal law permitting males serving in the military to claim wives as dependents in order to receive enhanced benefits, but requiring servicewomen to demonstrate that their husbands actually were dependent on them in order to receive the same benefits. Four Justices applied strict scrutiny, but could not attract a fifth vote. The remaining four Justices in the majority applied *Reed*'s rational basis with bite to invalidate the law. Those Justices declining to adopt strict scrutiny cited the pendency of the Equal Rights Amendment in the states as a reason for not embracing the more demanding standard of review.

After *Frontiero*, the Court continued to apply its searching form of rational basis review, invalidating classifications rooted in "archaic or overbroad" stereotypes. *See, e.g.*, Weinberger v. Wiesenfeld, 420 U.S. 636 (1975) (voiding provision entitling female, but not male, survivors to benefits based on earnings of deceased spouse); Stanton v. Stanton, 421 U.S. 7 (1975) (invalidating law requiring parental support of male children until age 21, but only until 18 for females). Not every gender classification was invalidated, however. The Court upheld a U.S. Navy rule permitting women a longer promotion period—during which one was either promoted or retired—than men, reasoning that policies such as the ban on women in combat furnished women with fewer opportunities to achieve promotion. Schlesinger v. Ballard, 419 U.S. 498 (1975); *see also* Kahn v. Shevin, 416 U.S. 351 (1974) (upholding property tax exemption for widows only, concluding that the exemption was a rational response to the demonstrated greater financial burden of women compared to men).

Finally, in *Craig v. Boren*, 429 U.S. 190 (1976), the Court acknowledged in fact what was apparent in practice—that it was scrutinizing gender classifications under a standard of review that was more demanding that the traditional rational basis review. Though the Court could not get a majority for strict scrutiny, there was a majority for the new intermediate standard of review. "To withstand constitutional challenge," Justice Brennan wrote, "previous cases establish that classifications by gender must serve important governmental objectives and must be substantially related to achievement of those objectives." *Craig*, 429 U.S. at 197.

The question presented in *Craig* was whether Oklahoma's law restricting sales of 3.2 percent beer to males 21 years old and older, but permitting sales to females 18 and older, violated the Equal Protection Clause. The interest asserted was the prevention of driving under the influence and other problems associated with drinking. While conceding the interest, the Court concluded that the classification was not substantially related to that objective. *Id.* at 199-200.

The state argued that because more men than women, and more men age 17 to 20, were arrested for driving under the influence and drunkenness, and were killed or injured in traffic accidents, it was reasonable to differentiate between the sexes regarding the purchase of beer. But although males between the ages of 17 and 20 were ten times as likely as females to be arrested for an alcohol-related driving offense (2 percent vs. 0.18 percent), the percentages meant that 98 percent and 99.92 percent of males and females, respectively, *weren't* arrested for those offenses. The Court found that "if maleness is to serve as a proxy for drinking and driving, a correlation of 2 percent must be considered an unduly tenuous 'fit.'" *Id.* at 202 (footnote omitted). Moreover, the Court observed that "when it is further recognized that Oklahoma's statute prohibits only the selling of 3.2 percent beer to young males and not their drinking the beverage once acquired (even after purchase by their 18-20-year-old female companions), the relationship between gender and traffic safety" was rendered even more suspect. *Id.* at 204.

QUESTION 11. D-i-v-o-r-c-e. The State of Ames imposes obligations of alimony following a divorce on husbands, but not on wives. According to the state, the intent is to provide financial assistance to needy women following the dissolution of a marriage. When Ken and Barbie divorced in Ames, the judge awarded alimony to Barbie, despite the fact that Barbie earns twice Ken's salary. Ken sued, claiming that the Ames statute violates the Equal Protection Clause. A reviewing court should:

A. Uphold the statute, because it is rationally related to an important governmental interest.
B. Invalidate the statute, because the imposition of alimony on men but not women is irrational.
C. Uphold the statue, because providing financial assistance to needy spouses is an important governmental interest.
D. Invalidate the statute, because it relies on outmoded gender stereotypes.

ANALYSIS. The facts here are taken from *Orr v. Orr*, 440 U.S. 268 (1979), in which the Supreme Court invalidated an Alabama statute similar to the one described. **A** and **B** can be eliminated quickly, because neither correctly states the standard of review. Intermediate scrutiny requires that a classification be *substantially* related to an important governmental interest. And while providing financial assistance to needy spouses following a divorce may be an important governmental interest, that's not what the statute does—it uses gender, specifically female gender, as a proxy for neediness. Therefore, **C** is incorrect. That leaves **D**, the best answer. Assuming, as the statute does, that following divorces females are always financially needy and that men never are is the kind of gender stereotype that the Court has repeatedly held to be unconstitutional.

2. *Intent, actual purpose, and real differences*

As is true of racial discrimination claims, mere disparate impact is not sufficient to make out a claim for sex discrimination. Intentional discrimination must be proven. In *Personnel Administrator v. Feeney*, 442 U.S. 256 (1979), the Court sustained a Massachusetts law creating a permanent preference for veterans when state civil service jobs were to be filled. Despite the fact that 98 percent of veterans were men, the Court refused to infer intentional discrimination from that fact. The Court noted that the veterans' preference excluded large numbers of men as well as women from consideration. *Feeney*, 442 U.S. at 275.

The Court has also made clear that states must rely on the *actual* purpose of the classification, not some purpose that was created ad hoc in order to defend the classification during litigation. The Court struck down Mississippi's "women-only" nursing school in *Mississippi University for Women v. Hogan*, 458 U.S. 718 (1982), declining to credit the state's asserted interest in compensating for past discrimination against women in higher education. Not only was there no evidence that the creation of MUW was actually to compensate women for past discrimination, but the Court noted that the exclusion of men from the nursing school tended to perpetuate gender stereotypes about appropriate career choices for men and women. *Mississippi Univ. Women*, 458 U.S. at 729.

At the other end of the spectrum from archaic stereotypes, however, are "real differences" between the sexes that the Court has permitted state and federal legislators to take into account. In *Michael M. v. Superior Court of Sonoma County*, 450 U.S. 464 (1981), for example, the Court upheld California's statutory rape law, which presumed that *females* under the age of 18 lacked the ability to consent to sexual intercourse.

Observing that it had upheld classifications that took account of situations in which "the sexes are not similarly situated," the Court noted that California had an interest in minimizing "illegitimate teen pregnancies" to prevent abortion and to avoid having unwanted children become "wards of the state." *Michael M.*, 450 U.S. at 469-471. Because only women could become pregnant, the Court reasoned, California could have concluded that men needed the additional disincentive provided by the statutory rape law to deter them from engaging in sexual intercourse with women under 18. *Id.* at 473. "A criminal sanction imposed solely on males . . . serves to roughly 'equalize' the deterrents on the sexes." *Id.* The majority brushed aside arguments that a gender-neutral statute would not hinder the state's aims in any significant way, observing that the question was not "whether the statute is drawn as precisely as it might have been, but whether the line chosen by the California Legislature is within constitutional limitations." *Id.* at 474. Absent from the majority opinion was proof that prevention of abortion and teen pregnancy was the *actual purpose* behind California's statutory rape law. Moreover, it is difficult to see why minor females are incapable of consenting to sexual intercourse while minor males are, without resort to at least some stereotypical notions of gender roles or the relative capacity of the sexes to consent prior to the age of majority.

The same year, the Court upheld the federal exclusion of women from registration for the draft. Rostker v. Goldberg, 453 U.S. 57 (1981). The Court deferred to Congress's expertise in military matters, and found that the registration of men only was substantially related to the important goal of raising and supporting armies. Because Congress excluded women from combat roles and because the draft was intended primarily to furnish combat troops, the Court reasoned, it made sense to exclude women from registering for the draft. *Rostker*, 453 U.S. at 75-77. "This is not a case of Congress arbitrarily choosing to burden one of two similarly situated groups, such as would be the case with an all-black or all-white, or an all-Catholic or all-Lutheran, or an all-Republican or all-Democratic registration," the Court wrote. *Id.* at 78. "Men and women, because of the combat restrictions on women, are simply not similarly situated for purposes of a draft or registration for a draft." *Id.* No inquiry was made, though, into the basis for the exclusion of women from combat, presumably because that question was not before the Court. The dissenters pointed out too that not every individual inducted into the army became a combat soldier, and that the government made no showing that including women in the registration would impede the registration's effectiveness. *Id.* at 83-84 (Marshall, J., dissenting).

The Court also upheld a federal statute conferring citizenship on an illegitimate child born abroad if the mother was a citizen; but where the father was a citizen, the statute required (1) legitimization, (2) acknowledgment of paternity, or (3) a court order of paternity before citizenship was conferred. Nguyen v. Immigration and Naturalization Service, 533 U.S. 53 (2001). The Court held that the policy served two important objectives: first, "assuring that a biological parent-child relationship exists" and second, to ensure "that the child and the citizen parent have some demonstrated opportunity or potential" to develop a relationship "consist[ing] of the real, everyday ties that provide a connection between child and citizen parent and, in turn, the United States." *Nguyen*, 533 U.S. at 62, 64-65. The Court found men and women were not similarly situated because establishing both parenthood and the "real, everyday ties" between a mother and child was easier, due to the biological fact of birth. The dissenters complained the majority ignored sex-neutral alternatives and accused it of relying on outmoded stereotypes about the relationships between mothers and children, as opposed to relationships between fathers and their children. *Id.* at 80-81, 89 (O'Connor, J., dissenting).

3. *A de facto "strict scrutiny" standard of review?*

The United States sued the Virginia Military Institute over its male-only policy in the mid-1990s. United States v. Virginia, 518 U.S. 515 (1996). Over only Justice Scalia's dissent,[6] the Court held that VMI must admit women; the language of the majority opinion, moreover, led some commentators to suggest that the Court had implicitly adopted strict scrutiny for gender-based classifications. Writing for the Court, Justice Ginsburg noted, quoting an earlier case, that those defending "gender-based government action must demonstrate an

---

6. Justice Thomas, whose son attended VMI at the time, recused himself.

'exceedingly persuasive justification' for that action." *Virginia*, 518 U.S. at 531. She continued that this meant the government must show, at a minimum, that the "classification serves 'important governmental objectives and that the discriminatory means employed' are 'substantially related to the achievement of those objectives.'" *Id.* at 533. Moreover, she emphasized, "[t]he justification must be genuine, not hypothesized or invented post hoc in response to litigation. And it must not rely on overbroad generalizations about the different talents, capacities, or preferences of males and females." *Id.* While acknowledging that "inherent differences" between men and women both exist and could serve as the basis for differentiation, "such classifications may not be used . . . to create or perpetuate the legal, social, and economic inferiority of women." *Id.* at 533-544.

The Court then concluded that Virginia could not meet the burden and that the remedy for the exclusion—the creation of a women-only "leadership academy" at nearby Mary Baldwin College—was not a sufficient remedy. While the Court did not dispute that single-sex education provided benefits, it concluded that neither "recent nor distant history bears out Virginia's alleged pursuit of diversity through single-sex educational options." *Id.* at 536. That rationale, suggested by the state, was not, the Court concluded, the "real purpose" for VMI's male-only policy. For example, following *Mississippi University for Women v. Hogan*, VMI spent two and a half years examining its policy, and decided to continue to exclude women. Whatever its purpose, the Court concluded, "we can hardly extract from that effort any [state] policy evenhandedly to advance diverse educational options." *Id.* at 539. As for the argument that VMI's "adversative training methods" are unsuited for female education, the Court noted that these are based on stereotypes about the capabilities and desires of men and women.

The Court was unimpressed by the Virginia Women's Institute for Leadership, finding it fell short of providing a remedy for the exclusion of females from VMI. By stripping the VWIL of the distinctive "adversative" elements of a VMI education, the state created a wholly different educational experience based, again, on generalizations of what men and women can and cannot handle. *Id.* at 549-551. Further, the Court noted that "VWIL's student body, faculty, course offerings, and facilities hardly match VMI's. Nor can the VWIL graduate anticipate the benefits associated with VMI's 157-year history, the school's prestige, and its influential alumni network." *Id.* at 551.

QUESTION 12. Bored of education. Ames City mandates that boys and girls in kindergarten through eighth grade be taught in separate classrooms. Data suggest that children of that age benefit from single-sex classrooms. If Ames City's policy is challenged in federal court, which of the following would be most helpful to the city's argument that its policy is constitutional?

A. Testimony that boys are more rambunctious and need to be active during the day, while girls are more focused and can sit still for longer periods of time.
B. Data showing a significant link between educational performance and lifetime income as well as data showing increases in educational performance in single-sex classes through the eighth grade.
C. Data showing a significant link between educational performance and lifetime income.
D. Testimony that separating school children by sex is a historical practice that has been maintained over the years.

ANALYSIS. This question was intended to test the Court's distinction between actual and pretextual purposes, as well as the Court's distinction between real differences and those rooted in stereotypes. The facts indicate that Ames City has a single-sex classroom policy for children through the eighth grade. Of the proffered choices, the *least* helpful would be **D**, because it suggests that the real reason for the separation has nothing to do with the educational achievement of children and is rooted, at best, in time-honored custom. **A** is not much better, because it is rooted in generalizations that approach the stereotypical. While **C** points to an important governmental purpose—preparing school-age children for success as adults—there's nothing to indicate that the separation is substantially related to that important purpose. That leaves **B**, which is the best answer: If the city can demonstrate both that it is in pursuit of that important purpose—adult success—and that the separation is related to that purpose, it would go far to justify its policy. If, in other words, the state can show not only that increased academic performance yields benefits down the road, but also that separating children by sex through the eighth grade increases academic performance, it has a stronger claim that its classification does not violate the Equal Protection Clause.

4. *Gender and illegitimacy*

The Court's treatment of laws penalizing illegitimacy have tracked its treatment of gender-based classifications. In the late 1960s and the late 1980s, the Court applied a searching form of rational basis review, invalidating, for example, a law prohibiting illegitimate children from suing for the wrongful death of their mother. Levy v. Louisiana, 391 U.S. 68 (1968); *see also* Gloria v. American Guarantee & Liability Insurance Co., 391 U.S. 73 (1968) (invalidating law prohibiting parents of illegitimate children from suing for child's wrongful death).

In 1988, however, the Court adopted intermediate scrutiny as the standard of review for laws classifying on the basis of legitimacy. Clark v. Jeter, 486 U.S. 456 (1988). The law in *Clark* invalidated a law establishing a six-year statute of limitations—which began running at birth—in order to obtain support from the birth father. The Court had invalidated shorter periods in earlier cases; even six years, it held, did not "provide a reasonable opportunity to assert a claim on behalf of an illegitimate child." *Clark*, 486 U.S. at 463; *see also* Pickett v. Brown, 462 U.S. 1 (1983) (invalidating two-year statute of limitations); Mills v. Habluetzel, 456 U.S. 1 (1982) (invalidating one-year statute of limitations).

E. Closer

QUESTION 13. The case of the Checkerboard Ordinance[7] A new town, New Utopia, incorporated in the State of Ames. New Utopia adopted a "Checkerboard Ordinance" under which every residential building lot within its corporate limits was classified as either "N" or "W" pursuant to a plan permitting "N" property to be acquired and occupied only by non-whites and "W" property only by whites. At a special ceremony, the Mayor of New Utopia flipped a coin to designate whether the first plot, at the extreme northeastern corner of the town's limits, would be N or W; thereafter, all other residential lots alternated between N and W, as the following map of residential plots indicates:

W	N	W	N
N	W	N	W
W	N	W	N
N	W	N	W

The ordinance makes any lease, contract for the sale of land, or other agreement invalid if its performance would lead to violation of the rules governing the acquisition and occupancy of the land. The town clerk is forbidden to accept for recordation any conveyance or lease that is not accompanied by proof that the buyer or tenant may lawfully acquire or occupy the land.

Jones, who is white, contracted to sell a lot designated W to Stevens, who is African American. The clerk of New Utopia refused to record the

7. This question is based on the hypothetical ordinance mooted in Boris I. Bittker, *The Case of the Checker-Board Ordinance: An Experiment in Race Relations*, 71 Yale L.J. 1387 (1962).

deed because Stevens is African American, and the town advised Jones that he would be treated as the owner of the land despite the sale. Jones and Stevens sued in federal court, claiming that the Checkerboard Ordinance violated the Equal Protection Clause of the Fourteenth Amendment because it prohibits the sale of the lot from Jones to Stevens and the recording of the deed in Stevens's name solely because of Stevens's race.

At trial, the town offers the following justifications for the ordinance:

I. The residents of New Utopia would benefit from the racial diversity that came from close proximity between members of different races.
II. The Checkerboard Ordinance is necessary to prevent racial isolation in schools that results from the tendency in residential neighborhoods to segregate by race.
III. The ordinance helps remedy past discrimination in housing as documented in surrounding communities.

Which of the following *could* supply a compelling governmental interest for the Ordinance?

A. I only.
B. II only.
C. III only.
D. II or III.

ANALYSIS. After reading *Parents Involved*, you might have found yourself looking for the "none of the above" choice! Let's start with the elimination that is easiest. Recall that the Court has repeatedly said that while remedying past discrimination can be a compelling governmental interest, government cannot attempt to remedy past *societal* discrimination that the government has had nothing to do with. New Utopia is a new town, with no history of discrimination against minorities. Moreover, as III notes, it is attempting to remedy discrimination *in surrounding communities*; again, the Court has repeatedly declined to hold that this is a compelling purpose as far back as Justice Powell's *Bakke* opinion. Therefore, neither **C** nor **D** is the right answer. You might have been drawn to justification I, because much of the Court's affirmative action jurisprudence concerns race-based preference in higher education, where much of the talk concerns the putative benefits of learning in a diverse atmosphere. But remember that in *Bakke*, and later in cases such as *Grutter*, the Court approved of the use of race as *one factor* in creating a diverse educational environment. It hasn't held that taking into account race for race's sake is permissible; nor has it held that achieving racial diversity alone is sufficient to employ the classification of race. Quite the opposite: The Court has suggested that racial diversity alone comes close to the inclination to take race into account for its own sake, which it has, in the past, condemned. So **A** isn't the best answer. "But wait!" I hear you saying, "Didn't the Court say that preventing racial isolation wasn't a sufficiently compelling interest in *Parents Involved*?" Recall that that portion of the opinion was written by only a *plurality* of the Court. Justice Kennedy refused to hold that prevention of racial isolation could *never* be a compelling governmental interest. Presumably, the other dissenters, many of whom would apply something less than strict scrutiny to benign racial classifications, would find that this motive passes muster. Therefore, **B** is the best answer of the four.

QUESTION 14. Bonus closer. Continuing Question 13, assuming that a compelling governmental interest could be found, a reviewing court would likely:

A. Invalidate the ordinance, because there is no evidence that race-neutral means of achieving the governmental interest were considered.
B. Invalidate the ordinance, because the Court has never upheld race-conscious remedies in cases other than those involving higher education.
C. Uphold the ordinance, because it is a necessary means of achieving the compelling interest.
D. Uphold the ordinance, because there is no quota involved.

ANALYSIS. As you will recall, satisfying the Court that the racial classification is in pursuit of a compelling governmental interest is only half the battle. The government must also prove that the classification is narrowly tailored to that compelling interest. Right away you should have spotted **B** as being incorrect: The Court *has* approved race-based remedies to compensate for past discrimination by governmental entities. But there is no evidence of past discrimination here. **C** is a possibility, but it is not the best answer, because it simply asserts the matter in question. **D** is not the best answer either. There *is* a quota, in the sense that New Utopia has reserved half of the residential lots for non-whites, just as the medical school in *Bakke* reserved a set number of its seats for minorities only. Of the available answers, then, **A** is the best. No evidence is given in the facts that New Utopia pursued race-neutral means of achieving any possible compelling interest. That failure is sufficient to support a finding that the ordinance is not narrowly tailored, and is therefore unconstitutional. The Court has held that the use of race ought to be one factor among several for securing diversity and that, in any event, race-neutral means ought to be investigated, even if their complete exhaustion is not constitutionally required.

Denning's Picks

1. **A**
2. **D**
3. **A**
4. **D**
5. **C**
6. **D**
7. **B**
8. **A**
9. **B**
10. **D**
11. **D**
12. **B**
13. **B**
14. **A**

5

The Equal Protection Clause of the Fourteenth Amendment, Part II: Fundamental Rights

A. Overview

Not only does the Equal Protection Clause of the Fourteenth Amendment restrict the government's ability to classify according to certain prescribed characteristics, such as race, it also restricts the government's ability to limit the ability of groups of persons to exercise certain (often unenumerated) "fundamental" rights. This aspect of equal protection doctrine has much in common with the doctrine of substantive due process discussed in Chapter 3.

For example, when the government denies a group of persons the ability to exercise a recognized fundamental right, grounds for the denial must satisfy strict scrutiny. That is, the government must prove that the denial is necessary or narrowly tailored to accomplish some compelling governmental interest. The difference between enforcing rights through the Equal Protection Clause as opposed to the Due Process Clause is subtle, but real. As one commentator put it: "If a law denies the right to everyone, then due process would be the best grounds for analysis; but if a law denies a right to some, while allowing it to others, the discrimination can be challenged as offending equal protection or the violation of the right can be objected to under due process." Erwin Chemerinsky, Constitutional Law: Principles and Policies 814 (4th ed. 2011).

This chapter will examine the three main fundamental rights vindicated by the Equal Protection Clause: the right to vote; the right to interstate travel; and the right of access to courts. You will notice that many of these rights were identified and protected by the Court around the same time, roughly from the mid-1960s to the mid- to late 1970s. It was during this time that the

Court appeared to flirt with the idea of guaranteeing individuals "positive" rights to a minimum standard of living. *See, e.g.,* Frank I. Michelman, *The Supreme Court, 1968 Term—Foreword: On Protecting the Poor Through the Fourteenth Amendment,* 83 Harv. L. Rev. 7 (1969). By the early 1970s, however, the Court appeared to have retreated from earlier efforts to make society more egalitarian through the use of judicial power. *See, e.g.,* San Antonio Independent School District v. Rodriguez, 411 U.S. 1 (1973) (refusing to recognize education as a fundamental right; *held,* state financing of schools through property taxes levied by local school districts did not violate the Equal Protection Clause because wealth was not a suspect classification). The Court seems to have called a halt to the recognition of new fundamental rights and their protection using the Equal Protection Clause, but considerable doctrine has formed around those rights that the Court previously recognized. We will look at each in turn.

B. Voting

1. *Introduction*

At the time of the Framing, qualifications for voting were left to state regulation; the Bill of Rights did not guarantee a right to vote. Beginning with the Fifteenth Amendment, however, the ability of states to restrict the franchise was subject to constitutional limitations. The Fifteenth Amendment barred restriction of the right to vote based on race in 1870. U.S. Const. amend. XV. It was another half-century, however, before female suffrage was guaranteed. U.S. Const. amend. XIX. The poll tax for *federal* elections was eliminated in 1964 by the Twenty-fourth Amendment. U.S. Const. amend. XXIV. In 1971, the franchise was extended to 18-year-olds. U.S. Const. amend. XXVI. In addition, by the mid-1960s, the Court recognized the right to vote as fundamental and began to scrutinize restrictions on that right closely. *See* Reynolds v. Sims, 377 U.S. 533, 555 (1964). Much of the Court's activity has occurred in three areas: (1) denial of the right to vote, (2) dilution of the right to vote through legislative malapportionment, and (3) the dilution of votes through gerrymandered voting district boundaries.

2. *Denial of voting rights*

Because voting "is of the essence of a democratic society" and "any restrictions on that right strike at the heart of representative government," *Reynolds,* 377 U.S. at 555, the Court has strictly scrutinized those restrictions. In *Harper v. Virginia,* 383 U.S. 663 (1966), for example, the Court invalidated state poll taxes (money voters had to pay to cast their votes), despite the fact that two years before the Twenty-fourth Amendment had banned poll taxes in federal elections. Restrictions on the franchise violated the Equal Protection Clause, the Court wrote, "whenever it makes the affluence of the voter or payment of any fee an election standard." *Harper*, 383 U.S. at 666. The Court further remarked that the "right to vote is too precious, too fundamental to be so burdened or conditioned." *Id.* at 670.

In addition to total denials, the Court has subjected selective or temporary denials of the franchise to strict scrutiny. For example, New York attempted to limit votes in school district elections to either parents of public school children or owners or lessees of real property; the Court invalidated that restriction. Kramer v. Union Free School District, 395 U.S. 621 (1969). No less than total deprivation, these selective denials had the potential to "deny[] some citizens any effective voice in the governmental affairs which substantially affect their lives." *Kramer*, 395 U.S. at 627. While the Court conceded the state's interest in limiting participation in the elections to those most interested or affected, it failed to see how exclusion of some residents was necessary to achieve that goal. *Id.* at 633.

QUESTION 1. "Bond . . . Municipal Bond." Ames City passed an ordinance prohibiting non-property-owning taxpayers from voting in favor of or against the issuance of municipal bonds out of the general revenue to fund the building, maintenance, or expansion of any public utility. Tom, a resident who rents property in Ames City, sued in federal district court, claiming that this was a violation of the Equal Protection Clause. A reviewing court would likely:

A. Uphold the ordinance, because the Constitution does not specifically guarantee everyone the right to vote.
B. Uphold the ordinance, because the restriction is rationally related to the government's legitimate interest in restricting the franchise to those who are most impacted by the outcome of the vote.
C. Invalidate the ordinance, because the exclusion of non-property owners from voting is not necessary to any compelling governmental interest.
D. Invalidate the ordinance, because restrictions on the fundamental right to vote can never pass constitutional scrutiny.

ANALYSIS. The facts in this question are similar to those in *City of Phoenix v. Kolodziejski*, 399 U.S. 204 (1970) (invalidating law permitting only property-owning taxpayers to vote in elections regarding the issuance of certain bonds), and *Cipriano v. Houma*, 395 U.S. 701 (1969) (same). But even without knowing how those cases came out, you could have narrowed down your choices. First, **A** is out because, as we've seen, even though voting is not explicitly guaranteed, the Court has recognized it as a fundamental right and applies strict scrutiny to state attempts to deny it to groups of people. Because strict scrutiny is the standard of review, **B** is not the correct answer; it employs a rational basis standard. **D**, on the other hand, goes too far—states can restrict the franchise to *residents*, for example. That leaves **C**, the correct answer: Even assuming that restricting the franchise to those most affected by the outcomes of votes, in the words of *Kramer*, property owners and non–property owners alike are affected by decisions to issue bonds to expand or repair utilities; the burdens and benefits are not restricted to property owners. Therefore, restricting the franchise to that group is not necessary to achieve that compelling interest.

In limited circumstances, however, the Court has approved the restriction of special-purpose elections to property owners uniquely affected by the outcome of an election. For example, in *Salyer Land Co. v. Tulare Lake Basin Water Storage District*, 410 U.S. 719 (1973), the Court permitted the state to limit voting in water district elections to property owners and then to allocate those votes on the basis of the value of assessed land within those districts. (The districts had reservoirs and canals to make water available for agriculture. The owners were charged an amount commensurate with the benefit received.) The Court reasoned that the property owners had a greater interest in the outcome of the election than others. *Salyer* was then expanded in *Ball v. James*, 451 U.S. 355 (1981), where the Court upheld a "one acre, one vote" rule for a water district election. Although the outcome of the election in *Ball* had a wider impact than that in *Salyer*, the Court still held that the impact on the landowners was disproportionately large relative to the impact on others. *Ball*, 451 U.S. at 371.

Even in special-purpose elections, however, the Court will not permit voters' participation to be restricted on the basis of race. *See* Rice v. Cayetano, 528 U.S. 495 (2000). *Rice* invalidated a law limiting the right to vote for trustees of the Office of Hawaiian Affairs to descendants of Hawaii's original inhabitants. 528 U.S. at 523-524. Racial limits on voting, the Court noted, were prohibited by the express language of the Fifteenth Amendment. *Id.* at 523.

QUESTION 2. Taxation and representation. Ames City just passed an ordinance requiring that one show proof of real property ownership to vote on property tax increases or decreases. Peter, who owns no property in Ames City, sues, claiming that the plan violates the Equal Protection Clause. A reviewing court would likely:

A. Uphold the ordinance, because government can limit the franchise to those most affected by a vote.

B. Uphold the ordinance, because the denial is limited to tax increases and decreases.

C. Invalidate the ordinance, because it denies citizens any effective voice in their government.
D. Invalidate the ordinance, because it is not necessary to achieve any compelling governmental interest.

ANALYSIS. It might have occurred to you to ask what the difference is between *Salyer* and *Ball* on the one hand, and *Kramer* on the other. Could a town limit votes on tax increases to property owners on the theory that they are more affected? While that is one reading of *Salyer* and *Ball*, it is probably too broad a reading. The difference seems to be that the cases in which a selective denial was upheld concerned water districts whose members were charged on the basis of water consumed. On the other hand, the decision to issue bonds or fund schools impacts all citizens, even if it impacts some—who may pay higher taxes—more than others. Going through the answers, then, **A** is not true for the reasons just given. The Court rejected those arguments in *Kramer*. **B** is incorrect as well; the denial in *Kramer* was limited to school board elections. **C** is incorrect on the facts because non–real property owners were not denied *all* effective voice; they were just denied votes on the question of tax hikes. That leaves **D**, the best answer: Even if there is some compelling reason to restrict the franchise to those who are most affected by a particular measure, the exclusion of non–property owners is not necessary to achieve that, which is the result the Court reached in *Kramer*.

Even temporary denials of the right to vote until a term of residency has been satisfied, once common in some states, have been invalidated. Dunn v. Blumstein, 405 U.S. 330 (1972). The Court held in *Blumstein* that such laws were not necessary to further aims such as ensuring that voters are knowledgeable. States may, however, permanently disenfranchise convicted felons. Richard v. Ramirez, 418 U.S. 24 (1974). The Court ruled, in part, that because the Fourteenth Amendment contemplated it, the deprivation of voting rights as punishment for being convicted of a crime was not a violation of the Equal Protection Clause.[1] Further, the Court has upheld laws requiring one to prove one's identity as a prerequisite to voting. Crawford v. Marion Cnty. Election Board, 553 U.S. 181 (2008).

In *Crawford*, Indiana required voters to produce a government-issued photo identification card before voting. If voters had no such identification,

1. *See* U.S. Const. amend XIV, § 2 (prescribing proportional reduction in representation in the House of Representatives if "the right to vote at any [federal or state] election . . . is denied to any of the male inhabitants of such State, being twenty-one years of age, and citizens of the United States, or in any way abridged, except for participation in rebellion, or other crime. . . .").

they could cast a provisional ballot; if they produce the requisite identification within ten days, it would be counted. *Crawford*, 553 U.S. at 185-186.

Indiana justified its requirement on the following grounds: (1) preventing fraud, especially because the state's voter rolls showed a number of people who were either dead or no longer residents of the state; and (2) safeguarding voter confidence in the integrity of the electoral system. *Id.* at 191.

Even though the record evinced little fraud in Indiana itself, the Court wrote that "[t]here is no question about the legitimacy or importance of the State's interest in counting only the votes of eligible voters. Moreover, the interest in orderly administration and accurate recordkeeping provides a sufficient justification for carefully identifying all voters participating in the election process." *Id.* at 196. Further, the Court found Indiana's voter rolls "unusually inflated," further justifying the identification requirement, which, the Court noted, was neutral and nondiscriminatory. *Id.* When balanced against those important interests, the burdens on voters, the Court concluded, were not serious, especially given the provisional ballot option. *Id.* at 198-199.

3. *Dilution of votes*

After *Baker v. Carr*, 369 U.S. 186 (1962), held that courts could hear Equal Protection Clause challenges to malapportioned state legislatures,[2] the Court still faced the problem of developing a baseline to measure deprivations of equality. In *Reynolds v. Sims*, 377 U.S. 533 (1964), the Court decided that "one person, one vote" was the standard, meaning that representation had to be apportioned according to population. *Sims*, 377 U.S. at 568. Thus, if a state had a population of 1 million and had 20 electoral districts, the districts needed to be drawn so that each included no more than 50,000 people. Otherwise, cities with larger populations could be underrepresented in legislatures, while sparsely populated rural districts would be overrepresented. This was the situation in many states, particularly in the South, until the Supreme Court intervened.

"Legislators," Chief Justice Warren wrote for the majority, "represent people, not trees or acres. Legislators are elected by voters, not farms or cities or economic interests." 377 U.S. at 562. He continued:

> [I]f a state should provide that the votes of citizens in one part of the State should be given two times, or five times, or 10 times the weight of votes of citizens in another part of the State, it could hardly be contended that the right to vote of those residing in the disfavored areas had not been effectively diluted.

Id. As a matter of equal protection, then, the Court held that "the seats in both houses of a bicameral state legislature must be apportioned on a population basis." *Id.* at 568.

---

2. See volume 1, Chapter 2, section C.4 for a discussion of *Baker* and the political question doctrine.

QUESTION 3. Upper house hijinks. Voters in the State of Ames recently amended their Constitution, by statewide majority vote, to apportion seats in the lower house of the Ames General Assembly by population but apportion seats in the upper house by geography. Voters who opposed the referendum sue, claiming that the new apportionment scheme violates the Equal Protection Clause. A reviewing judge should:

A. Invalidate the scheme, because it dilutes the votes of citizens electing members of the upper house of the Ames General Assembly.
B. Invalidate the scheme, unless the state demonstrates a compelling governmental interest.
C. Uphold the scheme, because it was passed by statewide referendum.
D. Uphold the scheme, because the malapportionment is not the result of the General Assembly's refusal to reapportion itself.

ANALYSIS. The "one person, one vote" rule applies even if the citizens themselves decide they prefer a different basis for representation, as Colorado found out in a companion case to *Sims.* Lucas v. Forty-fourth General Assembly, 377 U.S. 713 (1964). Colorado voters had approved a referendum apportioning seats in the lower house of the General Assembly by population and seats in the upper house by geography. The Court held that a majority of state voters had no authority to override the requirements of the Equal Protection Clause. 377 U.S. at 736-737. Even without knowing about the *Lucas* case, however, you could have reasoned your way through the choices to the correct answer. For example, **B** states the wrong standard of review. Vote dilution is apparently a per se violation of the Constitution. Moreover, because it is a constitutional mandate, states cannot override it, no matter how large the majority or supermajority. Therefore, **C** is not the right answer either. While it is true that many of the early apportionment cases arose out of state legislatures' refusal to reapportion following the census, the issue is not so much *how* the malapportionment came about, but rather whether it exists at all. So **D** isn't the best answer either. That leaves **A**, the correct answer. By apportioning seats in the upper house according to geography, the voters have ensured that some parts of the state will be overrepresented while the more populous parts of the state will be underrepresented in the Ames General Assembly. This would violate *Reynolds v. Sims*'s "one person, one vote" rule and is therefore unconstitutional.

The issue of vote dilution came up again in *Bush v. Gore*, 531 U.S. 98 (2000). In the course of litigating the closely contested election results in Florida, the Florida Supreme Court had ordered a manual recount only of "undervotes"—votes in which the machine-controlled tally failed to register a choice for President. Seven Supreme Court Justices found that this violated equal protection, but differed on the remedy. In a per curiam opinion, the Court wrote that "the State may not, by later arbitrary and disparate treatment, value one person's vote over that of another." *Bush*, 531 U.S. at 104-105.

The Court found that in an attempt to discern "the intent of the voter," no standards were specified for doing so, resulting in "unequal evaluation of ballots in various respects." *Id.* at 106. The Florida Supreme Court then, according to the Court, placed its imprimatur on that unequal treatment. "The recent process," the opinion continued, "in its features here described, is inconsistent with the minimum procedures necessary to protect the fundamental right of each voter in the special instance of a statewide recount under the authority of a single state judicial officer." *Id.* at 105-106.

4. *Gerrymanders*

Legislators seeking to reapportion for partisan political advantage have eagerly exploited the reapportionment requirement of *Baker v. Carr* and *Reynolds v. Sims.* With the aid of computers and maps, legislators can "pack" districts with large numbers of voters of one party and reduce their numbers elsewhere; or they can "crack" districts by dispersing voters of a particular party, leaving them in the minority in a number of districts. The question in *Davis v. Bandemer*, 478 U.S. 109 (1986), was whether such practices constitute unconstitutional vote dilution. A plurality of the Court held that an actionable claim would exist only where the "discrimination . . . is arrayed in a manner that will consistently degrade a voter's or a group of voters' influence on the political process as a whole." *Bandemer*, 478 U.S. at 132. Such a claim "must be supported by evidence of continued frustration of the will of a majority of the voters or effective denial to a minority of voters of a fair chance to influence the political process." *Id.* at 133.

Writing for two other Justices, Justice O'Connor argued that partisan gerrymanders were a nonjusticiable political question. *Id.* at 144 (O'Connor, J., dissenting). "The Equal Protection Clause," she wrote, "does not supply judicially manageable standards for resolving purely political gerrymandering claims[;] no group right to an equal share of political power was ever intended by the Framers of the Fourteenth Amendment." *Id.* at 147 (O'Connor, J., dissenting).

Almost 20 years later, four Justices (including Justice O'Connor and Chief Justice Rehnquist, who joined O'Connor's *Bandemer* dissent) came close to overruling *Bandemer.* Vieth v. Jubelirer, 541 U.S. 267 (2004). A plurality held that partisan gerrymanders were nonjusticiable political questions. Justice Kennedy, however, left open the possibility that some judicially manageable standards *could* be found, although he did not suggest what those standards might be. *Vieth*, 541 U.S. at 306 (Kennedy, J., concurring in judgment). In any event, he did not find a violation of equal protection on the facts in the case before the Court. *Id.* (Kennedy, J., concurring in the judgment).

The Court continued to fracture on the question of partisan gerrymanders in *League of United Latin American Citizens v. Perry*, 548 U.S. 399 (2006). Without revisiting the issue of justiciability, a splintered Court rejected the claim, even though there was evidence that partisan entrenchment was a primary motivation for mid-decade redistricting by Republicans in Texas. *LULAC*, 548 U.S. at 417, 477. Despite that motivation, there was also evidence that existing Democratic districts were left untouched. *Id.* at 417, 418.

While the Court has shied away from hearing cases involving partisan gerrymandering, *racial* gerrymanders—where district lines are drawn to dilute, disperse, or segregate voters based on their race—have long been strictly scrutinized and often held unconstitutional. *See, e.g.*, Gomillion v. Lightfoot, 364 U.S. 339 (1960) (concluding that a Tuskegee, Alabama, redistricting plan that resulted in the placement of all African American voters outside the city limits was motivated by racial discrimination and was, therefore, unconstitutional).

The more difficult question for the Court has been the constitutionality of drawing voting districts along racial lines to increase the chances of minority representatives being elected. When North Carolina attempted to do this by creating a majority black district that essentially followed the I-85 corridor, the state was sued. Shaw v. Reno, 509 U.S. 630 (1993). The Court held that "a plaintiff challenging a reapportionment statute under the Equal Protection Clause may state a claim by alleging that the legislation, though race-neutral on its face, rationally cannot be understood as anything other than an effort to separate voters into different districts on the basis of race" and that this "separation lacks sufficient" justification. *Shaw*, 509 U.S. at 649. Factors such as "compactness, contiguity, and respect for political subdivisions . . . may serve to defeat a claim that a district has been gerrymandered on racial lines." *Id.* at 647. "Racial gerrymandering," the majority warned, "even for remedial purposes, may balkanize us into competing racial factions; it threatens to carry us further from the goal of a political system in which race no longer matters." *Id.* at 657.

Two years later, in *Miller v. Johnson*, 515 U.S. 900 (1995), the Court noted that irregular district shape is not a necessary element to a racial gerrymandering claim, and evidence that race was the dominate legislative motive is sufficient. The Court wrote that the "plaintiff's burden is to show, either through circumstantial evidence of a district's shape and demographics or more direct evidence going to legislative purpose, that race was the predominant factor motivating the legislature's decision to place a significant number of voters within or without a particular district." *Id.* at 916. Those race-based districts were then subjected to strict scrutiny. *Id.* at 920. When the *Shaw* case came back to the Court in *Shaw v. Hunt*, 517 U.S. 899 (1996), the Court concluded that because the Voting Rights Act required neither race-based districting nor a specific shape for a district, the state had no compelling reason to use race.

Despite the hostility to majority-minority districts evinced in the *Shaw* and its progeny, more recent opinions suggest that an emerging majority of the Court will be more lenient in its adjudication of such districts. In *Easley v. Cromartie*, 532 U.S. 234 (2001), for example, the Court wrote that in cases involving majority-minority districts "where racial identification correlates highly with political affiliation, the party attacking the legislatively drawn boundaries must show at the least that the legislature could have achieved its legitimate political objectives in alternative ways that are comparably consistent with traditional districting principles." *Hunt*, 532 U.S. at 258. In addition, "[t]he party must also show that those districting alternatives would have brought about significantly greater racial balance." *Id.*

C. Interstate Migration

Among other constitutional provisions—such as the Privileges and Immunities Clause of Article IV[3]—the Court has held that the Equal Protection Clause of the Fourteenth Amendment protects individuals' right to interstate travel. The laws at issue in these cases usually involve residency requirements that must be satisfied before a new arrival in the state can access various forms of public assistance; the Court has invalidated most such laws.

In *Shapiro v. Thompson*, 394 U.S. 618 (1969), the Court invalidated a requirement that interstate migrants wait a year before receiving welfare. "[A]ny classification which serves to penalize the exercise of [a constitutional] right," the Court wrote, "unless shown to be necessary to promote a compelling governmental interest, is unconstitutional." *Shapiro*, 394 U.S. at 634. The Court followed up with *Memorial Hospital v. Maricopa Cnty.*, 415 U.S. 250 (1974), in which it invalidated an Arizona law denying free non-emergency medical care to indigents residing in the state for less than a year. "Arizona's durational residence requirement for free medical care penalizes indigents for exercising their right to migrate to and settle in that State." *Memorial Hospital*, 415 U.S. at 261-262.

A year later, however, the Court upheld a one-year Iowa residency requirement imposed on those seeking a divorce in that state. Sosna v. Iowa, 419 U.S. 393 (1975). The Court held that, unlike the budgetary interests asserted in the other cases, Iowa had a strong interest in not becoming a "divorce mill" and in avoiding "officious intermeddling in matters in which another State has a paramount interest, and in minimizing the susceptibility of its own divorce decrees to collateral attack." *Sosna*, 419 U.S. at 407.

Despite the Court's reluctance to expand the "fundamental rights" branch of its equal protection doctrine, it is still hostile to residency requirements imposed on the receipt of public assistance. In *Saenz v. Roe*, 526 U.S. 489 (1999), the Court invalidated a California law limiting new residents to

3. Discussed in volume 1, Chapter 5, section C.

whatever public assistance they would have received in their state of origin for their first year of residency in California. Drawing both on *Shapiro* and the Privileges or Immunities Clause of the Fourteenth Amendment, the Court held that the state's classification of the new citizens by "(a) the period of residency in California and (b) the location of the prior residences of the disfavored class members" was subject to strict scrutiny because it penalized the fundamental right to travel to and settle in a state. *Saenz*, 526 U.S. at 505. California's "entirely fiscal justification" was held to be insufficient to justify the residency requirements. The state could not classify "similarly situated citizens based on the location of their prior residence." *Id.* at 490.

D. Access to Courts

Finally, the Court has created a limited right not to be denied access to courts because of indigency. Although the Court has not always been clear in explaining the source of this right—specifically, whether it sounds in due process or equal protection—one commentator has written that "[t]he common thread in these decisions is the presence of a state-imposed economic barrier to court access where personal liberty or some other constitutionally fundamental liberty interest is at stake." Calvin Massey, American Constitutional Law: Powers and Liberties 835 (4th ed. 2013).

The Court started down this road in *Griffin v. Illinois*, 351 U.S. 12 (1956), in which it invalidated a law charging convicted criminals for the cost of their trial transcript, which was required for any appeal. The Court extended *Griffin* in *Douglas v. California*, 372 U.S. 353 (1963), requiring provision of counsel to indigent criminal defendants for the first appeal. There is no requirement, however, that free counsel be provided for discretionary appeals, such as those from an intermediate appellate court to the appellate court of last resort, such as a state supreme court. Ross v. Moffitt, 417 U.S. 600 (1974).

Indigent *civil* litigants have faced a tougher road in the Court. Litigants have usually obtained relief only when "the interest at stake was a constitutionally independent liberty interest." Massey, *supra*, at 836. In *Boddie v. Connecticut*, 401 U.S. 371 (1971), for example, the Court invalidated, as applied to indigents, the $60 filing fee required to initiate divorce proceedings. The Court relied solely on the Due Process Clause, with Justice Harlan writing that the "state['s] monopolization of the means for legally dissolving [the marriage] relationship" meant that, as a matter of due process, it could not "deny[], solely because of the inability to pay, access to its courts to individuals who seek judicial dissolution of their marriages." *Boddie*, 401 U.S. at 374. The Court similarly invalidated fees charged in paternity proceedings for blood tests as a matter of due process. Little v. Streater, 452 U.S. 1, 14 (1981). The Court cited the involvement of the state, the "'quasi-criminal' overtones" of the paternity proceedings, and the fact that blood testing alone overcame the disadvantages placed by state law on defendants in paternity cases in support of its conclusion that the interests were fundamental. *Little*, 452 U.S. at 10.

Again without clarifying whether it relied on the Due Process Clause or the Equal Protection Clause, the Court invalidated Mississippi's requirement that a party seeking to appeal the termination of parental rights to two minor children pay over $2,000 to prepare the record for appeal. M.L.B. v. S.J.L., 519 U.S. 102 (1996). The Court found that "the accusatory state action" against which M.L.B. was defending "is barely distinguishable from criminal condemnation in view of the magnitude and permanence of the loss she faces." *M.L.B.*, 519 U.S. at 119. Citing the importance of "[c]hoices about marriage, family life, and the upbringing of children," and the Court's prior cases, Justice Ginsburg concluded that "access to judicial processes in cases criminal or 'quasi criminal in nature'" cannot "turn on ability to pay." *Id.* at 116, 124. The Court noted that equal protection is implicated in cases such as *M.L.B.* because "due process does not independently require that the State provide a right to appeal." *Id.* at 104, 120.

QUESTION 4. A man of conviction. Frank is convicted of murder in an Ames state court. Frank appeals his conviction to the Ames Court of Criminal Appeals, which affirms it. Convinced that his conviction was erroneous, Frank seeks an appeal to the Ames Supreme Court. The court, however, requires a $250 filing fee to process a Petition for Leave to Appeal. Frank is indigent and cannot afford the fee; there is no exception for indigency, however. Frank sues in federal court, claiming that the filing fee requirement violates the Fourteenth Amendment. A reviewing court should:

A. Invalidate the filing fee requirement, because the right to appeal one's conviction to the state high court is fundamental.
B. Invalidate the filing fee requirement, because it impermissibly classifies on the basis of wealth.
C. Uphold the filing fee requirement, because Frank has no constitutional right to review by the state supreme court.
D. Uphold the filing fee requirement, because states have an interest in recouping costs associated with the administration of its judicial system.

ANALYSIS. The filing fee is a bit of a red herring. The fee is required for the filing of a Petition for Leave to Appeal with the state supreme court. Because one is not constitutionally entitled to a second appeal, the filing fee is valid. **C** is the best answer. **B** is incorrect because, as we have seen, wealth is not a protected class. **A** is also incorrect: There is no right to more than one appeal. **D** is not so much incorrect as irrelevant. Sure, states have an interest in recouping the costs of judicial administration, but it does not follow that there are no constitutional restrictions on what or whom they may charge.

By contrast, where no fundamental right is at stake, the Court has refused to invalidate fees or charges, even where they have the effect of, for example, burdening the ability of the indigent to file for bankruptcy. United States v. Kras, 409 U.S. 434, 446-447 (1973). The Court similarly upheld a $25 filing fee whose payment was required in order to secure review of eligibility for welfare benefits. Ortwein v. Schwab, 410 U.S. 656 (1973). Again, the lack of a fundamental right to receive the welfare benefits in question was decisive for the Court. *Ortwein*, 410 U.S. at 659.

QUESTION 5. **Fee simple?** Which of the following statutes is vulnerable to a constitutional challenge under the Fourteenth Amendment by an indigent plaintiff?

I. A state statute requiring a $50 fee in order to appeal an administrative eviction decision in a public housing project.
II. A state statute imposing a nonwaivable $100 fee for a marriage license.
III. A state statute imposing a $25 filing fee to file a civil suit in state court.

A. I only
B. II and III
C. II only
D. III only

ANALYSIS. Civil litigants generally receive relief only when an independent constitutional interest is at stake. Thus, of the three choices, the fee in neither I nor III would satisfy that test. Thus, neither **A**, **B**, nor **D** is correct. But in II, the state's conditioning the ability to marry—a fundamental right—on payment of a nonwaivable fee would seem vulnerable for the same reasons that the Court invalidated the fee for divorce in *Boddie*. Of the three choices, then, **C** is the best.

E. Closer

QUESTION 6. Borders. The State of Ames recently engaged in redistricting. As a result of the Ames General Assembly's efforts, one irregularly shaped district, District 1, contains over 30 percent of the state's African American population, making it the only district in the state in which a majority of voters are composed of a racial minority. (Caucasians comprise a majority in Ames.) The redistricting was challenged by African American residents of District 1, who claim that the redistricting is unconstitutional. Which of the following facts would be *least* helpful to their challenge?

A. Evidence that the redistricting was undertaken to pack minorities into a single district to lessen their voting strength in other districts.

B. Evidence that most African Americans in Ames vote Democrat, and that the Republican-controlled legislature generally sought to pack Democratic voters into districts that already tended to elect Democratic candidates.

C. The fact that the new District 1 stretched across several counties in Ames, carving minority voters out of particular neighborhoods.

D. Evidence that no other district in Ames now has more than 10 percent minority voters.

ANALYSIS. The Court has said that in racial gerrymandering cases, intent is everything. Intent, however, can be demonstrated by factors such as demographics, the odd shape of the district, or evidence of legislative purpose in the redistricting. But these are not necessary required, according to the Court. In determining which of the above is *least* helpful, then, **A** would be helpful to plaintiffs. Direct evidence of an intent to create districts based on the race of voters would be useful. So would **C**: An irregular shape, one that cuts across geographical boundaries, could also be helpful to plaintiffs. **D** too would be helpful. It strongly suggests that the legislature might have been "packing" minority voters into a single district, depriving them of the opportunity to elect candidates in other districts. That leaves **B**, which would be least helpful. If the state can show that race and party affiliation correlate closely, then the plaintiffs have to prove that the political objectives could have been obtained through other means that would have also resulted in a greater racial balance. That would, of course, increase the burden on plaintiffs seeking to invalidate or overturn the legislature's creation of District 1.

Denning's Picks

1. **C**
2. **D**
3. **A**
4. **C**
5. **C**
6. **B**

6

The First Amendment and Freedom of Expression

A. Overview

The First Amendment reads, in part, "Congress shall make no law . . . abridging the freedom of speech, or of the press; or the right of the people peaceably to assemble, and to petition the Government for a redress of grievances." U.S. Const. amend. I. This chapter discusses the First Amendment's protection of speech, the press, and the right to associate.[1] As you'll soon discover, however, the Court protects more than literal speech, which is why this chapter is titled "The First Amendment and *Freedom of Expression*." It will take you through the major doctrinal areas of freedom of expression: (1) unprotected and minimally protected speech; (2) content-neutral regulations of speech; (3) regulation of speech by government when it acts as owner, employer, or subsidizer; (4) prior restraint, vagueness, and overbreadth; (5) implicit rights of expression, such as the right to resist forced speech and the freedom of association; (6) campaign finance regulation; and (7) press freedoms. Despite the lack of robust enforcement by the Supreme Court prior to the twentieth century, from the First Amendment's freedom of expression protections have emerged a thick tangle of doctrinal branches. This chapter will, I hope, furnish you with a guide to navigating that thicket.

Before we plunge in, however, there are a few things that you should keep in mind as you read the sections that follow. First, despite the Amendment's being addressed to *Congress*, the speech, press, and assembly protections apply to *all* branches of the federal government. Neither the President nor a federal judge can violate the First Amendment's provisions any more than Congress can. Second, all the relevant provisions of the First Amendment have been incorporated through the Fourteenth Amendment and apply to states (and local governments) as well. Conversely, *private* individuals and institutions are *not* subject to the First Amendment's restrictions.

Third, you should understand a key distinction in the Court's free-speech jurisprudence: that between *content-based* and *content-neutral* regulation.

1. Of course, the Amendment also protects religious freedom by prohibiting religious "establishment" and guaranteeing the right to "free exercise." Those topics are addressed in Chapter 7, *infra*.

Content-based regulations are those that restrict or regulate speech based on the substance of its message—for example, an ordinance prohibiting the use of a municipal park for political rallies as opposed to, say, a concert or play. Because these substantive restrictions tend to be aimed at ideas, they are subject to strict scrutiny. The government bears the burden of proving it is pursuing a compelling governmental interest and that the regulation is narrowly tailored to achieve that interest using the least restrictive means. *Viewpoint* regulations, moreover, are a subset of content-based regulations and are even more disfavored. Not only do viewpoint-based regulations restrict the subject matter, they target a particular position. Instead of prohibiting *all* political rallies, imagine that the ordinance above prohibited all political rallies that criticize the government. That would be a viewpoint-based regulation; rallies praising the government would, by implication, be permitted.

Content-neutral regulations, on the other hand, impose limitations or restrictions on speakers regardless of the content of their message. So-called time, place, and manner restrictions imposed regardless of a speaker's message are the paradigmatic content-neutral regulations. To continue with our park ordinance example, an ordinance that merely prohibited the use of the park for live performances before 8 A.M. and after 8 P.M. would be a content-neutral regulation of speech. It does not matter whether the performer is a political agitator or a virtuoso guitarist; the ordinance does not address itself to the substance of the performance. It simply specifies hours when such performances are and are not permitted. Nevertheless, content-neutral regulations are still subject to a heightened standard of review. Courts apply intermediate scrutiny to content-neutral decisions, and the government—not the challenger—still bears the burden of proof. The government must prove (1) that the purpose of the regulation is not to suppress the content of speech (if that is a purpose, then it is evaluated as a content-based regulation of speech); (2) that the regulation is narrowly tailored to a significant governmental interest; and (3) that the regulation leave open ample alternative channels for communicating the information. Ward v. Rock Against Racism, 491 U.S. 781 (1989); United States v. O'Brien, 391 U.S. 367 (1968). The content-based/content-neutral distinction and the accompanying standards of review are summarized below:

Content-Based Regulation	Viewpoint-Based Regulation	Content-Neutral Regulation
• Compelling governmental interest • Narrow tailoring • Government bears burden of proof	• Same as content-based regulation	• Purpose must not be to suppress ideas • Narrowly tailored to achieve significant government interest • Leave open ample alternative channels • Government bears burden of proof

QUESTION 1. Signs. The Overbrook City Council recently passed an ordinance banning nonpolitical billboards from being erected within city limits. Political billboards were declared exempt for fear of running afoul of the First Amendment. Lacy Advertising, which owns a number of billboards in the city and sells advertising space to for-profit and nonprofit entities, sues in federal court, claiming that the new ordinance violates the First Amendment. The trial judge should:

A. Uphold the ordinance because there is no regulation of "speech."
B. Apply strict scrutiny because the ordinance is content-based.
C. Invalidate the ordinance if the challenger proves that the interest pursued is not substantial, that it is not narrowly tailored, or both.
D. Uphold the ordinance as a valid time, place, and manner regulation.

ANALYSIS. Because the ordinance differentiates between "political" billboards and all other kinds, it is not a content-neutral regulation; it is content-based. That means that strict scrutiny applies, requiring the government to prove that its regulation is narrowly tailored to some compelling governmental interest. **A** is incorrect because the printed matter on a billboard, while not vocal speech, is nevertheless protected by the First Amendment. **C** misstates both the standard of review and the burden of proof. Even under intermediate scrutiny—the standard cited in the distractor—the government, not the challenger, bears the burden of proof. **D** is also incorrect because the regulation goes beyond mere time, place, and manner, banning all billboards not carrying a political message. That is a content-based, not a content-neutral, restriction. That leaves **B**, which is the best answer.

QUESTION 2. Get yer ya-yas out of the park. Overbrook Park is a popular spot in Overbrook City. Among other features, it has a small amphitheater in which concerts are held in the spring and summer months. But Overbrook Park is located next to a tiny new subdivision, and the neighbors have recently complained about the noise from that venue, particularly late at night. In response, the Overbrook City Council passed an ordinance banning amplified sound in Overbrook Park before 8 A.M. and after 8 P.M. "Sticky Fingers," a Rolling Stones tribute band booked months ago to play a gig in Overbrook Park, objects to the new restrictions and sues in federal court, claiming that the noise ordinance violates the First Amendment. The band will likely:

A. Succeed, because there are no alternative avenues to get their message across.

B. Succeed, because the ordinance seeks to suppress speech.
C. Fail, because the ordinance is a valid time, place, and manner regulation.
D. Fail, because a concert performance is not protected by the First Amendment.

ANALYSIS. Again, let's start with the nature of the regulation. Overbrook City is not attempting to prohibit music or any particular type of music. It is just prescribing the times during which amplified music may be played in the park. This is a typical "time, place, and manner" regulation. Therefore, it is subject to intermediate scrutiny. Musical performances *are* protected by the First Amendment, so **D** is incorrect. **B** isn't really correct, for the reasons stated above: The City isn't banning speech altogether, but just setting the times during which it can be played in the park. Of the two remaining answers, **C** is better. It is true that content-neutral regulations must leave open ample alternative channels for expression, and the ordinance does that. Sticky Fingers is free to entertain folks with their music between the hours of 8 A.M. and 8 P.M. Therefore, **A** is not as good an answer as **C**.

Though the content-based/content-neutral distinction is the basic distinction in free speech jurisprudence, you'll see as you work through the chapter that free speech doctrine is a little more complicated than the summary above would suggest. For example, in the next section, you will learn that some speech lies outside of First Amendment protection altogether *because of its content*!

B. Unprotected and Low-Value Speech

1. Introduction

Since the Court began to enforce the First Amendment's free speech protections, there have been certain classes of speech regarded as lying outside the Amendment's protection altogether, based on the content of the speech. As one early Court put it:

> There are certain well defined and narrowly limited classes of speech, the prevention and punishment of which have never been thought to raise any Constitutional problem. These include the lewd and obscene, the profane, the libelous, and the insulting or "fighting" words—those which, by their very utterance, inflict injury or tend to incite an immediate breach of the

> peace. It has been well observed that such utterances are no essential part of any exposition of ideas, and are of such slight social value as a step to truth that any benefit that may be derived from them is clearly outweighed by the social interest in order and morality.

Chaplinsky v. New Hampshire, 315 U.S. 568, 571-572 (1942). Though the list has changed somewhat over the years, there are still entire classes of speech that are *not* protected by the First Amendment because of the implicit judgment that whatever value or worth the speech has is outweighed by its costs to the social order. We'll look at several of those here, as well as other categories of speech that, while not completely unprotected, have enjoyed less judicial protection than speech thought to be at the "core" of the First Amendment's protections.

The Court recently made clear, however, that it is skeptical of attempts to add to the list of subjects outside the protection of the First Amendment because of subject matter. United States v. Stevens, 559 U.S. 460 (2010). *Stevens* concerned the constitutionality of federal legislation prohibiting video depictions of animal cruelty. In response to the Government's argument that videos showing animal cruelty lacked expressive value and should be regarded as unprotected speech, the Court wrote that "[t]he First Amendment's guarantee of free speech does not extend only to categories of speech that survive an ad hoc balancing of relative social costs and benefits. The First Amendment itself reflects a judgment by the American people that the benefits of its restrictions on the Government outweigh the costs. Our Constitution forecloses any attempt to revise that judgment simply on the basis that some speech is not worth it." *Stevens*, 559 U.S. at 470. The Court declined to carve out an exception for animal cruelty and invalidated the statute as substantially overbroad. *Id.* at 482.[2] *See also* Brown v. Entertainment Merchants Association, 131 S. Ct. 2729, 2734 (2011) (rejecting attempts to characterize violent video games as "obscenity" to which minors' access could be limited; "[o]ur cases have been clear that the obscenity exception to the First Amendment does not cover whatever a legislature finds shocking, but only depictions of 'sexual conduct'").

2. *Incitement to commit crimes and true threats*

(a) Incitement The criminal law punishes speech based on content all the time. For example, it is illegal to communicate a threat to the life of the President. 18 U.S.C. § 871. This and similar laws are not thought to present any serious constitutional issues. But what if you are urging *others* to disobey the law or commit illegal acts? Can you be punished for inciting others to commit crimes? This question launched the Supreme Court's free speech jurisprudence during the First World War and the crackdown on communists, "syndicalists," and other political radicals that followed it.

2. For overbreadth, see *infra* section E.

The 1917 Espionage Act placed a number of restrictions on speech. Specifically, it prohibited the making of false statements with the intent to hinder military success. In addition, it outlawed the intentional fomenting of insubordination or mutiny among members of the armed services. It also prohibited obstruction of the draft. A number of defendants were convicted of violating the Espionage Act and sought to have those convictions reversed by the Court. In *Schenck v. United States*, 249 U.S. 47 (1919), for example, a socialist accused of interfering with the draft sought protection for his statements in the First Amendment. Noting that free speech does not prevent the prosecution of someone for "falsely shouting fire in a theater and causing a panic," Justice Oliver Wendell Holmes went on to write that the question was "whether the words used are used in such circumstances and are of such a nature as to create a clear and present danger that they will bring about the substantive evils that Congress has a right to prevent." *Schenck*, 249 U.S. at 52. The "clear and present danger" test governed incitement cases for the next half-century—with the Court often upholding convictions.

After *Schenck*, for example, the Court upheld the conviction of the author of articles in a German-language newspaper praising draft evaders. Frohwerk v. United States, 249 U.S. 204 (1919). Justice Holmes wrote the Court's opinion, concluding that the articles were published "in quarters where a little breath would be enough to kindle a flame." *Frohwerk*, 249 U.S. at 209. The Court also upheld the conviction of socialist presidential candidate Eugene V. Debs for his praise of several men jailed for draft resistance. Debs v. United States, 249 U.S. 211 (1919). Again the Court concluded that Debs's words had the "natural tendency" and the "reasonably probable effect" of producing draft resistance in his listeners.

Justice Holmes parted company with the Court's application of his test in *Abrams v. United States*, 250 U.S. 616 (1919), in which some anarchists were convicted of publishing a leaflet urging a general strike in response to the United States' intervention in Russia following the revolution there. While the Court found that "the plain purpose of their propaganda was to excite, at the supreme crisis of the war, disaffection, sedition, riots, and . . . revolution," Justice Holmes thought the defendants were "poor and puny anonymities" whose "silly leaflet[s]" posed little danger to anyone. *Abrams*, 250 U.S. at 623; *id.* at 628-629 (Holmes, J., dissenting).

Despite the arrival of peace after 1918, prosecutions under state "criminal syndicalism" statutes continued. Communists, anarchists, and other political radicals were often charged with advocating the violent overthrow of the government. Here again the Court tended to defer to state authorities and adopted a rather elastic definition of a "clear and present danger."

In *Gitlow v. New York*, 268 U.S. 652 (1925), the Court sustained the conviction of a man charged with distributing pamphlets urging revolution. His defense was that the pamphlets merely recited doctrine, and they did not incite anyone to anything. The Court was not persuaded, writing that states "may punish utterances endangering the foundations of organized government and threatening its overthrow by unlawful means." *Gitlow*, 268 U.S. at 667. Such calls, the Court continued, "by their very nature, involve danger to the public peace and to the security of the State. . . . And the immediate danger is none the less real and substantial, because the effect of a given utterance cannot be accurately foreseen." *Id.* at 669. The Court seemed to be saying that when the possible result was the end of civil authority, authorities might prosecute such calls regardless of how improbable the likelihood of success. Justice Holmes seized on the improbability of success in his dissent. "Every idea," he wrote, "is an incitement. . . . Eloquence may set fire to reason." *Id.* at 673 (Holmes, J., dissenting). But, he added, "the redundant discourse before us . . . had no chance of starting a present conflagration." *Id.* (Holmes, J., dissenting).

The Court went on to sanction punishment of mere membership in an organization whose tenets included violent overthrow of the government. Whitney v. California, 274 U.S. 357 (1927). Though concurring, Justices Louis Brandeis and Oliver Wendell Holmes wrote that when "the fundamental rights of free speech and assembly are alleged to have been invaded, it must remain open to a defendant to present the issue whether there actually did exist at the time a clear danger; whether the danger, if any was imminent; and whether the evil apprehended was one so substantial as to justify the stringent restriction interposed by the legislature." *Whitney*, 274 U.S. at 378-379 (Brandeis, J., concurring). In contrast to the elasticity of the majority's conception of the "clear and present danger" test and its deference to the state's evaluation of the threat and its immediacy, Justices Brandeis and Holmes seemed to argue that defendants ought to be able to introduce evidence that the danger was either not present, not imminent, or relatively minor.

For a brief moment, it looked as if Brandeis and Holmes's view would take root. The Court later overturned state convictions for merely belonging to groups that advocated the overthrow of lawful authority. Herndon v. Lowry, 301 U.S. 242 (1937); DeJonge v. Oregon, 299 U.S. 353 (1937). But following the end of the Second World War a second "Red Scare" swept the country. The federal Smith Act made membership in the Communist Party a crime; a plurality of the Court upheld convictions of the Party's leadership. Dennis v. United States, 341 U.S. 494 (1951). In language reminiscent of earlier decisions such as *Schenck* and *Gitlow*, the plurality held that a clear and present danger existed when "the gravity of the 'evil,' discounted by its improbability, justifies such invasion of free speech as is necessary to avoid the danger." *Dennis*, 341 U.S. at 510.

After the scare passed, the Court overturned several Smith Act convictions where no proof existed that the defendants themselves advocated the violent overthrow of the U.S. government, but merely *believed* it was necessary. *See, e.g.*, Yates v. United States, 354 U.S. 298 (1957). Later decisions required specific intent on the part of "active" members of parties advocating the violent overthrow of the government to attempt violence against the United States.

Scales v. United States, 367 U.S. 203 (1961). There was, to put it mildly, some tension between *Dennis* and the later cases.

This tension was resolved in *Brandenburg v. Ohio*, 395 U.S. 444 (1969), in which the Court established its contemporary test for incitement. The case concerned charges brought against members of the Ku Klux Klan, which held a rally in Ohio. An Ohio statute prohibited the advocacy of violence as a means of accomplishing political reform. Various speakers at the rally were heard to utter "scattered phrases . . . that were derogatory of Negroes and, in one instance, of Jews." *Brandenburg*, 395 U.S. at 446 (footnote omitted).

In an unsigned opinion the Court reversed the convictions and invalidated the Ohio law. Merely advocating the necessity or propriety of violence to achieve political aims is protected by the First Amendment, the Court held. "[T]he constitutional guarantees of free speech and free press do not permit a State to forbid or proscribe advocacy of the use of force or of law violation except [1] where such advocacy is directed to inciting or producing [2] imminent lawless action and [3] is likely to incite or produce such action." *Id.* at 447. The first element has been interpreted to require a specific intent on the part of the speaker to bring the lawless action about. Thus, in *Hess v. Indiana*, 414 U.S. 105, 107 (1973), the Court overturned the disorderly conduct conviction of a protester who, when ordered with the rest of the crowd to disperse by the police, allegedly said, "We'll take the fucking street later [or again]." At most, the Court held, the statement "amounted to nothing more than advocacy of illegal action at some indefinite future time." *Id.* at 108.

In *NAACP v. Claiborne Hardware Co.*, 458 U.S. 886 (1982), the Court cited *Brandenburg*'s imminence requirement to overturn an award of damages against participants in an economic boycott of a white-owned business in Mississippi. One of the speakers threatened those who defied the boycott with physical violence. And, indeed, an attack was made on a person seen to patronize one of the boycotted stores. Yet the Court overturned the jury's verdict imposing damages, in part because the "acts of violence . . . occurred weeks or months" after the inflammatory speech. *Claiborne Hardware Co.*, 458 U.S. at 928.

(b) True threats *Claiborne Hardware* provides a segue into another area of unprotected speech akin to incitement: so-called true threats. As noted above, federal law prevents, for example, threatening the life of the President. But not all threats are true threats, as *Watts v. United States*, 394 U.S. 705 (1969), demonstrates. In *Watts* the Court reversed the defendant's conviction for threatening the life of the President when he said, at a rally against the war in Vietnam, "If they ever make me carry a rifle the first man I want to get in my sights is L.B.J." The Court concluded that the remark was not a threat, but rather was "political hyperbole." *Watts*, 394 U.S. at 706. Among other things, the Court noted that the public nature of his statement suggested there was little likelihood that he intended to follow through with the threat.

The Court didn't revisit the relationship among threats, incitement, and the First Amendment until the 2003 case of *Virginia v. Black*, 538 U.S. 343 (2003). At issue were the convictions of two sets of defendants under a Virginia statute prohibiting cross burning with "an intent to intimidate a person or group of persons." *Black*, 538 U.S. at 347. Two defendants (Elliott and O'Mara) were convicted of burning a cross in a neighbor's yard following a dispute. Another defendant (Black) was convicted of leading a Ku Klux Klan rally on private property where a cross was burned. At Black's trial, the judge instructed the jury that it could infer intent to intimidate from the mere act of burning a cross. At Elliott's trial, by contrast, the judge did not instruct the jury on the meaning of "intimidate," nor did he invite the jury to infer intent to intimidate from the attempt to burn a cross. *Id.* at 350-351.

The Court assumed that the offense of burning a cross with the intent to intimidate was facially valid as a form of "true threat," which the Court defined as "statements where [1] the speaker means to communicate [2] a serious expression of intent to commit an act of unlawful violence [3] to a particular individual or group of individuals." *Id.* at 359. The Court added that "[t]he speaker need not actually intend to carry out the threat." *Id.* at 360.

A majority of the Court found that, as applied to Elliott and O'Mara, the statute was constitutional. "The First Amendment," the majority held, "permits Virginia to outlaw cross burning done with the intent to intimidate because burning a cross is a particularly virulent form of intimidation." *Id.* at 363.

A plurality of the Court, however, felt that the instruction given in Black's case rendered the statute unconstitutional. "The act of burning a cross may mean that a person is engaging in constitutionally proscribable intimidation. But that same act may mean only that the person is engaged in core political speech." *Id.* at 365. Blurring the line between the permissible and impermissible as the instruction did "chills constitutionally protected speech because of the possibility that [a state] will prosecute—and potentially convict—somebody engaging only in lawful political speech at the core of what the First Amendment is designed to protect." *Id.* Three other Justices concurred as to Black, but those same Justices felt that even Elliott and O'Mara's prosecution under the statute violated the First Amendment. They viewed the cross burning statute as content-based, because of its inextricable connection with "white Protestant supremacy," and thus inconsistent with the Court's decision in *R.A.V. v. City of St. Paul*, 505 U.S. 377 (1992) (invalidating ordinance prohibiting "hate speech" based on "race, color, creed, religion or gender" as impermissibly content-based).[3] *See Black*, 538 U.S. at 381 (Souter, J., concurring in part).

3. *R.A.V.* is discussed below in section B.5.

QUESTION 3. Alien nation. The Union of Solid Americans (USA) is a nativist organization dedicated to the eradication of illegal immigration. At a recent rally Gerry Swanson, the self-described "commander-in-chief" of the USA, said, "If I had my way, the fence we built along the border would be electric!" He made references to "fajitas" and "refried beaners" and closed his speech saying that "although I am a law-abiding citizen, the time may come when law-abiding citizens might have to take back our country from the illegals by any means necessary, including deadly force!" Swanson was arrested and charged with violating a state law making it a crime to "advocate the duty, necessity, or propriety of violence as a means for accomplishing political reform." Swanson claimed that his prosecution violated the First Amendment. A reviewing judge should rule for:

A. Swanson, because his speech was political.
B. The state, because his speech posed a clear and present danger of lawless action.
C. Swanson, because his speech did not include a call for imminent illegal acts.
D. The state, because advocacy of violence is not protected by the First Amendment.

ANALYSIS. Recall the elements of the *Brandenburg* test: The incitement to violence must have been intentional, the lawless action has to be imminent, and it has to have been likely to occur. You can eliminate **A**; just because he was speaking about a political issue does not ipso facto mean that the speech is protected. A threat against the President might be politically motivated, but it is still illegal. **B** is incorrect because it cites the wrong test. Though *Brandenburg* claimed it was merely restating the "clear and present danger" test, it is clear that the test itself changed as a result of *Brandenburg*. **D** is also incorrect. Mere advocacy of violence is *not* sufficient to qualify as incitement. That leaves **C** as the best answer. Here, as in *Hess*, Swanson's words are, at most, a call for some illegal activity to occur by someone at some unspecified future time.

QUESTION 4. Road rage. According to 18 U.S.C. § 875, it is illegal to "transmit[] in interstate commerce any communication containing any . . . threat to injure the person of another. . . ." Under binding Supreme Court precedent, this statute must be interpreted to apply only to those communications not protected by the First Amendment.

Adams telephoned Bonnie and threatened to assault her because of a traffic dispute they had earlier in the day. As a result, Bonnie became fearful and had to alter her daily routine. He is prosecuted and convicted under § 875. On appeal, Adams claims that he never had any intention of actually harming Bonnie; he was angry when he made the call, and he claims that prosecuting him for the phone call violates the First Amendment. On appeal, the Court should:

A. Affirm the conviction because his intentions regarding the threat are irrelevant.
B. Reverse the conviction because the content of his call was "hyperbole."
C. Reverse the conviction because he lacked the intent to cause Bonnie imminent harm.
D. Affirm the conviction because his threats constituted conduct, not speech.

ANALYSIS. *Black* tells us that making "true threats" involves directing a threat to a person (or group of people) with the intent of placing the victim in fear of bodily harm or death. The Court added, though, that the speaker need not intend to carry out that threat. While *Watts* suggests that there is a "political hyperbole" exception to the true threats doctrine, that case is distinguishable from one where, as here, the threat was communicated not in public in the course of a speech at a rally attended by a large group of people, but rather over the phone to someone with whom the speaker had an earlier dispute. **B**, therefore, is not the best answer. Whatever the "political hyperbole" exception's scope, it does not apply here. The imminence of the harm is likewise irrelevant to the true threat doctrine. Therefore, **C** is not correct. **D** is incorrect because Adams *is* being punished for his speech, not for conduct such as an actual assault. That leaves **A**, the correct answer. If the victim was in fear and he intended to place her in fear with his words, then the fact that he never actually intended to assault her is irrelevant.

QUESTION 5. McDonald-land massacre. During an anti-globalization protest in Washington, D.C., participants heard from a variety of speakers who denounced globalization in general and multinational corporations in particular. One speaker, David, pointed toward a McDonald's across the street from the park in which the protest was being held, called for "regime change in McDonald-land," and led the crowd in the following chant: "McDonald's is for clowns. We oughta burn it down." David then relinquished the microphone and left the stage without incident. The following week, the McDonald's was put to the torch by unknown persons. David is charged with violating a local law against inciting someone to damage the property of others. He is convicted. On appeal, David argues that his speech was protected by the First Amendment. The appeals court should:

A. Reverse his conviction because he was engaged in political speech.
B. Reverse his conviction if he did not actually intend anyone to do something unlawful.
C. Affirm his conviction because the restaurant burned as a result of his speech.
D. Affirm his conviction because his speech posed a clear and present danger that someone attending the rally would act on his words.

ANALYSIS. *Brandenburg* tightened the requirements for charging someone with incitement, despite the claim it was merely restating the "clear and present danger" test. Now incitement requires that the speaker intend to incite imminent lawless action and that such action be likely to occur. Recall that unlawful action occurring later (as in *Claiborne Hardware*) will not suffice. With that in mind, take a look at the choices. **D** can be eliminated because it does not state the correct standard of review after *Brandenburg*. You can discard **A** as well. Just because speech could be categorized as "political" does not confer immunity from prosecution based on that speech. A speaker inciting a mob to burn down city hall may be acting out of dissatisfaction with local government, but that doesn't enable her to claim First Amendment protection for her speech. Because the speech has to elicit *imminent* lawless action, **C** is incorrect. The restaurant did burn, but it burned down a week later. That leaves **B**, which is the correct answer. If David was just trying to turn a clever phrase and get the crowd riled up, and didn't actually intend for anyone to act on his words, then his speech is protected by the First Amendment.

QUESTION 6. An immoderate proposal. Jay Swift is a well-known columnist with a major newspaper. His "Modest Proposal" column is widely read for its trenchant political commentary. In a recent column Swift suggested that the country would be better off if someone killed the President. He ended by paraphrasing Ronald Reagan and asking, "If not now, when? If not me, who?" The column provoked nationwide outrage. Swift was arrested and charged with threatening the life of the President. Swift contends that his prosecution violates the First Amendment. He is convicted and appeals. A reviewing court should:

A. Affirm the conviction because threats to the President are not protected by the First Amendment.
B. Affirm the conviction because the column constitutes a true threat.
C. Reverse the conviction because Swift's column constitutes "political hyperbole."
D. Reverse the conviction because Swift's column is protected speech.

ANALYSIS. True threats represent another type of unprotected speech. True threats are those statements in which the speaker means to communicate a serious expression of intent to commit an act of unlawful violence to a particular individual or group of individuals. It doesn't matter, however, whether the person really intends to carry out the threat. But not all "threats" are true threats. The *Watts* case shows that even inflammatory rhetoric in which a speaker claims that he would take the life of the President can be protected, depending on the circumstances. Watts claimed that the first person he wanted in his sights if he were drafted and given a gun was Lyndon Johnson. The Court, however, held that his statement constituted "political hyperbole" and reversed his conviction for threatening the President. Looking at the answers, **A** can be eliminated; Watts's conviction, after all, was reversed on the ground that it constituted political hyperbole and was not a real threat. Recall that it does not matter whether Swift *intended* to carry out the threat; threats may be punished because of the fear and disruption they engender in the targets. Like Watts, it is unlikely that Swift really intended to put the President in fear for his life by communicating his "threat" to millions of his readers through a public newspaper column. Therefore, **B** is not the best answer; neither is **D**, because **C** is the better answer. Like Watts's threat against LBJ, Swift's "threat" against the President is likely designed to be deliberately provocative and not a serious communication of a threat of bodily harm.

3. *Fighting words*

The flip side to true threats are so-called fighting words, which the *Chaplinsky* Court described as words "which, by their very utterance, inflict injury or tend to incite an immediate breach of the peace." *Chaplinsky*, 315 U.S. at 571. Over the years, however, the Court has narrowed the category of fighting words to the point that the "phrase was no longer to be understood as a euphemism for controversial or dirty talk but [] required instead a quite unambiguous invitation to a brawl." John Hart Ely, Democracy and Distrust 114 (1980).

Chaplinsky itself involved the conviction of a Jehovah's Witness who was distributing literature in Rochester, New Hampshire, and denouncing religion as a "racket." When people complained, and the city marshal intervened to warn Chaplinsky he was angering the crowd, Chaplinsky rounded on the marshal, calling him a "God damned racketeer" and a "damned fascist," and declaring that the entire city government of Rochester was a nest of fascists. 315 U.S. at 569. He was convicted for violating a state law that prohibited directing "offensive, derisive, or annoying word[s] to any other person" on the street or in a public place. *Id.* This was construed by the state courts as prohibiting face-to-face epithets "plainly likely to cause a breach of the peace. . . ." *Id.* at 573. The Court upheld Chaplinsky's conviction, writing that it was "unnecessary to demonstrate that the appellations 'damn racketeer' and 'damn Fascist' are epithets likely to provoke the average person to retaliation, and thereby cause a breach of the peace." *Id.* at 574.

In *Cantwell v. Connecticut*, 310 U.S. 296 (1940), however, the Court reversed a conviction for inciting a breach of the peace in an appeal brought by another Jehovah's Witness, who had been playing anti-Catholic records on the streets of New Haven, Connecticut. As the Court noted, Cantwell had asked the two men permission to play the record; only after hearing its contents did they become offended and, they testified, were tempted to hit him. *Cantwell*, 310 U.S. at 308-309. The Court noted that Cantwell had a perfect right to be where he was, doing what he was doing. There was, in the Court's words, "no assault or threatening of bodily harm, no truculent bearing, no intentional discourtesy, no personal abuse" by Cantwell. *Id.* at 310. Because he did not pose a "clear and present menace to public peace and order" he could not be prosecuted. *Id.* at 311.

In later cases, the Court continued to narrow the category. In *Gooding v. Wilson*, 405 U.S. 518 (1972), the Court reversed the conviction for use of "opprobrious words or abusive language" of a protestor who told a police officer trying to move him: "White son of a bitch, I'll kill you. . . . You son of a bitch, I'll choke you to death." *Gooding*, 405 U.S. at 520 n. 1. The Court found that the statute under which the protestor was convicted was overbroad, meaning that its terms covered speech that was clearly protected as well as speech that might be actionable.

In the same term, the Court reversed other convictions under laws prohibiting the use of profane or vulgar language. The speaker in *Rosenfeld v. New Jersey*, 408 U.S. 901 (1972), used the word "motherfucker" at a public school board meeting, directing it at "the teachers, the school board, the town, and his own country." *Rosenfeld*, 408 U.S. at 910 (Rehnquist, J., dissenting). The same epithet was directed toward police officers who were arresting the son of the defendant in *Lewis v. New Orleans*, 408 U.S. 913 (1972), and also at the police in *Brown v. Oklahoma*, 408 U.S. 914 (1972).

Finally, in *Texas v. Johnson*, 491 U.S. 397 (1989), the Court invalidated Texas's flag desecration statute. Texas had argued that the prohibition of flag burning was necessary because such actions risked an immediate breach of the peace. The Court, however, noted that "[n]o reasonable onlooker would have regarded" the flag burning "as a direct personal insult or an invitation to exchange fisticuffs." *Johnson*, 491 U.S. at 409. Mere generic insults or the use of profanity is no longer sufficient to bring a speaker within the prohibition.

4. "*Offensive speech*"

(a) Profanity Cases like *Gooding, Rosenfeld*, and *Brown* were made possible by the Court's decision in *Cohen v. California*, 403 U.S. 15 (1971). The defendant was in the Los Angeles County Courthouse wearing a jacket on which was written "Fuck the Draft." He was charged with "maliciously and willfully disturb[ing] the peace or quiet of any neighborhood or person [by] offensive conduct" and sentenced to 30 days in jail. He testified that he wore the jacket to publicize his vehement opposition to the draft and to the war in Vietnam. *Cohen*, 403 U.S. at 16.

In his opinion for the Court, Justice Harlan first outlined what was and what was *not* at issue in the case. "The conviction," he wrote, "quite clearly rests upon the asserted offensiveness of the words Cohen used to convey his message to the public." *Id.* at 18. Moreover, it did not fall within any of the Court's other unprotected speech categories. It was not, for example, legally obscene. Nor did the use of the words on Cohen's jacket amount to "fighting words," because "[n]o individual actually or likely to be present could reasonably have regarded the words on appellant's jacket as a direct personal insult." *Id.* at 20. It was not intended to provoke a hostile reaction from a crowd. *Id.*

The Court rejected arguments that the law was enforced here to preserve courtroom decorum by observing that there was no "language in the statute that would have put [Cohen] on notice that certain kinds of otherwise permissible speech or conduct would [not] be tolerated in certain places." *Id.* at 19. Nor was the Court any more sympathetic to the notion that enforcement was proper to protect "unwilling or unsuspecting viewers" from Mr. Cohen's jacket. *Id.* at 21. "Those in the Los Angeles courthouse could effectively avoid further bombardment of their sensibilities simply by averting their eyes." *Id.*

The issue, for Justice Harlan, was whether the state could "excise, as 'offensive conduct,' one particular scurrilous epithet from the public discourse, either upon the theory . . . that its use is inherently likely to cause violent reaction or upon a more general assertion that the States, acting as guardians of public morality, may properly remove this offensive word from the public vocabulary." *Id.* at 22-23. The Court rejected the first condition, saying that the argument "amounts to little more than the self-defeating proposition that to avoid physical censorship of one who has not sought to provoke such a response by a hypothetical coterie of the violent and the lawless, the States may more appropriately effectuate that censorship themselves." *Id.* at 24. As to the second, Harlan was dubious about placing the state in the position of language police. "[O]ne man's vulgarity is another's lyric," and because that boundary is so difficulty to police, "the Constitution leaves matters of taste and style so largely to the individual." *Id.* at 25. Finally, Harlan noted that word choice is often inextricably bound with the content of the idea. "[W]ords are often chosen as much for their emotive as their cognitive force." *Id.* at 26.

In other words, the Court rejected the argument that the state—in the exercise of its police power—could bar certain words from public discourse. Permitting it to do so, Harlan maintained, was tantamount to giving it control over certain ideas or subjects, because many times the mode of communication, including language used, can't be separated from the *content* of the speech. If you doubt this, try this thought experiment: Imagine Cohen's jacket had said, "I Vehemently Disagree with the Draft" or even "To Hell with the Draft." Does either alternative formulation convey the depth of feeling about selective service that "Fuck the Draft" does?

QUESTION 7. Bumper sticker blues. DeKalb County, Georgia, has an ordinance prohibiting the display of "lewd" bumper stickers. "Lewd" is defined by the ordinance as "obscene or profane words or images likely to give offense, or to cause shock or alarm to the viewer or reader." Mary Martin was issued a ticket for violation of that order by a county sheriff for a bumper sticker on her car that read, "Shit Happens." She challenges the constitutionality of the ordinance. The judge should:

A. Invalidate the ordinance because it violates the First Amendment.
B. Uphold the ordinance because such speech is not protected by the First Amendment.
C. Invalidate the ordinance because it punishes a particular viewpoint.
D. Uphold the ordinance because preserving civility in public discourse is a compelling governmental interest.

ANALYSIS. The correct answer is **A.** The ordinance violates the First Amendment under current case law. *Cohen* stands for the proposition that merely offensive language can't be censored by the state, so **B** is not correct. **C** is incorrect because the ordinance doesn't punish the use of lewd bumper stickers that enlist on a particular side of an argument, though it is content-based. But, as we have seen, not all content-based restrictions violate the First Amendment. Indeed, the Amendment is held *not* to protect certain kinds of speech *because of* its content. **D** is incorrect, too. The First Amendment does not permit the state to prescribe baseline standards of decency and civility in speech and then punish those persons, like Cohen or Ms. Martin, who deviate from those standards.

QUESTION 8. Them's fightin' words (?). The State of Ames has made it a misdemeanor for "any person to address any offensive, derisive, or annoying words to any other person who is lawfully in any street or other public place, nor call him by any offensive or derisive name." The Ames Supreme Court has construed this statute to apply only to those situations "which by their very utterance inflict injury or tend to incite an immediate breach of the peace." In which of the following situations could someone, consistent with the First Amendment, be convicted under Ames's statute?

A. A frustrated driver who, exasperated with traffic, gestures toward cars that are impeding his progress and exclaims, "Why don't you fuckers learn how to drive!?"
B. A protestor wearing a shirt saying "Cops Are Pigs" outside a police station as part of a protest over allegations of police brutality.

C. A protestor at the Republican National Convention in Ames who burns a flag in front of the convention hall, saying to delegates and passers-by, "This is what I think of you and your party."

D. A protestor at a military base who taunts soldiers returning from Afghanistan and their families by confronting each of them individually and addressing them as "murderers" and "baby killers," and expressing the wish the soldiers had not returned alive.

ANALYSIS. If, as John Ely has written, fighting words must be tantamount to "a quite unambiguous invitation to a brawl," then only **D** fits the bill. **B** is clearly akin to *Cohen*, without the profanity. **C** is reminiscent of *Johnson*; no one is specifically being targeted or having flags snatched out of their hands for burning. Similarly, the driver in **A** is addressing everyone in general, and no one in particular. The protestors in **D**, however, are directly addressing individuals in a manner almost guaranteed to provoke a violent response. Of the four situations, only **D** is likely punishable consistent with the First Amendment.

(b) Hostile audiences California had defended its prosecution of Cohen in part on the likelihood that his jacket would provoke strong, possibly violent reactions on the part of observers. The problem of the "heckler's veto"—where speech is suppressed because of the actual or expected reaction of listeners—is one with which the Court has struggled. The results in these cases often depend on the specific facts.

In *Terminiello v. Chicago*, 337 U.S. 1 (1949), the Court reversed the conviction of a right-wing, former Roman Catholic priest who was convicted of disorderly conduct following a speech he gave that produced an unruly crowd of protesters. Justice Douglas, for the Court, wrote that one of the functions of free speech was "to invite dispute. It may indeed best serve its high purpose when it induces a condition of unrest, creates dissatisfaction with conditions as they are, or even stirs people to anger. Speech is often provocative and challenging. It may strike at prejudices and preconceptions and have profound unsettling effects as it presses for acceptance of an idea." *Terminiello*, 337 U.S. at 4. Because the ordinance permitted prosecution for "stirr[ing] people to anger, invit[ing] public dispute, or [bringing] about a condition of unrest," Douglas held, it could not stand. *Id.* at 5.

But just three years later, in *Feiner v. New York*, 340 U.S. 315 (1951), the Court upheld the disorderly conduct conviction of a man who addressed an outdoor meeting in Syracuse, New York, and, among other things, called President Truman a "bum" and the American Legion a "Nazi Gestapo," and urged African Americans in the audience to take up arms and fight for their rights. When one member of the audience approached a police officer and indicated that if the officer didn't remove Feiner from the stage, he would, the officer approached Feiner and asked him to discontinue his speech. When he refused he was arrested. Unlike the situation in *Terminiello*, the Court found that the officer's intent in taking him into custody was to protect him and not to suppress his ideas.

While the majority were "aware that the ordinary . . . objections of a hostile audience cannot be allowed to silence a speaker, and are also mindful of the possible danger of giving overzealous police officials complete discretion to break up otherwise lawful public meetings," the Court felt the latter was not at work here. *Feiner*, 340 U.S. at 320. "[W]hen the speaker passes the bounds of argument or persuasion and undertakes incitement to riot," the police were empowered to "prevent a breach of the peace." *Id.* at 321. The possibility of disorder and Feiner's "deliberate defiance of the police officers" counseled affirmation of the conviction. *Id.* Justice Black, dissenting, thought that before interfering with the speaker, "they first must make all reasonable efforts to attempt to protect him." *Id.* at 326 (Black, J., dissenting).

Subsequent cases have followed *Terminiello* rather than *Feiner*. Civil rights demonstrators in the 1960s were frequently subject to arrest for failing to disperse, even when neither the demonstration nor the crowd watching the demonstration posed any threat of violence. *See, e.g.*, Edwards v. South Carolina, 372 U.S. 229 (1963) (reversing the conviction of protestors in South Carolina). In *Cox v. Louisiana*, 379 U.S. 536 (1965), the Court reversed convictions of those protesting racial segregation and the arrest of students who had eaten at segregated lunch counters. Though there was no threat of violence from the protestors, who had complied with police requests to protest in a particular area, the sheriff ordered the protestors to disband because of the hostility of the white crowd observing them.

Finally, in *Gregory v. Chicago*, 394 U.S. 111 (1969), the Court reversed the disorderly conduct convictions of protestors who marched to Mayor Richard Daley's house to protest school segregation in the city. A hostile crowd gathered and threw rocks and eggs at the protestors, who refused to leave even when asked by the police. The Illinois Supreme Court had attempted a saving construction of the ordinance, confining it to instances in which violence is imminent and the police are unable to protect the demonstrators, who refuse to obey police requests to disperse. The Court rejected this construction because it was not given to the jury as part of its instructions. *Gregory*, 394 U.S. at 111-113.

QUESTION 9. I slam Islam. In response to worldwide violence over the publication of allegedly blasphemous depictions of the Prophet Muhammad, a "Free Speech Now!" rally was held in Ames City, the capital of Ames. One of the speakers, an outspoken conservative radio talk show host, said that the reaction of Muslims worldwide demonstrated that it was a backward and intolerant religion and that many Muslims are bent on proving they are enemies of freedom. He was scheduled to tour the State of Ames, repeating the same speech. In response, the Ames Muslim community warned that they would stage counter-demonstrations wherever he spoke. At one subsequent rally, supporters of the speaker and Ames Muslims clashed before he was scheduled to speak. In the midst of his speech, after refusing police requests to stop, the talk show host was arrested and charged with disorderly conduct. He was convicted after a trial, and he appealed his conviction. A reviewing court should:

A. Reverse his conviction because his speech was protected by the First Amendment.
B. Reverse his conviction because he did not use fighting words.
C. Uphold his conviction because Ames may constitutionally act to keep the peace.
D. Uphold his conviction because his statements were not protected by the First Amendment.

ANALYSIS. While the Ames constabulary can certainly act to keep the peace, the question here is whether they can, as part of keeping the peace, silence the talk show host. Though *Terminiello* and *Feiner* point in opposite directions, the former appears to have been more faithfully followed by the Court, meaning that the police have an obligation to protect the speaker and direct their energies to those who would silence him, even if it is more convenient or efficient to simply order him to stop talking. Thus, **C** is not the best answer. Neither is **D**, because his statements are precisely the sort of opinions that the First Amendment does protect, even if certain folks might find them offensive or objectionable. **B** is not the best answer because whether or not he used fighting words is not really relevant to the question whether the police can order him to stop speaking based on the reaction of the crowd. That leaves **A**, which is the best answer. Under current case law, the police are obligated to silence a speaker as a last resort, not the first, especially if he is doing nothing to incite the crowd to any sort of imminent violence.

(c) Broadcasting and offensive speech The Court has been somewhat more tolerant of attempts to regulate offensive speech in media broadcast to the public. In *FCC v. Pacifica Foundation*, 438 U.S. 726 (1978), the Court upheld a fine levied on a radio station that broadcast George Carlin's "Filthy Words" monologue during the daytime. Among the reasons given by the Court were (1) the broadcast media's "uniquely pervasive presence in the lives of all Americans" and (2) broadcasting's "unique[] accessibil[ity] to children, even those too young to read." *Pacifica Foundation*, 438 U.S. at 748-749. *But see* Federal Communications Comm'n v. Fox Television Stations, 132 S. Ct. 2307, 2317-2318 (2012) (holding that FCC's indecency policy was unconstitutionally vague because it failed to provide fined broadcasters with sufficient notice of what was proscribed).

The Court explained: "Patently offensive, indecent material present over the airwaves confronts the citizen, not only in public, but also in the privacy of the home, where the individual's right to be left alone plainly outweighs the First Amendment rights of an intruder." *Id.* at 748. The Court noted the difficulty of "unhearing" an offensive broadcast and the insufficiency of any warnings, since "the broadcast audience is constantly tuning in and out. . . ." *Id.* As for children, the Court noted that this particular broadcast "could have enlarged a child's vocabulary in an instant" and that "the ease with which children may obtain access to broadcast material" makes broadcasting a special case. *Id.* at 749-750. But it emphasized that its holding was a narrow one: "This case does not involve a two-way radio conversation between a cab driver and a dispatcher, or a telecast of an Elizabethan comedy." *Id.* at 750. The Court also emphasized that Pacifica was only being fined here and that the broadcast was during the daytime, when children would be more likely to inadvertently tune in. *Id. Pacifica Foundation*'s solicitude for individuals' privacy in their homes when broadcasting is pervasive and the special concerns of children have played out in different ways in the Court.

First, the Court has always recognized a right of individuals to be let alone, especially in their homes. As noted in *Pacifica Foundation*, this concern for privacy can trump the First Amendment rights of certain speakers. In *Rowan v. United States Post Office Department*, 397 U.S. 728 (1970), the Court upheld a law permitting individuals to stop mail of an "erotic" or "sexually arousing nature" as judged by the individual. The "mailer's right to communicate must stop at the mailbox of an unreceptive addressee," the Court wrote. *Rowan*, 397 U.S. at 737. The concern is that, in the home, an individual can become a "captive audience" unless empowered to stop unwanted mailings or solicitations.

Even outside the home, the Court has protected some captive audiences. In *Lehman v. Shaker Heights*, 418 U.S. 298 (1974), the Court upheld a ban on political advertisements on city buses. In part the Court relied on an earlier case, *Public Utilities Commission v. Pollak*, 343 U.S. 451 (1952), in which the Court upheld a ban on radio programming played on municipal transportation.

But the "captive audiences" doctrine has its limits. The Court invalidated a state order prohibiting the placement of fliers discussing "political matters," including arguments for nuclear power in utility bills. Consolidated Edison v. Public Service Commission, 447 U.S. 530 (1980). Consumers could avoid exposure to offensive material by "transferring the bill insert from envelope to wastebasket." *Consolidated Edison*, 447 U.S. at 542. Likewise, in *Bolger v. Youngs Drug Products Corp.*, 463 U.S. 60 (1983), the Court invalidated a federal ban on unsolicited advertisements for contraceptives on the theory that a brief "journey from mail box to trash can" was the proper remedy for the offensive material. *Id.* at 72.

The lesson of the cases regarding captive audiences seems to be that if it is possible for persons to engage in "self-help" to avoid offensive printed material, either by requesting that it not be delivered to them or by throwing away that which they do receive, individuals must do so. The First Amendment does not *preclude* government from aiding people in engaging in self-help by making it possible for them to request they not receive such material in the first place. And if the speech is impossible to escape or impossible to avoid, as is the case on public transportation, the Court will uphold limits on the speech to which individuals are subject.

Pacifica Foundation's other concern was with protecting children from exposure to indecent or offensive material. Actually, the concern is with protecting children from such material *unless their parents choose to expose them to it.* The principle can be traced to *Ginsberg v. New York*, 390 U.S. 629 (1968), in which the Court upheld a state law limiting minors' access to non-obscene pornography, even if similar restrictions would be unconstitutional if applied to adults.[4]

Still, even this principle has limits. When Congress attempted to ban non-obscene "dial-a-porn" telephone services to protect children, the Court held that the ban violated the First Amendment. Sable Communications, Inc. v. FCC, 492 U.S. 115 (1989). The Court conceded that protecting children from even non-obscene material was a compelling interest; it felt the total ban was not narrowly tailored and that less restrictive means existed to achieve that interest. *Sable Communications*, 492 U.S. at 131. In particular, the Court noted that the total ban meant that adults who were constitutionally entitled to hear the material would be kept from doing so. *Id. Pacifica Foundation* was distinguished in part because of the need for the listener to take affirmative actions to hear the messages, unlike radio broadcasts, which one might hear without warning. *Id.* at 127.

As *Sable Communications* demonstrates, the Court in recent years has had to adapt constitutional doctrines developed in a pre-cable, pre-Internet age to new technologies and to balance the First Amendment with, in many cases, the desire of parents not to have their children exposed to indecent or offensive material. The Court tends to be skeptical of absolute bans of subject matter to which adults are entitled access, even if children are not, unless the medium is so pervasive that it is difficult to shield children from inadvertent exposure.

In 1996, a badly fragmented Court variously upheld and invalidated parts of a federal law regulating non-obscene offensive material on cable television. Denver Area Educational Telecommunications Consortium (DAETC) v. FCC, 518 U.S. 727 (1996). The three sections of the challenged statute (1) authorized cable companies to refuse to carry offensive material, (2) mandated an opt-in provision for receiving channels on which such material was available, and (3) permitted cable companies to refrain from airing obscenity and

4. As we will see below, not all pornography is considered "obscene," which is a term of art.

"sexually explicit conduct" from public access channels that the companies were required to carry. *DAETC*, 518 U.S. at 734-735. A plurality upheld provision (1), relying on *Pacifica Foundation* and its concern for the pervasiveness and intrusiveness of the broadcast medium. *Id.* at 748.[5]

A majority of the Court, however, invalidated both the opt-in provision and the ban on indecent material on public access channels. The opt-in requirement was not narrowly tailored; other, less restrictive means were available to advance the government's interest in shielding children from indecent material, the Court held. *Id.* at 755. On the other hand, the government's interest in the ban on indecent material on public access channels was deemed "weak" because of the susceptibility of local governments to pressure regarding the content of public access channels. Local governments would run those channels and complaints about the content would be directed there, rendering them accountable for that content. *Id.* at 739.

The Telecommunications Act of 1996 required cable companies carrying channels broadcasting sexually oriented content either to completely block or scramble their programming or to "time-block" the material, broadcasting it only between the hours of 10 P.M. and 6 A.M. United States v. Playboy Entertainment Group, 529 U.S. 803 (2000). The Court again found this to be a content-based restriction and faulted Congress for not having considered less restrictive means—an opt-out provision for the programming, for example—to achieve the goal of protecting children. Because it was virtually impossible to completely block or scramble cable signals, the effect was to bar *anyone*, adults included, from viewing sexually explicit programming between 6 A.M. and 10 P.M. *Id.* at 806-807.

When the Court took its first case involving congressional regulation of the Internet, the question was whether it would view the Internet as akin to broadcasting and *Pacifica Foundation* or whether it would see it through the lens of *Sable Communications.* The Court adopted the latter position in *Reno v. ACLU*, 521 U.S. 844 (1997).

Congress passed the Communications Decency Act (CDA) in 1996 to protect minors from "indecent" and "patently offensive"—but not legally obscene—material on the Internet. One could escape liability for "knowingly" exposing minors to such material by either (1) making "good faith, reasonable, effective, and appropriate actions" to prevent minors from accessing the materials, or (2) restricting access by verifying the age of users through, for example, requiring the use of credit cards. *Reno*, 521 U.S. at 860-861.

Because the CDA was a content-based restriction, strict scrutiny applied; while the Court acknowledged that it had "repeatedly recognized the governmental interest in protecting children from harmful materials," the breadth of the CDA gave the Court pause. *Id.* at 875. "In order to deny minors access to

---

5. Justices Thomas and Scalia, with Chief Justice Rehnquist, joined the plurality, but on the ground that there was no First Amendment right to have one's content broadcast by an unwilling cable operator in the first place. 518 U.S. at 823 (Thomas, J., concurring in part and dissenting in part).

potentially harmful speech, the CDA effectively suppresses a large amount of speech that adults have a constitutional right to receive and to address to one another." *Id.* at 874. Nor did the Court think that the affirmative defenses worked to rescue the CDA. As for being able to "effective[ly]" bar minors from viewing the proscribed material, "[t]he Government recognizes that its proposed screening software does not currently exist." *Id.* at 881. As for requiring the use of a credit card or some other form of identification to verify age and view material covered by the CDA, the Court noted that "it is not economically feasible for most noncommercial speakers to employ such verification," rendering the defense of little use to those engaged in noncommercial, but covered, speech. *Id.*

5. *Hate speech*

Colloquially, "hate speech" is a term applied to speech that denigrates individuals based on identifiable characteristics such as race, gender, and sexual orientation. Polities and institutions—universities in particular—have attempted to curb hate speech over the last two decades. However, as we shall see, there is no "hate speech" exception to the First Amendment. It is really a form of offensive speech—unless it can be characterized as "fighting words" or a true threat.

One early case, *Beauharnais v. Illinois*, 343 U.S. 250 (1952), upheld an Illinois "group libel" statute that prohibited speech "which portrays depravity, criminality, unchastity, or lack of virtue of a class of citizens, of any race, color, creed, or religion" or which "expose[d] the citizens of any race, color, creed or religion to contempt, derision, or obloquy" or which was "productive of breach of the peace or riots. . . ." *Beauharnais*, 343 U.S. at 251. The statute was applied to an individual protesting the integration of residential neighborhoods in Chicago. *Id.* at 252.

Reasoning that because libel of individuals was not protected by the First Amendment, neither was libel of groups, the Court upheld the statute. The Court felt "precluded from saying that speech concededly punishable when immediately directed at individuals cannot be outlawed if directed at groups with whose position and esteem in society the affiliated individual may be inextricably involved." *Id.* at 263.

Though *Beauharnais* has never been explicitly overruled, doctrinal developments have eroded its underpinnings. First, as discussed below, libel, slander, and defamation are not categorically excluded from First Amendment protection. Second, after *Cohen*, it is not permissible to regulate speech that exposes one to derision or contempt or that one would find highly offensive. Third, after *Brandenburg*, it is not sufficient that speech have a "strong tendency" to cause violence or disorder. Speech must be intended to cause imminent lawless action; and that action must be likely to occur.

As the debate over the regulation of hate speech raged in the late 1980s and early 1990s, the city of St. Paul, Minnesota, passed an ordinance prohibiting the placement on public or private property of "a symbol, object, appellation, characterization or graffiti . . . which one knows or has reasonable grounds to know arouses anger, alarm or resentment in others on the basis of race, color, creed, religion, or gender commits disorderly conduct. . . ." R.A.V. v. St. Paul, 505 U.S. 377 (1992). The defendants were convicted under the ordinance of burning a crude wooden cross on the lawn of a black family living across the street from R.A.V.

The defendant appealed to the U.S. Supreme Court after his conviction was affirmed by Minnesota's high court, which interpreted the ordinance to reach only constitutionally unprotected fighting words. The Supreme Court invalidated the ordinance on the grounds that it was not only content based, but also viewpoint based. The Court noted that government may choose to proscribe only particularly offensive types of speech within a class outside First Amendment protection. For example, "[a] State might choose to prohibit only that obscenity which is the most patently offensive in its prurience. . . ." 505 U.S. at 388. But, the Court continued, "it may not prohibit . . . only that obscenity which includes offensive political messages." *Id.*

While St. Paul could have sought to ban particular types of fighting words, it could not punish fighting words dealing only with "race, color, creed, religion, or gender." Justice Scalia explained that under St. Paul's ordinance, "[d]isplays containing abusive invective, no matter how vicious or severe, are permissible unless they are addressed to one of the specified disfavored topics." *Id.* at 391. He noted that those using fighting words "in connection with other ideas—to express hostility, for example, on the basis of political affiliation, union membership, or homosexuality—are not covered." *Id.* Had St. Paul omitted the "race, color, creed, religion, or gender" language, then, its ordinance would have withstood scrutiny. Note, however, that Justice Scalia's opinion seems implicitly to reject the possibility that fighting words addressed to race, color, creed, religion, or gender *are* the most objectionable forms of fighting words. Just as the state could ban the most explicit forms of obscenity, but not necessarily all of it, the argument might be made that St. Paul considered these words the most harmful types of fighting words.

St. Paul's ordinance criminalized speech and other forms of expressive activity. The question in *Wisconsin v. Mitchell*, 508 U.S. 476 (1993), was whether a law increasing the penalties for intentionally selecting a victim on the basis of "race, religion, color, disability, sexual orientation, national origin or ancestry. . . ." *Mitchell*, 508 U.S. at 480. Some African Americans attacked a white person after seeing the film *Mississippi Burning*. Apparently, the victim was chosen because of his race. The defendants challenged the strengthened penalties, claiming that they violated *R.A.V.* A unanimous court rejected the argument. The Court noted that the ordinance in *R.A.V.* was aimed at expression; the Wisconsin statute was "aimed at conduct unprotected by the First Amendment." *Id.* at 487. The Court noted that it was reasonable for the state to seek to punish these crimes more than other crimes because hate crimes "are more likely to provoke retaliatory crimes, inflict distinct emotional harms on their victims and incite community unrest." *Id.* at 488.

QUESTION 10. Abate hate. In response to a rash of anti-homosexual graffiti and verbal taunts of Ames City's homosexual population, the City Council passes an ordinance banning the placement "on public or private property graffiti which one knows or has reason to know arouses anger, alarm, or resentment in others on the basis of their sexual orientation." Previous cases have interpreted the ordinance to cover "fighting words." Tim is prosecuted under the ordinance for writing "AIDS Kills Gays Dead" and "God Made Adam and Eve, Not Adam and Steve" on posters advertising an upcoming AIDS benefit. Steve's conviction should be

A. Upheld, because fighting words are not protected by the First Amendment.
B. Upheld, if the homosexual population of Ames City felt threatened or intimidated.
C. Overturned, because the ordinance regulates on the basis of viewpoint.
D. Overturned, because the ordinance criminalizes speech.

ANALYSIS. The ordinance criminalizes speech, to be sure; but not all speech is protected by the First Amendment. So **D** is incorrect. Among the types of speech excluded are "true threats" and "fighting words." But his graffiti wasn't directed at any particular person or group and did not communicate an intent to commit bodily harm against either, so **B** can't be correct. And while fighting words aren't protected by the First Amendment, *R.A.V.* holds that a viewpoint-based fighting words statute will violate the First Amendment. Therefore, **C** is a better answer than **A**.

6. *Obscenity*

Of all the areas addressed by the First Amendment, obscenity is the "intractable"[6] problem with which the Court wrestled for some time. This is the area of the law, after all, that led one justice to declare that although he could not define hard-core pornography, he "kn[e]w it when [he saw] it." Jacobellis v. Ohio, 378 U.S. 184, 197 (1964). Beginning in the late 1950s, the Court first wrestled with how legally obscene material should be defined, and it then struggled to apply the definition throughout the 1960s and 1970s.

At the outset, though, it is important to understand that "obscenity" is a term of art denoting sexually explicit material that is not protected by the First Amendment. It is not necessarily a synonym for sexually explicit material or even for "pornography" broadly defined. But it is precisely the difficulty of drawing a line between that material which is obscene and unprotected and that which is covered by the First Amendment that has bedeviled the Court.

6. Interstate Circuit, Inc. v. City of Dallas, 390 U.S. 676, 701 (1968) (Harlan, J., concurring and dissenting) ("These cases usher the Court into a new phase of the intractable obscenity problem. . . .").

The Court's first attempt to define "obscenity" occurred in a pair of cases known as *Roth v. United States*, 354 U.S. 476 (1957), which involved two separate convictions under federal and state law. In *Roth*, the question was whether a federal statute prohibiting the mailing of "obscene, lewd, lascivious, or filthy" materials violated the First Amendment. *Roth*, 354 U.S. at 491. The companion case involved a conviction under a California statute prohibiting the willful "creation, distribution, or advertising" of "obscene or indecent" material.

The Court first relied on history and current practice to conclude that obscenity was not protected by the First Amendment. *Id.* at 485-486. It made clear, however, that "sex and obscenity are not synonymous. Obscene material is material which deals with sex in a manner appealing to prurient interest." *Id.* at 487 (footnote omitted). A footnote explained that "prurient" meant that which had "a tendency to excite lustful thoughts." *Id.* at 486 n. 5. The Court rejected the English definition of obscenity, which, according to the Court, judged "obscenity by the effect of isolated passages upon the most susceptible persons" and could "encompass material legitimately treating with sex. . . ." *Id.* at 489. By implication, then, works alleged to be obscene had to be considered as a whole, and their prurience could not be assessed from the point of view of those with the most susceptible minds.

Justices Douglas and Black dissented; as they would for the remainder of their careers on the Court, they held the First Amendment to be absolute. They argued that attempting to assess the obscenity of any particular work was beyond the capacity of the Court and that it should simply not try to do so. *Id.* at 508 (Douglas, J., dissenting).

Roth was later restated by a plurality of three Justices in *Memoirs v. Massachusetts*, 383 U.S. 413 (1966). For a work to be legally obscene, it must be proven that "(a) the dominant theme of the material taken as a whole appeals to a prurient interest in sex; (b) the material is patently offensive because it affronts contemporary community standards relating to the description or representation of sexual matters; and (c) the material is utterly without redeeming social value." *Memoirs*, 383 U.S. at 418.

The *Roth* test, however, never attracted a majority of the Court. As a consequence, the Court simply relied on summary reversals of obscenity convictions when five Justices agreed that the material was not obscene. *See, e.g.*, Redrup v. New York, 386 U.S. 767 (1967).[7] This unsatisfactory state of affairs persisted until *Miller v. California*, 413 U.S. 15 (1973).

Miller involved a mass mailing of adult material for which the defendant was convicted under state law, and it furnished the opportunity for the Court to define the contours of constitutionally proscribable obscenity. First, the Court said, "statutes designed to regulate obscene materials must be carefully limited," meaning that they must apply to works that "depict or describe sexual

7. This state of affairs required the Justices to review material to assess whether or not it was obscene. For a hilarious description of "movie days" at the Court during this period, see Bob Woodward & Scott Armstrong, The Brethren 198-200 (1979).

conduct. That conduct must be specifically defined by the applicable state law, as written or authoritatively construed." *Miller*, 413 U.S. at 23-24. In other words, outlawing "lewd" or "filthy" works would no longer suffice. Statutes must spell out *which* depictions or descriptions of *what* sexual conduct it was regulating. The trier of fact must decide, according to the Court,

> (a) whether "the average person, applying contemporary community standards," would find that the work, taken as a whole, appeals to the prurient interest;
>
> (b) whether the work depicts or describes, in a patently offensive way, sexual conduct specifically defined by the applicable state law; and
>
> (c) whether the work, taken as a whole, lacks serious literary, artistic, political, or scientific value ("LAPS").

Id. at 24.

While *Miller* retained *Roth*'s emphasis on assessing the work as a whole, and its use of contemporary community standards to evaluate works, it rejected the "utterly without redeeming social value" test, presumably because it was so difficult to meet. In its place was the LAPS test—an inquiry into whether the material has serious literary, artistic, political, or scientific merit. It was the Court's hope that such a test, and the requirement that the proscribed sexual conduct be specifically described in the statute, would limit obscenity prosecutions only to so-called hard-core pornography. *Id.* at 27.

Later cases clarified that although juries applied contemporary community standards to questions of "prurient interest" and "patent offensiveness," their verdicts had to be subject to judicial review to ensure that those verdicts were aberrations produced by an unusually prudish jury. Jenkins v. Georgia, 418 U.S. 153 (1974) (overturning jury verdict finding Jack Nicholson film *Carnal Knowledge* to be legally obscene). By contrast, a jury deciding whether a work fails the LAPS test may *not* apply local community standards. The question, rather, is "whether a reasonable person would find such value in the material, taken as a whole." Pope v. Illinois, 481 U.S. 497, 501 (1987); *see also* Smith v. United States, 431 U.S. 291 (1977).

QUESTION 11. **Obscene scene.** The State of Ames prohibits the sale of "obscene" material, defined by statute as any material "that, considered as a whole, appeals to the prurient interest, and lacking serious literary, artistic, political, or scientific merit, depicts sex in a patently offensive manner according to contemporary community standards." Bill Bookseller is convicted of violating Ames's ordinance for selling "Girls Gone Crazy" videos in his bookstore, which feature amateurs posing nude for a video crew. Bill appeals his conviction. A court of appeals would likely:

A. Affirm the conviction because the Ames statute follows the *Miller* test.

B. Reverse the conviction because the Ames statute fails to follow the *Miller* test.

C. Affirm the conviction because the material at issue is low-value speech.
D. Reverse the conviction unless the material in question can be shown to lack any redeeming social value.

ANALYSIS. The statute under review is pretty close to the *Miller* test, but it lacks an important element. *Miller* requires that state law specifically define the sexual conduct that must be depicted or described in a "patently offensive way." Merely criminalizing "sex" won't do, according to the Court, because such laws will often be overbroad—that is, they would cover protected as well as unprotected material. The answer, therefore, is **B. D** includes part of the *Roth* test that *Miller* discarded; **C** is incorrect because if material is not "obscene" it is protected by the First Amendment. **A** is wrong for the reasons given.

QUESTION 12. **LAPS dance.** Assume that, as part of his appeal, Bookseller alleges error in the trial judge's instructions to the jury, which included an instruction that the jury apply contemporary community standards in considering whether the videos sold by Bookseller possessed any serious literary, artistic, political, or scientific merit. Was the trial judge's instruction proper?

A. Yes, because the jury is charged with applying contemporary community standards to make such assessments.
B. No, because the trial judge should have instructed the jury to apply national standards.
C. Yes, under the Supreme Court's *Miller* test.
D. No, because juries do not make independent assessments of literary, artistic, political, or scientific merit.

ANALYSIS. The Court has introduced procedural safeguards designed to ensure that *Miller* is applied correctly. One of these safeguards is judicial review of jury verdicts deciding that material *is* legally obscene. This is necessary to safeguard against one's being tried by a particularly sensitive jury that, although applying contemporary community standards, may have interpreted those standards more restrictively than is reasonable. The other safeguard is that the LAPS test is *not* assessed according to contemporary community standards; that is, the presence or absence of LAPS is judged from the point of view of a reasonable person viewing such material as a whole. The correct answer, then, is **D.** The other answers incorrectly state the law.

The Court has also addressed issues of *access* to obscene materials by individuals. In *Stanley v. Georgia*, 394 U.S. 557 (1969), the Court overturned the conviction of an individual for private possession of obscene material. However, two years later the Court refused to extend that right to encompass the right to *receive* such material. United States v. Reidel, 402 U.S. 351 (1971). The Court has also upheld a conviction for the interstate transportation of obscene material, even for private use, and the importation of obscene material for personal use. United States v. Orito, 413 U.S. 139 (1973) (transportation); United States v. Twelve 200-Foot Reels, 413 U.S. 124 (1973) (importation). The Court has also refused to extend *Stanley* to the private possession of child pornography. Osborne v. Ohio, 495 U.S. 103 (1990).

In a companion case to *Miller*, the Court held that states and municipalities could regulate the public exhibition of obscenity, even if it was confined to exhibition to adults. Paris Adult Theater I v. Slaton, 413 U.S. 49 (1973). Despite the lack of concrete evidence linking availability of obscene material with crime, the Court held that it was reasonable for the state to have "determine[d] that such a connection does or might exist." *Paris Adult Theater I*, 413 U.S. at 61. As long as the government followed the *Miller* test, nothing in the First Amendment precluded the regulation of businesses that exhibit obscene material. *Id.* at 53-54.

However, government is not permitted to censor films simply because they contain nudity. In *Erznoznik v. City of Jacksonville*, 422 U.S. 205 (1975), the Court overturned an ordinance prohibiting the public exhibition of films containing nudity that could be observed from public streets. Distinguishing cases involving invasion of privacy in the home and captive audiences, the Court emphasized that citizens had no right to be protected from all speech or expression they found offensive. "[T]he Constitution does not permit government to decide which types of otherwise protected speech are sufficiently offensive to require protection for the unwilling listener or viewer." *Erznoznik*, 422 U.S. at 210.

When it comes to child pornography, however, the Court has departed from the *Miller* test. The Court upheld a state statute criminalizing the production of child pornography that would not have met the *Miller* test for obscenity in *Ferber v. New York*, 458 U.S. 747 (1982). Specifically, the statute at issue prohibited the use of children under 16 in a "sexual performance," defined as "actual or simulated sexual intercourse, deviate sexual intercourse, sexual bestiality, masturbation, sadomasochistic abuse, or lewd exhibition of the genitals." *Ferber*, 458 U.S. at 765 n. 6.

The Court concluded that states should have more freedom to regulate pornographic material involving children. It refused to second-guess New York's conclusion that "the use of children as subjects of pornographic materials is harmful to the physiological, emotional, and mental health of the child." *Id.* at 758. Further, the Court concluded that child pornography is harmful to children because photographs and films are a "permanent record of the children's participation and the harm to the child is exacerbated by their circulation." *Id.* at 759. In addition, by attacking the supply side, officials may more effectively close down the distribution of child pornography generally. *Id.* The Court also held that the "value of permitting live performances and photographic reproductions of children engaged in lewd sexual conduct is exceedingly modest, if not de minimis" and would be unlikely to be required as part of a work with serious literary, artistic, political, or scientific merit. *Id.* at 762.

The Court did not completely defer to the state. It reaffirmed *Miller*'s requirement that the prohibited conduct "must be adequately defined by the applicable state law, as written or authoritatively construed," and limited to "works that visually depict sexual conduct by children below a specified age." *Id.* at 764. However, "[a] trier of fact need not find that the material appeal to the prurient interest of the average person; it is not required that the sexual conduct portrayed be done so in a patently offensive manner; and the material at issue not be considered as a whole." *Id.* The New York law at issue met each of the Court's criteria and affirmed the conviction.

Questions 13 and 14 concern the following facts: The State of Ames has a statute that makes it a felony to:

> use a child in a sexual performance by employing, authorizing, or inducing a child less than 16 years of age to engage in a sexual performance. "Sexual performance," as defined in this statute, means any performance that includes sexual conduct, which is defined as actual or simulated sexual intercourse, deviant sexual intercourse, masturbation, or lewd exhibition of the genitals. It shall also be a felony to possess or distribute any material that includes a sexual performance by a child less than 16 years of age.

QUESTION 13. **Pervy Paul.** Paul is charged under the Ames statute for distributing films that he concedes contain a "sexual performance by a child less than 16 years of age." He sold two such films to undercover police officers. At trial, he requests an instruction that, to convict him, the jury must find that the films "appeal to the prurient interest" taken as a whole, and that they must be found to be patently offensive. The trial judge should:

A. Refuse the instruction, because it does not accurately state the law in this area.
B. Give the instruction, in order to comply with the First Amendment.
C. Refuse the instruction, because the work need not be considered as a whole.
D. Refuse the instruction, because the judge will make those decisions as a matter of law.

ANALYSIS. Paul is requesting a jury instruction requesting three elements of *Miller* that the *Ferber* Court held were not required. **D** is incorrect, because neither the judge *nor* the jury is required to make those findings. **B** is also incorrect, because such instructions need *not* be given to comply with the First Amendment. **C** is correct, but **A** is the better answer because the work need neither be taken as a whole, appeal to the prurient interest, nor be found to be patently offensive.

QUESTION 14. A-Pauled. Following his conviction, Paul files an appeal alleging that the trial judge failed to find that the films lacked any serious literary, artistic, political, or scientific merit, and thus his conviction violated the First Amendment. The court of appeals should:

A. Reverse Paul's conviction, because the trial court failed to protect Paul's First Amendment rights.
B. Affirm his conviction, because the presence of literary, artistic, political, or scientific merit is no defense in Paul's case.
C. Reverse Paul's conviction, because one has a right to privately possess child pornography.
D. Affirm his conviction, because child pornography can never have literary, artistic, political, or scientific merit.

ANALYSIS. Again, *Ferber* held that states are not required by the First Amendment to exempt child pornography shown to have serious literary, artistic, political, or scientific merit. **D** is wrong because it is irrelevant; the Court didn't express an opinion one way or another whether such material could potentially have any merit. The state is simply not required to exempt it from prosecution. *Osborne v. Ohio* held that there was no right to possess child pornography for private use, refusing to extend *Stanley v. Georgia.* Therefore, **C** is not correct. Between the remaining answers, **A** incorrectly states the law, leaving **B** as the correct answer.

The chart below depicts the differences between the *Miller* test and that adopted by the Court in *Ferber.*

Miller	*Ferber*
The average person, applying contemporary community standards, must find that the work, taken as a whole, appeals to the prurient interest.	There is no need to consider the work as a whole or whether it appeals to the prurient interest of the average person.
The work must depict or describe, in a patently offensive way, sexual conduct specifically defined by the applicable state law.	Proscribed conduct must be defined in the statute, but it need not be depicted in a "patently offensive" manner.
Taken as a whole, the work must lack serious literary, artistic, political, or scientific value.	Even works with serious literary, artistic, political, or scientific merit may be proscribed.

Ferber presumed that the use of children in the production of pornography inflicts irreparable harm on the subjects—harm that far outweighs whatever value the material itself may have. But when Congress attempted to prohibit sexually explicit images that *appeared* to be of children, but in the making of which no children were actually used, the Court invalidated the ban on so-called virtual child pornography. Ashcroft v. The Free Speech Coalition, 535 U.S. 234 (2002).

Noting that the ban included material that did not meet *Miller's* test for obscenity, the Court rejected arguments that the ban be evaluated under the more lenient *Ferber* test. The Court noted that a rigorous application of the ban would, for example, prohibit production of *Romeo and Juliet.* Under *Ferber*, the Court wrote, it "recognized that the State had an interest in stamping [child sexual abuse] out without regard to any judgment about its content. The production of the work, not its content, was the target of the statute." *Free Speech Coalition*, 535 U.S. at 249.

The government argued that because some virtual child pornography was indistinguishable from actual child pornography, both needed to be banned; otherwise those prosecuted could always claim that what they were producing or possessing was the former and not the latter. The Court said this "turn[ed] the First Amendment upside down. The Government may not suppress lawful speech as the means to suppress unlawful speech." *Id.* at 255.

The Court has refused to extend *Ferber* to state regulation of the sale or rental of violent video games by minors, rejecting the state's argument that playing those video games inflicted harms on minors. Brown v. Entertainment Merchants Association, 131 S. Ct. 2729 (2011). The Court first noted that "the obscenity exception to the First Amendment [covers] only depictions of 'sexual content'" and then held that while "[n]o doubt a State possesses legitimate power to protect children from harm . . . that does not include a free-floating power to restrict the ideas to which children may be exposed." *Entertainment Merchants Ass'n*, 131 S. Ct. at 2736.

7. *Defamation*

In cases like *Chaplinsky* and *Beauharnais*, the Court assumed that libelous or defamatory material was unprotected by the First Amendment. In 1964, however, the Supreme Court constitutionalized the law of libel and slander, to the surprise of many observers. The landmark case of *New York Times Co. v. Sullivan*, 376 U.S. 254 (1964), inaugurated a series of cases in which the Court limited public officials' and private citizens' ability to control the public dissemination of truthful (and even inaccurate) information about them.

In this section, we'll look at the *Sullivan* decision as well as the numerous decisions it spawned as the Court attempted to differentiate between public and private citizens and between public and private matters. We'll also look at the related areas of intentional infliction of emotional distress and publication of private facts.

The *New York Times* ran an ad about a civil rights protest in Montgomery, Alabama, that included statements of fact later found to be untrue. The police commissioner of the state, Sullivan, sued for libel, claiming that the erroneous allegations about the actions of the police during the demonstration harmed his reputation—despite the fact he was not named in the ad. Sullivan was awarded $500,000 in damages, and the verdict was affirmed by the Alabama Supreme Court. The *Times* appealed to the U.S. Supreme Court; the newspaper was apparently in real danger of going bankrupt if it had to satisfy the verdict, as well as similar verdicts that were expected to follow. *Sullivan*, 376 U.S. at 256.

Dismissing earlier statements from *Chaplinksy* and other cases, Justice Brennan's majority opinion stated unequivocally that libel verdicts "must be measured by standards that satisfy the First Amendment." *Id.* at 269. He continued: "[D]ebate on public issues should be uninhibited, robust, and wide-open, and . . . it may well include vehement, caustic, and sometimes unpleasantly sharp attacks on government and public officials." *Id.* at 270. It may even include, he argued, erroneous statements; and, he added, toleration of those false statements "must be protected if the freedoms of expression are to have the 'breathing space'" necessary to make them effective. *Id.* at 271-272. If the state cannot criminalize false statements about the government or government officials, it cannot subject speakers to civil penalties through libel law.[8] And the fact that truth was a defense under Alabama law did not redeem the judgment. "[C]ompelling the critic of official conduct to guarantee the truth of all his factual assertions—and to do so on pain of libel judgments virtually unlimited in amount—leads to . . . 'self-censorship.'" *Id.* at 279.

According to Justice Brennan, the First Amendment required "a federal rule that prohibits a public official from recovering damages for defamatory falsehood relating to his official conduct unless he proves that the statement was made with actual malice—that is, with knowledge that it was false or with reckless disregard of whether it was false or not." *Id.* at 279-280. The Court then, instead of remanding the case, applied the standard to the facts of the case and held that the evidence "support[ed] at most a finding of negligence in failing to discover the misstatements, and is constitutionally insufficient to show the recklessness that is required for a finding of actual malice." *Id.* at 288.

Three years later the Court expanded *Sullivan* to cover "public figures" as well as public officials in two cases, *Curtis Publishing Co. v. Butts* and *Associated Press v. Walker*, both reported at 388 U.S. 130 (1967). The Court noted that "'public figures,' like 'public officials,' often play an influential role in ordering

8. Here Justice Brennan took time to retroactively condemn the 1798 Sedition Act, which criminalized "false, scandalous and malicious writing" against the government or its officials, as unconstitutional. 376 U.S. at 273.

society" and that "[o]ur citizenry has a legitimate and substantial interest in the conduct of such persons. . . ." 388 U.S. at 164.

Not until *Gertz v. Robert Welch, Inc.*, 418 U.S. 323 (1974), did the Court clarify who, precisely, was a "public figure." *Gertz* involved a suit by a lawyer against the John Birch Society for an article published in its magazine suggesting that the lawyer (Gertz) who represented the family of a man murdered by a Chicago policeman had framed the policeman for the crime. *Gertz*, 418 U.S. at 325-326. The article also claimed that Gertz had a criminal record and was a Communist. Gertz sued and won $50,000, which was set aside by the trial court judge, who applied the *Sullivan* standard.

The U.S. Supreme Court reversed, finding that Gertz was not a public figure. Announcing that "there is no constitutional value in false statements of fact," the Court acknowledged that "the compensation of individuals for the harm inflicted on them by defamatory falsehood" was the "legitimate state interest underlying the law of libel. . . ." *Id.* at 340-341. The Court distinguished between public officials and figures, who "usually enjoy significantly greater access to the channels of effective communication and hence have a more realistic opportunity to counteract false statements," and private individuals, who are thus "more vulnerable to injury," necessitating greater state protection. *Id.* at 344.

The Court then explained the difference between the two groups. Public officials "risk . . . closer public scrutiny than might otherwise be the case," while public figures "have thrust themselves to the forefront of particular public controversies in order to influence the resolution of the issues involved [, thus] invit[ing] attention and comment." *Id.* at 344-345. One not fitting either definition is a private figure and may be compensated for actual injury upon satisfaction of a negligence standard. *Id.* at 350. Awards for punitive damages would be supported only by evidence satisfying the actual malice standard. *Id.* at 334. While the Court did not define "actual injury," it held that the term included "impairment of reputation and standing in the community, personal humiliation, and mental anguish and suffering" as well as "out-of-pocket loss." *Id.* at 350.

In subsequent cases, the Court made clear that simply being involved in litigation that was itself the subject of publicity was not enough to make one a public figure. In *Time, Inc. v. Firestone*, 424 U.S. 448 (1976), for example, the Court rejected the argument that a socialite involved in a highly publicized divorce was a public figure because there was no evidence that she had thrust herself into the public eye. *Firestone*, 424 U.S. at 454-455. Similarly, having been convicted for refusing to testify before a grand jury did not render one a public figure, even though the topic on which the defendant was to testify was of some interest to the public. Wolston v. Reader's Digest Association, 443 U.S. 157 (1979). And finally, a scientist suing for defamation for being named in a senator's annual expose of allegedly wasteful spending was not a public figure. Hutchinson v. Proxmire, 443 U.S. 111 (1979).

QUESTION 15. Public enmity. Ken is a television host whose show "Ken's Korner" is a popular political talk show. An outspoken, self-proclaimed "independent," Ken prides himself on speaking truth to power regardless who is in political power. The local newspaper runs a story claiming that, in reality, Ken is on the payroll of a number of trade groups who pay Ken to publicize their agenda, and that he receives weekly talking points from lobbyists that he works into every show. A furor erupted following publication of the article. Ken's viewership plummeted and his show was canceled. Later the newspaper conceded that the reporter who wrote the story exaggerated the ties that existed between Ken and lobbying groups, making it look like he was doing their bidding. Ken sues the publisher of the newspaper for libel, claiming both actual and punitive damages. Which of the following statements is true?

A. Ken could recover actual and punitive damages if he proves that the publisher was negligent.

B. Ken could recover actual damages if he proves that the publisher was negligent, but must prove actual malice to receive punitive damages.

C. Ken could recover neither actual nor punitive damages because he is a public figure.

D. Ken could recover actual damages by demonstrating that the publisher knew the claims were false or published the claims with reckless disregard as to their truth or falsity.

ANALYSIS. The first question is whether Ken is a public official or public figure. From the facts he clearly appears to be someone who has "thrust [himself] to the forefront of particular public controversies in order to influence the resolution of the issues involved[, thus] invit[ing] attention and comment," in the words of the Court. *Sullivan*, along with *Butts* and *Walker*, say that public figures are subject to the actual malice rule. Therefore, **A** cannot be correct. **B** would be correct if Ken were a *private* figure, which he is not. **C** is incorrect: *Sullivan* does not foreclose recovery of damages by public figures; it just raises the standard required for libel in order to protect the First Amendment. That leaves **D**, which is the best answer. Ken could recover actual damages by satisfying the *Sullivan* standard.

But *Gertz* left open another question: What are the constitutionally required standards for speech about private figures on matters of purely *private* concern? That question was answered in *Dun & Bradstreet v. Greenmoss Builders*, 472 U.S. 749 (1985). A credit-reporting firm (D&B) erroneously published a report stating that Greenmoss Builders had declared bankruptcy. *Greenmoss Builders*, 472 U.S. at 751. The company recovered $350,000 in compensatory and punitive damages; the U.S. Supreme Court upheld the verdict. Noting that speech on matters of public concern was at the First Amendment's core, the Court contrasted with such speech "speech on matters of purely private concern," which it labeled "of less First Amendment concern." *Id.* at 759.

The Court went on to identify some characteristics supporting its conclusion that the speech was of purely private concern: The "credit report concerns no public issue. It was speech solely in the individual interest of the speaker and its specific business audience. [Further,] the credit report was made available to only five subscribers, who . . . could not disseminate it further. . . ." *Id.* at 762. The last factor, the Court stressed, was included to refute the notion that "the report involves any 'strong interest in the free flow of commercial information.'" *Id.* The Court concluded that "when the defamatory statements do not involve matters of public concern," the First Amendment did not require a showing of "actual malice" to support an award of compensatory and punitive damages. *Id.* at 763.

QUESTION 16. Queen Bea. Bea lives in Santa Barbara, California, gives and attends parties, and frequently appears in local magazines that cover the Santa Barbara social scene and include photographs of party attendees. She even hires a clipping service to keep track of the periodicals in which she appears. Recently, Bea divorced her husband. The local newspaper reported, erroneously, that the divorce was precipitated by her affair with the pool cleaner. Bea sues the newspaper for actual and punitive damages. A jury finds that it was negligent in publishing the story. Which of the following statements is true?

A. Bea should recover nothing, because negligence is not sufficient to warrant recovery.
B. Bea can recover actual damages, but not punitive damages.
C. Bea could recover both actual and punitive damages, because her divorce is a matter of purely private concern.
D. Bea can recover actual and punitive damages regardless of whether or not her divorce is a matter of private concern because she is a private figure.

ANALYSIS. These facts are similar to those in the *Firestone* case; the correct answer turns on whether Bea is a public or a private figure. You might assume, from the facts, that she is a public figure, because she sometimes is in the public eye. But under *Firestone*, simply being part of "society" and even having that fact recorded in the media is not sufficient to make one a public figure. Bea did not, for example, "thrust herself" into the public arena to influence the resolution of public controversies; she just went to some parties in the course of supporting charitable work. As a private figure, then, the next question is whether the matter is one of public or private concern. The Court has not provided much information on this issue, but a divorce seems closer to *Greenmoss*

Builders than, say, the high-profile lawsuit at issue in *Gertz.* It is difficult to see any public interest in knowing what precipitated Bea's divorce. When a private figure sues over false information published about a private matter, both compensatory and punitive damages are available upon a showing of negligence. The correct answer, therefore, is **C. D** is incorrect, because if it were a matter of public concern, punitive damages would require proof of actual malice. **A** is an incorrect statement of the law, as is **B.**

Note that under either *Sullivan* or *Gertz*, the burden of proof is borne by the plaintiff in the case, not by the defendant. Philadelphia Newspapers, Inc. v. Hepps, 475 U.S. 767 (1986). A matrix of the Court's libel and defamation rules might help you keep it all straight:

Libel Standards Summary

Plaintiff's Status	*Definition*	*Issue Status*	*Applicable Standard*
Public official or public figure	Persons running for or serving in public office, and persons who have "thrust themselves to the forefront of particular public controversies in order to influence the resolution of the issues"	N/A	Actual malice
Private figure	Persons who have *not* "thrust themselves to the forefront of particular public controversies in order to influence the resolution of the issues"	Matter of public concern	Negligence required for actual damages; actual malice required for punitive damages
		Matter of private concern	Actual and punitive damages may be recovered on proof of negligence

There are a handful of other torts that implicate the First Amendment that might be labeled as violating "the right to stop people from speaking about you."[9] These include torts for intentional infliction of emotional distress, false-

9. *See* Eugene Volokh, *Freedom of Speech and Information Privacy: The Troubling Implications of a Right to Stop People from Speaking About You*, 52 Stan. L. Rev. 1049 (2000).

light invasion of privacy, public disclosure of private facts, and misappropriation of expression.

The Court's imposition of limits on torts for intentional infliction of emotional distress is probably the best known of these, owing to the colorful personalities involved in *Hustler Magazine v. Falwell*, 485 U.S. 46 (1988). *Hustler* magazine ran a parody ad featuring the Reverend Jerry Falwell, at the time a well-known conservative minister and political activist. The ad—which was labeled as a parody—suggested that the first time Reverend Falwell had sex was in an outhouse with his mother. *Falwell*, 485 U.S. at 48. Falwell sued when the ad appeared and was awarded compensatory and punitive damages totaling $200,000. The question for the Court was "whether a public figure may recover damages for emotional harm caused by the publication of an ad parody offensive to him, and doubtless gross and repugnant in the eyes of most." *Id.* at 50. The Court held that he could not.

Echoing *Sullivan*, the Court noted that public figures and officials were going to be the subject of sharp attacks and harsh criticism for their actions. "Such criticism, inevitably, will not always be reasoned or moderate. . . ." *Id.* at 51. The Court rejected Falwell's argument that when the intent was to cause emotional injury, "it is of no constitutional import whether the statement was fact or opinion, or whether it was true or false." Adopting that standard, the Court predicted, would mean that "political cartoonists and satirists would be subjected to damage awards without any showing that their work falsely defamed its subject." *Id.* at 53. The Court concluded that "public figures and public officials may not recover for the tort of intentional infliction of emotional distress by reason of publications [like the ad] without showing in addition that the publication contains a false statement of fact which was made with 'actual malice.' . . ." *Id.* at 56.

Relying in large part on the *Falwell* case, the Court invalidated a verdict for intentional infliction of emotional distress against members of the Westboro Baptist Church, who picket at soldiers' funerals and declare that military deaths in Iraq and Afghanistan are divine retribution for American tolerance of homosexuality. Snyder v. Phelps, 131 S. Ct. 1207 (2011). The Court held that where, as here, the speech concerned a matter of public concern, "that speech is entitled to 'special protection' under the First Amendment. Such speech cannot be restricted simply because it is upsetting or arouses contempt." *Snyder*, 131 S. Ct. at 1219. That protection, the Court continued, could not be overridden by a jury's decision that the expressive conduct was outrageous.

In addition to parodies, which do not claim to be communicating facts, there are "false light" torts in which statements about a person tend to invite inferences that are not true and violate that individual's privacy interest. In *Time, Inc. v. Hill*, 385 U.S. 374 (1967), for example, the Court applied *Sullivan* to a New York statute granting a cause of action for making false but non-defamatory statements about things that happened to the plaintiff. When *Time* magazine covered a play based on the real-life hostage taking of the Hill family, the article left readers with the impression that the events of the play—which included acts of violence perpetrated against the family—actually happened to the Hills. They sued under the New York cause of action and won, but their verdict was reversed by the Court, which required a showing of actual malice. *Hill*, 385 U.S. at 386-387. It is an open question, after *Gertz*, whether the Court applied the correct standard. The Hills, after all, were not public figures, though perhaps their kidnapping and the subsequent play about their ordeal were matters of public concern.

Still further removed from defamation is the public release of true facts that are allegedly private, which violates an individual's "right to be left alone," as the famous article by Brandeis and Warren puts it. As far as the Court is concerned, if the facts are of interest to the public, are obtained from public sources, and are true, then the publisher cannot be held civilly liable for airing them. In *Cox Broadcasting Corp. v. Cohn*, 420 U.S. 469 (1975), the Court refused, on First Amendment grounds, to impose civil liability on a broadcaster for releasing the name of a deceased rape victim. The Court wrote that "once true information is disclosed in public court documents open to public inspection, the press cannot be sanctioned for publishing it." *Cohn*, 420 U.S. at 496. Similarly, the Court rejected civil liability for a newspaper's decision to publish the name of a rape victim obtained from police reports. Florida Star v. B.J.F., 491 U.S. 524 (1989).

The Court even invalidated a federal statute attaching civil and criminal liability to disclosure of an illegally intercepted communication, if the person knew (or had reason to know) that the interception was, in fact, illegal. Bartnicki v. Vopper, 532 U.S. 514 (2001). The case arose after a talk radio host broadcast the recording of a call between a union negotiator and the union's president that included references to blowing up the porches of school board members to convince them to bend to teachers' demands. The call occurred during heated contract negotiation talks between the union and the school board. *Vopper*, 532 U.S. at 518-519. While protecting the privacy of communications was important, the Court felt that under the circumstances the application of those statutes sanctioned "the publication of truthful information of public concern" and that liability for doing so violated the First Amendment. *Id.* at 533-534.

8. *False statements of fact*

Just as the Court has offered constitutional protection for making false statements about public figures, as long as the speaker or publisher doesn't do so with actual malice, the Court recently refused categorically to hold that conveying false information about one's self could be criminally punished. United States v. Alvarez, 132 S. Ct. 2537 (2012). At issue was the constitutionality of the Stolen Valor Act, punishing false claims about winning military awards with fines and jail time. The Act included an enhanced penalty for falsely claiming to have won the Medal of Honor. *Alvarez*, 132 S. Ct. at 2542.

The Court first rejected the government's argument that false speech ought to receive no First Amendment protection. There was no such general exception, nor should there be, it held, observing that "some false statements are inevitable if there is to be an open and vigorous expression of views in public and private conversation, expression the First Amendment seeks to guarantee." *Id.* at 2544. The Court distinguished criminalization of perjury and impersonation of federal officials, noting that in both instances, the law sought to preserve the integrity of the underlying trial and of government processes. *Id.* at 2546. By contrast, "[p]ermitting the government to decree this speech to be a criminal offense, whether shouted from the rooftops or made in a barely audible whisper, would endorse government authority to compile a list of subjects about which false statements are punishable. That governmental power has no clear limiting principle." *Id.* at 2547.

Because the law punished false speech about military honors, the Court applied the strict scrutiny it reserves for content-based regulations. While the Court was willing to accept the government's interests—recognizing and expressing gratitude for heroism and protecting "the integrity of the military honors system in general, and the Medal of Honor in particular"—the Court found the Act lacked narrow tailoring. *Id.* at 2549. First, the government failed to establish "a direct causal link" between false claims and the integrity of the honors system. "The Government points to no evidence," the Court wrote, "to support its claim that the public's general perception of military awards is diluted by false claims such as those made by Alvarez." *Id.* at 2549. It also failed to show how counterspeech could be an effective remedy. *Id.* Finally, the criminalization of false claims was not the least restrictive means available. The Court suggested a database could be established that would allow for the verification of claims about military honors. *Id.* at 2551. In dissent, Justice Alito accused the majority of breaking "from a long line of cases recognizing that the right to free speech does not protect false statements that inflict real harm and serve no legitimate interest." *Id.* at 2557 (Alito, J., dissenting).

9. *Commercial speech*

Over the last 35 years commercial speech has gone from completely unprotected to nearly fully protected under the First Amendment. In *Valentine v. Chrestensen*, 316 U.S. 52, 54 (1942), the Court stated categorically that the First Amendment placed no "restraint on government as respects purely commercial advertising." By the mid-1970s the Court was beginning to distinguish between "purely" commercial advertising and advertising that—while having a commercial component—involved an individual constitutional right. Thus, in *Pittsburgh Press Co. v. Pittsburgh Commission on Human Relations*, 413 U.S. 376 (1973), the Court upheld a ban on single-sex employment advertisements because they constituted "no more than a proposal of possible employment." But because a ban on the advertisement of abortion services involved an independent constitutional right, the Court invalidated that ban in *Bigelow v. Virginia*, 421 U.S. 809 (1975).

The year after *Bigelow*, the Court revisited the issue of "pure" commercial speech, hearing a challenge to a Virginia ban on the advertisement by pharmacists of the prices of their prescription drugs. Virginia Board of Pharmacy v. Virginia Citizens Consumer Council, 425 U.S. 748 (1976). The Court first pointed out that many parties in free speech cases had economic motives. "The interests of the contestants in a labor dispute," the Court pointed out, "are primarily economic, but it has long been settled that both the employee and employer are protected by the First Amendment when they express themselves on the merits of the dispute in order to influence its outcome." *Virginia Citizens Consumer Council*, 425 U.S. at 762. A consumer's interest in "the free flow of commercial information . . . may be as keen, if not keener . . . than his interest in the day's most urgent political debate." *Id.* at 763. The Court drew a connection between the availability of information to consumers and the efficient allocation of resources in a free market system. *Id.* at 764-765. The Court discounted the impact that permitting price advertising would have on professional standards among pharmacists, especially given the state's tight regulation. "The advertising ban does not directly affect professional standards one way or the other." *Id.* at 769. The advantage the state was claiming was to protect its citizens by keeping them in ignorance. These paternal concerns, the Court felt, did not outweigh the First Amendment interest of pharmacists in communicating, and customers in receiving, truthful information about drug prices. *Id.* at 770.

Still, the majority did not hold that all commercial speech was beyond regulation. For example, the Court suggested advertising regulation that was a true "time, place, and manner" restriction would pass muster if the regulation "serv[ed] a significant governmental interest, and . . . [left] open ample alternative channels for communication of the information." *Id.* at 771. It also suggested that the state was free to regulate false or misleading advertising or those advertising illegal transactions. *Id.* at 771-772. "What is at issue is whether a State may completely suppress the dissemination of concededly truthful information about entirely lawful activity, fearful of that information's effect upon its disseminators and recipients." *Id.* at 773. The Court decided it could not.

The factors mentioned by Justice Blackmun were restated, in *Central Hudson Gas & Electric Corp. v. Public Service Commission*, 447 U.S. 557 (1980), as a multi-part test. The case arose over a New York public service commission regulation prohibiting promotional advertising by electrical utilities. The view of the commission was that such promotional messages were antithetical to the state's desire to see consumers conserve electricity. *Central Hudson*, 447 U.S. at 558-559.

For the Court, Justice Powell first took another crack at defining commercial speech: "[E]xpression related solely to the economic interests of the speaker and its audience." *Id.* at 561. He then articulated the standard of review, acknowledging that "[t]he Constitution . . . accords a lesser protection to commercial speech than to other constitutionally guaranteed expression." *Id.* at 563.

> For commercial speech to come within [the First Amendment] it at least must concern lawful activity and not be misleading. Next, we ask whether the asserted governmental interest is substantial. If both inquires yield positive answers, we must determine whether the regulation directly advances the governmental interest asserted, and whether it is not more extensive than is necessary to serve that interest.

Id. at 566.

Applying the test, the Court found there was no question that the advertisement was for a lawful transaction and was not misleading. Likewise, it found the government's interest in incentivizing energy conservation to be substantial and that the ban directly advanced the interest, because of the connection between advertising and energy consumption. *Id.* at 566-569.

But the "critical inquiry" was "whether the Commission's complete suppression of speech ordinarily protected by the First Amendment is no more extensive than necessary to further the State's interest. . . ." *Id.* at 569-570. The Court concluded that the commission's total ban swept too broadly. For example, the Court noted that the ban would prevent utilities from encouraging their customers to upgrade to more energy-efficient appliances or to appliances whose use would not result in increased consumption. *Id.* at 570. "The Commission . . . has not demonstrated that its interest in conservation cannot be protected adequately by more limited regulation of [Central Hudson's] commercial expression." *Id.*

QUESTION 17. Burger blues. Concerned over the effects of obesity on children in society, Ames passes a law banning billboards containing advertisements for fast food from being erected within 500 feet of a school or playground. Adams Advertising, which has contracts with Friar's Fat Burger to erect billboards with the fast-food company's advertising, challenges the law in federal district court. The district court should:

A. Uphold the statute because commercial speech is not protected by the First Amendment.

B. Invalidate the statute because it is not narrowly tailored to a compelling governmental interest.

C. Invalidate the statute because there are means of advancing the state's interest that do not involve as much restriction of speech.

D. Uphold the statute because the regulation is content-neutral.

ANALYSIS. Remember that commercial speech is afforded less protection than other forms of speech or expressive conduct precisely because of its content. Therefore, **D** is incorrect. The statute bans fast-food advertising; it is not content-neutral. Nevertheless, **A** is not true: Current doctrine affords some First Amendment protection to commercial speech. But **B** states the incorrect standard of review. *Central Hudson* requires that the government's interest in regulating truthful, nonmisleading advertising directly advance a substantial governmental interest and suppress no more speech than is necessary to effectuate that interest. The language in **B** describes the test for content-based speech regulations. That leaves **C**, which is the best answer. Even assuming that a ban on fast-food advertising directly advances Ames's interest in combating childhood obesity, the state has options open to it—education, taxation, direct regulation on sales—that do not involve the suppression of speech.

QUESTION 18. Beat it. *MetroBeat* is a free weekly newspaper published in Ames City. Ames City has an ordinance prohibiting both prostitution and solicitation of prostitution. *MetroBeat* is known for its classified ads for "adult services" in the back of the paper, including "escort services," which Ames City claims is a thinly veiled front for prostitution rings. Ames City charges the publisher and editor of *MetroBeat* with solicitation of prostitution because of the ads in the back of the newspaper. The paper responds by claiming that the prosecutions violate the First Amendment and seeks to have the charges dismissed. A reviewing judge is likely to:

A. Dismiss the charges, because they violate the First Amendment.
B. Dismiss the charges, unless the government can prove that it is barring no more speech than necessary.
C. Allow the prosecution to go forward because the advertisements are for illegal transactions.
D. Allow the prosecutions to go forward because the advertisements relate solely to the economic interests of *MetroBeat*.

ANALYSIS. Although the advertisements relate to the economic interest of the newspaper, that does not exclude it from First Amendment protection. Thus, **D** is incorrect. The First Amendment does protect commercial speech, just not quite as much as non-commercial expression. But the threshold question is whether the commercial speech is in fact not misleading and proposes transactions that are legal. That is at issue here. Assuming that the state proves that the escort service ads are advertisements for prostitution, which is illegal under Ames City ordinances, **C** is the correct answer. **B** is incorrect, because one does not evaluate the strength of the government's interest, and the fit between the regulation and that interest, until it is established that the commercial speech at issue is not misleading and proposes a transaction that is itself legal. **A** is incorrect as well. Prosecuting the newspaper for advertising illegal activities is not a violation of the First Amendment.

A subsequent decision held that the "no more extensive than necessary" prong of the *Central Hudson* test does *not* require the state to use the "least restrictive alternative" available to it. So the Court held in *Board of Trustees, SUNY v. Fox*, 492 U.S. 469 (1989). A public university barred students from running businesses on campus, which meant that students could not hold Tupperware parties in the dorms. *Fox*, 492 U.S. at 471-473. Applying *Central Hudson*, the Court found that the commercial speech neither was misleading nor offered an illegal transaction. It also found the university's interests—protecting students and maintaining a proper educational atmosphere on campus—to be substantial and directly advanced by the ban. *Id.* at 475. But Justice Scalia wrote that requiring government's regulation to be no more extensive than necessary to achieve its goal did not require it to use the least restrictive means, "[b]ut, as we have put it in . . . other contexts . . . a means narrowly tailored to achieve the desired objective." *Id.* at 480.

Even so, the Court is skeptical of total bans on the communication of information, as shown by *Thompson v. Western States Medical Center*, 535 U.S. 357 (2002), in which the Court invalidated a ban on the advertisement of "compounded drugs"—whereby pharmacists blend or combine ingredients to produce a tailor-made drug. The ban was justified on a couple of grounds: (1) to prevent subversion of the new drug approval process from which compounded drugs are exempt while (2) enabling those who need them to obtain compounded drugs. *Id.* at 768. Again, while conceding the substantial nature of the concerns and that the ban was directly related to advancing those interests, the Court nevertheless struck down the ban, finding that it swept more broadly than necessary. The Court noted that the government could more strictly regulate the compounding of drugs, placing limits on the amount available by volume or sale. *Id.* at 372. The government, it wrote, "has not offered any reason why these possibilities, alone or in combination, would be insufficient to prevent compounding from occurring on such a scale as to undermine the new drug approval process." Moreover, there was no evidence the government even considered such alternatives. *Id.* at 373.

Western States Medical Center confirms something of a pattern in recent commercial speech cases: The government restricts nonmisleading commercial speech about transactions that are not in and of themselves illegal; the Court concedes the importance of the government interest, and the direct advancement of that interest by the regulation, but concludes nevertheless that the regulation swept too broadly and restricted more speech than necessary. *See also* Sorrell v. IMS Health, Inc., 131 S. Ct. 2653 (2011) (invalidating prohibition on disclosure of physician prescribing practices for marketing purposes; conceding importance of governmental objectives of lowering costs of drugs and promoting health, but concluding that ban did not "directly advance" those interests because information could be disclosed widely for non-marketing purposes).

This trend arguably began with *44 Liquormart, Inc. v. Rhode Island*, 517 U.S. 484 (1996). In *44 Liquormart*, the Court invalidated Rhode Island's ban on liquor price advertising. Four Justices held that Rhode Island's "blanket prohibition against truthful, nonmisleading speech about a lawful product" did not "significantly advance" the state's interest in promoting temperance because the state failed to show that the advertising ban reduced consumption. *44 Liquormart*, 517 U.S. at 504-505. Further, the plurality found that the ban was a more extensive limitation of speech than was necessary. "It is perfectly obvious," Justice Stevens wrote, "that alternative forms of regulation that would not involve any restriction on speech would be more likely to achieve the State's goal of promoting temperance." *Id.* at 507. The plurality suggested higher taxes, limits on per capita purchases, and educational campaigns as alternatives. *Id.*

Another severe advertising ban, this one on tobacco, was invalidated in *Lorillard Tobacco Co. v. Reilly*, 533 U.S. 525 (2001). Massachusetts had prohibited outdoor tobacco advertising within 1,000 feet of a school or playground. The regulations also prohibited indoor advertising of tobacco lower than 5 feet from the ground within 1,000 feet of a school or playground and prohibited indoor advertising visible from the outside. *Lorillard Tobacco Co.*, 533 U.S. at 534-535.

While the Court accepted the importance of the interest in preventing underage smoking and that the ban directly advanced that interest, it held that the outdoor advertising ban effectively eliminated outdoor tobacco advertising in most parts of the state. This near-total ban on truthful information about a lawful product went too far. The government cannot keep from adults truthful information about products it is lawful for them to buy, even in an attempt to keep those items out of the hands of children. *Id.* at 562-564.

The indoor advertising regulations also failed to pass muster, both because of the amount of speech they suppressed and because the state failed to show how its interest was directly advanced by the 5-foot height requirement. The Court pointed out that many underage children are 5 feet tall or taller; those who are not could simply look up to see the advertising. *Id.* at 566. The Court did, however, uphold regulations requiring that tobacco products be placed behind the counter and that customers purchase them from a salesperson. *Id.* at 570.

Central Hudson and its progeny have been usefully summarized in the chart below:

Is the information true, not misleading and proposes a lawful transacton?

- Government must show a *substantial* interest, and
- That the regulation *directly advances* that interest, and
- The regulation must *not be more extensive than necessary* to achieve the interest.
- "No more extensive than necessary" ≠ "least restrictive means"
- *But* total bans of advertising for legal products or service that are true and not misleading are disfavored

QUESTION 19. Under the gun. Under pressure from gun control groups, which claim studies show that gun owners are more likely to be killed or injured with the guns they own than they are to use them successfully in self-defense, the State of Ames has made it unlawful to advertise firearms in print or on television. It is legal to sell, buy, and possess firearms in Ames. The statute is challenged by Bolt Firearms, which manufactures the Homemaker, a lightweight, easy-to-handle firearm that it markets to first-time gun owners who want a firearm for home defense. The trial court judge finds that the content of the ad—that the Homemaker is lightweight and easily handled by someone not familiar with firearms—is true. He nevertheless upholds the ad ban. On appeal, the reviewing court should hold the ban to be:

A. Unconstitutional, because the regulation is based on the content of the ad.

B. Constitutional, because it directly advances the state's substantial interest in preventing gun violence.

C. Constitutional, because advertisements about the gun's utility for home defense are misleading.

D. Unconstitutional, because the ban on truthful, nonmisleading advertising sweeps too broadly.

ANALYSIS. From reading this section, you know that **A** is incorrect. Commercial speech is one of the areas of speech that is afforded somewhat less protection *because of* its content. **B** is partially true, but misses the prong of the *Central Hudson* test requiring that the regulation go no farther than necessary to advance the state's interest. Although they need not be the least restrictive means, total advertising bans have been subject to considerable skepticism from the Court, which has often found that the state had alternatives available to it other than the suppression of speech. **C** could be true under different facts. Ads have to be true and not misleading, but nothing in the facts suggests that the ad makes specific claims about the utility of the gun for home defense. According to the facts, the ad says that the gun is lightweight and easy to use. The best answer, then, is **D**. The state, for example, might require gun owners to pass a proficiency test. It might regulate gun sales directly or engage in an advertising campaign warning against buying guns for self-defense if you don't know how to use them. Any of those alternatives would not require the suppression of the ads.

Before leaving commercial speech, let's look briefly at advertising by lawyers. Initially, even members of the Court desirous of extending First Amendment protections to some commercial speech held the opinion that "different factors would govern were we faced with a law regulating or even prohibiting advertising by the traditional learned professions of medicine or law." *Virginia Citizens Consumer Council,* 425 U.S. at 774 (Burger, C.J., concurring). The next year, however, the Court invalidated a state ban on price advertising by lawyers in *Bates v. State Bar,* 433 U.S. 350 (1977). The Court later extended *Bates* to invalidate restrictions on the truthful and nonmisleading solicitation of clients through direct mail. Shapero v. Kentucky Bar Association, 486 U.S. 466 (1988).

In two cases, the Court upheld restrictions on commercial speech by lawyers. In the first, *Ohralik v. State Bar,* 436 U.S. 447 (1978), the Court upheld a ban on in-person solicitation by lawyers. Because of the danger of coercion and overreaching, the Court held that the in-person ban was permissible under the First Amendment. (The lawyer in the case had approached an accident victim about representation while the victim was still in the hospital, then refused to withdraw from representation when the client attempted to fire him.)

The Court also upheld Florida's restriction on direct mail solicitation of personal injury victims or their relatives for 30 days following an injury. Florida Bar v. Went For It, Inc., 515 U.S. 618 (1995). The ban was implemented in response to what the bar perceived as a negative public reaction to solicitation by lawyers following mass tort incidents in the state. The bar thought the ban necessary to prevent further decline of the bar's reputation. *Went For It,* 515 U.S. at 625. The Court held that the regulation went no further than necessary because there were other channels than direct mail for soliciting clients and because the ban was only temporary. *Id.* at 633-634.

C. Content-Neutral Regulation

1. *Introduction*

As noted in the overview to this chapter, free speech doctrine turns, as a general rule, on whether government is attempting to regulate speech based on its content. Assuming that the material in question is not one of the aforementioned areas of speech or expression that is either not protected by the First Amendment or given somewhat lesser protection, content-based regulation is subject to strict scrutiny. Content-*neutral* regulation, by contrast, is subject to intermediate scrutiny. The paradigmatic content-neutral regulations are those that place "time, place, and manner" restrictions on speech.

We will look at content-neutral regulations in this section. In some cases, the question arises whether seemingly content-neutral restrictions are, in fact, content-based and thus subject to strict scrutiny. In addition, this section looks at restrictions placed on expressive conduct—that is, actions that have an expressive component—as well as the so-called secondary effects doctrine, in which the Court has permitted the regulation of expressive activity not because of its content but because of the effects produced by it.

To review quickly, *United States v. O'Brien* set forth the standard of review for content-neutral regulation of speech or expressive activity:

- Regulation cannot be based on content.
- The purpose of the regulation must not be to suppress ideas.
- Regulation must be narrowly tailored to achieve a significant government interest.
- Regulation must leave open ample alternative channels.

2. *Content-neutral time, place, and manner restrictions*

Ward v. Rock Against Racism, 491 U.S. 781 (1989), furnishes a good example of the application of neutral time, place, and manner restrictions. In an effort to address complaints arising from the use of the band shell in New York City's Central Park as a live music venue, the City of New York imposed sound regulations on bands performing there. The regulations stated that performers had to use the city's sound equipment, as well as a sound technician employed by the city. *Rock Against Racism*, 491 U.S. at 787-789. This was alleged to violate performers' First Amendment rights; the Court disagreed.

First, the Court noted that musical performances were protected under the First Amendment. *Id.* at 790. The sound amplification restrictions, the Court concluded, were aimed at protecting residents around Central Park from unwanted noise and were unrelated to the content of the performance. Because it was a valid time, place, and manner restriction, the government need only prove that it was narrowly tailored to a significant governmental interest. The Court had little trouble concluding that safeguarding the privacy and solitude of nearby residents was significant. The question was whether the regulations were narrowly tailored.

The lower court had equated "narrow tailoring" with "least restrictive means," which the Court held to be in error. "[O]ur cases quite clearly hold that restrictions on the time, place, or manner of protected speech are not invalid 'simply because there is some imaginable alternative that might be less burdensome on speech.'" *Id.* at 797. Narrow tailoring, the Court held, was satisfied as long as a regulation "'promotes a substantial government interest that would be achieved less effectively absent the regulation.' . . . So long as the means chosen are not substantially broader than necessary to achieve the government's interest," the regulation won't be invalidated simply because another, less restrictive regulation would be just as substantially effective. *Id.* at 799-800.

As applied to the case at bar, the Court concluded that other potential means of dealing with the noise problem would be less effective than the requirement that bands use the city's sound equipment and engineer. Because "the guideline allows the city to control volume without interfering with the performer's sound mix, it is not 'substantially broader than necessary' to achieve the city's legitimate ends. . . ." *Id.* at 802.

QUESTION 20. Noises off. Ames City has a vibrant downtown area known as The Flatts, which is home to a number of bars, restaurants, and clubs. In recent years, vacant buildings in The Flatts have been converted to condominiums and lofts, which are occupied by professionals attracted by The Flatts' proximity to Ames City's central business district. However, the professionals occupying the new real estate have complained about the noise emanating from the bars and clubs. In response, the Ames City Council passed a noise ordinance prohibiting amplified music audible from the street after 11:00 P.M. on Sunday through Wednesday, after 12:00 A.M. on Friday night, and after 2:00 A.M. on Saturday night. A local band, the Dixie Pixies, sued, claiming that the ban violated the First Amendment. A reviewing judge should:

A. Invalidate the ordinance, unless the city demonstrates that it is the least restrictive means available to it to control noise.
B. Invalidate the ordinance, because there is no significant governmental interest at stake.
C. Uphold the ordinance, because it is a valid time, place, and manner restriction.
D. Uphold the ordinance, because musical performance is not "speech" protected by the First Amendment.

ANALYSIS. First, the ordinance makes no distinction based on the content of the performance. It appears to be—and there is no evidence to the contrary—content-neutral. Therefore, intermediate scrutiny, as opposed to strict scrutiny, applies. You also know from *Ward* that musical performance is not excluded from First Amendment protection, so **D** is incorrect. *Ward* also instructs you that **A** is incorrect: The reference to "narrow tailoring" in the description of intermediate scrutiny does not require the government to prove that the regulation is the least restrictive means possible; rather, it need only show that its efforts at regulating the end would be less effective if it weren't able to use the particular means chosen. Nor is **B** correct; protecting the ability of residents of The Flatts to enjoy peace and solitude when in their homes (as New York City sought to do in *Ward*) is a significant interest. That leaves **C**, the correct answer. No speech is absolutely restricted; the city has just specified when amplified music may be played to reduce the impact on surrounding residents.

So what time, place, and manner restrictions *would* sweep too broadly? The Court has historically expressed reservations about total media bans, even when apparently content-neutral. In *Ladue v. Gilleo*, 512 U.S. 43 (1994), the Court invalidated a city's ban on all signs displayed in or on residences. "[P]rohibitions foreclosing entire media may be completely free of content or viewpoint discrimination [but] the danger they pose to the freedom of speech is readily apparent—by eliminating a common means of speaking, such measures can suppress too much speech." *Gilleo*, 512 U.S. at 55. On the other hand, the Court upheld a ban on the picketing of private residences in *Frisby v. Schultz*, 487 U.S. 474 (1988). The ban was enacted in response to the picketing of a physician's residence by abortion opponents; the Court found that the ban was content- (and viewpoint-) neutral and was narrowly tailored to the substantial purpose of protecting the home as a refuge from unwanted speech. The Court also noted the presence of ample alternative forms of communication picketers might use to express their opposition to abortion. *Schultz*, 487 U.S. at 58-59.

Schultz, though, raises another issue: that of facially neutral bans that may be motivated by opposition to the particular ideas being expressed. According to *O'Brien*, such regulations are subject to strict scrutiny. When Colorado barred persons within 100 feet of a health care facility from "'knowingly approach[ing]' within eight feet of another person, without that person's consent," to communicate with them orally or through handbills or signs, abortion opponents claimed that they were being targeted—that despite its facial neutrality, the ban was content-based. Hill v. Colorado, 530 U.S. 703, 707 (2000). The Court rejected this argument, holding that the ban was content-neutral, left ample alternative channels open, and was narrowly tailored to the significant governmental interest of preserving access to medical services and protecting citizens from unwanted speech. *Hill*, 530 U.S. at 725-726. The dissenting Justices complained that the facially neutral law was actually content-based and aimed at suppressing ideas. *Id.* at 742-743 (Scalia, J., dissenting).

In contrast to the holding in *Hill*, the Court invalidated a Massachusetts law that prohibited "sidewalk counselors" who sought to dissuade woman from having abortions from approaching within 35 feet of clinic entrances. McMullen v. Coakley, 2014 WL 2882079 (2014). Though the Court, consistent with *Hill*, found the restriction to be content- and viewpoint-neutral and subject only to intermediate scrutiny, the majority found the law restricted too much speech in service of the government's interests in "public safety, patient access to healthcare, and the unobstructed use of public sidewalks and roadways." *McMullen*, 2014 WL 2882079, at *15.

> At each of the three Planned Parenthood clinics where petitioners attempt to counsel patients, the zones carve out a significant portion of the adjacent public sidewalks, pushing petitioners well back from the clinics' entrances and driveways. The zones thereby compromise petitioners' ability to initiate the close, personal conversations that they view as essential to "sidewalk counseling."

Id. Writing for himself and Justices Kennedy and Thomas, Justice Scalia argued that *Hill* should be overruled, and that the law should be deemed content-based and invalidated using strict scrutiny. *Id.* at *21 (Scalia, J., concurring).

QUESTION 21. A-sign-ment. In 2005, developers broke ground on Ames Garden, a high-end subdivision on the outskirts of Ames City. Luxury homes were sold as fast as builders could erect them. As it turned out, however, many of the purchasers were unable to make their mortgage payments once the recession hit. According to one estimate, two out of every three houses are in foreclosure. Remaining residents are worried about how the high number of foreclosed and bank-owned properties will affect their property values. They persuaded Ames City to ban all yard signs, except those of candidates for political office or "for sale" signs that list the realtor's name and contact information. During the debate on the ordinance several residents of Ames Garden spoke up about how demoralizing it was to see so many "Foreclosure" and "Bank Owned" signs, how they feared that the empty houses would become magnets for criminals and vandals, and how they worried about the impact of all this on their own property values. After the ordinance passed, however, Ames Realty, the largest realtor in town, and the First Bank of Ames, which now owns a substantial number of foreclosed homes, sued in federal court, claiming the ordinance violated the First Amendment. (Ames Realty is employed by the First Bank of Ames to sell the houses that the bank now owns.) If a reviewing judge strikes down the ordinance, it will likely be because:

A. The ordinance is content-based.
B. The ordinance does not further a significant governmental interest.
C. The ordinance is not narrowly tailored.
D. The ordinance does not regulate protected speech.

ANALYSIS. This one is a little tricky. First, yard signs *are* protected speech, so the First Amendment applies. Therefore, **D** is incorrect. (Remember *Ladue* *v. Gilleo.*) Now, look carefully at the ordinance. It begins by banning *all* yard signs, which seems content-neutral, but then exempts both political signs and certain "for sale" signs. Those exemptions render the ordinance content-based, not content-neutral. Therefore, the correct answer is **A**. Answers **B** and **C** are incorrect because they describe the standard of review for a truly content-neutral sign.

QUESTION 22. A bill in the hand. Ames City recently passed an ordinance prohibiting the distribution of handbills or leaflets anywhere within the city limits. Supporters of the ordinance describe it as an effort to combat littering and to encourage conservation of paper. Does this ordinance violate the First Amendment?

A. Yes, because it does not further a compelling governmental interest.
B. Yes, because it is not narrowly tailored.
C. No, because the prevention of littering and conservation are significant governmental interests.
D. No, unless the government can prove that the ban is the least restrictive means available to further its interest.

ANALYSIS. Now, this ordinance *is* content-neutral; but it also is a total media ban, which the Court has disfavored. Because it is content-neutral, intermediate scrutiny applies and thus **A** is incorrect. The ordinance needs to pursue significant governmental interests, and the prevention of littering and encouragement of conservation are two such interests. But **C** isn't the best answer, because it is incomplete. In addition to achieving a significant governmental interest, the ordinance needs to be narrowly tailored—and that does *not* mean that government must prove that its regulation is the least restrictive means available to it. Therefore, **D** is not correct. That leaves **B**, which is the correct answer. The Court is skeptical of total media bans and has invalidated several. Here, there appear to be means open to combat littering and encourage conservation that don't involve an abridgement of free speech rights. The city could develop recycling programs, impose stiff penalties for littering, and so on.

3. *Expressive conduct*

First Amendment doctrine sometimes distinguishes between "conduct" that government may regulate, even if it has an expressive component, and "speech." For example, in *Wisconsin v. Mitchell*, the Court upheld an enhanced sentence for certain crimes committed against victims chosen because of, inter alia, their race. The sentence enhancement did not violate *R.A.V. v. St. Paul* because the enhancement targeted conduct that was not protected by the First Amendment, that is, assault and battery. In *Nevada Commission on*

Ethics v. Carrigan, 131 S. Ct. 2343 (2011), to take another example, the Court upheld a recusal provision that prohibited a public official from voting on, or advocating the passage or defeat of, a measure where a prior commitment to another person could cause the official's independent judgment to be called into question. The Court held that the recusal provision did not affect public officials' free speech rights because "a legislator's vote is the commitment of his apportioned share of the legislature's power to the passage or defeat of a particular proposal. The legislative power thus committed is not personal to the legislator but belongs to the people; the legislator has no personal right to it." *Carrigan*, 131 S. Ct. at 2350. The Court rejected the notion that a vote was symbolic speech: "But the act of voting symbolizes nothing. It *discloses*, to be sure, that the legislator wishes . . . that the proposition on the floor be adopted, just as a physical assault discloses that the attacker dislikes the victim. But neither the one nor the other is an act of communication." *Id.*

In the more difficult cases, the conduct and the expressive message are intertwined such that the regulation of the former burdens the latter. In *O'Brien*, for example, although Congress had forbidden the burning of one's draft card, O'Brien burned his to communicate his opposition to the war in Vietnam. The Court assumed that O'Brien's action had an expressive component and then held that because the ban was not content- or viewpoint-based, it was subject to intermediate, as opposed to strict, scrutiny. In a recent case, the Court made clear that only "inherently expressive" conduct is protected. Rumsfeld v. FAIR, 547 U.S. 47 (2006). In *FAIR*, the Court rejected an argument from law schools that their inferior treatment of military recruiters was "inherently expressive," even though that treatment was a result of the law schools' disapproval of the military's ban on service by persons who were openly homosexual.

QUESTION 23. Playing army. As part of a protest against continued American military involvement in Iraq and Afghanistan, Stark Young staged a play in which the main character, played by Young, was vampire who wore a U.S. Army uniform and preyed on innocent young women who represented various countries in which the Army was conducting military operations. Young was convicted under a federal statute that prohibited the use of uniforms or insignia of the United States armed forces in plays, movies, or on television in any manner that "tended to discredit" the military or its members. The statute is likely to be found:

A. Unconstitutional, because it is viewpoint-based.
B. Constitutional, because it proscribes conduct.
C. Unconstitutional, because it does not further a legitimate governmental interest.
D. Constitutional, because it furthers a compelling governmental interest and is substantially related to furthering that interest.

ANALYSIS. The facts here are similar to those in *Schacht v. United States*, 398 U.S. 58 (1970). Not only does this statute regulate expressive conduct based on content—the wearing of a uniform—but it is also viewpoint-based. Only those depictions of members of the military that would "tend to discredit" the military are prohibited. That means the statute is subject to strict scrutiny. **A** is the correct answer. **B** is not correct, because the wearing of uniforms in a play or movie constitutes expressive conduct. **C** and **D** are incorrect because they misstate the appropriate standard of review. Content- and viewpoint-based restrictions require the government to demonstrate a compelling governmental interest and narrow tailoring.

In what is probably the most famous recent expressive conduct case, the Court invalidated Texas's prohibition on "desecration" of public monuments, graves, and flags, as applied to someone who publicly burned a U.S. flag at the 1984 Republican National Convention in protest against nuclear weapons. Texas v. Johnson, 491 U.S. 397 (1989). First, the Court asked whether the conduct was expressive and protected by the First Amendment; it concluded that it was. Concluding that the flag burning came as the "culmination" of a political protest, "[t]he expressive, overtly political nature of this conduct" was obvious. *Johnson*, 491 U.S. at 406.

Second, the Court had to determine whether "Texas has asserted an interest in support of Johnson's conviction that is unrelated to the suppression of expression." *Id.* at 407. It concluded that it had not. Texas argued that conviction was necessary to (1) prevent breaches of the peace and (2) preserve the flag as a symbol of national unity. As to the first, the Court found no evidence in the record that any "disturbance of the peace actually occurred or [was] threatened . . . because of Johnson's burning of the flag." *Id.* at 409.[10] The second goal, however, was related to suppression of expression. Noting that burning of the flag is sanctioned if the flag is soiled or worn, the Court pointed out that Texas's statute was directed "only against impairments [of the flag] that would cause serious offense to others." *Id.* at 411. But a "bedrock principle" of the First Amendment is that speech or expressive conduct may not be banned simply because others might find it offensive. *Id.* at 414. In the uproar that followed *Johnson*, a federal statute was passed that barred, inter alia, the mutilation or physical defilement of the American flag. The Court invalidated this ban as well. United States v. Eichman, 496 U.S. 310 (1990). Contrary to claims that the federal statute was content-neutral, the Court found that "[t]he Government's interest in protecting the 'physical integrity' of a privately owned flag rests upon a perceived need to preserve the flag's status as a symbol of our Nation and certain national ideals" and "suppresses expression out of concern for its likely communicative impact." *Eichman*, 496 U.S. at 317. For the reasons given in *Johnson*, the Court concluded that the federal law was invalid.

---

10. The Court also rejected the argument that flag burning constitutes a form of "fighting words." *Id.* at 409.

4. *Secondary effects*

The "secondary effects" doctrine holds that when expressive activity is regulated not because of the message that it communicates, but rather because of activities closely associated with the speech or conduct but not directly produced by it, the regulation will be deemed content-neutral. The doctrine arose out of government attempts to regulate certain non-obscene, adult-oriented establishments, such as adult bookstores and strip clubs. Both the materials in adult bookstores and nude dancing are protected activities under the First Amendment. *See, e.g.*, Erie v. Pap's A.M., 529 U.S. 277 (2000). However, the Court has approved efforts to zone adult businesses in an attempt to combat public ills including public drunkenness, drug dealing, and prostitution, which are often associated with such establishments.

When Renton, Washington, barred adult theaters from operating within 1,000 feet of residences, churches, parks, or schools, forcing the theaters to concentrate in a small part of the town, theater owners sued, claiming the zoning violated the First Amendment. Renton v. Playtime Theaters, Inc., 475 U.S. 41 (1986). Relying in large part on *Young v. American Mini Theaters*, 427 U.S. 50 (1976), the Court analyzed the ordinance "as a form of time, place, and manner regulation." *Renton*, 475 U.S. at 46.

The Court explained that though the ordinance applied only to "adult motion picture theaters," it was not content-based because the ordinance was "aimed not at the content of the films shown . . . but rather at the *secondary effects* of such theaters on the surrounding community." *Id.* at 56. The inquiry for the Court was whether "the Renton ordinance is designed to serve a substantial governmental interest and allows for reasonable alternative avenues of communication." *Id.* at 50. The Court noted that, first, ameliorating the effects of those establishments and protecting the quality of life in Renton was a substantial interest. Further, "the ordinance leaves . . . more than five percent of the entire land area of Renton, open to use as adult theater sites." *Id.* at 53.

A later case clarified that to satisfy the "substantial interest" prong of the secondary effects test, the evidence must "fairly support" the reasons for the law. Los Angeles v. Alameda Books, 535 U.S. 425, 438 (2002) (plurality). Plaintiffs seeking to overcome this support must show that the evidence does not support the rationale or that the evidence is in dispute. If either is established, the burden shifts to the government to provide additional evidence.

It is an open question whether the secondary effects doctrine applies in cases not involving adult entertainment establishments. The Court rejected an attempt to invoke the doctrine in support of a District of Columbia law barring displays of signs that bring a foreign government into "public odium" or "public disrepute" within 500 feet of that country's embassy. Boos v. Barry, 485 U.S. 312 (1988). A plurality of the Court explained that reactions to the signs are not "secondary effects"; rather, they are the result of the impact of the speech on the audience. By attempting to regulate messages designed to evoke those reactions, the D.C. law was content-based and subject to strict scrutiny.

QUESTION 24. Papers please. Concerned that the patchwork of state laws governing the issuance of drivers' licenses and other forms of identification were a threat to national security, Congress passed a law requiring all U.S. citizens and resident aliens to obtain and carry with them at all times a national ID card, which must be produced when requested by state, local, or federal law enforcement personnel. A number of people vigorously objected to what they saw as "Big Brotherism" run amok; several began to burn their ID cards publicly, in protest. Federal law prohibits "forging, altering, or knowingly destroying or mutilating" one's ID card. When Alex O'Brien is convicted of violating this provision by burning his card in a protest against "big government," he appeals, claiming that the law is unconstitutional. Which of the following scenarios would be most helpful to his claim?

A. The destruction provision applies *only* to destruction or mutilation done as a means of protest.
B. Legislative history demonstrates that the purpose behind the destruction and mutilation provision was to deter those who might protest the national ID from doing so in that manner.
C. Both A and B.
D. Neither A nor B because O'Brien is solely engaged in conduct, which is not protected by the First Amendment.

ANALYSIS. If you've read this section carefully, you know that you can discard **D**. O'Brien may be engaged in conduct, but that conduct undoubtedly has an expressive element. The question is whether the law is content-based or content-neutral. If, as in **A**, the conduct described applied only to burning or mutilating in protest, that fact would be helpful to O'Brien's case, because the statute would then be not only *content*-based, but *viewpoint*-based, meaning that strict scrutiny would apply. Similarly, if the true purpose behind the statute is to punish protestors, as in **B**, even if the statute is facially neutral, then that, too, would be helpful because it would mean that the purpose was the suppression of ideas. Again, the statute would be reviewed under strict scrutiny. That means that **C** is the best answer.

D. Government-Subsidized Speech and Speech on Government Property

1. *Introduction*

Generally speaking, individuals and private institutions can restrict the speech of their employees, decide what messages they endorse, and control access to their property, along with other rights. Public institutions and other state actors, however, are bound by the First Amendment. So what happens when the *government* attempts to restrict access to its property, control the speech of its employees, refuse to subsidize certain messages, or control the behavior of young people put in its charge? As this chapter makes clear, while governments are usually not completely free to regulate speech when they wear the hat of property owner or employer, neither are they completely fettered by the First Amendment. We'll begin by looking at the government's ability to control access to its property. Then we'll look at the free speech rights in public education, the speech rights of public employees, and the scope of government's right to choose which messages it will support.

2. Government as property owner: the public forum doctrine

Originally, government was held to have the same rights to exclude as private property owners. This view was well expressed by Oliver Wendell Holmes when he was on the Massachusetts Supreme Judicial Court. He wrote that for the government to forbid someone from speaking on a highway or in a public park "is no more an infringement of the rights of a member of the public than for the owner of a private house to forbid it in his house." Massachusetts v. Davis, 162 Mass. 510, 511 (1895). Nearly a half-century later, however, the U.S. Supreme Court repudiated this view; in dicta, Justice Roberts wrote that regardless who held legal title to streets and parks "they have immemorially been held in trust for the use of the public and . . . have been used for purposes of assembly, communicating thoughts between citizens, and discussing public questions." Hague v. CIO, 307 U.S. 496, 515 (1939). This observation spawned what is now known as the "public forum doctrine." The Court has recognized four types of fora, each having its own standard of review for regulations restricting speech. They are summarized below.

Type of Forum	*Definition*	*Example(s)*	*Standard of Review*
Traditional public forum	Government property traditionally available for public expression	Park, street corner	Restrictions on speech must be narrowly tailored to achieve a compelling governmental interest, but may impose time, place, and manner restrictions on speech

Type of Forum	*Definition*	*Example(s)*	*Standard of Review*
Designated public forum	Property the government has opened for expressive activity for all or part of the public or for certain kinds of expressive activity; once it is opened, government is not required to keep forum open	Public meeting hall	Restrictions on speech must be narrowly tailored to achieve a compelling governmental interest
Limited public forum	Any property limited to use by groups or dedicated to discussion of certain subjects	University meeting facilities, city-owned theater	Restrictions permitted that are reasonable and viewpoint-neutral
Nonpublic forum	All remaining public property	Military base, governmental offices, jails and prisons	Regulations must be reasonable and viewpoint-neutral

In an early case, *Perry Educational Association v. Perry Local Educators' Association*, 460 U.S. 37 (1983), the Court upheld restrictions placed on access to teachers' mailboxes. A rival teachers' union sought access as a way to communicate with potential supporters; the existing collective bargaining agreement gave another union the exclusive right to communicate with teachers through the school mail system. *Perry Educational Association*, 460 U.S. at 39-41. Using the classification described in the chart above, the Court concluded that the school mail system was a nonpublic forum, and thus the restrictions on its use need only be reasonable, as long as there is no viewpoint discrimination. *Id.* at 49. Here, the Court concluded, there was no such discrimination. The distinction drawn was between the union designated the official bargaining unit and everyone else. *Id.* at 50-52. Dissenters pointed out, however, that some other groups were permitted access and that the opponents of the current union's positions were excluded from using the mail system. Therefore, they argued that the exclusion was, in effect, viewpoint-based. *Id.* at 55-56 (Brennan, J., dissenting).

QUESTION 25. Park it. A section of Main Street in Ames City is a pedestrian thoroughfare offering easy, traffic-free access to public and private buildings. There is a grassy area in the square in which the city has placed benches. All citizens are encouraged to use the area, and local artists have been allowed to display and sell their artwork there. Occasionally, individuals give speeches near the area, in which many people gather. What term best characterizes the space?

A. A nonpublic forum.
B. A designated public forum.
C. A traditional public forum.
D. A limited public forum.

ANALYSIS. This looks like a trick question, but it isn't. The facts suggest that this area has been there for some time; the City did not just create it. Moreover, the area itself incorporates a pedestrian thoroughfare and a park. The best answer, then, is **C**: This area appears to be a traditional public forum of the sort people have used for expressive activity since, in the Court's words, "time out of mind." **A** is not correct because public access isn't restricted or limited. Neither **B** nor **D** appears to be correct on the facts given. It is not as if the government created the street and park area, then sought to open it or restrict it to certain uses or speakers.

QUESTION 26. Mayor McSqueeze. In response to a series of speakers criticizing the mayor, Ames City passes an ordinance prohibiting political speeches in the park described in Question 25. Which of the following statements about the new ordinance is likely to be true?

A. It would be valid.
B. It would be subject to strict scrutiny.
C. It is a valid time, place, and manner restriction.
D. It is valid as a reasonable restriction on speech.

ANALYSIS. In answering this question it is important to correctly characterize the regulation. An ordinance banning "political speeches" is a content-based regulation; it is not a content-neutral time, place, and manner restriction. Therefore, even if you weren't sure whether the forum at issue was a traditional public forum or a designated public forum, strict scrutiny would still apply. **B**, therefore, is the correct answer. **C** would not be true, for the reasons stated above. **A** is unlikely to be true, because of the high burden the government bears demonstrating that its regulation is narrowly tailored to a compelling governmental interest. **D** misstates the standard of review:

Reasonable regulations of non-viewpoint-based speech restrictions are valid if imposed in *non*public fora.

In two important public forum cases, *International Society for Krishna Consciousness, Inc. v. Lee*, 505 U.S. 672 (1992) (*ISKCON I*), and *Lee v. International Society for Krishna Consciousness, Inc.*, 505 U.S. 830 (1992) (*ISKCON II*), the Court was called on to evaluate the constitutionality of a ban on the solicitation of money and the distribution of leaflets in New York–area airports.

The Court upheld the solicitation ban in airport terminals. Writing for the Court, Chief Justice Rehnquist rejected the notion that airport terminals were traditional public fora. "Reflecting the general growth of the air travel industry, airport terminals have only recently achieved their contemporary size and character. But given the lateness with which the modern air terminal has made its appearance, it hardly qualifies for the description of having 'immemorially . . . time out of mind' been held in the public trust and used for purposes of expressive activity." *ISKCON I*, 505 U.S. at 680. The Court similarly rejected arguments that airport terminals ought to be considered the equivalent of other "transportation nodes" in which expressive activity *had* occurred in the past. Airports had security concerns, among other differences, that rendered them unique, in the Court's opinion. *Id.* at 681-682.

As a nonpublic forum, then, the restrictions need only be reasonable and non-viewpoint-based. The Court felt that the restriction on solicitation was reasonable given the inconvenience to passengers and disruption to business that such solicitations present. *Id.* at 683-684. "In addition, face-to-face solicitation presents risks of duress that are an appropriate target of regulation." *Id.* at 684. The Court noted that the Port Authority permitted solicitation on sidewalk areas outside the terminals, which was "frequented by an overwhelming percentage of airport users." *Id.* In a per curiam opinion, however, the Court upheld the lower court's invalidation of the ban on distribution of literature. *ISKCON II*, 505 U.S. at 831. The Court was badly fractured, however. Justice Kennedy, for example, felt that airport terminals *were* public fora; but he concurred with the solicitation ban as an appropriate time, place, and manner regulation of expressive activity. *ISKCON II*, 505 U.S. at 693 (Kennedy, J., concurring). On the other hand, three Justices, led by Justice Souter, would have invalidated both bans. *ISKCON II*, 505 U.S. at 716 (Souter, J., concurring and dissenting).

The Court, however, upheld a postal regulation barring distribution of literature on a sidewalk connecting the post office to a parking lot used solely by post office customers. United States v. Kokinda, 497 U.S. 720 (1990). The sidewalk was not open to the public and was not, therefore, a traditional public forum. As a reasonable, content-neutral restriction of speech on a nonpublic forum, then, the regulation was upheld.

Other cases involving public property that is not a public forum include *Adderly v. Florida*, 385 U.S. 39 (1966), in which the Court upheld trespass convictions of protestors who blocked a jail entrance used by sheriff's deputies. A plurality of the Court similarly held that public transit vehicles were not a public forum; the Court upheld the public transportation system's refusal to accept paid political advertising on its buses. Lehman v. Shaker Heights, 418 U.S. 298 (1974). The government can also close off access to parts of military bases for "political speakers," on the ground that the base itself is not a public forum, even if portions of it are open to the public. Greer v. Spock, 424 U.S. 828 (1976). Not even Internet access at a public library is a public forum, or so a plurality held in *United States v. American Library Association*, 539 U.S. 194 (2003), in which the Court upheld the requirement that filters be placed on Internet access in public libraries receiving federal money for the provision of such access. As in *ISKCON I*, the Court relied on the recent advent of Internet access to rebut arguments that a "traditional" governmental forum existed. Further, because the library did not acquire Internet access with the intent to open its property as a public forum, it was not a designated or limited public forum either.

In many ways, identifying designated public fora is one of the most difficult areas in an already difficult doctrine. A limited or designated public forum is created when the government agrees to open land up to certain speakers or for certain kinds of events, but not for others. What is clear, however, is that the decision to permit some users or some messages, but not others, cannot be made according to viewpoint. So, for example, a state university may not make its facilities available for groups other than those engaging in "religious worship or religious teaching." Widmar v. Vincent, 454 U.S. 263, 265 (1981). Such viewpoint-based regulations will be subject to strict scrutiny. *See also* Rosenberger v. Rector and Visitors of the University of Virginia, 515 U.S. 819 (1995) (invalidating Virginia's provision of student funds for student publications other than those that were religiously themed).

Widmar has been extended to public elementary and secondary schools. *See, e.g.*, Lamb's Chapel v. Center Moriches Union Free School District, 508 U.S. 384 (1993). In other words, public schools may not permit the chess club to use school facilities during non-instructional time, but deny the Bible club similar use. Milford Central School tried to do just this and, on the strength of cases like *Lamb's Chapel*, the Court held that the school was engaged in impermissible viewpoint discrimination by refusing to allow the Good News Club to use facilities after school. Good News Club v. Milford Central School, 533 U.S. 98 (2001). The school had argued that the exclusion of the Good News Club was required to prevent the school from committing an Establishment Clause violation; the Court rejected that argument.[11]

---

11. The Establishment Clause is discussed in Chapter 7. The Court rejected a similar argument by the University of Virginia in the *Rosenberger* case. *See* 515 U.S. at 839-840 (holding that the Establishment Clause posed no barrier to the school's funding of religiously themed, student-edited publications).

In *Christian Legal Society v. Martinez,* 130 S. Ct. 2971 (2010), the Court upheld the University of California, Hastings College of Law's nondiscrimination policy for student organizations as applied to a group whose national policy was to deny membership to homosexuals. The opportunity to form a registered student organization and enjoy benefits provided to RSOs by the University constituted a limited public forum. The nondiscrimination policy, a majority concluded, was reasonable and viewpoint-neutral. *Martinez,* 130 S. Ct. at 2993. The dissent claimed that the policy that the majority found constitutional was quite different from that which was actively applied to the group. *Id.* at 3004-3005 (Alito, J., dissenting).

The public forum decisions are often confusing—the product of fractured Courts whose majorities failed to agree on the reasons for the decisions. But to sum up, it is helpful to remember that most government property—other than street corners or parks—is either a designated public forum (because the government created it for a particular purpose) or a nonpublic forum (includes all public property that is neither a traditional nor designated public forum). Restrictions of speech in either traditional or designated public fora, other than content-neutral time, place, and manner restrictions, must satisfy strict scrutiny. Restrictions in nonpublic fora must be "reasonable" but cannot be viewpoint-based.

3. *Public education*

The Court has also struggled with the speech rights of students at public schools—at public middle and high schools in particular—and how those should be balanced with the need to keep order and facilitate instruction and education. In *Tinker v. Des Moines School District,* 393 U.S. 503 (1969), the Court reversed the suspension of school-aged children who wore black armbands to school to protest the Vietnam War. Declaring that neither students nor teachers shed their rights at the schoolhouse gates, the Court held that in the absence of evidence that the wearing of armbands either actually or potentially disrupted the school environment, the school's interest in maintaining order did not trump the children's rights to free expression. "There is here no evidence," Justice Fortas wrote, "of petitioners' interference, actual or nascent, with the schools' work or of collision with the rights of other students to be secure and to be let alone." *Tinker,* 393 U.S. at 508. In response to the school's claim that it feared such a disruption, the Court replied that "undifferentiated fear or apprehension of disturbance is not enough to overcome the right to freedom of expression." *Id.* at 508. It also noted that the school permitted the wearing of other symbols, including an Iron Cross, and singled out the students' armbands. *Id.* at 510.

Fifteen years later, the Court returned to the issue in *Bethel School District No. 43 v. Fraser,* 478 U.S. 675 (1986). There it upheld the suspension of a student who gave a nominating speech at a school assembly that was rife with crude—if juvenile—sexual innuendo. Labeling the speech "plainly offensive" to students and teachers, the Court upheld the ability of the school to punish the student for his "vulgar and lewd" speech, especially because his punishment was "unrelated to any political viewpoint." *Fraser*, 478 U.S. at 683, 685. In addition, there was evidence that the speech caused disruption both during and after the assembly. *Id.* at 677-678. Justice Brennan concurred, writing that "in light of the discretion school officials have to teach high school students how to conduct civil and effective public discourse, and to prevent disruption of school educational activities, it was not unconstitutional for school officials to conclude . . . [that Fraser's] remarks exceeded permissible limits." *Id.* at 687-688 (Brennan, J., concurring).

The Court again ruled against students in *Hazelwood School District v. Kuhlmeier*, 484 U.S. 260 (1988), in which it upheld a principal's decisions to spike two stories slated for publication in a high school newspaper: one on teen pregnancy and the other on the effects of divorce on children. Surprisingly, the Court eschewed *Tinker*'s inquiry into the stories' disruptiveness, holding instead that the school newspaper—published as part of a journalism class—was a nonpublic forum, and that speech restrictions therefore need only be reasonable. *Kuhlmeier*, 484 U.S. at 267. "[E]ducators," the Court wrote, "do not offend the First Amendment by exercising editorial control over the style and content of student speech in school-sponsored expressive activities so long as their actions are reasonably related to legitimate pedagogical concerns." *Id.* at 273. The Court found the principal's concern over student privacy (in the teen pregnancy article) and fairness (in a story in which one student criticized her father following her parents' divorce) to be reasonable. *Id.* at 274. It was also reasonable for the principal to be concerned about the appropriateness of the stories' content in light of the age of some of the students at the school. *Id.* In addition, the Court noted that the newspaper also bore the school's imprimatur and was part of the school curriculum. As a result, the school should be able to disassociate itself from work that is either unsuitable for its intended audience or of insufficient quality. *Id.* at 271.

Finally, there is the recent case of *Morse v. Frederick*, 551 U.S. 398 (2007), in which the Court upheld the disciplining of a student who held up a banner at a school social event that read, "BONG HITS 4 JESUS." Though the banner was not disruptive, the school defended its decision to discipline Frederick on the grounds that it was offensive and undermined the school's educational mission. *Morse*, 551 U.S. at 399.

The Court agreed, though on narrower grounds. Instead of synthesizing its prior cases, the Court opted for designating another category of speech—speech encouraging illegal drug use—that schools could punish. The Court specifically rejected the notion that schools had authority to sanction all speech officials found "offensive" or that undermined what the school determined was encompassed by its "educational mission." *Id.* at 406. The Court also refused to apply *Kuhlmeier*, concluding that no reasonable observer could have attributed Frederick's banner to the school. *Id.* at 405.

Concluding that Frederick's banner was an endorsement of drug use, the Court held that the school could punish the speech, even though it was not disruptive, because "deterring drug use by schoolchildren is an 'important—indeed, perhaps compelling' interest" and that "the government interest in stopping student drug abuse . . . allow[s] schools to restrict student expression that they reasonably regard as promoting illegal drug use." *Id.* at 407-408.

In the absence of a unifying principle in the school speech cases, it is probably best to summarize the holdings according to speech that is protected and that which is unprotected by the First Amendment:

Student Speech after *Morse v. Frederick*

Unprotected	*Protected*
• On-campus speech causing widespread disruption • Sexually suggestive or sexually explicit speech in classes or in school assemblies • Speech bearing the school's imprimatur from which the school wishes to disassociate itself • On-campus speech advocating or celebrating the use of illegal drugs	• Otherwise protected speech made off school grounds and not part of school activity or otherwise bearing the school's imprimatur • Non-disruptive, on-campus speech not otherwise unprotected (including speech that administrators merely find offensive)

QUESTION 27. *Hair* today, gone tomorrow. The Ames City High School Drama Club performs two shows a year. Its spring show is, by tradition, a musical. The students have discretion in the selection and production of the performances, but are supervised by a drama teacher. All students receive academic credit for participating in the club. When the principal learns that the students have decided to perform the 1960s musical *Hair*, she orders the students to halt production, citing the play's references to drug use and sex, as well as its nude scene, as inappropriate for a high school–age audience. The students sue the school in federal court, alleging that the principal's actions violate their First Amendment rights to free speech. A reviewing judge should:

A. Order the school to permit the production, unless the school can prove it is disruptive.
B. Order the school to permit the production, because schools may not suppress merely "offensive" speech.
C. Find for the school, because students do not have the same free speech rights as adults.
D. Find for the school, because its concerns about the content were reasonable.

ANALYSIS. The drama production, like the school newspaper, is part of the school curriculum and carries the school's "imprimatur." According to *Kuhlmeier*, that means both that the production is a nonpublic forum and that the school can choose to disassociate itself from inappropriate or poor-quality content. More relevant to the choices listed, the *Kuhlmeier* Court held that the *Tinker* regime did not apply. That eliminates **A** and **B**. Between the remaining answers, **D** is the better one. **C** is not so much wrong as beside the point. True, students do not possess adult free speech rights at school, but neither do they relinquish all rights to free expression.

QUESTION 28. Burger flippin'. Bart, a student at Ames High School, encounters Ken, his biology teacher, at the local KrustyBurger restaurant one day after school has been dismissed. Bart makes an obscene gesture at Ken, whom he does not like; Ken sees Bart do this. At school the next day, Bart is called to the principal's office and suspended for "inappropriate, disrespectful, and vulgar conduct toward school personnel," which is forbidden by the Ames High School code of conduct. If, after Bart files a lawsuit challenging his suspension, a judge rules for him, and orders his suspension lifted and his record cleared, it would likely be because:

A. The school failed to prove that Bart's conduct was disruptive.
B. The school cannot punish conduct it merely found to be offensive.
C. Bart's conduct was fully protected by the First Amendment.
D. None of the above; the school can punish Bart for his obscene gesture.

ANALYSIS. This one was a little trickier. First, recall that Bart is not at school and the incident occurs after school hours. While it is true that Bart's gesture is not disruptive, it's questionable whether that even matters since the student and teacher are not on school grounds during instructional time. **A**, therefore, is not the best answer. **B** is not quite right either. Though *Frederick* held that schools could not claim that speech was "offensive" and then punish it, regardless of its content, *Fraser* at least stands for the proposition that sexually explicit or sexually themed speech during school may be punished, either because it is disruptive or simply because the school can require some standards of decorum from its students. Between the two remaining answers, **C** is the best. Whatever the limits of the school's power over students while in school or at school-sponsored events, none of the cases suggest that the school controls student conduct after instructional time and outside the school building when students are not attending school events. Bart may be in trouble had he done this at a football game, but he is likely off the hook in the KrustyBurger parking lot.

Two other issues are worth mentioning. First, there is reason to believe that many of the grounds restricting the expression of public primary and secondary school students would not apply to students at public universities. *See, e.g.*, Papish v. Board of Curators, 410 U.S. 667 (1973) (voiding expulsion of student for distributing newspaper with political cartoon depicting rape of Statue of Liberty and using vulgar language).

Second, the Court has ruled that schools have some discretion in making acquisition decisions for their libraries, including the removal of books that become the subject of controversy. According to the Court, as long as the school removes the book after a good-faith determination that the material is inappropriate or otherwise unsuitable for its students, the First Amendment has not been violated. Island Trees Union School District v. Pico, 457 U.S. 853 (1982). Removing books because of disagreement with the ideas expressed in them is constitutionally problematic, however. The constitutionality of the removal turns, then, on the state of mind of school officials, which could be difficult to prove.

4. *Public employment*

When government acts as an employer regulating the workplace, it is afforded more leeway in regulating speech. While this power is not unlimited—and certainly not as expansive as the rights of *private* employers to regulate employee speech—recent Court decisions have tended to give more discretion to public employers and have expressed a fear of constitutionalizing public workplace disputes.

Initially, public employees were deemed to have no rights of expression while on the clock. As Justice Holmes put in when he served on the Massachusetts Supreme Judicial Court, a person "may have a constitutional right to talk politics, but he has no constitutional right to be a policeman." McAuliffe v. New Bedford, 155 Mass. 216, 220 (1892). Beginning in the late 1960s, however, the Court acknowledged that, not unlike public school students, public employees cannot be made to surrender their right to free expression in exchange for a government job.

The plaintiff in *Pickering v. Board of Education*, 391 U.S. 563 (1968), was fired for writing a letter to a newspaper criticizing expenditures related to a recent bond issue. For the Court, Justice Marshall wrote that citizens can't be punished for "comment[ing] on matters of public interest in connection with the operation of the public schools in which they work." *Pickering*, 391 U.S. at 568. While acknowledging the right of government as employer to ensure that its employees do the jobs they were hired to do, the Court said that a balance needs to be struck between that interest and the interest of its employees "in commenting upon matters of public concern."[12] *Id.* Absent a showing that the

12. These protections extend not only to formal employees, but to independent contractors as well. *See* Board of Commissioners v. Umbehr, 518 U.S. 668 (1996).

plaintiff's speech had "impeded the teacher's proper performance of his daily duties" or interfered with the operation of the school in general, the employee was permitted to speak his mind about the school board's financial decisions. *Id.* at 573-574.

Following the language in *Pickering*, the Court in *Connick v. Myers*, 461 U.S. 138 (1983), understood the threshold question to be whether an employee was commenting on a matter of public concern. If not, then one does not engage in *Pickering* balancing. At issue in *Connick* was the disciplining of an assistant district attorney upset at reassignment who undertook extensive questioning of her co-workers on a variety of topics, most of which concerned the supervision of the office by the district attorney. *Connick*, 461 U.S. at 140-141. One question, however, asked whether members of the office had felt pressure to work on political campaigns.

According to the Court, when "a public employee speaks not as a citizen upon matters of public concern, but instead as an employee upon matters of personal interest . . . a federal court is not the appropriate forum in which to review the wisdom of a personnel decision taken by a public agency," at least absent unusual circumstances. *Id.* at 147. But the Court nevertheless engaged in *Pickering* balancing, because it felt that the question about pressure to participate in political campaigns *was* a matter of public concern, measured by "the content, form, and context of [the] statement, as revealed by the whole record." *Id.* On the whole, though, much of the employee's speech was "an employee grievance concerning internal office policy." *Id.* at 154. The statements "touched upon matters of public concern only in a most limited sense" and were outweighed, in the Court's opinion, by the district attorney's reasonable belief that her actions "would disrupt the office, undermine his authority, and destroy close working relationships." *Id.*

Later cases seemed to narrow the government's power to restrict the speech rights of lower-level public employees. In *Rankin v. McPherson*, 483 U.S. 378 (1987), a clerical worker in a constable's office was overheard wishing that another assassination attempt on President Ronald Reagan's life would take place and be successful. The employee was discharged and the Court held that the discharge violated the First Amendment. First, the Court noted that the employee was speaking on a matter of public concern. It also noted that she had no "confidential, policymaking, or public contact role" and suggested that absent such roles, government has little interest in suppressing the speech of its employees.

Similarly, in *United States v. National Treasury Employees Union*, 513 U.S. 454 (1995), the Court invalidated a ban on honoraria collected by low-level government employees for speeches and articles. The plaintiff-employees all spoke on matters of public concern unrelated to their government employment. The Court found that the ban constituted a significant burden on speech, which was not outweighed by concerns about abuse and corruption, which is what motivated the ban in the first place, at least as applied to the plaintiffs who were low-level executive branch employees. *National Treasury Employees Union*, 513 U.S. at 468-470.

Recent cases not only confirm that whether speech is a "matter of public concern" is a threshold question that must be answered before a court undertakes *Pickering* balancing, but have also seemed to define "public concern" rather narrowly.

A policeman who wore his uniform while making lewd films that he distributed over the Internet was fired for his actions. San Diego v. Roe, 543 U.S. 77 (2004). The Court upheld his dismissal, noting both that the speech was not on a matter of public concern and that the use of his policeman's uniform could harm his employer. The Court wrote that speech of public concern "is something that is a subject of legitimate news interest; that is, a subject of general interest and of value and concern to the public at the time of publication." *Roe*, 543 U.S. at 83-84.

Then, in *Garcetti v. Ceballos*, 547 U.S. 410 (2006), the Court refused to reverse the discipline of a deputy district attorney who became involved in a dispute within his office about an affidavit used to obtain a search warrant. *Garcetti*, 547 U.S. at 413-415. The question for the Court was whether an employee could be disciplined for speech made pursuant to his official duties. Ceballos argued that the speech was on a matter of public concern and that *Pickering* ought to apply. The Court disagreed, writing that "when public employees make statements pursuant to their official duties, the employees are not speaking as a citizen for First Amendment purposes, and the Constitution does not insulate their comments from employer discipline." *Id.* at 421.[13]

The Court distinguished *Pickering*, noting that the employee's speech there came in the form of a letter to the newspaper. The Court noted that public employees can exercise their First Amendment rights in the public sphere, but observed that "[e]mployers have heightened interest in controlling speech made by an employee in his or her professional capacity." *Id.* at 422. In addition, the Court worried that a contrary rule would enmesh federal courts in countless employee disputes. *Id.* at 423. But the Court qualified its decision with two observations: First, when considering the scope of an employee's duties, courts should consider the realities of the employee's duties and not rely on formal job descriptions. Further, the Court conceded that a different rule might be necessary for professors and teachers, given the independent protection afforded academic freedom by the First Amendment. *Id.* at 424-425.

---

13. The Court recently held that claims brought by public employees pursuant to the First Amendment's Petition Clause would be governed by the rules developed for the Amendment's Free Speech Clause. Borough of Duryea v. Guarnieri, 131 S. Ct. 2488, 2500 (2011) ("The framework used to govern Speech Clause claims by public employees, when applied to the Petition Clause, will protect both the interests of the government and the First Amendment right. If a public employee petitions as an employee on a matter of purely private concern, the employee's First Amendment interest must give way, as it does in speech cases.... When a public employee petitions as a citizen on a matter of public concern, the employee's First Amendment interest must be balanced against the countervailing interest of the government in the effective and efficient management of its internal affairs.").

The Court recently clarified that "[t]ruthful testimony under oath by a public employee outside the scope of his ordinary job duties is speech as a citizen for First Amendment purposes." Lane v. Franks, 2014 WL 2765285 (2014). The petitioner in *Franks* was fired, allegedly in retaliation for testifying against a public official in her corruption trial. *Lane*, 2014 WL 2765285, at *4-*5. Reversing lower court decisions, the Court held that *Pickering*, not *Garcetti*, controlled. Lane's testimony was speech as a citizen because it was outside the scope of his job responsibilities (that is, testifying in court was not part of his job description) even though the subject of his testimony was related to his employment. *Id.* at *8. It was, moreover, a matter of public concern, dealing as it did with "corruption in a public program and misuse of state funds . . . ." *Id.* at *9. Applying the balancing test prescribed by *Pickering*, the Court concluded that "the employer's side of the *Pickering* scale [was] entirely empty" compared with the public interest in ensuring the integrity of programs and probity of those charged with handling public monies. *Id.* at *10.

QUESTION 29. Teaching the teacher. Lois, an untenured public school teacher, wrote a letter to the local newspaper expressing opposition to a pending bill that would substantially reform health care in the United States. When it had been published, her principal told her, "Well, since you hate government so much, why don't you just find a job in the private sector?" and proceeded to dismiss her. Lois sues in federal court, claiming that her dismissal violated the First Amendment. A reviewing judge would likely:

A. Find for the school, because Lois has no right to be a public school teacher.
B. Find for the school, because Lois was not commenting on a matter of public concern.
C. Find for Lois, because her letter in no way inhibited her effectiveness in the classroom.
D. Find for Lois, unless the school can prove that her discipline was the least restrictive means to ensuring her efficacy in the classroom.

ANALYSIS. Unlike the old days, employees aren't completely bereft of constitutional rights when the state is their employer. So **A** is incorrect. *Pickering* et al. give public employees some protection when they speak out on matters of public concern as citizens (as opposed to speaking out on the job about internal, job-related matters). Lois's writing a letter to the newspaper opposing health care reform is certainly a matter of public concern, and she is speaking as a private citizen, not as a teacher. Therefore, **B** is incorrect as well. Moreover, the standard of review mentioned in **D** is what the Court employs to decide whether dismissal because of party affiliation is permissible. That leaves **C**, the best answer: Unless the school could somehow demonstrate that the letter inhibits Lois's efficacy in the classroom, her speech would be protected and a judge would likely find in her favor.

QUESTION 30. Employees on the loose. Adrian works for the Ames Department of Public Health as a nurse. When his supervisor reassigns Adrian against Adrian's wishes, he begins to e-mail his co-workers complaining of the supervisor's dictatorial and high-handed management style. After being warned, Adrian is terminated for insubordination. Adrian sues in federal court, claiming that he was the victim of retaliation for exercising his First Amendment rights. A reviewing judge would likely:

A. Find for Adrian, because there is no evidence that he was a less effective nurse as a result of his speech.
B. Find for Adrian because he lacked a confidential, policymaking, or public contact role.
C. Find for the Department, because Adrian's speech was not about a matter of public concern.
D. Find for the Department, because the state is entitled to regulate the speech of its employees.

ANALYSIS. First, **D** is incorrect, because, as this section illustrates, government's ability to control the speech of its employees is not unlimited, even if it does have more leeway than when regulating the speech of its citizens. The threshold question is whether the employee's speech is on a matter of public concern or is essentially an employment dispute. The facts here, like those in *Connick v. Myers*, appear to point to the latter. **C**, therefore, is the best answer. **A** is incorrect, because the impact of the speech on job performance is an issue only if the speech is a matter of public concern. **B**, which borrows language from *Rankin v. McPherson*, suggests that the state's interest in regulating employees' speech on matters of public concern is not as weighty if the employee lacks a "confidential, policymaking, or public contact role." (Moreover, it might be questioned whether the public health nurse did in fact interact with the public as part of his job.)

A final line of cases involving public employees concern the extent to which employees can be discharged simply because they lack the correct political affiliation. Prior to the advent of civil service protections for government employees, it was common, following an election, for entire offices of employees with the "wrong" party affiliation to be fired. These practices began to change in the twentieth century with statutes like the Hatch Act, which prohibits executive branch officials from actively campaigning.[14]

14. The Hatch Act has been challenged as a violation of the First Amendment, but the challenges were unsuccessful. *See, e.g.*, United States Civil Service Commission v. National Association of Letter Carriers, 413 U.S. 548 (1973); United Postal Workers v. Mitchell, 330 U.S. 75 (1947).

In addition, the Court began to use the First Amendment to restrict dismissal on patronage grounds. According to *Elrod v. Burns*, 427 U.S. 347 (1976), party affiliation may be a basis for dismissal only when it is necessary for the effective performance of an employee's duties.[15] The burden is on the government to prove the connection between job efficacy and party affiliation. *See also* Branti v. Finkel, 445 U.S. 507 (1980) (reversing dismissal of assistant public defenders because they were Republicans). A later decision clarified both that the *Elrod-Branti* rule applied to sanctions that fell short of dismissal and that the test was whether dismissal or sanction for party affiliation was "narrowly tailored to further vital government interests." Rutan v. Republican Party of Illinois, 497 U.S. 62, 74 (1990). Justice Scalia, with two others, dissented, arguing that patronage was a historic practice known to the Framers of the First Amendment and that *Elrod* and *Branti* should be overruled. *Rutan*, 497 U.S. at 94-97 (Scalia, J., dissenting).

QUESTION 31. Controversial professor. Drew Chamberlin, a professor at the public Ames State University, writes an op-ed for the local newspaper in praise of suicide bombers' "resistance" to American and "Zionist" attempts at "hegemony" in the Middle East. He apparently airs these views in his "History of the Middle East" class on a regular basis. Outraged over Chamberlin's statements, as well as a classroom incident in which he publicly berated a returning veteran who took his class as being a "tool of the oppressor class," trustees and members of the public demand Chamberlin's ouster. In response to political pressure, Chamberlin is not fired, but is reassigned to less controversial classes. Chamberlin sues, claiming that his reassignment violates his First Amendment rights. If a judge agrees and orders him reinstated, it would likely be because:

A. Concerns about academic freedom warrant different rules for college professors.
B. Chamberlin was speaking about a matter of public concern.
C. Chamberlin was not speaking as a public employee pursuant to his official duties.
D. The statements had no impact on his efficacy in the classroom.

ANALYSIS. In *Garcetti*, the Court held that public employees making statements pursuant to their official duties were not speaking as citizens for First Amendment purposes. They could be subject to discipline for such statements. This is true even when their statements might conceivably touch on a matter

15. Or an independent contractor's duties. *See* O'Hare Truck Services, Inc. v. Northlake, 518 U.S. 712 (1996) (reinstating tow truck operator taken off the city's "rotation list" of companies to summon for a traffic tow because the operator failed to support the incumbent mayor and supported his opponent).

of public concern. Therefore, **B** is incorrect. **C** may be true in relation to the letter to the editor, but not to the statements made by Chamberlin while he was teaching his class. Finally, it is unclear how much **D** matters if an employee is making statements not as a public citizen, but as a public employee after *Garcetti*. Of the answers, the best one is **A**: The Court suggested in *Garcetti* that different rules have to apply to teachers engaging with controversial subjects as part of their official duties. Presumably, academic freedom allows teachers—particularly university professors—to provoke and even anger when engaging controversial materials.

To recap: Public employees who (1) speak as citizens (2) about matters of public concern (i.e., those matters that are the subject of legitimate news interest or of value and concern to the public when published or made) are entitled to speak without being disciplined as long as their speech (3) does not harm their employer, impede their official duties, or interfere with the operation of the workplace. Further, the absence of "confidential, policymaking, or public contact roles," reduces the government's interest in regulating that employee's speech.

By contrast, a public employee who speaks not as a citizen, but as an employee, about *matters of personal interest* or *pursuant to her official duties* may be disciplined for that speech. The Court is concerned in those instances about judicial interference in the administration of the workplace and management of employees.

Finally, dismissals or other sanctions of public employees (or independent contractors) for party affiliation must be narrowly tailored to further a vital governmental interest. The government has the burden of proving the connection between effective job performance and party affiliation.

5. *Public support for speech*

There is an old saying, "He who pays the piper, calls the tune," meaning that if you're paying someone to do something, you have considerable input into how they perform what you hired them to do. But in constitutional law the state's ability to call the tune is somewhat limited. Government can demand that an advertising agency it hires to design a campaign to increase military recruiting not create a campaign that would *discourage* recruitment. Conversely, simply because government chooses to spend money on, say, a military recruiting campaign, it is not obliged to similarly subsidize a campaign promoting pacifism. *See, e.g.*, Regan v. Taxation with Representation of Washington, 461 U.S. 540 (1983) (upholding federal law denying tax deductions for donations made to charitable organizations that lobby the government; *held*, rules merely reflect Congress's decision not to subsidize lobbying activities by nonprofits and was neither a "penalty" nor an attempt to "suppress dangerous ideas").

On the other hand, government cannot require citizens, as a condition of receiving unemployment benefits, to support the incumbent President and actively campaign against his opponent in an election. *See, e.g.*, Speiser v. Randall, 357 U.S. 513 (1958) (invalidating denial of veteran's property tax benefit to those refusing to state they didn't favor the overthrow of the government).

Balancing the right of government to ensure that taxpayer money is spent wisely on the ends for which it was appropriated, while protecting citizens against coerced surrender of constitutional rights by linking them with government largesse, is the subject of this section. But, as we shall see, the distinction between a constitutional "subsidy" and an impermissible "penalty" is not clear-cut, even for the Court.

This difficulty is illustrated by *FCC v. League of Women Voters*, 468 U.S. 364 (1984), in which the Court invalidated a portion of a law prohibiting public radio or television stations receiving federal money from engaging in "editorializing." The majority saw this as a penalty: stations were barred for expressive activity in exchange for receiving less than 1 percent of their budgets from the federal government. Nor could stations use privately raised funds for editorializing. *League of Women Voters,* 468 U.S. at 400. To the dissenters, however, this was a simple decision not to subsidize such activity, indistinguishable from *Regan.* For them, when "the government is simply exercising its power to allocate its own public funds, we need only find that the condition imposed has a rational relationship to Congress['s] purpose in providing the subsidy and that it is not primarily 'aimed at the suppression of dangerous ideas.'" *Id.* at 407 (Rehnquist, J., dissenting). The disagreements between majority and dissent in these cases turn, as did *League of Women Voters,* on how each side frames the regulation.

Rust v. Sullivan, 500 U.S. 173 (1991), involved restrictions placed by the Department of Health and Human Services (HHS) on recipients of family planning funds (known as Title X funds). Under the restrictions, recipients were prohibited from counseling women about or discussing abortion as a family planning option. They were permitted to offer a range of advice regarding childbirth and prenatal care. *Rust,* 500 U.S. at 178-179. While it was possible for a Title X recipient to provide the proscribed services, there had to be both physical and fiscal separation between the Title X recipient and the portion of the organization providing services that the HHS regulations forbade. Health care providers challenged these regulations as an impermissible penalty on their right to speak freely with patients about health care options.

For the Court, Chief Justice Rehnquist wrote that "[g]overnment can, without violating the Constitution, selectively fund a program to encourage certain activities it believes to be in the public interest, without at the same time funding an alternative program which seeks to deal with the problem in another way." *Id.* at 193. This isn't viewpoint discrimination, the Court explained, but merely a choice "to fund one activity to the exclusion of the other." *Id.* The majority also pointed out that because provision of abortion counseling was permissible if the organization maintained a separation between the Title X parts of the organization and others, the regulations did not condition receipt of benefits on the relinquishment of a constitutional right. *Id.* at 198.

But when the University of Virginia attempted to rely on *Rust* to defend its decision to fund the printing cost of student publications, except for those with an explicitly religious viewpoint, the Court found that refusal violated the First Amendment. Rosenberger v. Rector & Vistitors of University of Virginia, 515 U.S. 819 (1995). The Court labeled the refusal to fund periodicals with explicitly religious editorial viewpoints as constituting viewpoint discrimination. It rejected the analogy to *Rust* because, here, it was not the University of Virginia that was speaking. *Rosenberger*, 515 U.S. at 833-834. "When the government disburses public funds to private entities to convey a governmental message, it may take legitimate and appropriate steps to ensure that its message is neither garbled nor distorted by the grantee," the Court wrote. *Id.* at 833. But "[i]t does not follow [that] viewpoint-based restrictions are proper when the University does not itself speak or subsidize transmittal of a message it favors but instead expends funds to encourage a diversity of views from private speakers." *Id.* at 834. Query: Would the average patient have understood the doctors in *Rust* to be speaking for the federal government?

However when the government makes grants to artists through the National Endowment for the Arts, it may require that the awarding body take account of "general standards of decency and respect for the diverse beliefs and values of the American people." National Endowment for the Arts v. Finley, 524 U.S. 569 (1998). The Court rather unconvincingly held that the standards were merely guidelines that the awarding panel was to "consider" when reviewing grant proposals. It concluded that the government can "allocate competitive funding according to criteria that would be impermissible were direct regulation of speech or a criminal penalty at stake." *Finley*, 524 U.S. at 587-588. Only Justice Souter thought the guidelines constituted *Rosenberger*-like viewpoint discrimination. *Id.* at 613-615 (Souter, J., dissenting).

QUESTION 32. War game. Congress has passed a bill granting veterans of the wars in Afghanistan and Iraq free college or graduate school tuition if they have been honorably discharged from service. However, the grant comes with the condition that recipients must not take part in anti-war protests or otherwise publicly criticize the government's conduct of the war either in speech or in print. Would such a restriction be constitutional?

A. Yes, because it reflects Congress's decision not to subsidize criticism of a war that it is currently prosecuting.
B. No, because it penalizes the speech of recipients.
C. Yes, because there is no constitutional right to receive the education benefit.
D. No, Congress may never use its power of subsidies to restrict the speech of recipients.

ANALYSIS. One touchstone of the government-subsidized speech cases is that conditions may not be meant to suppress "dangerous ideas" or attach penalties to the exercise of constitutional rights. At the same time, the Court has conceded Congress's ability to choose to subsidize certain messages and not others. **D** therefore, cannot be correct. Moreover, simply because one is not entitled to the education benefit does not mean there are no restrictions on government's ability to attach conditions to that benefit if it is created. So **C** is likewise incorrect. Certainly, one way to look at the condition is to say that Congress is merely choosing not to subsidize protest by those who are benefiting from government largesse—that the condition requires recipients not to bite the feeding hand. But **B** is a better answer than **A**, because of the aforementioned rule against suppressing dangerous ideas. Conditioning receipt of federal programs on not criticizing the government is a paradigmatic "unconstitutional condition" that seeks to suppress certain ideas.

Congress prohibited lawyers receiving money from the Legal Services Corporation from challenging existing welfare laws. Specifically, the lawyers agreed not to claim that state law was preempted by federal statutes or that either state or federal welfare laws violated the Constitution. Legal Services Corp. v. Velazquez, 531 U.S. 533 (2001). In a somewhat surprising decision, given the Court's approach in *Rust*, it invalidated the provision. The LSC program, the Court wrote, "was designed to facilitate private speech, not to promote a governmental message. Congress funded LSC grantees to provide attorneys to represent the interests of indigent clients." *Velazquez*, 531 U.S. at 542. Moreover, the Court accused Congress of "us[ing] an existing medium of expression and to control it" by "distort[ing] its usual functioning." *Id.* at 543. "By seeking to prohibit the analysis of certain legal issues and to truncate presentation to the courts, the enactment under review prohibits speech and expression upon which courts must depend for the proper exercise of the judicial power." *Id.* at 545. It is unclear, though, why the "distortion" found by the Court in the LSC regulation didn't apply with the same force to the gag rule at issue in *Rust*, a point made forcefully in Justice Scalia's dissent. *Id.* at 562-563 (Scalia, J., dissenting).

But arguments that the placement of Internet filters on computers at public libraries receiving federal funds to provide such access "distorted" the role of public libraries were unavailing. United States v. American Library Association, 539 U.S. 194 (2003). Instead, a plurality of the Court analogized the filtering requirement to the decision not to subsidize abortion-related services in *Rust*. Libraries have traditionally excluded pornography from their collections; thus "Congress could reasonably impose a parallel limitation on its Internet assistance program." *American Library Association*, 539 U.S. at 212. *Velazquez* was inapposite because "[p]ublic libraries . . . have no comparable role that pits them against the Government," unlike courts and attorneys representing clients. *Id.* at 213.

Finally, the Court held in *Pleasant Grove City v. Summum*, 555 U.S. 460 (2009), that the City of Pleasant Grove, Utah, did not engage in impermissible viewpoint discrimination when it refused to accept a religious sect's offer of a monument to display in a public park. The Court concluded that by accepting some monuments, the city had not created a public forum open to all comers; rather, it was choosing which messages to make its own by accepting the monuments. Because the government was, in a sense, the speaker, "the Free Speech Clause has no application." *Pleasant Grove*, 555 U.S. at 467.

The Court's approach to government-subsidized speech is not a model of consistency. As noted above, framing is everything; many cases, moreover, can be framed in multiple ways, producing different results. One commentator has suggested that there are a couple of generalizations that emerge from the cases: "First, the government is entitled to hire people to present its own views. . . . Second, the government cannot condition a completely unrelated benefit on speech activities." Daniel A. Farber, The First Amendment 203 (3d ed. 2010). As for the hard cases in between these extremes, Farber suggests that "[t]he basic principle seems to be that the government can condition use of its facilities or employment on forbearance from speech that interferes with the purpose of the government program," with government having "to make a plausible claim that particular speech falls outside the legitimate scope of the program." *Id.* The catch is determining whether or not "the government's definition of the program has been distorted by impermissible hostility to disfavored ideas." *Id.*

Recently, the Court attempted to harmonize its cases. In *Agency for Int'l Development v. Alliance for Open Society Int'l, Inc.*, 133 S. Ct. 2321 (2013), the Court invalidated a portion of a congressional act that made funds available for combatting HIV/AIDS worldwide, but conditioned receipt of the money on (1) prohibiting grant recipients from using the funds to advocate for the legalization of prostitution or sex trafficking and (2) requiring recipients to have an explicit policy opposing prostitution and sex trafficking. *Alliance for Open Society*, 133 S. Ct. at 2322. The Court invalidated the second requirement as unconstitutional forced speech. Summarizing its cases, the Court held that "the relevant distinction that has emerged from our cases is between conditions that define the limits of the government spending program—those that specify the activities Congress wants to subsidize—and conditions that seek to leverage funding to regulate speech outside the contours of the program itself." *Id.* at 2328. The Court distinguished *Rust* by noting that there the recipients had the opportunity to engage in the proscribed speech if it was conducted by an entity that did not receive any of the federal funds. *Id.* at 2331. The invalidated regulation, by contrast, prohibited grant recipients from deviating from the government's message, even if it used private money.

E. Overbreadth, Vagueness, and Prior Restraints

This section addresses doctrines used to invalidate statutes that either cover constitutionally protected activity along with activity that government may regulate (overbreadth) or give insufficient detail as to what is and is not permissible under the law (vagueness). Both doctrines have special purchase when it comes to speech and expression. This section also addresses the problem of prior restraints, whereby speech or expression is enjoined before it occurs. Owing in part to the experience of the Framers, prior restraints are regarded with profound skepticism by the Court.

1. *Overbreadth*

Substantially overbroad statutes are unconstitutional. "An overbroad statute regulates constitutionally unprotected conduct by also regulating protected conduct." Calvin Massey, American Constitutional Law: Powers and Liberties 973 (4th ed. 2013). In *Broadrick v. Oklahoma*, 413 U.S. 601 (1973), the Court upheld an Oklahoma statute prohibiting civil servants from taking part in the management or affairs of political parties or of any political campaign except to vote or privately express an opinion. The law also barred civil servants from soliciting political campaign contributions. *Broadrick*, 413 U.S. at 602. Plaintiffs claimed that the statute was overbroad, that it potentially barred things such as wearing campaign buttons or having a bumper sticker on one's car. *Id.* at 609-610. The plaintiffs themselves, however, were charged with impermissibly soliciting campaign contributions and conceded that their activities could constitutionally be regulated. Nevertheless, they claimed the right to escape punishment because of what they argued was the statute's overbreadth. (Overbreadth challenges are something of an exception to the usual rule that litigants can't raise claims of third parties. Plaintiffs alleging overbreadth can challenge a statute on its face, even when it is clear that the plaintiffs' conduct may constitutionally be regulated.)

The Court was unsympathetic. While acknowledging the First Amendment's need for "breathing space" and noting that statutes burdening First Amendment rights "must be narrowly drawn and represent a considered legislative judgment that a particular mode of expression has to give way to other compelling needs of society," the Court thought that a narrow construction of the law was available here. *Id.* at 611-612. A statute must thus not only be overbroad, but be *substantially* overbroad to permit plaintiffs like those in *Broadrick* to invoke that doctrine and escape punishment when there is consensus their actions were covered and could be regulated by the state. *Id.* at 615. The law here, the Court concluded, was not substantially overbroad. It sought "to regulate political activity in an even-handed and neutral manner" and "regulates a substantial spectrum of conduct that is . . . subject to state regulation. . . ." *Id.* at 616. The examples invoked by the plaintiffs, the Court concluded, could be dealt with on a case-by-case basis, presumably through as-applied challenges. *Id.* at 622.

Two other cases illustrate the possibilities. *Village of Schaumburg v. Citizens for a Better Environment*, 444 U.S. 620 (1980), concerned an ordinance banning in-person solicitation by an organization that used less than 75 percent of its contributions for charitable purposes. The Court invalidated the ordinance, holding that the justification (prevention of fraud)—while substantial—was not sufficiently related to the charitable use requirement. It was also unable to effect a narrowing construction on the ordinance.

In *Brockett v. Spokane Arcades, Inc.*, 472 U.S. 491 (1985), by contrast, the Court narrowly construed an obscenity law regulating material that "incites lasciviousness and lust"[16] and invalidated it as applied to the Arcade, an adult bookstore, despite the bookstore's facial challenge. The Court concluded that because a narrowing construction was available to the Arcade, the Court was not required to invalidate the ordinance in toto. *Spokane Arcades*, 472 U.S. at 506.

QUESTION 33. LAX rules. The Los Angeles Airport Commission adopted a regulation prohibiting "First Amendment activities within the Central Terminal Area at Los Angeles International Airport." A group of plaintiffs, including a group that wished to proselytize passengers inside the terminal, challenged the ordinance on its face as a violation of the First Amendment. A reviewing judge should:

A. Uphold the regulation, because proselytizing is not protected by the First Amendment.
B. Uphold the regulation as long as a narrowing construction is possible.
C. Invalidate the ordinance as applied to the proselytizing plaintiffs.
D. Invalidate the ordinance on its face as substantially overbroad.

ANALYSIS. Believe it or not, these are the facts of an actual case, *Board of Airport Commissioners of Los Angeles v. Jews for Jesus, Inc.*, 482 U.S. 569 (1987). It is difficult to imagine a more substantially overbroad regulation—it would prohibit reading, talking, or even silently wearing a message-carrying T-shirt or button! Given the breadth of the regulation (i.e., it specifically prohibits "all First Amendment activities"), it is hard to imagine how a court could adopt a narrowing construction. Therefore, **D** is the best answer. **A** is not correct: Proselytizing *is* protected by the First Amendment. **B** isn't the best answer for the reason given above: A narrowing construction doesn't seem to be available. If a narrowing construction is not available, then plaintiffs should be able to mount a facial challenge to the regulation, meaning that **C** isn't the best answer either.

---

16. The ordinance's definition did not follow the *Miller* standard, described in section B.6 of this chapter.

QUESTION 34. Houston, we have a problem. A Houston ordinance makes it illegal to "assault, strike, or in any manner oppose, molest, abuse, or interrupt any policeman in the execution of his duty." While a policeman was questioning his friend, Hill shouted, "Why don't you pick on someone your own size?" and was arrested and charged with violating the ordinance. On appeal, a reviewing court should:

A. Sustain the conviction, because the purpose of the ordinance is to protect police officers, not to chill freedom of expression.
B. Sustain the conviction, because the ordinance reaches only criminal conduct unprotected by the First Amendment.
C. Reverse the conviction, because the ordinance regulates speech.
D. Reverse the conviction, because the ordinance covers constitutionally protected expression.

ANALYSIS. These facts are also based on a real case, *City of Houston v. Hill*, 482 U.S. 451 (1987). In *Hill* the Court invalidated the ordinance as overbroad, noting that it both reached quite a bit of protected speech and raised the specter of selective enforcement by vesting in police nearly unfettered discretion to arrest people who annoy them. Even if you weren't familiar with the case, though, you could have worked your way through the distracters to the correct answer. **A** and **C** are red herrings. It may not be the *intent* of the ordinance to chill expression, but that's rather beside the point. The fact of the matter is that is precisely what the ordinance effectively does. Similarly, as you're probably aware by now, not every regulation of speech is unconstitutional. **B** is not correct because is mischaracterizes the ordinance, which prohibits "oppos[ing]" or even "interrupt[ing]" a police officer. That means the officer could arrest you for asking for directions, if he thought you were interrupting him in the execution of his duties. **D**, thus, is the best answer—and the one the Court gave for striking the ordinance down on its face.

2. *Vagueness*

An unconstitutionally vague statute requires "persons of common intelligence [to] necessarily guess at its meaning and differ as to its application." Connally v. General Construction Co., 269 U.S. 385, 391 (1926). Laws must provide "sufficiently definite warning as to the proscribed conduct when measured by common understanding and practices," or else they are vague and deny those prosecuted under them due process of law. Jordan v. De George, 341 U.S. 223 (1951). For example, in *Smith v. Goguen*, 415 U.S. 566 (1974), the Court invalidated as vague a law criminalizing contemptuous treatment of the U.S. flag in public.

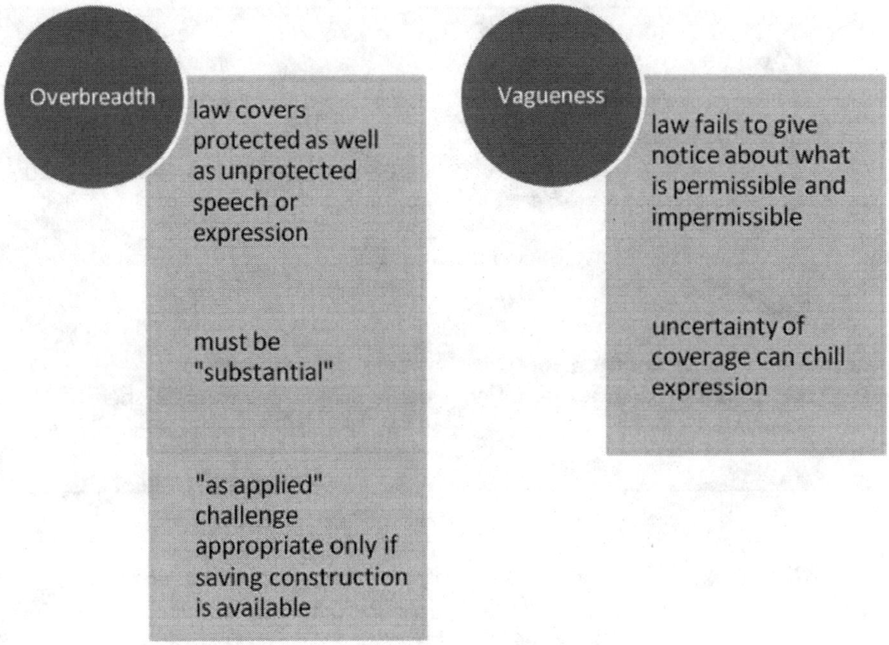

Overbreadth and Vagueness at a Glance

Vague laws are of particular concern where free expression comes into play because of the potential for such laws to chill expression and invite covert viewpoint-based prosecutions. As a doctrine, vagueness often overlaps with overbreadth. *See, e.g.,* Coates v. Cincinnati, 402 U.S. 611 (1971), in which the Court invalidated an ordinance that prohibited three or more people from congregating on a street corner and annoying passersby. The Court found the ordinance to be vague because it "subject[ed] the exercise of the right of assembly to an unascertainable standard, and unconstitutionally broad because it authorizes the punishment of constitutionally protected conduct." *Coates,* 402 U.S. at 614. *See also* Federal Communications Comm'n v. Fox Television Stations, 132 S. Ct. 2307, 2317-2318 (2012) (holding that FCC's indecency policy was unconstitutionally vague because it failed to provide fined broadcasters with sufficient notice of what was proscribed).

3. *Prior restraint*

A prior restraint is "an administrative or judicial order that prohibits speech before it occurs, and it does so on the basis of the speech's content." Calvin Massey, American Constitutional Law: Powers and Liberties 1075 (4th ed. 2013). Prior restraints are disfavored by the Supreme Court and are presumptively void. Many historians believe that whatever else the First Amendment was meant to do, it was meant to curb the practice of prior restraint, though not necessarily to immunize the speaker or publisher from liability after publication. The most common forms of prior restraints are licensing regimes and injunctions. Licensing regimes require would-be speakers to get permission from governmental authorities before engaging in speech or expression. Injunctions are court orders that prohibit speech or expression from taking place. Both are regarded with skepticism by the Court.

(a) Licensing The Supreme Court has invalidated licensing laws that confer unlimited discretion on governmental officials to grant or withhold permission to engage in First Amendment activities. The fear is that such discretion might be abused, resulting in the silencing of unpopular speakers in a form of hidden viewpoint-based discretion. *See, e.g.,* Lovell v. Griffin, 303 U.S. 444 (1938). In a later case, *Lakewood v. Plain Dealer Publishing Co.,* 486 U.S. 750 (1988), the Court invalidated a law empowering the mayor to license news racks on the sidewalk on terms the mayor "deemed necessary and reasonable." Such standardless discretion, the Court held, was always facially invalid. *Lakewood,* 486 U.S. at 769.

Four years later the Court applied *Lakewood* to a Georgia county ordinance granting the county administrative discretion to vary license fees for parades or protests according to the expected expense of preserving the public peace. Forsyth Cnty. v. The Nationalist Movement, 505 U.S. 123 (1992). The Court noted that this could impose a heckler's veto, in effect, over unpopular speakers or marchers who could attract a hostile or unruly crowd.

Conversely, when government officials charged with issuing licenses have their discretion cabined by standards, the Court is more tolerant, unless the regime is applied in a discriminatory manner. *See, e.g.,* Cox v. New Hampshire, 312 U.S. 569 (1941) (upholding time, place, and manner rules regarding protests).

Once upon a time, motion picture exhibiters were required to obtain permission from local government licensing boards before running movies, to ensure the movies weren't obscene. While conceding that local governments had the power to require pre-screening of movies, the Court in *Freedman v. Maryland,* 380 U.S. 51 (1965), required procedural safeguards to ensure that the discretion employed by government censors wasn't standardless. The Court required that the censor have the burden of proving the movie was obscene, and that only a judicial finding of obscenity could justify an order that the movie not be exhibited. *Freedman,* 380 U.S. at 58. *Freedman,* however, applies when the licensing requirement is content-based. *Thomas v. Chicago Park District,* 534 U.S. 316 (2002), held that a content-neutral permit ordinance did not raise the censorship concerns that motivated the Court to lay down the procedural rules it did in *Freedman. Thomas,* 534 U.S. at 322-323. However, the Court stressed that "time, place, and manner regulation[s] contain adequate standards to guide the official's decision and render it subject to effective judicial review." *Id.* at 323. The Court again stressed that unfettered discretion raised the specter of content-based regulation by regulators that could go undetected. *Id.* at 324.

QUESTION 35. **Mayor, may I?** After Ames City dedicated its new park, the Mayor's office promulgated rules and regulations regarding its use. Concerts, rallies, protests, and other mass gatherings required permission and payment of a fee to cover the costs of clean-up and security. The City Manager had authority to deny permits if, based on objective evidence, the gathering was unlawful or dangerous, or was likely to result in serious damage to the park or severely impede other users' enjoyment of the park. Decisions of the City Manager could be appealed to the Mayor directly. When the Big Cat Owners of Ames City were denied a permit to host their annual Big and Exotic Cat Show in the park on the ground that having so many large cats (including tigers, ocelots, and panthers) in an enclosed area would pose a danger to both attendees and the public at large, the BCOAC filed suit in district court, claiming that the denial violated their First Amendment rights. A reviewing court would likely:

A. Uphold the permit regulation as a valid time, place, and manner regulation that sufficiently limits discretion.
B. Uphold the permit regulation because there is a right to appeal to the Mayor.
C. Invalidate the permit regulation because it vests the City Manager with standardless discretion.
D. Invalidate the permit regulation as an invalid prior restraint on speech.

ANALYSIS. Remember that the difference between a permissible time, place, and manner restriction on speech and impermissible prior restraint often turns on the extent to which the discretion to grant or withhold the license is confined by some criteria. Here the City Manager does have the ability to deny a permit, *but* the regulation goes on to specify the grounds for which denial is appropriate. Thus, **C** is incorrect. Further, the Manager must base the decision on "objective evidence" *and* there is an appeal to the Mayor—though, contrary to the suggestion in **B**, this would not be enough by itself to sustain a regulation that does not constrain discretion. **D** is incorrect largely for the same reason as **C**: A valid time, place, and manner regulation is not a prior restraint on speech. That leaves **A**, which is the best answer.

(b) Injunctions For a court to issue an order, which one must obey or be held in contempt of court, is a serious matter; injunctions restraining publication or expression will be upheld only under the most serious of circumstances. The Court was reluctant to uphold an order enjoining publication even before it was otherwise robustly enforcing the First Amendment. *Near v. Minnesota*, 283 U.S. 697 (1931), arose when a judge enjoined a newspaper from publishing after it ran a series of articles alleging wrongdoing and corruption in Minneapolis. (A prosecutor sought the injunction based on a state law prohibiting the mailing of "malicious, scandalous and defamatory" newspapers.)

The Court quashed the order, suggesting that only the most dire of situations justified prior restraints. "No one would question," wrote the Court, "that a government might prevent actual obstruction to its recruiting service or the publication of the sailing dates of transports or the number and location of troops." *Near*, 283 U.S. at 716. Similarly, government may seek to prevent obscenity or "incitements to acts of violence and the overthrow by force of orderly government." *Id.* But none of those situations were present in the facts before it. While baseless charges of corruption against public officials are not without cost, the fact that freedoms can be abused was not a license to engage in prior restraint, the Court concluded. Libel and defamation penalties, the Court felt, could adequately compensate victims after the fact. That truth was a defense would do nothing to sustain the ordinance, because of the potential chilling effect on publishers, the Court held. *Id.* at 722-723.

So what *would* warrant a prior restraint on publication? Many of *Near*'s examples concerned national security (sailing of transports, number and location of troops); but, as *New York Times v. United States*, 403 U.S. 713 (1971), demonstrated, simply invoking "national security" was insufficient for the Court to bar publication of the so-called Pentagon Papers, a detailed historical examination of the United States' role in Vietnam dating back to the late 1940s. A divided court ruled that the government had not presented enough evidence to enable it to overcome the presumption against prior restraint, though the Justices had different opinions regarding what evidence would have sufficed. A few years later, though, a district court enjoined the *Progressive* from publishing what the judge termed a "recipe for a nuclear bomb" in its pages. United States v. Progressive, Inc., 467 F. Supp. 990 (W.D. Wis. 1979).

Finally, the Court has rejected attempts to restrain publication of information regarding an ongoing criminal trial ordered by a judge in the name of preserving the defendant's right to a fair trial. Nebraska Press Association v. Stuart, 427 U.S. 539 (1976). While conceding that a judge might be faced with the need to issue a prior restraint to preserve a defendant's fair trial rights, the Court felt in this case that the judge had not explored alternatives such as change of venue, postponement, jury sequestration, and the like, which would not have occasioned the need to issue the injunction. *Nebraska Press Association*, 427 U.S. at 563-564. These alternatives, along with the probability of an unfair trial and the efficacy of the prior restraint in ensuring a fair trial, were the factors the Justices suggested should guide trial judges in similar situations. *Id.* at 565.

F. Implicit Rights of Free Expression

1. *Right to associate*

Implicit in the right to freely express oneself is the right to associate with like-minded people and, by extension, to exclude from one's group those with whom one does *not* wish to associate. Similarly, the Court has recognized that one has a right not to be associated with certain messages. This section addresses these implicit rights of free expression: the right of association and the right not to have the government put words in one's mouth.

For example, the Court held in *NAACP v. Alabama*, 357 U.S. 449 (1958), that Alabama could not force the NAACP to disclose its membership list because of the danger that forced disclosure would expose those members to discrimination, harassment, and possibly physical violence. "[F]reedom to engage in association for the advancement of beliefs and ideas," the Court wrote, was "an inseparable aspect [of] freedom of speech." *NAACP*, 357 U.S. at 460. The Court found Alabama's interest—allegedly to determine whether the group was conducting business in the state without having registered as a foreign corporation—was not sufficiently compelling to overcome the presumption against disclosure. *Id.* at 465.

On the other hand, the Court upheld disclosures of campaign contributions required by the Federal Election Campaign Act. Buckley v. Valeo, 424 U.S. 1 (1976) (per curiam). While subjecting the disclosure requirements to "exacting scrutiny," the Court found three interests sufficiently important to sustain the act: (1) informing voters of the source of campaign funds, (2) deterring corruption and the appearance of corruption, and (3) gathering data to detect violations of rules governing contribution limits. *Buckley*, 424 U.S. at 66-68. The Court found that the disclosure rules directly advanced the "substantial governmental interests" behind disclosure.

In addition to the core political associational interests protected in *NAACP* and *Buckley*, the Court has recognized that one has associational rights that don't involve political advocacy or activism. These rights can sometimes be forced to give way when balanced against other important society interests, however. In general, the Court subjects laws requiring admission to expressive groups and requiring speech to strict scrutiny. To override individual free expression rights, the government must demonstrate that its law is narrowly tailored to some compelling governmental interest.

The issue in *Roberts v. United States Jaycees*, 468 U.S. 609 (1984), was whether a Minnesota antidiscrimination law barring places of public accommodation from discriminating on the basis of sex could be enforced against a private male-only organization. A state court had concluded that the Jaycees, which excluded women from membership at the time, were a place of public accommodation and thus subject to the state human rights act. The U.S. Supreme Court concluded that the application of the act to the group was permissible.

First, the Court distinguished the rights of intimate association recognized in cases involving the family from what it termed the "freedom of expressive association" at issue in the case. The former involved "the formation and preservation of certain kinds of highly personal relationships" in groups that were small, selective, and exclusive. *Roberts*, 468 U.S. at 618-620. The latter, like the Jaycees, involved associations that were "large and basically unselective groups" involving "the participation of strangers." *Id.* at 621. The Court recognized even this form of association as "implicit in the right to engage in activities protected by the First Amendment" and acknowledged that such a right was "plainly implicated in this case." *Id.* at 622.

The Court went on to detail the ways in which government could interfere with the right. It could, for example, "impose penalties or withhold benefits from individuals because of their membership in a disfavored group. . . ." In the alternative, it could "require disclosure of the fact of membership in a group favoring anonymity" or "interfere with the internal organization or affairs of the group." *Id.* at 622-623. Here, the state was doing the last of these things. "There can be no clearer example of an intrusion into the internal structure of affairs of an association than a regulation that forces the group to accept members it does not desire." *Id.* at 623.

However, the Court also held that the association rights of groups could be infringed if the state's regulations "serve[d] compelling state interests, unrelated to the suppression of ideas, that cannot be achieved through means significantly less restrictive of associational freedoms." *Id.* The Court was convinced that the state's "compelling interest in eradicating discrimination against its female citizens justifie[d] the impact" on the group's associational freedom. *Id.* The state was not trying to suppress particular viewpoints and, in any event, "the Jaycees . . . failed to demonstrate that the Act imposes any serious burdens on the male members' freedom of expressive association," though it was unclear why it was the group's responsibility to bear that burden. *Id.* at 626.Perhaps more important for the Court was its conclusion that requiring the admission of women "impose[d] no restrictions on the organization's ability to exclude individuals with ideologies or philosophies different from those of its existing members." *Id.* at 627. Later cases upheld application of *Roberts* to the Rotary Club, *Board of Directors of Rotary International v. Rotary Club of Duarte*, 481 U.S. 537 (1987), and to private clubs in New York City whose membership exceeded 400 and that provided meal service. New York State Club Association v. New York, 487 U.S. 1 (1988).

QUESTION 36. Going clubbing. Following the *Roberts* decision, a group of former Jaycees resign and form another club dedicated to the proposition that men are best suited to the world of work and that women should stick to maintenance of the domestic sphere. This club, the PeeGees, does not admit women as members and promotes the business interests of its members. Could a state with a human rights act similar to Minnesota's validly enforce it against the PeeGees, assuming that the club, as was the Jaycees, is found to be a place of public accommodation?

A. Yes, the state still has a compelling interest in eliminating discrimination.

B. Yes, because associational rights do not include the right to discriminate against others.

C. No, because the ban does not plainly serve any valid compelling state interest.

D. No, because enforcement of the statute against the PeeGees would impede the group's ability to disseminate its views.

ANALYSIS. Remember that the Court in *Roberts* held that there was nothing inherent in the Jaycees that prevented the granting of full membership to women. Here, on the other hand, it appears that the PeeGees were established with the *purpose of* excluding women because of its members' beliefs about the proper roles of men and women. The question isn't so much whether the state has a continuing interest in the elimination of discrimination, as suggested by **A**, but whether that interest can override the associational freedoms of the PeeGees. **B** is not the best answer, because it is not correct: Associational freedoms *do* include the right to exclude, in some circumstances, those who do not subscribe to your message or who otherwise inhibit the transmission of your message. **C** is not correct either. *Roberts* said that the elimination of discrimination *is* a compelling state interest. That leaves **D**, which is the best answer: Forcing a group to admit women as full members, when that group was established for the purpose of advocating for the *exclusion* of women from the business sphere, would likely inhibit it in the spreading of its message.

The foregoing question provides a good segue into the case of *Boy Scouts of America v. Dale*, 530 U.S. 640 (2000), in which the Court reversed the New Jersey Supreme Court's finding that the Boy Scouts had violated state antidiscrimination law when it discharged an openly gay assistant scoutmaster. The Court held that a group's engaging in any expressive activity was sufficient to trigger the protections of the First Amendment—it need not have been constituted for the express purpose of engaging in that particular expressive activity. *Dale*, 530 U.S. at 655. Therefore, the Court held that the BSA's urging that its members lead "clean" and "morally straight" lives was sufficiently incompatible with homosexuality to significantly affect its ability to communicate its viewpoint. *Id.* at 652-653. This meant that, unlike the situation in *Roberts*, the compelling interest in eliminating discrimination could *not* override the Boy Scouts' associational freedoms. *Id.* at 656. The dissenters disputed the notion that hostility to homosexuality was part of the Scouts' core message. *Id.* at 665 (Stevens, J., dissenting).

When law schools and their faculties tried to make use of *Dale* to justify excluding military recruiters from their campuses because of the military's policy against permitting service by openly gay servicemen and women, the Court balked. Rumsfeld v. Forum for Academic and Institutional Rights, Inc., 547 U.S. 47 (2006). The Solomon Amendment made funding for colleges and universities contingent on granting military recruiters the same access to school facilities and students as other recruiters. The Forum for Academic and

Institutional Rights (FAIR) complained that this violated a school's right to exclude those who interfered with its antidiscrimination message. *FAIR*, 547 U.S. at 52-53.

The Court first noted that the Solomon Amendment was addressed primarily at conduct, not speech. *Id.* at 57. Schools, the Court pointed out, were free to say anything they wished—as long as they offered military recruiters the same access as other recruiters. This led to a second point: Unlike the case in *Dale*, the Court reasoned, schools' associational rights were not affected. "To comply with the statute, law schools must allow military recruiters on campus and assist them in whatever way the school chooses to assist other employers. Law schools therefore 'associate' with military recruiters in the sense that they interact with them. But recruiters are not part of the law school." *Id.* at 69. They are, by definition, outsiders and don't enter the law school in order to become a part of its expressive community. "Unlike the public accommodations law in *Dale*, the Solomon Amendment does not force a law school 'to accept members it does not desire.'" *Id.*

The contours of the Court's associational jurisprudence can be stated with some certainty. First, the First Amendment is implicated when a group engages in expressive activity (speech or conduct), even if it was not constituted for the sole purpose of propagating a particular message. If government attempts to force a group to associate with persons or messages that severely impinge on the group's ability to communicate that message, then the associational rights of the group will generally trump even a compelling governmental interest. If, however, the impact on the ability of the group to communicate its message is slight or if the government's regulation does not require a group to incorporate persons into its expressive community, then the associational rights will generally give way to any compelling governmental interest that can be demonstrated.

2. *Forced speech*

Just as government generally can't prohibit individuals from speaking, it can't *force* citizens to speak either. As Justice Robert Jackson put it in *West Virginia State Board of Education v. Barnette*, 319 U.S. 624 (1943), when the Court invalidated West Virginia's mandatory flag salute law: "If there is any fixed star in our constitutional constellation, it is that no official, high or petty, can prescribe what shall be orthodox in politics, nationalism, religion, or other matters of opinion or force citizens to confess by word or act their faith therein." *Barnette*, 319 U.S. at 642.[17] He concluded that "compelling the flag salute and

17. *Barnette* represented a fairly dramatic reversal from *Minersville School District v. Gobitis*, 310 U.S. 586 (1940). Decided just three years prior, the *Gobitis* Court had upheld a similar law. The plaintiffs in both cases were Jehovah's Witnesses who objected to what they saw as worshiping graven images. Jehovah's Witness children were expelled for failing to salute the flag—subjecting them to being adjudicated delinquent, and their parents to fines and imprisonment for not having their children enrolled in school.

pledge transcends constitutional limitations on [official] power and invades the sphere of intellect and spirit which it is the purpose of the First Amendment to our Constitution to reserve from all official control." *Id.*

Nearly 35 years later, the Court again vindicated the rights of Jehovah's Witnesses when it held that New Hampshire could not prosecute someone for covering up a portion of the state license plate reading "Live Free or Die." Wooley v. Maynard, 430 U.S. 705 (1977). The defendants were accused of violating a state law prohibiting the "obscuring" of the state motto. The Court framed the question as whether "the State may constitutionally require an individual to participate in the dissemination of an ideological message by displaying it on his private property in a manner and for the express purpose that it be observed and read by the public." *Wooley*, 430 U.S. at 713.

Deciding that the state could not, the Court rooted the right *not* to speak in the First Amendment as interpreted by *Barnette.* "The right to speak and the right to refrain from speaking are complementary components of the broader concept of 'individual freedom of mind.'" *Id.* at 714. The state, the Court observed, was presenting the defendants with a choice: "use their private property as a 'mobile billboard' for the State's ideological message—or suffer a penalty. . . ." *Id.* at 715. Applying strict scrutiny, the Court concluded that the state's interests—facilitating the identification of vehicles and promoting "appreciation of history individualism, and state pride"—were either insufficiently compelling or inconsistent with the First Amendment. *Id.* at 716-717.

First, the Court noted that the license plates "normally consist of a specific configuration of letters and numbers, which makes them readily distinguishable from other types of plates, even without reference to the state motto." *Id.* at 716. Moreover, the appreciation-of-history interest was not "ideologically neutral," according to the Court. Though the state may do this in some ways, it may not do so by trammeling "an individual's First Amendment right to avoid becoming the courier for such message." *Id.* at 717.

QUESTION 37. A penny for your thoughts. The U.S. Code prohibits the defacing of U.S. currency. Madelyn, an atheist, is incensed by the words "In God We Trust," which appear on U.S. coins and currency. She scratches those words out on coins, and marks through them on bills with a permanent marker. She is charged with and convicted of defacing U.S. currency; she appeals her conviction, claiming that carrying money with the motto violated her First Amendment rights. If a reviewing court rules against Madelyn, it would likely be because:

A. Protecting the integrity of United States currency as a valuable medium of exchange is a compelling governmental purpose.

B. Unlike license plates on personal cars, money changes hands frequently and does not force an individual to serve as a billboard for the state.

C. Laws against currency's defacement are narrowly tailored to the compelling governmental purpose of protecting the integrity of United States currency.
D. Any of the above.

ANALYSIS. The best answer is **D**. In a footnote to *Wooley*, the Court distinguished the "In God We Trust" motto from the license plates by noting that, unlike license plates, which are affixed to personal property, money is a medium that we pass back and forth freely. The latter qualities of currency, for the Court, suggested that it was not as "personal" as a motto you were required to carry around with you at all times on your property. (Moreover, though the Court didn't mention it, Madelyn could avoid using money by, say, using credit cards or writing checks.) Further, even if a court were to apply strict scrutiny, a likely compelling purpose would be to prevent counterfeiting or other things that could impair the integrity of U.S. currency; prohibiting defacement would be narrowly tailored to that purpose. **A**, **B**, and **C**, therefore, are all possible reasons for rejecting Madelyn's suit.

The California Public Utilities Commission required private utilities to include messages from another private organization critical of utilities and their rate-making procedures. Pacific Gas & Electric Co. v. Public Utilities Comm'n, 475 U.S. 1 (1986). Pacific Gas & Electric (PG&E) objected, claiming that the First Amendment barred the state from forcing it to be associated with messages with which it disagreed. The Court agreed and invalidated the Commission's order.

The Court framed the issue as one of "compelled access" that "both penalizes the expression of particular points of view and forces speakers to alter their speech to conform with an agenda they do not set." *PG&E*, 475 U.S. at 9. The Court found that the Commission's order was viewpoint-based, and "limited to persons or groups . . . who disagree with [PG&E's] views [and] who oppose [PG&E] in Commission proceedings." *Id.* at 13. Because access is triggered by PG&E's taking a position on particular issues, the Court concluded that the forced access could have a chilling effect on PG&E's free expression rights.

Again applying strict scrutiny, the Court considered the Commission's justifications, rejecting each in turn. While conceding that the State's "interest in fair and effective utility regulation may be compelling," it held that the state could pursue that in ways other than burdening PG&E's First Amendment rights—by subsidizing advocacy groups, for example. *Id.* at 19. Further, it dismissed the state's argument that it was "promoting speech by making a variety of views available" because of the viewpoint-based nature of the regulation. *Id.* at 20. "Moreover," it added, "the means chosen to advance variety tend[ed] to inhibit expression of [PG&E's] views in order to promote" those of their opponents. *Id.*

The *PG&E* decision relied heavily on an earlier case, *Miami Herald Publishing Co. v. Tornillo*, 418 U.S. 241 (1974), in which the Court invalidated a Florida "right of reply" statute requiring that newspapers give candidates whose character or record they attacked equal space in which to respond. As in *PG&E*, the Court held that such a rule of forced access could deter newspapers from speaking out in the first place, lest that trigger a requirement to serve as a platform for messages with which they disagreed. *Tornillo*, 418 U.S. at 256-257. The Court also held that the law impermissibly interfered with newspapers' exercise of editorial control and judgment. *Id.* at 258. *See also* Agency for Int'l Development v. Alliance for Open Society Int'l, Inc., 133 S. Ct. 2321 (2013) (invalidating a portion of a congressional act that made funds available for combatting HIV/AIDS worldwide, but conditioned receipt of the money on (1) prohibiting grant recipients from using the funds to advocate for the legalization of prostitution or sex trafficking and (2) requiring recipients to have an explicit policy opposing prostitution and sex trafficking; *held*, the second condition was unconstitutional forced speech).

QUESTION 38. Fair and balanced. The Federal Communications Commission imposes a regulation on all broadcasters to furnish equal air time to persons whose points of view differ from the editorial viewpoints of the broadcaster. Ralph Honcho is a popular talk-radio host whose show is heard nationwide by tens of millions of people. He sues the FCC in federal district court, claiming that the so-called fairness doctrine violates his First Amendment rights. If a reviewing judge *upheld* the doctrine, it would likely be because:

A. The regulation is content-neutral.
B. The Court has given the government more leeway in the regulation of broadcast media in light of broadcast spectrum scarcity.
C. The regulation does not force the speaker to say anything.
D. The regulation ensures accuracy in broadcasting.

ANALYSIS. Before it was repealed during the Reagan administration, the fairness doctrine bound both television and radio broadcasters. The Supreme Court turned back a challenge to that doctrine in *Red Lion Broadcasting Co. v. FCC*, 395 U.S. 367 (1969), based on the government's authority to regulate a diminishing publicly owned resource: the broadcast spectrum. (Recall the leeway the Court gave the FCC in the *Pacifica Foundation* case.) The best answer, therefore, is **B**. Even if you weren't familiar with *Red Lion*, you could have discerned the correct answer through a process of elimination. **A** is not correct, because the regulation is not content-neutral; in fact, it is viewpoint-based, in a sense. The rule mandates the inclusion of views contrary to those of the broadcaster. It does not require access for people whose views are complimentary or identical to the broadcaster. While **C** may be true in a formal sense, the regulation does require the broadcaster to, in effect, subsidize messages with which it disagrees, or to eschew positions for which equal access must be afforded in the first place. **D** is not the best answer, because there are other, less intrusive means to ensure accuracy. Libel laws are one example that would not entail forcing broadcasters to include messages with which they disagree.

Aspects of both forced association and forced speech combined in *Hurley v. Irish-American Gay, Lesbian and Bisexual Group of Boston* (GLIB), 515 U.S. 557 (1995). Massachusetts sought to require a private group that staged the annual St. Patrick's Day parade to include GLIB members among the marchers. While the group did not object to members of GLIB marching in the parade *as individuals,* it refused to permit GLIB to march with an identifying banner. The Court found that the order violated the group's First Amendment rights. *Hurley,* 515 U.S. at 573.

First, the Court found that parades were protected by the First Amendment. It noted that GLIB's wish to participate and express its viewpoint conflicted with the organizer's desire not to have the group identify itself during the parade. The state's order, the Court concluded "violates the fundamental rule of protection under the First Amendment, that a speaker has the autonomy to choose the content of his own message." *Id.* "Disapproval of a private speaker's message," the Court added, "does not legitimize use of the Commonwealth's power to compel the speaker to alter the message by including one more acceptable to others." *Id.* at 581.

Finally, the law schools that objected to being required to host military recruiters on their campuses on pain of loss of federal funding claimed that this requirement was a form of forced speech. Rumsfeld v. Forum for Academic and Institutional Rights, Inc., 547 U.S. 47 (2006). As it did with all of FAIR's arguments, the Court unanimously rejected this one. The recruiting assistance that the schools were compelled to furnish (sending e-mails and posting notices on behalf of recruiters) "is a far cry from the compelled speech in *Barnette* and *Wooley*. . . . There is nothing in this case approaching a Government-mandated pledge or motto that the schools must endorse. . . ." *FAIR,* 547 U.S. at 62. The Court also noted that unlike its other forced speech cases, "accommodating the military's message does not affect the law schools' speech, because the schools are not speaking when they host interviews and recruiting receptions. . . . A law school's recruiting services lack the expressive quality of a parade, a newsletter, or the editorial page of a newspaper . . . ." *Id.* at 64. The Court noted as well that nothing in the Solomon Amendment affects what schools may say about the military's policies with which they disagree. *Id.* at 65.

Both freedom to associate and freedom *not* to speak are summarized below.

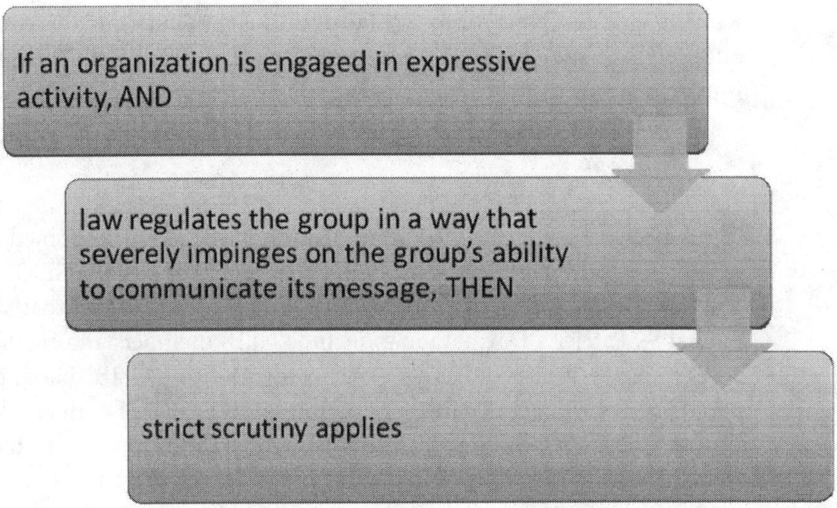

Freedom of Association Summary

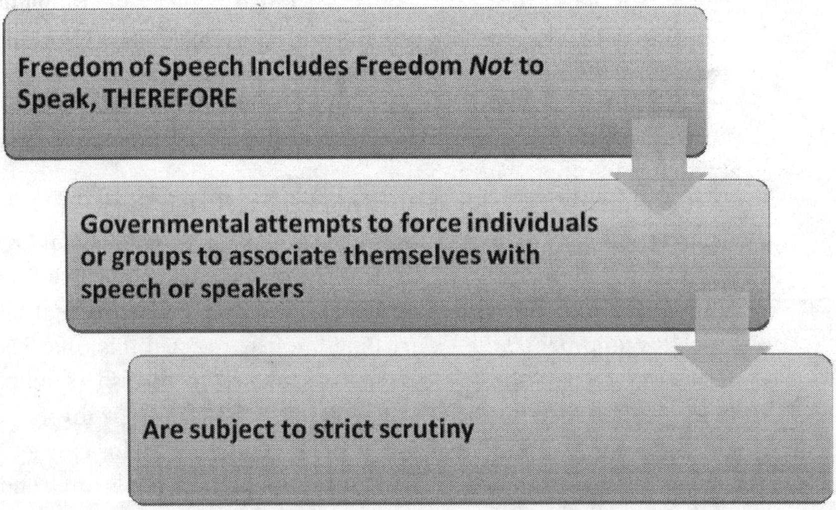

Forced Speech Summary

QUESTION 39. The fine print. A regulation of the Food and Drug Administration requires makers of "herbal supplements" and other vitamins that have not been through the FDA's drug approval process to use a disclaimer in their advertisements. Manufacturers must explain that "[t]he statements and products referred to in this advertisement have not been evaluated by the FDA. They are not intended to diagnose, treat, cure or prevent any disease or condition." Manufacturers of a drink made from snozzberry juice ("SNOB") attest to a variety of health benefits from regular consumption of SNOB. They claim to have conducted scientific research backing up these allegations and would prefer not to run the FDA-approved disclaimer. If they challenge the regulation on First Amendment grounds, would a reviewing judge likely rule for them?

A. No, because the speech involved was an advertisement.
B. No, because the disclaimer requirement was narrowly tailored to further a compelling interest in consumer protection.
C. Yes, because there is a rational basis for the disclaimer requirement.
D. Yes, because the government is compelling the manufacturers to endorse a message with which they disagree.

ANALYSIS. Upon reading this question, you might have thought it was misplaced—that it ought to be in the commercial speech section. Well, you can be forgiven for thinking so. This question is parked squarely at the intersection of commercial speech and forced speech. And the Court has never quite reconciled the two areas completely. While it is a regulation of commercial speech, the regulation is furthered through the mandatory use of a disclaimer, as opposed to prohibition of certain speech in advertising. And while it is forced speech of a sort, the disclaimer sits alongside the speech that the manufacturer wishes to use. In other words, the manufacturer is not prohibited from making its claims; it just has to disclose that those claims haven't been vetted by the FDA. Considering the choices, then, two can be eliminated fairly quickly: **A**, as you now know, is incorrect because advertisements and other forms of commercial speech *are* protected by the First Amendment. **C** is not correct because it states an inappropriate standard of review. Unless speech is completely unprotected by the First Amendment, the Court does not employ the rational basis test in the First Amendment context. **D** is true, but somewhat incomplete. The Court evaluates even forced speech cases using strict scrutiny; just because the Court is forcing someone to speak does not, ipso facto, mean the regulation is unconstitutional. Of the answers, then, **B** is the best. Consumer protection *is* a compelling governmental interest; and the disclaimer requirement doesn't prohibit speech or even force the manufacturer to contradict its own claims about SNOB. It simply requires the factual disclosure that the FDA has not conducted an independent evaluation of the health claims. Thus, it is narrowly tailored relative to regulations in other forced speech cases, such as *Wooley* and *Barnette.*

G. The First Amendment and the Political Process

1. *Introduction*

As we have seen, the First Amendment guarantees our right to associate with like-minded people to collectively advance our views on a variety of topics. Political parties are one example of such organization, and the First Amendment protects the rights of individuals to organize, support candidates, and run for office. At the same time, federal, state, and local governments regulate aspects of the political process to guarantee the integrity of parties and the electoral system and to ensure a modicum of fairness in the political process. This section examines three areas in which the First Amendment has often come into conflict with governmental efforts to regulate the political process: the financing of political campaigns, the regulation of elections, and the regulation of campaign speech.

2. *Campaign finance regulation*

The Watergate scandal brought about some of the first comprehensive federal campaign finance reform measures. The Federal Election Campaign Act of 1974 (FECA), among other things, limited contributions to and expenditures by candidates for federal elective office. Specifically, FECA limited total campaign contributions to $25,000/year, limited contributions to individual candidates to $1,000/year, restricted donations "relative to a clearly identified candidate" to $1,000/year, and imposed spending limitations on the candidates themselves. The regulations in FECA were challenged; in a per curiam decision, the Supreme Court upheld the contribution limits while invalidating those limits imposed on candidates' expenditures. Buckley v. Valeo, 424 U.S. 1 (1976).

In a decision that remains controversial, the Court held that spending and donating money were expressive activities protected by the First Amendment, especially because the money went to fund political speech long deemed to be at the core of the First Amendment. *Buckley*, 424 U.S. at 15-18. Limitations on expenditures necessarily reduced the amount of expression, the Court held, because they "restrict[ed] the number of issues discussed, the depth of their exploration, and the size of the audience reached." *Id.* at 19. The Court invalidated both the limits on individual expenditures as well as those imposed on the spending of personal or family money by candidates.

The individual spending limits "impose direct and substantial restraints on the quantity of political speech" and were insufficiently connected with the prevention of the actuality of or potential for corruption to outweigh someone's interest in spending money "relative to a clearly identified candidate." *Id.*

at 39. The Court noted too that individuals could spend unlimited amounts of money on "issue ads" that did not specifically call for the election or defeat of a particular candidate. It concluded that the interest in preventing corruption, moreover, was insufficient to outweigh individuals' First Amendment rights.

As for limitations on expenditure of the candidates' money or that of their families, the Court found *no* connection with the interest in preventing corruption. The "First Amendment," the Court wrote, "simply cannot tolerate [this] restriction upon the freedom of a candidate to speak . . . on behalf of his own candidacy." *Id.* at 54. Further, the Amendment "denies the government the power to determine that spending to promote one's political views is wasteful, excessive, or unwise." *Id.* at 57. The Court did uphold the availability of public financing for candidates who voluntarily submitted to limits on expenditures.

But the Court took a different tack with contributions. Those, it felt, "entail[ed] only a marginal restriction upon the contributor's ability to engage in free communication." Candidates would simply have to raise smaller amounts of money from more donors; in any event, the Court noted that only a small percentage of donations were larger than the statutory maximum per candidate. *Id.* at 20-22. This marginal limitation was outweighed by the important interest served by FECA: "to limit the actuality and appearance of corruption resulting from large individual financial contributions. . . ." *Id.* at 26.

Buckley remains a foundational case in the Court's analysis of campaign finance regulation, which did not stop with FECA. In general, the Court's subsequent cases have addressed the areas originally regulated by FECA—contribution and expenditure limits—supplemented by cases concerning coordinated expenditures and political spending by corporations, each of which is discussed below. In addition, *Buckley* furnished the winning justification for subsequent campaign finance regulation limiting contributions: controlling actual or apparent corruption in the political process. Moreover, the Court has continued to adhere to *Buckley*'s rejection of another possible justification for regulation: the desire to "level the playing field" among candidates.

(a) Contribution limits Following *Buckley*, the Court upheld federal limits on contributions to political action committees (PACs) that furnish money to multiple candidates. California Medical Association v. Federal Election Commission, 453 U.S. 182 (1981). The Court also upheld contribution limits for *state* elections in *Nixon v. Shrink Missouri Government PAC*, 528 U.S. 377 (2000), invoking *Buckley*'s "combating corruption" rationale. But the Court invalidated an ordinance limiting contributions to groups opposing or supporting ballot measures. Citizens Against Rent Control v. City of Berkeley, 454 U.S. 290 (1981). In the latter case, the Court regarded the limit as a substantial restriction of political speech not outweighed by any concern over actual or apparent corruption. *But see* McCutcheon v. Federal Election Comm'n, 134 S. Ct. 1434 (2014) (holding that federal limits on the aggregate amounts given to candidates and to party committees violated the First Amendment).

(b) Limits on expenditures The Court struck down a law barring PACs from spending more than $1,000 in support of a presidential candidate, finding the limit burdened speech and that there was an insufficient risk of actual or apparent corruption. It also invalidated limits on party expenditures that were made independently of candidates and their campaigns. Colorado Republican Federal Campaign Committee v. Federal Election Commission, 518 U.S. 604 (1996). *See also* Meyer v. Grant, 486 U.S. 414 (1988) (invalidating the use of paid workers to gather signatures to place a constitutional amendment on the ballot). The Court underlined its skepticism of expenditure limits in *Arizona Free Enterprise Club's Freedom Club PAC v. Bennett*, 131 S. Ct. 2806 (2011). Arizona had a provision that permitted publicly funded candidates to receive additional money once preset spending limits were exceeded by candidates who declined public funds or by independent groups opposing the publicly funded candidate. Subjecting the provisions to strict scrutiny, the Court held that leveling the playing field among candidates was *not* a compelling governmental interest. *Freedom Club PAC*, 131 S. Ct. at 2825-2826. The Court also rejected attempts to link the provision to an interest the Court has recognized as compelling in the past—combating the appearance of corruption. The Court noted that Arizona had "ascetic contribution limits, strict disclosure requirements, and the general availability of public funding"; therefore, it was "hard to imagine what marginal corruption deterrence could be generated by the matching funds provision." *Id.* at 2827.

(c) Coordinated expenditures The Court has upheld limits on coordinated expenditures—the spending of money by independent groups on behalf of a candidate that is coordinated with the candidate's campaign. Colorado Republican Federal Campaign Committee v. Federal Election Commission, 518 U.S. 604 (1996); *see also* Federal Election Commission v. Colorado Republican Federal Campaign Committee, 533 U.S. 431 (2001). The Court concluded that large contributions to parties that, in turn, spent money on behalf of candidates in conjunction with their campaigns could create a sense of obligation on the candidate's part, which ran the risk of actual or apparent corruption.

Reformers' next target was a ban on so-called soft money—money donated directly to political parties for purposes other than influencing elections. A great deal of soft money had been going toward the purchase of political ads that did not explicitly advocate the election or defeat of a particular candidate. The Bipartisan Campaign Reform Act of 2002 closed this "loophole" and banned soft money contributions. BCRA also banned "electioneering communications," running a certain number of days before the election, which allowed the advertisements, often purchased with soft money, that did not explicitly urge the election or defeat of a particular candidate. The Act also barred corporate and union disbursements for electioneering communications, restricted coordinated expenditures, imposed record-keeping requirements, and banned donations by persons under 17 years old. A badly fractured

Court upheld some of the restrictions and invalidated others in *McConnell v. Federal Election Commission*, 540 U.S. 93 (2003), a decision that itself was partially overruled just a few years later.

As it had in the past, the Court upheld the bans on soft money contributions, concluding that the ban had "only a marginal impact on the ability of contributors, candidates, officeholders, and parties to engage in effective political speech." *McConnell*, 540 U.S. at 138. On the other hand, the interest in combating the appearance of corruption was compelling; the Court thought it likely that the donation of large amounts to parties, who in turn would spend it to benefit certain candidates, would engender in those candidates a feeling of obligation and would feed the perception that money bought access and influence. *Id.* at 143.

The Court also upheld restrictions on "electioneering communications" (the issue ads that did not explicitly say "vote for" or "vote against" a candidate), bans on corporate and union disbursements for electioneering communications, restrictions on coordinated expenditures, and certain record-keeping requirements. The Court, however, invalidated the ban on donations by minors, finding it an infringement of their First Amendment rights. *Id.* at 231. The Court, however, was badly fractured, with various members writing different parts of the opinion for the Court on particular issues. Opponents of campaign finance regulation, sensing that the Court was closely divided, pressed the issue in subsequent cases.

In *Randall v. Sorrell*, 548 U.S. 230 (2006), the Court invalidated Vermont's restrictions on campaign contributions and expenditures to and on behalf of candidates for state office, which were some of the lowest in the country. The limits on contributions included the incurring of expenses by campaign volunteers. The Court found that *Buckley* controlled on the expenditure issue, and that the contribution limits were so low as to be a significant infringement on free speech. *Sorrell*, 548 U.S. at 248-249. In particular, the Court found that the law's including volunteer expenses as "contributions" harmed political parties by discouraging volunteer activity. *Id.* at 253.

The Court then invalidated the application of BCRA to an ad protesting the filibustering of judicial appointments. Chief Justice John Roberts, along with Justice Alito, concluded that the ad, while an electioneering communication as defined by the Act, was not the "functional equivalent" of "express advocacy." Federal Election Commission v. Wisconsin Right to Life, Inc., 551 U.S. 449, 476 (2007). They were joined by Justices Scalia, Kennedy, and Thomas, who urged the Court to overrule *McConnell* and declare the electioneering communication provision facially invalid.

Another provision of BCRA—the so-called Millionaire's Amendment—provided that the opponent of any candidate spending more than $350,000 of her own money could solicit triple the statutory amount from each contributor, while the self-funded candidate was bound by the statutory limits. Davis v. Federal Election Commission, 554 U.S. 724 (2008).

The Court invalidated this asymmetry, finding that it placed a "substantial burden on the exercise of the First Amendment right to use personal funds for campaign speech." *Davis*, 554 U.S. at 740. The Court held that leveling the playing field between candidates of unequal financial resources was not a compelling interest and that the limits were not sufficiently connected to the combating of actual or apparent corruption. *Id.* at 741-742.

In 2009, the Court revisited BCRA's ban on corporate and union expenditures for electioneering communications. Overruling that portion of *McConnell* that upheld that provision, the Court concluded that those provisions infringed corporations' and unions' First Amendment rights and were invalid. Citizens United v. Federal Election Commission, 130 S. Ct. 876 (2010).

The ad in question was a feature-length movie entitled *Hillary!* made before the 2008 primaries by a nonprofit corporation. The Court described the film as "a feature-length negative advertisement that urges viewers to vote against Senator Clinton for President." *Citizens United*, 130 S. Ct. at 890. In addition to BCRA, which barred such electioneering communications, and *McConnell*, which upheld those restrictions, the Court had decided prior cases pointing in different directions. In *First National Bank of Boston v. Bellotti*, 435 U.S. 765 (1978), the Court affirmed that corporations were protected by the First Amendment and invalidated a restriction on corporate contributions to influence outcomes of ballot measures. But in *Austin v. Michigan Chamber of Commerce*, 494 U.S. 652 (1990), the Court upheld a state law prohibiting expenditures to elect or defeat a candidate for political office made from general corporate funds. The Court held that the state had a compelling interest in preventing the "distorting effects" of corporate monies on the political process. *Austin*, 494 U.S. at 679-680.

The Court acknowledged this conflict and, in the end, rejected *Austin*'s "anti-distortion" rationale and overruled *Austin*, as well as that portion of *McConnell* that upheld the corporate ban in BCRA. "Speech restrictions based on the identity of the speaker are all too often simply a means to control content," the Court wrote. *Citizens United*, 130 S. Ct. at 889. The Court noted that media corporations were exempt from regulation, but that technology was blurring the lines separating "media" corporations from other types of corporations. "The First Amendment protects speech and speaker, and the ideas that flow from each." *Id.*

The Court also rejected claims that the ban was necessary to combat real and apparent corruption in the political process. *Buckley*'s concern was with "quid pro quo" corruption—that is, the trading of legislative favors for campaign contributions or the offer of contributions in return for favors. Merely having some "influence" over or "access" to officials was not tantamount to corruption. *Id.* at 910. The Court also found the ban unnecessary to protect shareholders, noting that it was both over- and underinclusive. It was underinclusive because the exception for media corporations did not protect the interest of those shareholders; it was overinclusive because some corporations that wished to contribute funds had few shareholders. *Id.* at 911. There was a vigorous dissent from Justice Stevens, and even President Obama publicly chided the majority for its decision during the 2010 State of the Union Address. *See also* American Tradition Partnership v. Bullock, 132 S. Ct. 2490 (2012) (per curiam) (invoking *Citizens United* to invalidate a state statute prohibiting campaign expenditures by corporations to elect or oppose political candidates).

Campaign finance regulation is very much a moving target these days. It is unlikely that *Citizens United* will be the Court's last word; it remains to be seen whether the distinction between contributions and expenditures, central to the *Buckley* decision, will survive, or whether the Court, as urged by its more conservative members, will treat both as speech and subject both to strict scrutiny. Here's a short summary of where the Court stands now:

Expenditures	Contributions
• Fully protected by the First Amendment • Court has rejected "levelling" rationales to limit self-funding • Most limits invalidated • Mandated disclosure permitted	• Limits on money to candidates and parties upheld • Limits cannot be too low • Countering apparent/actual corruption compelling interest • Court suggests that corruption must be "quid pro quo"; "influence" and "access" not sufficient • Corporations and unions may contribute • Record-keeping and disclosure permitted

3. *Governmental regulation of elections*

States exercise significant regulatory authority over voters and elections, including party primaries. Not surprisingly, this means that states can exercise some authority, albeit indirectly, over political parties themselves. At the same time, as we've seen, the First Amendment protects the associational rights of groups. Occasionally, the state's regulatory authority and parties' associational rights come into conflict, usually in cases involving who is eligible to vote in a party's primary and thus to select that party's standard-bearer in the general election.

Occasionally, a party will try to tightly limit access to its primary, to ensure that the party faithful select who they wish to represent them. In states with "closed" primaries—in which only registered party members may vote—parties have sometimes attempted to prescribe a minimum amount of time within which one must be registered to be eligible for a primary ballot. In *Rosario v. Rockefeller,* 410 U.S. 752 (1973), the Court upheld New York's requirement that one be on the rolls 8 to 11 months prior to the primary. However, the Court found that a law prohibiting voting in a party primary if one had voted in another party's primary in the preceding 24 months was unconstitutional. Applying strict scrutiny, the Court found that the state had a compelling interest in maintaining the party's integrity by preventing "poaching" of its candidates, but that the length of the ban substantially infringed on voters' free association rights.

Parties do have substantial leeway in structuring the way they select candidates. For example, trial judges in New York are selected by conventions made up of delegates, each of whom is required to obtain 500-plus signatures of party members within a 37-day period. New York State Board of Elections v. Lopez Torres, 552 U.S. 196 (2008). The Court upheld this practice, saying that it was akin to the Court's decisions requiring persons to demonstrate a "significant modicum of support" before being granted access to a general election ballot. *Lopez Torres,* 552 U.S. at 204. In addition, the Court invalidated—in the name of preserving the party's right to decide who votes in its primary—a law requiring all voters in a party's primary to be registered members of that party. Tashjian v. Republican Party, 479 U.S. 208 (1986). The Court also invalidated a law barring political parties from endorsing, supporting, or opposing any candidate for the party's nomination to a partisan, elected office. Eu v. San Francisco Democratic Committee, 489 U.S. 214 (1989). In all these cases, the Court applied strict scrutiny to laws that trammeled on the party's associational rights.

The flip side of laws requiring exclusion of voters or candidates from primaries are laws requiring their *inclusion* despite the party's wishes. In an effort to encourage "moderate" candidates who might appeal to voters across a broad spectrum, California adopted a blanket primary whereby all the candidates, regardless of party, are listed on one ballot received by all primary voters. California Democratic Party v. Jones, 530 U.S. 567 (2000). The candidate winning the most votes becomes that party's candidate in the general election.

The parties objected, especially because many of them, prior to the passage of the initiative establishing the blanket primary, had used closed primaries to select nominees. Applying strict scrutiny, the Court invalidated the blanket primary. "Proposition 198," the Court wrote, "forces political parties to associate with—to have their nominees, and hence their positions, determined by—those who . . . have refused to affiliate with a party, and [may have] expressly affiliated with a rival." *Jones,* 530 U.S. at 577. This interference violated the parties' First Amendment rights of association.

The state offered seven interests furthered by Prop 198; the Court found them either not compelling or not narrowly tailored. The state had argued that the blanket primary encouraged candidates to address problems other than those of narrow interest to the party, thus ensuring that the candidates were "more representative" of the electorate as a whole. The Court responded that this was simply another way of saying "we want candidates other than the party's." *Id.* at 581. Ensuring the "effective" vote of voters in "safe" districts was also deemed insufficient. Voters could simply switch parties to ensure that their voice was heard in the selection of the dominant party's candidate. *Id.* at 583-584. The other four interests—ensuring fairness, increasing choice, increasing participation, and protecting privacy—were not "automatically out of the running," wrote the Court, "but neither are they, *in the circumstances of this case*, compelling." *Id.* at 584. Further, "[r]espondents could protect them all by resorting to a *nonpartisan* blanket primary." *Id.* at 585.

Not all state regulation of primaries, however, have been found unconstitutional. *Clingman v. Beaver*, 544 U.S. 581 (2005), saw the Court uphold a "semi-closed" primary, in which the party's own voters and unaffiliated independent voters can vote, but not voters registered as members of another party. The Court distinguished its *Tashjian* decision by contrasting the imposition on voters, which the Court found was slight. *Washington State Grange v. Washington State Republican Party*, 552 U.S. 442 (2008), upheld, against a facial challenge, a primary election law requiring candidates to disclose their party preference, but permitting voters to vote for any candidate, and then restricting the general election to the top two vote-getters, candidates' party preference notwithstanding. *Id.* at 447-448. Because the party was still free to nominate its preferred candidate, its associational rights were protected, despite the fact of the party's inability to designate its official nominee. *Id.* at 453. The Court also left open the possibility of an as-applied challenge if voters were confused by the party preference designation, but said claims of widespread voter confusion were, at this point, "sheer speculation." *Id.* at 454.

4. *Regulation of campaign speech*

Finally, there is the issue of campaign speech. Few would question that statements candidates make while seeking office are located squarely at the core of political speech protected by the First Amendment, and that all efforts to regulate that speech will be closely scrutinized. Indeed, the Court confirmed this in *Brown v. Hartlage*, 456 U.S. 46 (1982), in which it held that promises to voters could not be constitutionally prosecuted under state laws prohibiting promising anything of value in exchange for support in an election.

A number of states with elective judgeships, however, had long regulated *judicial* campaign speech. Indeed, the American Bar Association's code of judicial ethics—adopted by many states—held that certain campaign speech was unethical and that a candidate engaged in such speech was subject to discipline. Minnesota similarly barred candidates for judicial office from "announcing [the candidate's] views on disputed legal and political issues." The Court, viewing this as a content-based speech restriction, applied strict scrutiny and struck it down. Republican Party of Minnesota v. White, 536 U.S. 765, 788 (2002).

The state offered two justifications for the "announce rule": (1) preservation of impartiality and (2) preservation of the appearance of impartiality in the administration of justice. Writing for the Court, Justice Scalia pointed out that there were at least three ways one might interpret "impartiality."

First, one might mean impartiality between parties. But in that case, the announce rule would not be narrowly tailored because "it does not restrict speech for or against particular *parties*, but rather speech for or against particular *issues*." *White*, 536 U.S. at 776. Impartiality might also mean "lack of preconception in favor of or against a particular *legal view*." *Id.* at 777. But this interest was not compelling because "it is virtually impossible to find a judge who does not have preconceptions about the law." *Id.* Finally, there is impartiality as open-mindedness—a willingness to be persuaded. But the Court pointed out that the announce rule was not adopted for this purpose, because it only applied to judges' statements during elections. At other times, judges were encouraged to state their views about the law in a variety of public fora. *Id.* at 778-779. The Court detected in the rule an aversion to judicial elections in general; the First Amendment, it concluded, "does not permit [the state] [to] leav[e] the principle of elections in place while preventing candidates from discussing what the elections are about." *Id.* at 788.

An open question is what impact *Caperton v. A.T. Massey Coal Co.*, 556 U.S. 868 (2009), might have on *White*. In *Caperton* the Court held that the Due Process Clause of the Fourteenth Amendment required recusal of a judge who was elected due to "significant and disproportionate" campaign donations or expenditures on the candidate's behalf by a donor with a stake in a case before that judge. Whether the Due Process Clause could require recusal of a judge based on campaign positions the First Amendment guarantees her the right to express remains to be seen.

H. The First Amendment and Press Freedoms

In addition to guarding against governmental abridgement of "freedom of speech," the First Amendment adds "or of the press." The question for the Court in a number of recent cases is whether the Constitution's singling out of the press creates special protections for newspapers, broadcasters, and reporters compared with those provided to ordinary citizens. Of course, some of the Court's decisions—specifically, its constitutionalization of libel and slander—benefit the press immensely. By and large, however, the Court has not been willing to use the "press clause" of the First Amendment as a source of additional protections for the institutional press. At the same time, however, the Court has been keen to protect the press from special disabilities.

While some states have enacted so-called shield laws that protect reporters from being forced to testify before grand juries or reveal confidential sources, the Court has held that no such immunity is required by the Constitution. In *Branzburg v. Hayes*, 408 U.S. 665 (1972), a reporter was asked to testify before a grand jury about various drug transactions he had witnessed while covering a story. He refused, but the Supreme Court held that the First Amendment did not "exempt the newsman from performing the citizen's normal duty of appearing and furnishing information relevant to the grand jury's task." *Branzburg*, 408 U.S. at 691. Whatever interest a reporter might have in protecting her sources was outweighed, the Court reasoned, by the government's interest in investigating and prosecuting crime. *See also* Herbert v. Lando, 441 U.S. 153 (1979) (refusing to shield publisher being sued for defamation from inquiry into editorial policies and procedures).

The Court has also held that if a search of a newspaper's office complies with the Fourth Amendment, then the First Amendment imposes no additional barrier to law enforcement. Zurcher v. Stanford Daily, 436 U.S. 547 (1978). *Zurcher* involved a police search of a college newspaper for photographic evidence that might help identify persons who had assaulted police during a student demonstration. The newspaper sued after the search, which uncovered no evidence, claiming that the search violated press freedom. In response to *Zurcher*, Congress passed a statute limiting federal and state officials' power to use search warrants to obtain information from the news media.[18]

One area in which the media have had success is in obtaining access to trials and other government—especially judicial—proceedings, and in publishing what they observe. This "right of access" dates to *Richmond Newspapers, Inc. v. Virginia*, 448 U.S. 555 (1980), in which the Court upheld the right of individuals and the press to attend criminal trials. It's worth noting, however, that the rights of access are generally the same for members of the press and for the general public—again the Court seems disinclined to accord to the press special protections under the First Amendment.

A defendant being tried for murder for the fourth time petitioned to have his trial closed to the public. The judge granted the motion, relying on a statute permitting the exclusion from trial of persons whose presence would prevent a fair trial. *Richmond Newspapers*, 448 U.S. at 559-560. The judge's order was upheld by the Virginia Supreme Court, but reversed by the U.S. Supreme Court, which began its opinion by noting that the openness of criminal trials was "an indispensible attribute of the Anglo-American trial," aiding fairness and deterring misconduct. *Id.* at 569. Dismissing the state's argument that the right to attend trials was not explicitly given in the Bill of Rights, the Court held that "the right to attend criminal trials is implicit in the guarantees of the First Amendment; without the freedom to attend such trials . . . important aspects of freedom of speech and 'of the press could be eviscerated.'" *Id.* at 580.

---

18. 42 U.S.C. § 2000aa.

In the Court's opinion, the reasons for public exclusion were inadequate—indeed, the judge never gave any. He "made no findings to support closure; no inquiry was made as to whether alternative solutions would have met the need to ensure fairness; there was no recognition of any right under the Constitution for the public or press to attend the trial." *Id.* at 580-581. Sequestration of witnesses might be one way to prevent exposing them to prejudicial information while preserving the trial's openness, the Court suggested. Without "an overriding interest articulated in findings," the Court concluded, "the trial of a criminal case must be open to the public." *Id.* at 581.

The interest in openness is stronger even than a state's interest in sparing a minor victim of a sex crime from further trauma, the Court held in *Globe Newspaper Co. v. Superior Court*, 457 U.S. 596 (1982). *Richmond Newspapers* was extended to voir dire of a jury pool in the trial of a defendant accused of raping and murdering a teenager. Press-Enterprise Co. v. Superior Court, 464 U.S. 501 (1984). The Court again expanded *Richmond Newspaper*'s scope to cover access to transcripts of a preliminary hearing in the same case. Press-Enterprise Co. v. Superior Court, 478 U.S. 1 (1986).

The Court has been more solicitous of state restrictions on access by the press to incarcerated persons. In *Pell v. Procunier*, 417 U.S. 817 (1974), the Court upheld a California ban on face-to-face interviews with prisoners. *See also* Saxbe v. Washington Post, 417 U.S. 843 (1974) (upholding similar federal policy). In *Houchins v. KQED, Inc.*, 438 U.S. 1 (1978), the Court upheld much of a policy restricting access to a county jail that, among other things, closed a portion of the jail to all visitors and banned cameras and recorders. The Court invalidated the ban on cameras and recorders, and required the county to conduct more frequent tours, but it held that the First Amendment does not "guarantee the press any basic right of access superior to that of the public generally." *Houchins*, 438 U.S. at 16.

But if the Court has not been willing to infer from the First Amendment special rights for members of the press, it has accorded close scrutiny to laws apparently designed to single out or penalize the press. Minnesota imposed a sales tax on retail sales and a "use tax" on goods purchased elsewhere but consumed or stored in Minnesota and on which no sales tax was paid. Minneapolis Star & Tribune Co. v. Minnesota Commissioner of Revenue, 460 U.S. 575 (1983). For a time, Minnesota exempted periodicals from both the sales and use taxes; in 1971, however, it imposed a use tax on the cost of ink and paper used in production. In 1974, the legislature passed an exemption for the first $100,000 used per year by any publication. *Minneapolis Star & Tribune*, 406 U.S. at 577-578. As a result, the tax applied to 11 publishers and 14 newspapers in the state.

The U.S. Supreme Court invalidated the tax. First it noted that the use tax did not protect the sales tax, as use taxes usually do. The "special use tax," the Court noted, "has singled out the press for special treatment. . . . A tax that burdens rights protected by the First Amendment cannot stand unless the burden is necessary to achieve an overriding governmental interest." *Id.* at 582.

Reciting the dangers of selective taxation to a free press, the Court considered and rejected the reason given by the state for the tax: to raise revenue. "[A]n alternative means of achieving the same interest without raising concerns under the First Amendment is clearly available," the Court wrote. "[T]he State could raise the revenue by taxing businesses generally, avoiding the censorial threat implicit in a tax that singles out the press." *Id.* at 586. It noted that the state offered no justification for using the use tax as opposed to a retail sales tax; and "even assuming that the legislature did have valid reasons for substituting another tax for the sales tax," the Court was "hesitant to fashion a rule that automatically allowed the State to single out the press for a different method of taxation as long as the effective burden was no different from that on other taxpayers or the burden on the press was lighter than on other businesses." *Id.* at 588. This reticence was reinforced by the Court's admitted inability "to evaluate with precision the relative burdens of various methods of taxation." *Id.* at 589. The Court was further troubled by the fact that the tax "targets a handful of newspapers" because of the $100,000 exemption. *Id.* at 591.

Note, however, that the Court's concerns in *Minneapolis Star & Tribune* do not extend to differential tax rates on different media. Leathers v. Medlock, 499 U.S. 439 (1991). The Court upheld Arkansas's extending of its sales tax to cable television while retaining exemptions for newspapers, magazines, and satellite broadcasting. The Court found that the extension was content- and viewpoint-neutral and didn't make distinctions within classes of publications as the Minnesota legislature had. *Leathers,* 499 U.S. at 447-449.

When legislatures go after media based on content or message, however, the Court has been more skeptical. The Court invalidated a tax exemption for newspapers as well as "religious, professional, trade and sports journals." Arkansas Writers' Project, Inc. v. Ragland, 481 U.S. 221 (1987). The exemption, the Court noted, "depends entirely on its content." *Arkansas Writers' Project,* 481 U.S. at 229. The Court also invalidated a New York law confiscating income from one "accused or convicted of a crime" derived from books or other publications about the crime. The income was to be held in trust to satisfy civil judgments arising out of the crime. Simon & Schuster, Inc. v. New York State Crime Victims Board, 502 U.S. 105 (1991). The Court found that the law was not narrowly tailored to its alleged interest in compensating victims. The Court noted, for example, that the law applied to those merely "accused" of a crime, whether or not convicted. *Simon & Schuster,* 502 U.S. at 121-123.

Generally applicable laws, however, do not raise constitutional concerns, even if there is some incidental burden on the press. In *Cohen v. Cowles Media Co.,* 501 U.S. 663 (1991), the Court upheld a damage award to a whistle-blower who gave information to a newspaper in return for a promise of confidentiality. The paper then exposed the identity of the informant, who lost his job and sued under a theory of promissory estoppel. *Cowles Media,* 501 U.S. at 665-666. The Court held the verdict was the result of a content-neutral application of contract law and was not barred by the First Amendment. *Id.* at 668-670.

The chart below sums up press freedoms. In general, the Court has not interpreted the Press Clause to confer special rights, but protects the press from being singled out.

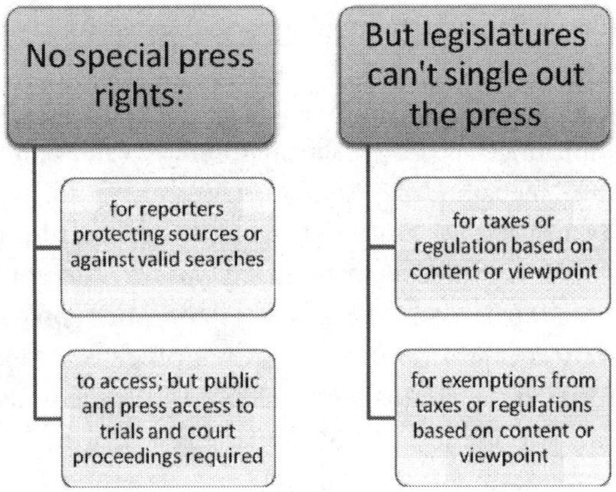

I. Closer

QUESTION 40. Fenced pickets. In response to the activities of the East Hills Church—which pickets the funerals of soldiers killed in Iraq and Afghanistan, alleging that the soldiers were killed in retaliation for American toleration of homosexuality—Ames City adopts an ordinance that prohibits "picketing activity within 100 feet of a funeral, burial, memorial service, or funeral procession." Members of the East Hills Church challenge the law, alleging that it violates their First Amendment rights. Which of the following would be *most* helpful to the Church in seeking to have the ban struck down?

A. It applies only to funeral picketing.
B. The fact that it is content-neutral.
C. Proof that the ban was enacted by the City with the Church specifically in mind.
D. That it was passed to preserve the sanctity of funerals and to protect the privacy of mourners.

ANALYSIS. The Court has tended to interpret picketing bans, at least those that don't specify what *kind* of picketing is being prohibited, as content-neutral regulations (recall *Frisby v. Schultz* and *Hill v. Colorado*, discussed above). If that is true, then the government need prove only that the regulation was narrowly tailored to a significant governmental interest, and that ample alternative channels of communication remain open. If, however, the regulation was passed with the purpose of suppressing particular ideas, then the Court will apply strict scrutiny, as it does with content-based regulations. Of the choices, then, **C** is the best answer, because it looks as if, despite its facial neutrality, the ordinance was passed to suppress the activities of the East Hills Church because of the viewpoint they have adopted. Forcing Ames City to defend its ordinance under a strict scrutiny standard of review would be more difficult compared with intermediate scrutiny. The fact that it applies to funeral picketing only (choice **A**) is not helpful, because that suggests that numerous channels remain for the Church to express its opposition to homosexuality. **B** likewise is not helpful, because it lowers the standard of review the government has to satisfy. **D** is not helpful either, because protecting the privacy of mourners and the sanctity and solemnity of funerals is likely a significant—and maybe even a compelling—governmental interest.

Denning's Picks

1. **B**
2. **C**
3. **C**
4. **A**
5. **B**
6. **C**
7. **A**
8. **D**
9. **A**
10. **C**
11. **B**
12. **D**
13. **A**
14. **B**
15. **D**
16. **C**
17. **C**
18. **C**
19. **D**
20. **C**
21. **A**
22. **B**
23. **A**
24. **C**

25. **C**
26. **B**
27. **D**
28. **C**
29. **C**
30. **C**
31. **A**
32. **B**
33. **D**
34. **D**
35. **A**
36. **D**
37. **D**
38. **B**
39. **B**
40. **C**

7

First Amendment Protection of Religious Freedom

A. Overview

In addition to protecting speech and expression, the First Amendment prohibits Congress and the states[1] from making any "law respecting an establishment of religion, or prohibiting the free exercise thereof...." U.S. Const. amend. I. Neither guarantee generated much Supreme Court doctrine until the 1940s, though both have generated scores of cases since then. The difficulty has been how to resolve the tension between the two sets of rights. On the one hand, the Free Exercise Clause appears to require the state to be at least neutral, if not somewhat accommodating, when it comes to citizens' religious observance. On the other, though, if the state is too accommodating, or if it seems to endorse or privilege one religion or one denomination over another, the Establishment Clause is implicated. The chart below shows the ways in which a court might interpret both Clauses.

Quadrant 1, which represents a position the Supreme Court has never adopted, implies strong enforcement of the Establishment Clause (think literal enforcement of the "wall of separation" metaphor) so that little or no accommodation of religion by government would be tolerated. Consequently, the level of protection required by the Free Exercise Clause would be quite weak, giving government broader range to incidentally burden religious belief or conduct.

1. Both the Free Exercise Clause and the Establishment Clause have been incorporated through the Fourteenth Amendment and applied to the states. *See* Cantwell v. Connecticut, 310 U.S. 296 (1940) (free exercise); Everson v. Board of Education, 330 U.S. 1 (1947) (establishment). For more on incorporation, see Chapter 3, *supra*.

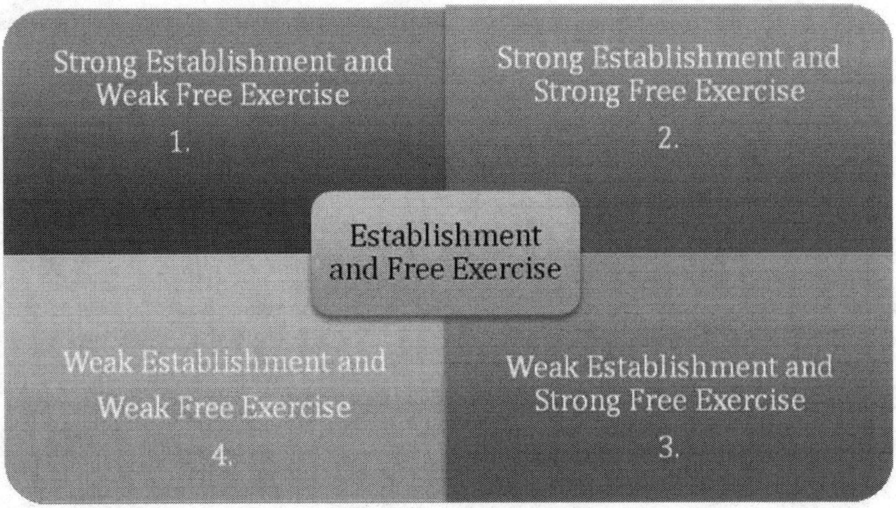

Interpretive Possibilities for Establishment and Free Exercise

Quadrant 2, by contrast, signifies strong enforcement of *both* the Establishment Clause and the Free Exercise Clause. Though something of an oversimplification, this quadrant describes the Supreme Court's pattern of enforcement of both Clauses from the late 1960s into the 1980s.

Quadrant 3 suggests a weak Establishment Clause, which would permit a wide range of interaction between government and religion along with strong enforcement of the Free Exercise Clause. The Supreme Court, to date, has not adopted this position.

Finally, Quadrant 4 reflects, more or less, where the Court is at present. Relative to the 1970s and even the early 1980s, the Court permits much more governmental involvement with religion (weak Establishment Clause), with a corresponding *narrowing* of what the Free Exercise Clause requires the government to accommodate (weak Free Exercise Clause).

The Court's oscillation over the years, in some sense, reflects an inability to settle on a unifying theory of the religion clauses. This is hardly surprising given the fact that the Court's jurisprudence in this area is the product of many different Courts and Justices, and has developed over six decades, during which time the nation's attitude toward religion has evolved. If the fit between the Court's line of Establishment and Free Exercise Clause cases is not a particularly tidy one, it is largely a reflection of the untidy nature of doctrinal development in the Supreme Court generally.

This chapter will cover first the evolution of the Court's approach to the Free Exercise Clause. As we will see, the Court's approach underwent a sea change following the 1989 case of *Employment Division v. Smith*, 494 U.S. 872 (1990). The second half of the chapter will chart the course of the Court's Establishment Clause jurisprudence, with particular attention to government funding of religion, prayer in schools, and display of religious symbols in public schools and in public buildings.

We begin with a threshold question: What is "religion"? It may surprise you to know that not only has the Court never really attempted to answer the question, it has even suggested that trying to do so would run afoul of the Establishment Clause! The Court will, thus, not inquire into the substance of beliefs, only into whether the beliefs are sincerely held. *See, e.g.,* United States v. Seeger, 380 U.S. 163 (1965); United States v. Ballard, 322 U.S. 78 (1944). If beliefs are sincerely held, then they are eligible for protection under the First Amendment.

Further, the Court has declined to weigh in on suits over church property spawned by church splits over religious doctrine or practice. Jones v. Wolf, 443 U.S. 595 (1979). Only if "neutral principles" of trust and property law can be applied will the Court intervene. *See also* Presbyterian Church v. Mary Elizabeth Blue Hull Church, 393 U.S. 440 (1969) (courts cannot resolve property disputes based on construction of religious dogma).

In addition to refusing to inquire into the substance of religious beliefs or settling property disputes by employing religious dogma, the Court also recently affirmed that the Free Exercise and Establishment Clauses limited the Court's ability to rule on who is and is not covered by the ministerial exception that bars certain discrimination claims against religious institutions. Hosanna-Tabor Evangelical Lutheran Church and School v. EEOC, 132 S. Ct. 694 (2012). The plaintiff in *Hosanna-Tabor* filed a complaint with the EEOC after being discharged from her job as a teacher at a religious school. The school, in turn, invoked "the 'ministerial exception'" and argued "that the suit was barred by the First Amendment because the claims at issue concerned the employment relationship between a religious institution and one of its ministers." *Hosanna-Tabor*, 132 S. Ct. at 701. The school claimed that the petitioner was a minister and that her pastoral duties were inseparable from her classroom teaching duties. *Id.* at 707-708.

A unanimous Supreme Court held both that a ministerial exception existed, was rooted in the First Amendment, and that it barred the teacher's employment discrimination claim. Government's ability to dictate who is or isn't a religious organization's minister "infringes the Free Exercise Clause, which protects a religious group's right to shape its own faith and mission through its appointments." *Id.* at 705. Moreover, "[a]ccording the state the power to determine which individuals will minister to the faithful also violates the Establishment Clause, which prohibits government involvement with such ecclesiastical decisions." *Id.* The Court declined "to adopt a rigid formula for deciding when an employee qualifies as a minister." *Id.* at 708. Because of "the formal title given to [the plaintiff] by the Church, the substance reflected in that title, her own use of that title, and the important religious functions she performed for the Church," however, the Court concluded that the ministerial exemption applied to her. *Id.* at 708.

B. Free Exercise Clause

1. *Laws explicitly targeting religious belief or conduct*

The paradigmatic violation of the Free Exercise Clause occurs when the government discourages or penalizes religious conduct or belief *as* religious conduct or belief (or non-belief). For example, the Court invalidated a Maryland law requiring public officials to swear belief in the existence of God. Torcaso v. Watkins, 367 U.S. 488 (1961). The Court also invalidated a Tennessee law barring clergy members from holding public office. McDaniel v. Paty, 435 U.S. 618 (1978).

2. *Generally applicable laws burdening religious observance*

The more difficult situation arises when a generally applicable law—that is, one aimed at conduct generally, not just religious conduct or belief—incidentally burdens an individual's religious beliefs. A ban on the sale and consumption of alcohol, for example, would inhibit the belief and conduct of Roman Catholics, Episcopalians, and Jews, all of whose liturgy calls for the sacramental use of wine.

The old view was that this was not a problem. In *Reynolds v. United States*, 98 U.S. 145 (1879), the Court upheld a ban on polygamy in a suit brought by Mormons. Exempting Mormons from compliance, in the Court's words, "would . . . make the professed doctrines of religious belief superior to the law of the land, and in effect . . . permit every citizen to become a law unto himself." *Reynolds*, 98 U.S. at 167.

By the mid-twentieth century, however, the Court was more solicitous of Free Exercise claims, and more skeptical of governmental actions that burdened religious beliefs, though skepticism did not mean automatic invalidation. In *Braunfeld v. Brown*, 366 U.S. 599 (1961), for example, the Court upheld Pennsylvania's Sunday closing law against a challenge from a Jewish shopkeeper who closed on Saturday to observe the Sabbath. The Court did, however, apply a heightened standard of review.

Two years later, again applying strict scrutiny, the Court invalidated South Carolina's denial of unemployment compensation to a sabbatarian who refused to accept employment on Saturday. Sherbert v. Verner, 374 U.S. 398 (1963). The Court applied this test somewhat unevenly over the next 25 years, however, so that different lines of precedent began to develop.

Under one line of cases, strict scrutiny was still the rule. The Court upheld the Free Exercise claims of persons denied unemployment compensation in cases that resembled *Sherbert v. Verner. See, e.g.*, Frazee v. Employment Security Dep't, 489 U.S. 829 (1989); Hobbie v. Unemployment Appeals Comm'n, 480 U.S. 136 (1987); Thomas v. Review Bd., 450 U.S. 707 (1981). In addition, the Court invalidated compulsory school attendance laws as applied to the Old

Order Amish, whose beliefs mandated their children leave school a couple of years prior to the state's minimum age for dropping out. Wisconsin v. Yoder, 406 U.S. 205 (1972). In other cases, Free Exercise claims were rejected after the Court found that the laws in question satisfied strict scrutiny. *See* Bob Jones Univ. v. United States, 461 U.S. 574 (1983) (upholding denial of tax-exempt status to private religious schools that practiced racial discrimination); United States v. Lee, 455 U.S. 252 (1982) (upholding imposition of Social Security tax on wages of Amish).

In another line of cases, usually involving those in the military or in prison, the Court applied—without seeming to acknowledge it explicitly—a more deferential standard of review. *See, e.g.,* O'Lone v. Estate of Shabazz, 482 U.S. 342 (1987) (upholding prison regulations that prevented Friday midday prayer by Islamic prisoners); Goldman v. Weinberger, 475 U.S. 503 (1986) (upholding military discipline of Orthodox Jewish Air Force officer, an ordained rabbi, for wearing yarmulke)[2]; Johnson v. Robinson, 415 U.S. 361 (1974) (upholding the exclusion of conscientious objectors who performed alternative service from veterans' benefits); *see also* Lyng v. Northwest Indian Cemetery Protection Ass'n, 485 U.S. 439 (1988) (upholding Forest Service plan to build logging road through area regarded as sacred by Indian tribes).

The Court clarified its test in the seminal case of *Employment Division v. Smith,* 494 U.S. 872 (1990). On the facts, the case looked quite similar to *Sherbert v. Verner* and the other unemployment compensation cases. The plaintiffs were counselors at a drug rehabilitation clinic and members of the Native American Church, whose members engage in the sacramental use of the hallucinogen peyote. *Smith,* 494 U.S. at 874. After failing a drug test, the plaintiffs were dismissed for cause from their jobs. Their for-cause dismissal, moreover, rendered them ineligible for unemployment benefits. *Id.* They sued, claiming that the denial of benefits violated their free exercise rights.

The Court, however, framed the issue differently. According to the Court, the question was whether the plaintiffs had a free exercise right to be exempt from a "neutral, generally applicable law," the prohibition of the use of peyote. "We have never held," the Court wrote, "that an individual's religious beliefs excuse him from compliance with an otherwise valid law prohibiting conduct that the State is free to regulate." *Id.* at 878-879.

The Court distinguished earlier cases, like *Yoder,* as "hybrid" cases combining a free exercise claim with another right, such as the right to control the raising of one's child without governmental interference. Such a hybrid situation was not present in *Smith,* the Court concluded. *Id.* at 881-882. Should plaintiffs wish to be exempt from the general criminal laws of the state, they may appeal to the legislature, the Court noted. *Id.* at 890.

2. In the aftermath of *Goldman,* Congress passed a law permitting the wearing of unobtrusive religious headgear by active-duty military personnel.

QUESTION 1. Playing chicken. A state statute prohibits the killing of any animal "in a manner which causes unnecessary pain or suffering of said animal." Dobson is prosecuted for violating the statute by strangling a chicken as part of a religious ritual in which he participated. Dobson defends on the ground that the state statute as applied in his case unconstitutionally interferes with his free exercise of religion. Consider the following statements:

I. The judge may consider whether Dobson is sincere in his belief that his religion requires the strangling of a chicken.
II. The judge may consider whether the requirement of strangling a chicken is reasonable.
III. The judge may not consider the sincerity of Dobson's belief under the Establishment Clause.

Which of these statements is true?

A. I only
B. II only
C. III only
D. II and III

ANALYSIS. Recall the initial discussion about the definition of "religion." Attempts to separate "true" religions from those that are "false" themselves violate the Establishment Clause. Therefore, the Court has long held that the only inquiry permitted to courts is whether a particular adherent's beliefs are sincere. Thus statement I is correct while II is not. And if I is correct, then III cannot be correct. Of the choices then, **A** is the correct answer. **B** is incorrect, because passing judgment on the reasonableness of particular practices or beliefs gets courts close to the forbidden inquiry into their truth. **C** is irrelevant to the question whether a practice is protected by the First Amendment. Because neither statement II or III is correct, **D** cannot be the correct answer.

QUESTION 2. Sikh, and ye shall find. Devout Sikhs are required to wear a *kirpan*, a ceremonial dagger, wherever they go. Recently, a Sikh boy was suspended from a public school in the State of Ames, under a school policy that prohibits the carrying of knives to school. The policy specifically prohibits the carrying of items that are or can be used as weapons, and covers guns, explosive devices, pellet guns, as well as knives and other items with sharp blades. The school has a "zero tolerance" policy for the carrying of weapons; violation of this school policy carries a mandatory ten-day suspension. The suspended student and his parents sue the school, claiming that his suspension violates the Free Exercise Clause. The trial judge should rule:

A. For the student, as long as his belief is sincere.
B. For the student, unless the school demonstrates a compelling governmental interest and that its policy is narrowly tailored.
C. For the school, because the policy is neutral and generally applicable.
D. For the school, because of the need to protect other students.

ANALYSIS. According to the facts, the policy is neutral and generally applicable. There does not seem to be evidence that it sought to target Sikhs or that it is being enforced against them exclusively. In that case, despite the incidental burden on religious observance, the law or policy cannot be said to violate the Free Exercise Clause. Thus, **C** is the correct answer. **D** is not as good an answer, insofar as it suggests that "protection of others" is a sufficient reason to uphold a law against a free exercise challenge. **A** is incorrect, because sincerity of belief is irrelevant in these cases; the only question is whether the law is generally applicable. **B**, moreover, employs the wrong standard of review. *Smith* tells us that the proper standard of review for a generally applicable law that incidentally burdens religious conduct or observance is the rational basis test.

3. *Facially neutral laws aimed at religious conduct or beliefs*

Despite *Smith*, simple facial neutrality is not sufficient to avoid strict scrutiny, if a law has been passed with the purpose or the effect of targeting a particular religious belief or practice. In *Church of the Lukumi Babalu Aye v. City of Hialeah*, 508 U.S. 520 (1993), the Court invalidated a series of ordinances passed by the City of Hialeah, Florida aimed at discouraging the establishment of a Santeria church. Santeria is an Afro-Caribbean religion that mixes elements of Christianity and voodoo. Some rites call for the ritual sacrifice of animals to appease various spirits.

Hialeah passed ordinances that forbade the ritual animal sacrifice, but in a way that affected only adherents of Santeria. (Kosher or halal slaughter was exempt, for example.) *Church of the Lukumi Babalu Aye*, 508 U.S. at 526-528. According to the Court, the "suppression of the central element of the Santeria worship service was the object of the ordinances." *Id.* at 534. It noted that "few if any killings of animals are prohibited other than Santeria sacrifice, which is proscribed because it occurs during a ritual or ceremony and its primary purpose is to make an offering . . . not food consumption." *Id.* at 536. The ordinances, moreover, swept broadly, "prohibit[ing] Santeria sacrifice even when it does not threaten the city's interest in public health." *Id.* at 538-539.

Four Justices also found that the ordinances' *purpose* was to outlaw Santeria, and that this was sufficient to invalidate them. Quoting extensively from the meeting at which the ordinances were considered and passed, the plurality showed that hostility to Santeria and its practice generally predominated over genuine concerns about animal welfare or public safety. *Id.* at 540-542.

But just as facial neutrality isn't sufficient to insulate laws from strict scrutiny, explicit discrimination against religion isn't sufficient to trigger it. The Washington Constitution placed limits on state aid to religious organizations that were more stringent than those imposed by the Establishment Clause of the First Amendment. Locke v. Davey, 540 U.S. 712 (2004). As a result of those limitations, state law excluded students "pursuing a degree in devotional theology" from a state-funded college scholarship program. *Id.* at 715. Students could attend religious schools, even major in religion, just not take a degree that prepared them for the ministry. *Id.* at 724-725.

But the Court distinguished *Lukumi* and other cases, like *McDaniel v. Paty*. The state "imposes neither criminal nor civil sanctions on any type of religious service or rite." *Id.* at 720. "That a State would deal differently with religious education for the ministry than with education for other callings is . . . not evidence of hostility toward religion." *Id.* at 721. The Court noted that students could still take courses in devotional theology, even if they could not major in the subject. *Id.* at 724-725.

The majority seemed as concerned with federalism as it did with freedom of religion. While it noted that the state could, without running afoul of the Establishment Clause, choose to include students majoring in devotional theology in its scholarship program, the Court was reluctant to hold that, as a matter of free exercise, it was *required to do so*—especially when the state's constitution imposed stricter limits on governmental support of religion. "The State's interest in not funding the pursuit of devotional degrees," the Court wrote, "is substantial and the exclusion of such funding places a relatively minor burden on Promise Scholars." *Id.* at 725. The Court described this gray area where the Free Exercise Clause would not mandate what the Establishment Clause would not prohibit as embodying a necessary "play in the joints." *Id.* at 718.

Justice Scalia, joined by Justice Thomas, penned a vigorous dissent. He argued that "when the State withholds [a] benefit from some individuals solely on the basis of religion, it violates the Free Exercise Clause no less than if it had imposed a special tax." *Id.* at 726-727 (Scalia, J., dissenting).

QUESTION 3. **Snakes alive!** Consider the following state statute:

Handling snakes so as to endanger life—Penalty.

It shall be unlawful for any person, or persons, to display, exhibit, handle, or use any poisonous or dangerous snake or reptile in such a manner as to endanger the life or health of any person; provided, however, that this provision shall not apply to persons engaged in the scientific or zoological study or display of such snakes or reptiles and those persons under their direct supervision. Any person violating the provisions of this section shall be guilty of a misdemeanor and punished by a fine of not less than fifty dollars ($50.00) nor more than one hundred and fifty dollars ($150), or by confinement in jail not exceeding six (6) months, or by both such fine and imprisonment, in the discretion of the court.

Jeff Brown is a member of a fundamentalist Christian sect that believes the Bible commands the faithful to take up serpents and drink poison. He argues that the statute violates the Free Exercise Clause. If he files a motion for declaratory judgment that the statute is unconstitutional, a judge is likely to:

A. Uphold the statute, because it is facially neutral and generally applicable.
B. Invalidate the statute, because an exception is not available for the religiously scrupulous.
C. Invalidate the statute, unless the state can demonstrate a compelling governmental interest and that it is narrowly tailored.
D. Uphold the statute, unless there is evidence of discriminatory purpose or effects.

ANALYSIS. *Smith* tells us that generally applicable statutes are not required to exempt the religiously scrupulous from their operation. The question is whether the exemption for scientists and zoo personnel renders this *not* generally applicable. *Church of the Lukumi Babalu Aye*, moreover, tells us that evidence of discriminatory purpose or effect can trigger strict scrutiny of even an ostensibly facially neutral statute. Therefore, **A** isn't the best answer. Neither is **B** because such an exemption is not required. **C** recites the wrong standard of review, unless a discriminatory purpose or effect is demonstrated; for example, if Jeff could prove that the statute was passed to give law enforcement a tool to use against members of his sect, he could prove discriminatory purpose and have the law invalidated, despite its facial neutrality. That means that of the answers, **D** is the best.

QUESTION 4. **Free exercise potpourri.** Which of the following practices would likely be found to violate the Free Exercise Clause?

A. A state statute authorizing college scholarships for needy citizens of the State of Ames, but excluding students wishing to pursue studies in devotional theology.
B. A state statute prohibiting the possession or use of marijuana as applied to a devout Rastafarian for whom the use of marijuana is a sacrament.
C. A city ordinance prohibiting the ritual slaughter of animals that exempts hunting and the kosher butchering of animals.
D. A military regulation prohibiting the wearing of religious headgear while in uniform.

ANALYSIS. Time for a quick review. We know that *Smith* held that there was no free exercise right to be exempt from generally applicable laws, even if they incidentally burden religious belief or conduct. That being the case, **B** is not the right answer. *Smith* says that minority religions must petition the legislature, not courts, for exemptions. At the other end of the spectrum, though, *Locke* held that even if the Establishment Clause would not prohibit some government funding or support of religion, the Free Exercise Clause—under the theory of "play in the joints"—does not mandate that support, should the government withhold it. Therefore, **A** is not the correct answer. That leaves **C** or **D**. A facially neutral law proscribing conduct must be truly neutral; it cannot have either the purpose or effect of targeting a particular religion or religious practice or belief. The facts in **C** resemble those in the *Church of the Lukumi Babalu Aye*, where a practice is outlawed, with exceptions made for certain cases but not others (e.g., no exception for halal butchering). The carve-outs raise the concern that it either was motivated by an intent to discriminate or has that effect, whatever the motivation. Of the two remaining answers, then, **C** is the better of the two. Recall that the Court upheld a military regulation similar to that in **D**, though Congress later legislatively changed the military's policy by statute.

QUESTION 5. Back tax. Ames City exempts "charitable institutions" from paying property taxes. The definition of charitable institutions includes churches and other houses of worship. In an effort to close a huge budget deficit, Ames City decides to eliminate the church property tax exemption. A study found that churches and other religious buildings occupied some of the most valuable land in Ames City and constituted nearly 90 percent of the claimants for the exemption. Churches and synagogues in the city sue, claiming that excluding them—and only them—from the exemption violates the Free Exercise Clause. A reviewing court would likely:

A. Uphold the repeal, because Ames City is not required to exempt religious groups under the Free Exercise Clause even if it does exempt secular institutions.
B. Uphold the repeal, if it is narrowly tailored to advance a compelling governmental interest.
C. Invalidate the repeal, because it is discriminatory.
D. Invalidate the repeal, because it is tantamount to a tax on religious organizations, which is forbidden by the Free Exercise Clause.

ANALYSIS. If I had asked this question immediately after the discussion of *Church of the Lukumi Babalu Aye*, you might have immediately been drawn to the "invalidate the repeal" choices. But because you remember *Locke*, you see that the simple fact that religious organizations were not included in the exemption—or, rather, had their exemptions revoked—wouldn't necessarily trigger strict scrutiny. First, it's clear from *Smith* that neutral, generally applicable taxes, such as property taxes, would not be subject to strict scrutiny simply because they imposed a financial burden on churches and their congregants, right? Exemptions, then, are often granted as a matter of legislative grace, just as Justice Scalia advocated in *Smith*. Once granted, can they be revoked *for churches only* without violating the Free Exercise Clause? The answer, after *Locke v. Davey*, is yes. Therefore, **A** is the best answer. There are no facts to suggest that the repeal was motivated by hostility; therefore, strict scrutiny would not be triggered. Accordingly, **B** is incorrect, because its premise (strict scrutiny would apply) is wrong. **C** is also incorrect, because even if we conceded that the repeal for churches and no other institutions is "discriminatory" in some sense of the word, a very similar measure was upheld in *Locke*. **D**, which summarizes Justice Scalia's dissent in *Locke*, is also incorrect. With the exemption withdrawn, churches are put in no different position than other owners and businesses that must pay property taxes. While there is no constitutional bar to granting them an exemption, *Locke*'s principle of "play in the joints" suggests that state and local governments are not obliged to provide that exemption as a matter of free exercise.

QUESTION 6. Scarf snafu. Disturbed by the prospect of religious conflict in its increasingly diverse public school system, the Ames General Assembly passes a law prohibiting the wearing of religious ornamentation at school, defined as any "item of clothing, headgear, jewelry, or other accessory worn on the body that symbolizes, announces, advertises, or signifies attachment to a particular religion, religious sect, or denomination." If challenged, the law would likely be:

A. Upheld, as a neutral, generally applicable law that applies to all religious attire.

B. Upheld, because while public schools could permit religious clothing to be worn without violating the Establishment Clause, they are not required to permit the wearing of religious clothing as a matter of free exercise.

C. Invalidated, because it targets religious, but not secular, conduct or belief.

D. Invalidated, because it burdens religious belief or conduct.

ANALYSIS. Though the statute applies to *all* religious clothing, headgear, jewelry, etc., it applies *only* to items that are identifiable with religion. That means it is not neutral and generally applicable within the meaning of *Smith*. Therefore, **A** is not the right answer. **B** is not correct either because while not everything that is permitted by the Establishment Clause is required by the Free Exercise Clause, it does not follow that *nothing* permitted by the Establishment Clause has any free exercise implications. At a minimum, targeting religious belief or conduct because of its religious character is at least subject to strict scrutiny, and a government would have a difficult time justifying such a ban. That means that of the remaining answers, **C** is the best; merely burdening conduct, as in **D**, is not sufficient for a Free Exercise Clause violation.

C. Establishment Clause

1. *Introduction*

The Court's Establishment Clause jurisprudence seeks to answer the following question: To what extent is government permitted to support, directly or indirectly, religion or religious observance? One's answer to that question turns at least in part on what one thinks "establishment of religion" means. Recent scholarship, endorsed by at least one Supreme Court Justice, suggests that the Establishment Clause was largely a "federalism" provision designed to ensure that there was no *national* official church, but was not designed to prevent *states* from establishing official churches. In fact, at the time the Bill of Rights was ratified there were still official churches, the last of which wasn't disestablished until the first half of the nineteenth century. On this reading, the Establishment Clause permits anything short of outright coercion—physical or financial—on the part of government to force its citizens to support a particular sect or denomination.

At the other extreme are those who favor Jefferson's "wall of separation" metaphor, which sums up a much broader conception of establishment. For "separationists," most governmental support for or involvement in religion or religious observance is at least constitutionally suspect. A strict separationist approach—which the Court has never embraced—would lead to absurd results—for example, the fire department can't put out church fires because to do so would be to indirectly support religion. More difficult questions involve, say, permitting tax deductions for donations to religious organizations. By permitting such deductions, the government is, at least indirectly, subsidizing religion. In the middle is "neutrality," where the government is not set in opposition to religion, nor may it appear to support or endorse one sect or denomination over others—or even support religion over a lack of belief. Until the late 1980s, neutrality, as represented by the so-called *Lemon* test, summarized the Court's approach to Establishment Clause cases in general.

In the much-maligned *Lemon* test, named for *Lemon v. Kurtzman*, 403 U.S. 602 (1971), the Court synthesized its prior cases and articulated a three-part test that laws must pass. In the Court's words: "First, the statute must have a secular legislative purpose; second, its principal or primary effect must be one that neither advances nor inhibits religion; finally, the statute must not foster an excessive government entanglement with religion." *Lemon*, 403 U.S. at 612-613.

Lemon has its critics, notably Justice Scalia, who once compared it to "some ghoul in a late-night horror movie that repeatedly sits up in its grave and shuffles abroad, after being repeatedly killed and buried," but none of its proposed replacements have to date garnered the votes of five Justices. Lamb's Chapel v. Center Moriches Union Free School Dist., 508 U.S. 384, 398 (1993) (Scalia, J., concurring). In recent years, though, the test has undergone some apparent evolution; in some cases, it is completely absent. Nevertheless, if you don't have a case on point, and need somewhere to begin an analysis, *Lemon* remains a good place to start.

The remainder of this chapter will take up three general subjects: government aid to religions; government endorsement of religion; and governmental accommodation of religion. Governmental endorsement will differentiate between governmental endorsement in public schools and that endorsement occurring elsewhere in the public square.

2. *Government aid to religions*

If one were to look for evidence of greater tolerance of religion in the Court's case law, its journey from stringent separation to accommodation in the area of government aid would furnish a number of examples.

As it happens, the font of the Court's Establishment Clause jurisprudence involved a funding case. New Jersey had a program to reimburse the parents of parochial school children for the cost of transporting those students to their schools. (Public school children were transported for free on school buses.) Everson v. Board of Educ., 330 U.S. 1, 3 (1947). This program was challenged as violating the Establishment Clause. Though Justice Black, writing for the majority in *Everson*, invoked the "wall of separation" language, he and four other Justices upheld the program. The legislation, he explained, "does no more than provide a general program to help parents get their children, regardless of their religion, safely and expeditiously to and from accredited schools." *Everson*, 330 U.S. at 18. Though the Establishment Clause "requires the State to be [] neutral in its relations with groups of religious believers and non-believers" it "does not require the state to be their adversary." *Id.*

Important for the *Everson* Court was the fact that the aid was indirect—the money was paid to parents, not to the schools directly. For many years, the direct/indirect aid distinction often meant the difference between upholding aid and invalidating it, even when the aid was the in-kind contribution of instructional materials as opposed to cash. *See, e.g.*, Wolman v. Walter, 433 U.S. 229 (1977) (voiding loan of materials other than books on the ground that materials could be adapted for religious instruction); Meek v. Pittenger, 421 U.S. 349 (1975) (invalidating provision of maps and lab equipment). One exception was *Board of Education v. Allen*, 392 U.S. 236 (1968), in which the Court upheld a program that loaned textbooks used to teach secular subjects in parochial schools.

Beginning in the 1980s, the Court began to move toward a more accommodating approach, one that approved indirect support for religious schools if the support was offered on a neutral basis (i.e., not exclusively to religious schools) and benefited those schools indirectly, as a result of choices parents made. Thus, a tax credit offered only to parochial school parents was invalidated in *Committee for Public Education v. Nyquist*, 413 U.S. 756 (1973), while a similar credit offered to both parochial *and* public school parents to offset educational costs was upheld in *Mueller v. Allen*, 463 U.S. 388 (1983).

The *Mueller* Court rejected the plaintiffs' "establishment in effect" argument, which asked the Court to recognize that private, not public, school parents would take advantage of the tax credit and that most private schools were parochial or sectarian. "We would be loath to adopt a rule grounding the constitutionality of a facially neutral law on annual reports reciting the extent to which various classes of private citizens claimed benefits under the law." 463 U.S. at 401.

The Court also upheld aid to *students*, even if those students attended religious schools. *Witters v. Washington Department of Services for the Blind*, 474 U.S. 481 (1986), upheld the award of a scholarship for handicapped students to a blind student attending a Christian college in preparation for the ministry. *Zobrest v. Catalina Foothills School District*, 509 U.S. 1 (1993), upheld the state's provision of a sign language interpreter for a deaf student attending Catholic school. A common theme in the two cases was that the aid was awarded on a neutral basis to all students; it wasn't available *only* to students attending religious schools.

Initially, however, the Court was still reluctant to permit direct state aid to religious schools. In *Aguilar v. Felton*, 473 U.S. 402 (1985), and *Grand Rapids School District v. Ball*, 473 U.S. 373 (1985), the Court invalidated a federal program that provided money to parochial schools to hire remedial math and reading teachers. Though the program included extensive regulations to ensure that it did not, in the language of *Lemon*, "advance" religion—including removing religious symbols from walls and surprise inspections—the Court concluded that the elaborate monitoring fostered "excessive entanglement" between the religious schools and the government. *Aguilar*, 473 U.S. at 413.

Twelve years later, however, the Court reversed course in *Agostini v. Felton*, 521 U.S. 203 (1997), overruling *Aguilar* and *Ball* and permitting direct aid. The Court concluded that the programs were neutral and this neutrality meant that the aid was less likely to advance religion. *Agostini*, 521 U.S. at 243-235. No longer would the Court regard direct aid to parochial schools as presumptively unconstitutional. *Id.* at 235. The Court further rejected *Aguilar*'s and *Ball*'s assumption that paying for secular teachers in parochial schools promoted entanglement: "Not all entanglements . . . have the effect of advancing or inhibiting religion. Interaction between church and state is inevitable, and we have always tolerated some level of involvement between the two."

Id. at 233. Following *Agostini*, many observers wondered whether *Lemon* was on its way out. Presumably the inquiry would then be—in funding cases at least—whether the aid was offered neutrally, that is, to secular and sectarian recipients alike. If so, then the Establishment Clause would not prohibit the inclusion of sectarian institutions.

Neutrality, however, failed to garner five votes in *Mitchell v. Helms*, 530 U.S. 793 (2000), though the Court in that case did uphold the inclusion of religious schools in a federal program providing media and library materials, including computers and software to schools. *Helms* overruled *Meek* and *Wolman*, but Justice O'Connor declined to make neutrality the only criterion for assessing the constitutionality of aid to parochial schools. *Helms*, 530 U.S. at 838-840 (O'Connor, J., concurring).

A bare 5-4 majority, moreover, upheld Ohio's voucher program enabling students of underperforming schools to enroll in participating private schools, including parochial schools. Zelman v. Simmons-Harris, 536 U.S. 639 (2002). Analogizing the program to the system of tax credits in *Mueller*, the majority found that the fact the money went to parochial schools as a result of parents' individual choices meant that the effect of the program was not to advance religion. *Zelman*, 536 U.S. at 652. The Court explained that

> where a government aid program is neutral with respect to religion, and provides assistance directly to a broad class of citizens who, in turn, direct government aid to religious schools wholly as a result of their own genuine and independent private choice, the program is not readily subject to challenge under the Establishment Clause.

Id.

With regard to aid, then, it appears that the Court's latest cases alter *Lemon* somewhat, or create some presumptions when it comes to aid furnished to secular and religious organizations on a neutral basis. First, the neutrality usually means that there's little doubt that the aid furthers a secular purpose. Second, neutrality likewise seems to create a presumption that the aid is not intended to advance or inhibit religion. Third, this lack of advancement means that there is little danger of "excessive entanglement." The upshot is that the Court has gradually moved from a stance of skepticism toward direct or indirect funding of religious schools or institutions, to one of more accommodation.

QUESTION 7. **Oh my darlin' *Lemon*-tine.** Which of the following statements about the *Lemon v. Kurtzman* test is true?

A. It looks to governmental purpose to ascertain the constitutionality of a law.

B. It has been replaced by the Court with a test that examines the "neutrality" of laws.

C. It requires total separation between church and state.

D. It is no longer good law.

ANALYSIS. Though *Lemon* has been much maligned, it has never been overruled or replaced explicitly with another test. At most, the Court has simply declined to use it or has disclaimed reliance on it in particular cases. Therefore, **B** and **D** are incorrect. Moreover, even though *Lemon* represents the high-water mark for the Court's requirement that government be "neutral" toward religion, it was never a test that required strict separation; in fact, the Court has never adopted that position. Therefore, **C** is incorrect. What *Lemon* does require is that a law (1) have a secular purpose, (2) not have the effect of advancing or inhibiting religion, and (3) not promote excessive entanglement between government and religion. Because the first prong looks to the purpose of the law, **A** is the best answer.

QUESTION 8. E-lab-oration. Concerned that its school-age children are falling behind those elsewhere in the United States and in the world, the State of Ames has passed legislation providing funding for updating science labs and for hiring experienced science teachers in both public and private schools. Opponents noted that 90 percent of private schools in Ames are sectarian schools, and that including those schools would violate the Establishment Clause. The amended bill passed and was immediately challenged in federal court by a civil liberties group as unconstitutional. A reviewing court would likely:

- **A.** Invalidate the statute, because, in effect, it benefits religious schools only.
- **B.** Invalidate the statute, because it results in the state's excessive entanglement with religion.
- **C.** Uphold the lab equipment, but invalidate the provision for funding teachers' positions, because paying teachers would result in excessive entanglement.
- **D.** Uphold the bill, because it is part of a general scheme of aid offered to both public and private schools.

ANALYSIS. Such a program would likely have been invalidated in the mid-1980s, but by the mid-1990s the Court was much more amenable to aid—even direct aid—that was offered on a neutral basis to private and public schools alike. First things first: The information about the percentage of private schools that are parochial versus sectarian is a red herring. As far back as *Mueller* the Court has refused to consider an "establishment in effect" argument against the New York tax credit designed to reimburse parents for school-related expenses. Therefore, **A** is incorrect. Further, as made clear in *Agostini v. Felton*, the Court has begun to collapse the "advancement" and "entanglement" tests when aid is offered on a neutral basis. In other words, when aid is offered to all schools, the Court now presumes that means it is less likely that it will advance religion, which, in turn, means that there is little chance of excessive entanglement. This is true even if the aid flows directly to the school. Therefore, **B** and **C** are incorrect. That leaves **D**, which is the best answer. The *Helms* case endorsed the provision of materials directly to schools, overturning earlier cases like *Wolman* and *Meek*. Therefore, the materials for updating science labs in parochial schools would be fine. As noted earlier, *Agostini* would mean that the aid for paying teachers to teach science would likely pass muster, too.

QUESTION 9. A matter of degree. The State of Ames sponsors a scholarship program that awards ten scholarships to outstanding students in the state. The scholarship provides for four years of college, including room, board, tuition, and books, as well as a summer abroad during that four years. One of this year's winners enrolls at a private, religious college and takes on a degree program preparing him for the ministry. After he is interviewed by a local paper, suit is filed to force the state to exclude those studying for the ministry from the scholarship program. The suit claims the would-be minister's inclusion violates the Establishment Clause. Would a reviewing court likely agree?

A. Yes, because the program involves excessive entanglement between the state and religion.
B. Yes, because the program provides direct financial aid to religious organizations.
C. No, because the scholarship program is offered on a neutral basis and religion benefits, if at all, indirectly and through the exercise of individual choice.
D. No, because there is no state coercion of religious belief or observance involved.

ANALYSIS. It's déjà vu all over again! These facts ought to remind you a bit of those in *Locke v. Davey*. There the question, though, was whether the Free Exercise Clause *prohibits* the state from excluding students like our would-be minister from a scholarship program, where the state's own version of the Establishment Clause required the exclusion. Citing the need for "play in the joints" between the Free Exercise and Establishment Clauses, the Court said inclusion was not required as a matter of constitutional law. Here the question is whether a state could choose to *include* the would-be minister in that scholarship program. First, you'll notice that the aid is offered on a non-preferential basis to all students, regardless of where they enroll or in what they major. According to the Court in *Agostini*, *Helms*, and *Zelman*, this neutrality eliminates any concern that the effect is to advance religion and any possibility of excessive entanglement. Thus, **A** is incorrect. Moreover, note that the aid flowing to religious schools occurs because of the exercise of individual choice, a fact that caused the Court in *Mueller* and *Zelman*, as well as *Everson*, to uphold the aid programs. **B**, then, is incorrect, because it states that the aid was direct. In any event, after *Helms* and *Agostini*, direct aid to parochial schools, if part of a general aid package available to all, is no longer presumptively unconstitutional. **D** is incorrect because the Establishment Clause prohibits more than actual coercion of religious belief or observance. That leaves **C**, which is the best answer. The Court upheld a program similar to the one described above in *Witters v. Washington Department of Services for the Blind*, 474 U.S. 481 (1986).

3. Governmental endorsement of religion

(a) Public schools There is a notable exception to the Court's gradual shift toward the "accommodation" side of the Establishment Clause spectrum: government endorsement of religion in public schools. In general, the Court has not been receptive to arguments that some religious observance or instruction should be tolerated in public schools. Not surprisingly, given the relatively religious nature of the United States citizenry, these decisions are among the Court's most controversial and, in some parts of the country, likely the most flouted as well.

The year after the *Everson* case, the Court invalidated a "release time" program in which public school students who elected to do so left their secular classes to receive religious instruction from clergy on school grounds. McCollum v. Board of Education, 333 U.S. 203 (1948). Following *McCollum*, the practice was altered so that students wishing to receive religious instruction would be released from classes and receive the instruction off school grounds; other students would remain in study hall during that time. A divided Court upheld this practice in *Zorach v. Clauson*, 343 U.S. 306 (1952). The Court observed that "[t]his 'released time' program involves neither religious instruction in public school classrooms nor the expenditure of public funds." *Zorach*, 343 U.S. at 308-309. The Court rejected the notion that the First Amendment required church and state to "be aliens to each other—hostile, suspicious, and even unfriendly." *Id.* at 312.

A decade later, the Court passed on the constitutionality of the common practice of opening public school with a teacher-led prayer or Bible verse reading. The Court invalidated both. Engel v. Vitale, 370 U.S. 421 (1962) (prayer); School Dist. of Abington v. Schempp, 374 U.S. 203 (1963) (Bible reading). The Court was later to invalidate Alabama's "moment of silence" statute, which authorized one minute of silence for "meditation or voluntary prayer" after evidence emerged that the statute had been amended to include "voluntary prayer" in an effort to reintroduce prayer in school. The General Assembly's motive, the Court concluded, was impermissible. Wallace v. Jaffree, 472 U.S. 38 (1985).

Even when schools have attempted to replace teacher-led prayers with prayers led by non-school officials or by students at school events, the Court has invalidated them. In *Lee v. Weisman*, 505 U.S. 577 (1992), the Court invalidated the practice of having a non-denominational prayer at a public middle school graduation. The majority concluded that forcing students to sit silently through the prayer at an event, like graduation, that most would feel compelled to attend was a form of psychological coercion. Coercion to acquiesce or participate in a prayer or other religious observance is at the heart of what the Establishment Clause forbids, according to the Court. *Lee*, 505 U.S. at 592-594. "Finding no violation under these circumstances," the Court concluded, "would place objectors in the dilemma of participating, with all that it implies, or protesting. . . . [T]he State may not, consistent with the Establishment Clause, place primary and secondary school children in this position." *Id.* at 593.

The Court next struck a student-led prayer at high school football games in *Santa Fe Independent School District v. Doe*, 530 U.S. 290 (2000). Again the Court's concern was for those students—athletes, band members, and cheerleaders—who had to attend the games and sit through the prayer, or forgo extracurricular activities altogether. *Santa Fe Indep. School Dist.*, 530 U.S. at 311-312.

QUESTION 10. Lunchroom liturgy. The student body of a high school in Ames City has elected a student "chaplain" to the student council. The new student chaplain begins a practice of saying grace in the cafeteria before the lunch period. It is student-led, but faculty and staff have tolerated the practice, even participating by standing with the students and bowing their heads. A group of students and their parents object, claiming that the practice violates the Establishment Clause. The group files suit in federal court. The judge hearing the case will likely:

A. Enjoin the practice, because prayer is never permitted in school.
B. Dismiss the suit, because no school officials are involved in the selection of the student or the prayer itself.
C. Enjoin the practice, because students are required to be in school and are likely to feel psychological coercion to participate or sit in respectful silence.
D. Dismiss the suit because participation is voluntary.

ANALYSIS. The Court is suspicious of organized, government-sponsored religious observances in public schools, even "voluntary" ones. The Court assumes that, unlike adults, children are subject to subtle coercion to conform (as well as the more direct kind that requires them to attend school). Therefore, simply because the pre-meal prayer is voluntary would not be sufficient to insulate it from an Establishment Clause challenge. Even the schoolchildren in the 1960s were, theoretically, able to excuse themselves from prayer and Bible reading if they did not wish to participate. Thus, **D** is incorrect. But

A goes too far: Individual students can pray at school if they wish (as long as they are not disrupting class). **B**, too, is incorrect, because having student-led prayer or prayer led by a non–school official is no protection against an Establishment Clause challenge, as both *Lee v. Weisman* and the *Doe* case make clear. That leaves **C**, which accurately captures the Court's presumptions about students and school prayer.

A second area in which the Court has been quite active in public schools concerns the introduction of religious symbols into schools or of religious content into the curriculum. Symbols placed in schools because of their religious content or message (as opposed to those in a textbook or classroom display for historical purposes) are forbidden by the Establishment Clause. The Court invalidated Kentucky's attempt to place the Ten Commandments in public school classrooms in *Stone v. Graham*, 449 U.S. 39 (1980). The Court was not persuaded by arguments that they were placed there as historical documents. *Stone*, 449 U.S. at 41.

The Court has also held firm against attempts either to bar the teaching of the theory of evolution or to force those teaching evolution to teach alternative theories like "creation science" or its successor "intelligent design" alongside evolution. In *Epperson v. Arkansas*, 393 U.S. 97 (1968), the Court invalidated a state law that prohibited the teaching of evolution. The Court concluded that the law's purpose was to promote a particular sectarian viewpoint. *Epperson*, 393 U.S. at 107-108.

Twenty years later the Court struck down a Louisiana law mandating the teaching of "creation science" if the theory of evolution was taught. The Court refused "to be blind" to "the legislature's preeminent religious purpose in enacting [the] statute. There is a historic and contemporaneous link between the teachings of certain religious denominations and the teaching of evolution." Edwards v. Aguillard, 482 U.S. 578, 590 (1987). The Court found "no clear secular purpose for the Louisiana Act." *Id.* at 585. It rejected arguments that the Act was intended to protect academic freedom, observing that "requiring schools to teach creation science with evolution does not advance academic freedom. The Act does not grant teachers a flexibility that they did not already possess." *Id.* at 587. It also noted that there was a discriminatory preference in favor of creation science and against evolution: While the Act contained guarantees for creation science and those who taught it, there were no comparable protections for evolution or its teachers. *Id.* at 588.

As noted in the Free Exercise section, however, because the Free Exercise Clause bars schools from *discriminating* against religious groups when it makes its premises available before or after school hours to student groups, a school does not violate the Establishment Clause by doing so. *See, e.g.*, Good News Club v. Milford Central School, 533 U.S. 98 (2001).

QUESTION 11. Curricular kerfuffle. The State of Ames legislature recently passed a law requiring all biology classes to teach "intelligent design" if the theory of evolution is taught. Intelligent design rejects evolution, arguing that it is scientifically impossible for living things to have evolved through numerous genetic mutations. Which of the following could a court rely on to support a finding that the legislature's law violated the Establishment Clause?

A. A legislative finding that evolution is one of many theories concerning the origins of life and that students should be encouraged to think critically about scientific theories, and explore their strengths and weaknesses.
B. Legislative statements from the floor debate over the law in which supporters claimed evolution was "anti-Christian" and theories like intelligent design had to be introduced to combat the influence of "secular humanism."
C. A past committee report that sought intelligent design's inclusion so that students could explore the "scientific method" and compare evolution and intelligent design to decide which, if either, fits the definition of a scientific theory.
D. The fact that some proponents of intelligent design believe that aliens were the "intelligent designers."

ANALYSIS. In the Court's cases dealing with evolution and creation science, much turns on the purpose of the legislature. In *Epperson* and *Aguillard* the Court was suspicious of reasons for either banning the teaching of evolution altogether or requiring that "creation science" be taught along with evolution. In neither case could the Court find a valid secular purpose, as required by the *Lemon* test. Of the choices here, **A** and **C** would not support a decision to invalidate, because both recite plausible secular purposes for including intelligent design in the curriculum. **D** wouldn't support a decision to invalidate either. That leaves **B**, which is the best answer, because the statements suggest an intent to promote a particular sectarian point of view by forcing intelligent design to be taught.

(b) Other governmental endorsement If the Court has been fairly consistent in its approach to religious observance in public schools, its approach in cases involving government endorsement of religion or religious displays on governmental property outside of public schools has not been a model of consistency, to put it mildly.

On the one hand, the Court has upheld Sunday closing laws, accepting the argument that prescribing a uniform day of rest is a valid secular purpose. McGowan v. Maryland, 366 U.S. 420 (1961). The Court, citing historical practice, also upheld Nebraska's practice of opening legislative sessions with a prayer led by a chaplain paid for with public funds. Marsh v. Chambers, 463 U.S. 783 (1983). The Court recently extended *Marsh* to encompass a town's practice of opening town board meetings with a prayer led by local volunteer ministers. Town of Greece v. Galloway, 2014 WL 1757828 (2014). Challengers attempted to distinguish *Marsh* on two grounds: first, that the town meeting prayers were sectarian; and second, that those in attendance might be subject to subtle coercive pressure to participate or at least not leave the room in order to avoid offending officials before whom they might have business. *Town of Greece*, 2014 WL 1757828, at *8.

A majority of the Court rejected those arguments. "An insistence on nonsectarian or ecumenical prayer as a single, fixed standard," Justice Kennedy wrote, "is not consistent with the tradition of legislative prayer outlined in the Court's cases." *Id.* at *9. The Court cited a number of examples, both old and new, that ran counter to that tradition. The majority did note that the tradition had limits. "If the course and practice over time," Kennedy added, "shows that the invocations denigrate nonbelievers or religious minorities, threaten damnation, or preach conversion, many present may consider the prayer to fall short of the desire to elevate the purpose . . . and to unite lawmakers in their common efforts." *Id.* at *11. Such prayers "would present a different case than the one presently before the Court." *Id.*

For Justices Thomas and Scalia, that was that; neither joined the second part of Kennedy's opinion, in which he rebutted arguments that *Marsh* was inapplicable because the town meeting prayer was subtly coercive. *Id.* at *25 (Thomas, J., concurring) ("[T]o the extent coercion is relevant to the Establishment Clause analysis, it is actual legal coercion that counts—not the 'subtle coercive pressures' allegedly felt by respondents in this cases . . . ."). In a portion of his concurring opinion that Justice Scalia did not join, Justice Thomas reiterated his view that the Establishment Clause "probably prohibits Congress from establishing a national religion" and nothing more. *Id.* at *23 (Thomas, J., concurring).

Kennedy's plurality opinion concluded that, on the facts, "the Court is not persuaded that the town . . . through the act of offering a brief, solemn, and respectful prayer to open its monthly meetings, compelled its citizens to engage in a religious observance," but conceded that the inquiry was a fact-sensitive one. *Id.* at *14. He noted in particular that board members did not "direct[] the public to participate in the prayers," single out the nonobservant for "opprobrium," or "indicate[] that their decisions might be influenced by a person's acquiescence in the prayer opportunity." *Id.* at *15. He also distinguished the case from *Lee v. Weisman* because, unlike in *Lee*, those not wishing to participate in the prayer were free to leave the room, or arrive after the ceremony was concluded. It was also relevant that the respondents in the case were adults, not schoolchildren at a graduation ceremony. *Id.* at *16.

The principal dissent, written by Justice Kagan, faulted the town for not being sufficiently inclusive of other faiths in inviting clergy to deliver the monthly invocation. *Id.* at *30. (Kagan, J., dissenting). Moreover, on her reading of the facts, the prayers delivered were impermissibly sectarian and could send the message that the outcome of any matters one had before the town council might be affected by one's participation (or not) in the prayer. *Id.* at *32 (Kagan, J., dissenting). What occurred monthly in Greece's meetings was, in her opinion, different than the opening prayer in *Marsh. Id.* at *34 (Kagan, J., dissenting).

The Court's reaction to religious displays on public property, however, has been more equivocal, as the decisions in *Lynch v. Donnelly*, 465 U.S. 668 (1984), and *Allegheny County v. Greater Pittsburgh ACLU*, 492 U.S. 573 (1989), demonstrate. In *Lynch*, a nativity scene (crèche) was included as part of a larger Christmas display in a public park in Pawtucket, Rhode Island. As described by the Court, the display included the crèche along with "a Santa Claus house, reindeer pulling Santa's sleigh, candy-striped poles, a Christmas tree, carolers, cutout figures representing such characters as a clown, an elephant, and a teddy bear, hundreds of colored lights [and] a large banner that read[] 'SEASONS GREETINGS' . . . ." 465 U.S. at 671.

While declining to be bound to apply *Lemon* in all Establishment Clause cases, the Court proceeded to more or less apply the *Lemon* test to Pawtucket's display. First, the Court concluded that "there is insufficient evidence to establish that the inclusion of the crèche is a purposeful or surreptitious effort to express some kind of subtle governmental advocacy of a particular religious message." *Id.* at 680. Rather, the Court concluded, the city was simply acknowledging an event of historical significance for many people.

The Court was also "unable to discern a greater aid to religion deriving from inclusion of the crèche," concluding that there was no significant advancement. It explained that "display of the crèche is no more an advancement or endorsement of religion than the Congressional and Executive recognition of the origins of the Holiday itself. . . ." *Id.* at 683. Summing up, the Court was "satisfied that the city has a secular purpose for including the crèche, that the city has not impermissibly advanced religion, and that including the crèche does not create excessive entanglement between religion and government." *Id.* at 685.

Justice O'Connor concurred, proposing that the test be "whether Pawtucket has endorsed Christianity by its display of the crèche." *Id.* at 690 (O'Connor, J., concurring). But she never got four other Justices to adopt her endorsement test.

In contrast to *Lynch*, the Court in *Greater Pittsburgh ACLU* invalidated part of a Christmas display in a courthouse. One display included a crèche alone in the public space of a county courthouse. Another display included a menorah alongside a Christmas tree and a sign saluting liberty. 492 U.S. at 578. A fractured Court approved of the menorah while finding that the crèche violated the Establishment Clause. Four Justices would have approved both displays; three Justices would have found both to violate the Establishment

Clause. Justices O'Connor and Blackmun, however, found that the prominence of the crèche in the courthouse public space conveyed endorsement in a way that the menorah didn't. *Id.* at 632-633. In their view, the menorah's religious element was diluted by the presence of the Christmas tree and the banner. *Id.*

The Court has also struggled with the issue of private speech on public land. In *Capitol Square Review & Advisory Board v. Pinette*, 515 U.S. 753 (1995), the Court found that a cross placed in a public forum on public property by private persons did not violate the Establishment Clause. A plurality held that neutral treatment of private religious speech in a public forum could not violate the Establishment Clause. *Pinette*, 515 U.S. at 769. A number of Justices emphasized the presence of the disclaimer at the foot of the cross indicating that it was placed there by private, not public, parties. *Id.* at 782.

Salazar v. Buono, 559 U.S. 700 (2010), appeared to furnish an opportunity for the Court to clarify the status of the endorsement test in a case involving a large war memorial cross placed in the Mohave National Preserve by the Veterans of Foreign Wars (VFW) to honor American war dead. A lower court held that the cross on public land could be perceived as governmental endorsement of Christianity. During the appeal, Congress transferred the property to the VFW in exchange for privately held land elsewhere. A divided Court that produced no clear majority opinion reversed the appeals court and remanded the case to decide, among other things, whether the transfer of land was permissible.

The final group of cases concerns the display of the Ten Commandments. Though *Stone v. Graham*, 449 U.S. 39 (1980), struck down their display in public schools, the Court has been reluctant to require that all similar displays—whatever their origin or history—be removed from public buildings. Indeed, the Supreme Court building itself includes Moses and the Ten Commandments in a "lawgivers" frieze. Two cases from 2005 show that the Court will be sensitive to the context in which religious displays are exhibited and will probe governmental motives in establishing them. *See* McCreary Cnty. v. ACLU, 545 U.S. 844 (2005); Van Orden v. Perry, 545 U.S. 677 (2005).

McCreary County involved attempts by two Kentucky counties to place copies of the Ten Commandments in courthouses, either alone or grouped with other documents alleged to support the claim that the Commandments are a touchstone for law and its development in the United States. 545 U.S. at 850. *Van Orden*, on the other hand, concerned a Ten Commandments display located on the grounds of the Texas State Capitol along with a number of other historic markers and monuments, placed there by the Fraternal Order of Eagles in the early 1960s. 545 U.S. at 681-682. Both displays were the subject of Establishment Clause challenges; in a split decision, the Court invalidated the Kentucky display while allowing the Texas monument to remain.

In the *McCreary County* case, the key for the Court was the lack of a secular purpose motivating the original display, and the insufficiency of subsequent attempts to cure it by adding "historical" documents to the Commandments display. While the County argued that only its last display should be evaluated, Justice Souter responded that "the secular purpose required has to be genuine, not a sham" and that "the world is not made brand new every morning, and the Counties are simply asking us to ignore perfectly probative evidence; they want an absentminded objective observer, not one presumed to be familiar with the history of the government's actions. . . ." 545 U.S. at 864, 866.

The undeniably sectarian atmosphere of the first display (during which a pastor spoke about the Commandments' religious message) was not cured by the subsequent additions. The Court declined to hold that government's "past actions forever taint any effort on their part to deal with the subject matter," or that integration of religious elements into governmental displays on the subject of law were presumptively invalid. *Id.* at 873-874. It did emphasize that context mattered, and "an implausible claim that governmental purpose has changed should not carry the day in a court of law any more than in a head with common sense." *Id.* at 874. Further, it commented that the more "neutral" a display, i.e., one that includes secular figures along with sectarian ones, the less likely an observer would be to think that government was endorsing a particular religious point of view.

In *Van Orden*, however, Justice Breyer voted with the *McCreary County* dissenters (Rehnquist, Thomas, Scalia, and Kennedy) to make a majority, which held that the Texas monument could stay. The plurality opinion by Chief Justice Rehnquist emphasized the historical nature of the monument, and the presence of similar Ten Commandments displays in government buildings (including the Supreme Court). Justice Breyer began his opinion by noting that "the Establishment Clause does not compel the government to purge from the public sphere all that in any way partakes of the religious." 545 U.S. at 699 (Breyer, J., concurring). Responding to dissenters' concerns that the display, and similar monuments, could prove divisive in a religiously pluralistic society, Justice Breyer observed that "40 years passed in which the presence of this monument, legally speaking, went unchallenged." *Id.* at 702 (Breyer, J., concurring). For Justice Breyer, that length of time "suggest[ed] more strongly than can any set of formulaic tests that few individuals, whatever their system of beliefs, are likely to have understood the monument" as governmental endorsement. *Id.* (Breyer, J., concurring). He contrasted that quiescence with the controversy that erupted over the McCreary County display. Justice Breyer closed by remarking that divisiveness is a two-way street—that by striking down any and all such displays, the Court could create the divisiveness over religious issues that the dissenters were trying to avoid.

It is difficult to get a definitive handle on the religious monument cases. The Court's latest—*Salazar v. Buono*—was marred by peculiar procedural facts that prevented the Court from coalescing around a test that could garner five votes. Nevertheless, it is clear that the history and context of the display are central. In general, the longer a religious display has been around without generating significant controversy, the less likely the Court will be to vote to require its removal. If, on the other hand, a new display is installed in circumstances suggesting a sectarian purpose, the Court will be suspicious of attempts to cure the initial defect by inclusion of secular symbols to "dilute" the religious significance.

QUESTION 12. **Poetic justice?** The State of Ames recently completed a new state judicial building. In the building's rotunda is an immense sculpture of a blindfolded female holding scales and a sword. The statue is a traditional representation of Justice, who in turn derives from the Greek goddess Themis and the Roman goddess Justitia. The statue was selected because the planning commission wanted there to be a representation of the law or of justice as a centerpiece in the new building. After a competition, the Themis/Justitia statue was selected. A group of Christian attorneys and courthouse workers file suit, claiming that the statue constitutes an unconstitutional establishment of religion. The suit sought an injunction forcing the State to remove the statute from the rotunda. The injunction should be:

A. Denied, because the average observer would not understand the state to be endorsing Greek or Roman polytheism.
B. Granted, because the display did not include other items that would dilute the statue of its religious significance.
C. Denied, because the display is not coercive.
D. Granted, because there is state action.

ANALYSIS. This is a little tricky. As noted above, the Court has not settled on a formula for adjudicating religious monument cases. The fate of the "endorsement" test is somewhat uncertain since Justice O'Connor's retirement, but Justice Kennedy sometimes favors it. Nevertheless, **A** is the best answer compared with the others. **B** is not the best answer, because the Court has never indicated that religious symbols *require* dilution by the inclusion of other, less sectarian elements in a display. The Court seemed to regard the presence of other elements either as reducing the chances that anyone would perceive endorsement or that the presence of a religious display (like a crèche) in a larger display was unlikely to advance religion appreciably, especially when the larger display was intended merely to mark the event itself (a secular purpose) as opposed to celebrating the religious significance that many attach to a holiday like Christmas. **C** is incorrect not only because lack of actual coercion is not sufficient to escape scrutiny under the Establishment Clause, but also because the concept does not usually come into play in the religious display cases. **D** is also incorrect. While state action is an essential element of an Establishment Clause claim, it is only the beginning of that inquiry, not its end. The question is whether the state action itself somehow violates the Establishment Clause.

QUESTION 13. Display drama. It's Christmas in Ames City! To celebrate the season, the city regularly displays banners that hang from the lampposts along Main Street. Each banner bears a separate seasonal symbol and the banners are alternated among the lampposts. Banners include Santa Claus, Mrs. Claus, Frosty the Snowman, Rudolph the Red-Nosed Reindeer, and a baby in a manger, intended to represent the baby Jesus. Which of the following would constitute an argument in favor of the display's constitutionality?

A. The presence of secular symbols offsets or dilutes the manger banner's possible religious significance.
B. The city chose the symbols in order to acknowledge the holiday.
C. The average observer would not understand the display to convey a religious message.
D. Any of the above.

ANALYSIS. If you paid attention to the last answer, this should be easy! The answer is **D**: Any of the arguments would go a ways to support the display's constitutionality. In *Lynch*, the Court concluded that by electing to have a display to acknowledge an historic holiday, as suggested in **B**, Pawtucket was pursuing a secular end. Moreover, including the manger banner as one among other representations of the seasons (as in **A**) suggests, according to *Lynch*, that there is little chance that religion would be significantly advanced as a result. Further, to the extent that "endorsement" is still at play for the Court, the proliferation of seasonal symbols would tend to reduce the chances of an objective observer understanding that the City was endorsing any particular conception of Christmas (**C**). Any of those answers would support a finding that the display was constitutional; therefore, **D** is the best answer.

QUESTION 14. Creche-endo. Assume that instead of the banner display in Question 13, Ames City has erected a Nativity scene in the county courthouse, along with a sign that reads, "A King is Born!" Does the city's display violate the Establishment Clause?

A. Yes, because it appears the city is endorsing Christianity.
B. No, because the display is not coercive.
C. No, under the test in *Lemon*.
D. Yes, because no religious imagery is permitted in courthouses.

ANALYSIS. In contrast to the last question, the display here is something of a problem. Not only does the crèche stand alone, but the centrality of it is reinforced by a banner that proclaims the identity of the child in the manger as the Messiah. A reasonable observer could believe that the prominence of the display, coupled with the unambiguously *Christian* message, suggests some level of endorsement. **B** is incorrect because the degree to which the display is "coercive" does not really figure into the analysis. Similarly, **C** isn't a good answer, because one might question whether there is a secular purpose in placing the crèche with the banner in so prominent a public building. This is not the display in *Lynch*, with its mishmash of seasonal symbols. The facts here seem closer to the display invalidated in *Greater Pittsburgh ACLU*. **D** isn't accurate; as noted above, the Supreme Court building itself contains representations of the Ten Commandments. That leaves, **A**, which is the best answer. Though we don't know the precise status of the endorsement test, and while it has not replaced the *Lemon* test, it is often employed by a plurality of Court members to evaluate the constitutionality of religious monuments in public buildings.

4. *Governmental accommodation of religion*

We conclude where the chapter began, really: What limits does the Establishment Clause place on governmental efforts to accommodate religion? In the funding context, we saw that the Court has moved to a more accommodationist approach, at least if religion is included in a funding program that awards money to secular and sectarian institutions on a neutral basis. What about in other areas? In general, the Establishment Clause is not a bar to legislative exemptions for the religiously observant. For example, exempting conscientious objectors from military service—but only those who object to *all* war, as opposed to those who believe that a particular war is unjust—did not violate the Establishment Clause. Gillette v. United States, 401 U.S. 437 (1971). Similarly, the Court has upheld exemptions from Title VII's antidiscrimination provisions for religious institutions. Corporation of Presiding Bishop v. Amos, 483 U.S. 327 (1987); *see also* Hosanna-Tabor Evangelical Lutheran Church and School v. EEOC, 132 S. Ct. 694, 708 (2012) (concluding that First Amendment compelled a "ministerial exception" from antidiscrimination laws and that exception applied to minister-teacher's employment discrimination claim). Further, in *Cutter v. Wilkinson*, 544 U.S. 709 (2005), the Court upheld the Religious Land Use and Institutionalized Persons Act (RLUIPA), which requires the application of strict scrutiny to any burden on free exercise imposed on a person in a federal institution (such as a prison). The Court found RLUIPA to be a permissible accommodation offered to all religiously observant persons. The Court also held that religious accommodations do not violate the Establishment Clause simply because the non-observant do not benefit from them. *Wilkinson*, 544 U.S. at 724.

On the other hand, the Court has invalidated laws that force *private* businesses to accommodate the religiously observant or that delegate governmental power to religious organizations or institutions. So, in *Estate of Thornton v. Caldor, Inc.*, 472 U.S. 703 (1985), the Court invalidated a Connecticut law prohibiting employers from firing someone for refusing to work on the person's Sabbath. Similarly, in *Larkin v. Grendel's Den, Inc.*, 459 U.S. 116 (1982), the Court invalidated a Massachusetts law giving churches the power to veto applications for liquor licenses for establishments located within 500 feet of a church. In *Board of Educ. of Kiryas Joel Sch. Dist. v. Grumet*, 512 U.S. 687 (1994), the Court invalidated a New York law authorizing a Hasidic sect to form its own school district so that it could provide special education services in its religious schools.

The Court also invalidated an exemption for religious periodicals only in *Texas Monthly v. Bullock*, 489 U.S. 1 (1989). The plurality decision relied on the fact that no other publications were eligible for the exemption. The opinion distinguished earlier cases, including *Walz v. Tax Commission*, 397 U.S. 664 (1970), in which the Court upheld the charitable deduction for donations to churches. Unlike in *Texas Monthly*, the plurality noted that the deduction in *Walz* was part of a larger package of benefits that furthered secular goals, not simply religious ones. *Texas Monthly* is a little difficult to reconcile with more recent cases like *Wilkinson*. It is unclear how they are to be reconciled, if indeed they can be.

D. The Closer

QUESTION 15. Court-ing controversy. The State of Ames is building a new appellate court building that will house the Ames Supreme Court, and the courts of civil and criminal appeals. The Chief Justice of the State of Ames calls seeking your advice on the decoration of the courthouse atrium, through which all persons working in, visiting, or doing business with the courts will enter. She has some discretion to purchase furnishings for the public areas, and she would like to place excerpts from the Magna Carta, the Declaration of Independence, and Lincoln's Gettysburg Address, plus a copy of the Ten Commandments along the walls facing the entrance. She says that each document has special significance in the life and development of American law, and she wants to celebrate the Anglo-American commitment to the rule of law. But, she adds, she wants to know if the inclusion of the Ten Commandments is constitutional. She insists that the inclusion of the Ten Commandments represents part of our legal heritage, and that is why she wants it included. A group calling itself Citizens for a Secular Court files suit, claiming that the Chief Justice's Ten

Commandments display is unconstitutional. Which of the following would be most helpful to the group's case?

A. The fact that the display was not visible to those entering the courthouse.
B. The fact that the U.S. Supreme Court has a similar display in its courthouse.
C. The fact that the Chief Justice gave a speech emphasizing the importance of recognizing "God's Law" in the adjudication of cases.
D. The fact that the display replicates a display in the old appellate court building, which was built in the early twentieth century.

ANALYSIS. We know from the display cases that context matters. Of the choices given, only one stands out as *helpful* to those opposing the Chief Justice's display. **A** is not it, because the lack of visibility would be a mark in favor of the Chief Justice. If no one can see it, how could an observer make a judgment whether there is endorsement or not? **B** is not helpful to either side; that the Supreme Court has some element of the display in its building does not necessarily mean it will survive scrutiny if the context in which the display was erected suggests endorsement of religion. On the other hand, in cases like *Van Orden* and *Marsh*, in upholding both the Texas Ten Commandments monument and Maryland's legislative prayer, the Court has noted that it both displays the Ten Commandments and opens its sessions with a kind of prayer. In any event, there is a better answer. But it isn't **D**, which would not be helpful either: That a religious monument has been in place for a long time, without controversy, is evidence that no one perceives it as having a governmental imprimatur. That leaves **C**, which is the best answer. If it appeared that, despite what she told you, the Chief Justice has given evidence of some sectarian purpose through her words or actions, that would be evidence that the display is impermissible.

Denning's Picks

1. **A**
2. **C**
3. **D**
4. **C**
5. **A**
6. **C**
7. **A**

8. **D**
9. **C**
10. **C**
11. **B**
12. **A**
13. **D**
14. **A**
15. **C**

8

The Second Amendment and the Right to Keep and Bear Arms

A. Overview

The Second Amendment reads, "A well regulated Militia, being necessary to the security of a free State, the right of the people to keep and bear Arms shall not be infringed." Few other constitutional provisions have given rise to such intense disagreement over their meaning and scope. Unlike most constitutional provisions, moreover, the debate over gun rights, gun control, and the Second Amendment has occurred with virtually no meaningful guidance from the Supreme Court. Until 2008, the leading twentieth-century case interpreting the Second Amendment, *United States v. Miller*, 307 U.S. 174 (1939), was notable largely for its delphic ambiguity. Scholars, moreover, have tended to treat the Amendment as an embarrassment. *See* Sanford Levinson, *The Embarrassing Second Amendment*, 99 Yale L.J. 637 (1989) (challenging academics to take the Amendment seriously).

In 2008, however, the Court returned to the issue, nearly six decades after the *Miller* decision, in *District of Columbia v. Heller*, 554 U.S. 570 (2008). While *Heller* answered several questions scholars had debated over the years—the most important of which was whether the Amendment guaranteed an individual right, like the right of free speech, or whether it guaranteed some sort of collective right of states to retain armed militia—it raised a number of other questions that the Court did not answer. The most important of these, whether the Amendment would be incorporated through the Fourteenth Amendment and applied to state and local governments, was answered two years later in *McDonald v. Chicago*, 130 S. Ct. 3020 (2010).

The remainder of this chapter surveys the Court's treatment of the Second Amendment in *Miller* and *Heller*. The chapter concludes with a discussion of Second Amendment incorporation in *McDonald*.

B. The Second Amendment and the Federal Government

Although the Court had addressed the Second Amendment in a few cases in the nineteenth century, *United States v. Miller*, 307 U.S. 174 (1939), was, prior to *Heller*, the only modern case dealing with the right to keep and bear arms. *Miller* arose when two men were indicted for possessing a sawed-off shotgun in violation of federal law. A federal district court judge quashed the indictment, ruling that the federal law violated the Second Amendment. Under the rules of the time, when a district court judge invalidated a federal law on constitutional grounds, the ruling could be appealed directly to the Supreme Court; thus, there was no court of appeals decision.

In its brief, the government (which was the only side to appear) argued that (1) the Second Amendment did not guarantee rights that individuals could invoke, and that the Amendment guaranteed only the right of states to maintain armed militia; as a fallback, it argued that (2) even if the Amendment *did* guarantee an individual right, sawed-off shotguns were not the sorts of "arms" whose possession the Amendment guaranteed. Without resolving the first issue explicitly, the Court disposed of the case by accepting the government's second argument:

> In the absence of any evidence tending to show that possession or use of a "shotgun having a barrel of less than eighteen inches in length" at this time has some reasonable relationship to the preservation or efficiency of a well regulated militia, we cannot say that the Second Amendment guarantees the right to keep and bear such an instrument. Certainly it is not within judicial notice that this weapon is any part of the ordinary military equipment or that its use could contribute to the common defense. . . .

Miller, 307 U.S. at 178.

Commentators and scholars were left to fight over what *Miller* meant, and the Court did not deign to clarify matters until 2008, when it heard a challenge to a District of Columbia ordinance that all but prohibited private ownership of a handgun, the favored self-defense weapon by many. In a lengthy opinion that parsed nearly every word of the Second Amendment, seeking its meaning in the context of contemporary and post-ratification history, Justice Scalia's majority opinion concluded first that "the Second Amendment right is exercised individually and belongs to all Americans."[1] *Heller*, 554 U.S. at 581. Further, the Court concluded that the right "to keep and bear arms" meant "the individual right to possess and carry weapons in case of confrontation." *Id.* at 592.

---

1. Indeed, even the dissenting opinions agreed that the Second Amendment guaranteed a right that individuals not officially members of any organized militia could invoke in federal court. Thus, the Court unanimously interred the "collective rights" or "state's right" theory of the Amendment that was the foundation of the government's primary argument in *Miller*.

The Court noted that this right, like all constitutional rights, was not unlimited. Justice Scalia stressed that

> nothing in our opinion should be taken to cast doubt on longstanding prohibitions on the possession of firearms by felons and the mentally ill, or laws forbidding the carrying of firearms in sensitive places such as schools and government buildings, or laws imposing conditions and qualifications on the commercial sale of arms.

Id. at 626-627. The Court also stressed that the Amendment guarantees the right to keep and bear "the sorts of weapons . . . 'in common use at the time'" and did not include "the carrying of 'dangerous and unusual weapons.'" *Id.* at 627.

As applied to the D.C. ordinance, the Court found that "the law totally bans handgun possession in the home" and that the ban "amounts to a prohibition on an entire class of 'arms' that is overwhelmingly chosen by American society" for the purpose of "the inherent right of self-defense [that] has been central to the Second Amendment right." *Id.* at 628. Because the ordinance "makes it impossible for citizens to use [handguns] for the core lawful purpose of self-defense in the home" it was held to be unconstitutional. *Id.* at 630. Though the Court did not explicitly state a particular standard of review, in a footnote the Court noted, in response to Justice Breyer's comment that the ordinance would have passed the rational basis test, that if that were the operative standard of review, "the Second Amendment would . . . have no effect." *Id.* at 628 n. 27.

QUESTION 1. Rage against the machine (gun). Under 18 U.S.C. § 922(o) the possession of fully automatic machine guns by individuals is prohibited. Dave challenges this ban as an infringement of his Second Amendment rights. He argues that he would like to keep a machine gun in the home for self-defense; he further argues that machine guns are analogous to the weapons that militia members would have possessed at the time of the Framing. Dave's suit in federal district court would likely:

A. Succeed, because *Heller* prohibits absolute bans like § 922(o).
B. Fail, because machine guns could be considered dangerous and unusual weapons for individuals to own.
C. Fail, because machine guns are not necessary for self-defense.
D. Succeed, unless the government demonstrates that the ban furthers some compelling governmental interest.

ANALYSIS. You might have initially been drawn to **A** because *Heller* did, after all, overturn the district's ban on handguns. But note that categorical bans—either on classes of persons who can own weapons or even on classes of weapons themselves—were not necessarily all called into question. Therefore, it is not the best answer. **C** isn't either. Handguns themselves aren't "necessary" for self-defense; however, the Court noted that many people found them useful and that they were the self-defense weapon of choice among many, even where other firearms, like shotguns, might serve just as well. **D** is incorrect because *Heller* did not hold that strict scrutiny was the proper standard of review. While it rejected the notion that the Second Amendment could be satisfied by federal laws that were "rational," the Court did not specify the precise standard of review by which it was evaluating the D.C. ban. That leaves **B**, which is the best answer. Recall that the "safe harbor" language of Justice Scalia mentioned a number of laws that should not be regarded as presumptively unconstitutional in the wake of *Heller*. Among these are bans on "dangerous and unusual" weapons. If the ban is upheld, it could be because of the feeling that fully automatic weapons are dangerous and unusual.

QUESTION 2. Misdemeanor mandate. 18 U.S.C. § 922(g)(9) prohibits anyone convicted of a domestic violence misdemeanor from possessing a firearm. Carl pled guilty ten years ago to misdemeanor assault against a girlfriend and is unable to purchase a handgun to use for self-defense in his home. Carl sues in federal district court, challenging the constitutionality, under *Heller*, of § 922(g)(9). If a court rejects his suit, it will likely be because:

A. Domestic violence misdemeanants are a class of individuals, like felons and the mentally ill, whose Second Amendment rights may be limited.
B. The law is rationally related to a legitimate governmental interest.
C. When weighed against the societal interest in protecting persons from domestic violence, the burden on Carl's Second Amendment rights is minimal.
D. Protecting victims of domestic violence from further violence is a compelling governmental interest, and prohibiting those convicted of domestic violence from possessing firearms is a narrowly tailored means of achieving that interest.

ANALYSIS. As noted above, *Heller*'s majority opinion was not clear on the exact standard of review to be employed by courts in assessing laws restricting individuals' gun rights. However, if you read the description of the case carefully, you can easily eliminate some of the choices here. First, it is clear that the majority did not apply a rational basis test; in fact, Justice Scalia dismissed as irrelevant Justice Breyer's dissenting observation that the D.C. gun ordinance would pass the rational basis test, saying that this would render the Second Amendment a dead letter. So **B** does not seem as if it could be the correct answer. Further, the weighing of the interest of the government against the individual's right to keep and bear arms cited in **C** was the "interest-balancing approach" adopted not by the majority but by Justice Breyer's opinion. It is not correct either. On the other hand, nor did the majority endorse strict scrutiny. Thus, **D** is not the better of the remaining answers. That leaves **A.** If you recall, the Court included a paragraph giving a non-exclusive list of laws *not* called into question by its decision. This categorical approach—whereby certain individuals are excluded from the Second Amendment's protections based on their status (ex-felon, mentally ill, etc.)—has been used by courts called on to evaluate laws such as the domestic violence misdemeanor ban to turn back Second Amendment challenges.

C. The Second Amendment and the States

Immediately after the decision in *Heller* was announced, litigants challenged gun control ordinances in Chicago and Oak Park, Illinois, which were as restrictive as the District of Columbia's and, among other things, banned possession of handguns. *McDonald,* 130 S. Ct. at 3026.

As was expected, the plaintiffs lost in the lower courts. Twice in the nineteenth century the U.S. Supreme Court held that the Second Amendment did not apply to the states. First in *United States v. Cruikshank,* 92 U.S. 542, 544-545 (1875), and later in *Presser v. Illinois,* 116 U.S. 252, 265 (1886), the Court held that the Second Amendment applied only to the federal government. However, both cases were decided before the Court began to incorporate *any* provisions of the Bill of Rights. *Cruikshank,* for example, also held that the right to assemble peaceably, guaranteed by the First Amendment, applied only to the federal government. But this did not stop the Court, in *DeJonge v. Oregon,* 299 U.S. 353, 364 (1937), from incorporating that right. Thus a majority of the Court in *McDonald v. Chicago* did not feel that prior case law doomed petitioners' claims that the right recognized in *Heller* ought to be incorporated against state and local governments. *Id.* at 3031 ("We follow the same path here and thus consider whether the right to keep and bear arms applies to the States under the Due Process Clause.").

A plurality of the Court concluded that it did, using the selective incorporation framework articulated in *Duncan v. Louisiana,* 391 U.S. 145 (1968). Under *Duncan,* those provisions of the Bill of Rights that are "fundamental to *our* scheme of ordered liberty and system of justice" Are incorporated through the Due Process Clause and applied to the states. *Id.* at 3034.

First, the plurality observed that *Heller* recognized that "[s]elf-defense is a basic right, recognized by many legal systems from ancient times to the present day," that self-defense was the "central component" of the Second Amendment's right to arms, and that it was deeply rooted in our history and traditions. *Id.* at 3036. Further, as of the time of Reconstruction and the framing of the

Fourteenth Amendment, "[e]vidence . . . only confirms that the right to keep and bear arms was fundamental." *Id.* at 3042. Justice Alito also noted that "[t]he right to keep and bear arms was also widely protected by state constitutions at the time when the Fourteenth Amendment was ratified. In 1868, 22 of the 37 States in the Union had state constitutional provisions explicitly protecting the right to keep and bear arms." *Id.* He concluded that "the Due Process Clause of the Fourteenth Amendment incorporates the Second Amendment right recognized in *Heller*." *Id.* at 3050. The Court then remanded the case to the lower court for reconsideration.

Justice Thomas concurred in the judgment. He agreed that the Second Amendment was incorporated through the Fourteenth Amendment and applied to state and local governments, but he would have used, as the vehicle for incorporation, the Amendment's Privileges or Immunities Clause. *See id.* at 3058-3059 (Thomas, J., concurring) ("I write separately because I believe there is a more straightforward path to this conclusion, one that is more faithful to the Fourteenth Amendment's text and history."). Because he agreed with the plurality that the Second Amendment applied to the states, Justice Thomas's vote meant that a majority held the Amendment to bind the states, even though Justice Thomas relied on a different provision of the Fourteenth Amendment than did the plurality opinion.[2]

Like *Heller*, however, *McDonald* was not explicit about the standard of review lower courts should employ when assessing the constitutionality of gun control laws. The plurality did, however, reject balancing, as it had in *Heller*. "In *Heller* . . . we expressly rejected the argument that the scope of Second Amendment rights should be determined by judicial interest balancing." *Id.* at 3047. On the other hand, the plurality referred to the "*Heller* safe harbor," described above, in which the Court enumerated a few laws that were not presumptively unconstitutional, including bans on possession of arms by felons and the mentally ill. "We repeat those assurances here," Justice Alito wrote, adding that "[d]espite [the respondents'] doomsday proclamations, incorporation does not imperil every law regulating firearms." *Id.*

In response to the ambiguity and uncertainty in both *Heller* and *McDonald*, many lower courts are reviewing gun control laws under something akin to intermediate scrutiny. *See, e.g.*, United States v. Skoien, 614 F.3d 638 (7th Cir. 2010) (en banc) (upholding federal law banning gun possession by those convicted of domestic violence misdemeanors). However, even settling on a standard of review does not resolve questions over the proper application of that standard. For example, what counts as an "important governmental interest"? How heavy should the government's burden be to prove that interest or to prove that the challenged regulation is "substantially related" to that interest?

2. *See also* Marks v. United States, 430 U.S. 188, 193 (1977) ("When a fragmented Court decides a case and no single rationale explaining the result enjoys the assent of five Justices," the holding of the Court may be viewed as that position taken by those Members who concurred in the judgments on the narrowest grounds.).

See Skoien, 614 F.3d at 651-654 (Sykes, C.J., dissenting) (criticizing the majority's application of intermediate scrutiny). Unless and until the Supreme Court decides another Second Amendment case, these controversies are likely to persist in the lower courts.

D. Closer

QUESTION 3. Wait! The State of Ames requires prospective purchasers of firearms, including handguns, rifles, and shotguns, to wait five days before completing the purchase. The state justifies the time not only to enable the seller to complete an extensive background check that goes beyond that required by federal law, but also to ensure a "cooling off" period between the decision to purchase the firearm and the sale completion. Gordon, a prospective handgun buyer, argues that the Ames statute violates his Second Amendment right to keep and bear arms. He sues in federal district court for the district of Ames. Which of the following arguments would be *most* helpful to the state in making its case that the law should be upheld?

A. It is rational that requiring a waiting period could reduce gun violence.
B. The Second Amendment does not apply to state and local regulations of firearms.
C. The regulation is not a total ownership prohibition, but is merely a condition on the commercial sale of arms.
D. The burden on the right is minimal compared to the potential for saving lives lost to gun violence.

ANALYSIS. Before *McDonald*, Gordon would not have had a case because *Heller* applied only to *federal* regulations of firearms. But because the Second Amendment has been incorporated, Ames's statute is open to constitutional challenge as well. Therefore, **B** can be eliminated right off the bat. **A** can be eliminated as well, because both *Heller* and *McDonald* made clear, while not committing the Court to a particular standard of review, that rational basis was not it; *any* regulation could satisfy a rational basis standard. Similarly, the kind of interest-balancing standard set forth in **D**, which is Justice Breyer's favored approach, was also rejected in both cases by the Court, which found such approaches inconsistent with its ordinary treatment of constitutional rights—as "trumps" that limit the scope of or check governmental action in cases, not as mere "interests" to be balanced away. That leaves **C**, which is the best answer. Recall that in *Heller*, the Court enumerated a non-exclusive list of laws that were not presumptively unconstitutional in light of *Heller*'s holding. Among these were the regulation of and placement of conditions on the commercial sale of arms. Ames's waiting period does not absolutely prevent anyone from owning a gun for self-defense; it simply makes you wait for it. Its inclusion, moreover, in the *Heller* safe harbor makes it a strong argument for the state to deploy in its defense.

Denning's Picks

1. **B**
2. **A**
3. **C**

9

State Action and the Constitution

A. Overview

The Bill of Rights as well as the Fourteenth and Fifteenth Amendments apply only to the federal or state government, not to private individuals. In the *Civil Rights Cases*, 109 U.S. 3 (1883), for example, the Court invalidated the Civil Rights Act of 1875, which prohibited certain forms of private racial discrimination. The Court held that Congress had no authority to pass the act, despite § 5 of the Fourteenth Amendment,[1] because the Fourteenth Amendment governs the actions only of states, not of private individuals. The Court's holding is commonly referred to as the "state action doctrine."

In most cases, state action is easy to discern, because it is clear whether or not the government is acting; but occasionally actions by a putatively private party will be charged by courts to the state. Even when it is clear that parties are state actors, they have to have taken some sort of *action*; inaction or failure to act is not generally a ground for suit, as the tragic case of *DeShaney v. Winnebago County Department of Social Services*, 489 U.S. 189 (1989), made clear. In *DeShaney*, a young boy was beaten by his father, who had custody of him. He suffered brain damage so severe as to require his institutionalization for life. His mother sued the state for failure to remove him from his father's custody, even after having received and investigated reports of abuse. Though there was no question that state actors had failed to remove the child, the Court held that the failure to remove the boy from the custody of his father did not violate the Due Process Clause. Because, the Court wrote,

> the Due Process Clause does not require the State to provide its citizens with particular protective services, it follows that the State cannot be held liable under the Clause for injuries that could have been averted had it chosen to provide them. As a general matter, then, we conclude that a State's failure to

1. U.S. Const. amend. XIV, § 5 ("The Congress shall have power to enforce, by appropriate legislation, the provisions of this article.").

> protect an individual against private violence simply does not constitute a violation of the Due Process Clause.

DeShaney, 489 U.S. at 196-197.

The Court has developed exceptions to the state action doctrine for situations in which ostensibly private action will be held to constitute state action. In the words of the Court, private action will equal state action when "there is a sufficiently close nexus between the State and the challenged action" of a private entity "that the action of the latter may be fairly treated as that of the State itself." Jackson v. Metropolitan Edison Co., 419 U.S. 345, 351 (1971). This section will discuss the main lines of cases in which the Court has imputed private action to the state.

At the outset, however, it should be made clear that the path of the Court's state action doctrine has not been a straight one. One eminent constitutional law professor wrote in the late 1960s that the doctrine was, in fact, a "conceptual disaster area." Charles L. Black, Jr., *The Supreme Court, 1966 Term—Foreword: "State Action," Equal Protection, and California's Proposition 14*, 81 Harv. L. Rev. 69, 95 (1967). There are situations in which the Court finds state action in one case, only to decline to find it in another case with quite similar facts.

These difficult-to-distinguish cases bring up another point: The Court's state action doctrine is bound up with its attempts in the second half of the twentieth century to eliminate racial discrimination. The *Civil Rights Cases* notwithstanding, the Court has often adopted a broad definition of state action in the service of racial equality, only to narrow or distinguish the earlier definitions in later cases that *don't* seem to involve race or racial discrimination.

To take one famous example of the former, the Court repeatedly found state action in private organizations' attempts to keep African Americans from voting in Texas after invalidating a state law expressly barring blacks from voting in the Democratic primary. Nixon v. Herndon, 273 U.S. 536 (1927). When the state delegated power to the parties to set their voting qualifications and the Democratic Party excluded black voters, the Court struck down that as well. Nixon v. Condon, 286 U.S. 73 (1932). When the Democratic Party, on its own, adopted a rule excluding blacks from voting, the Court struck that down, after an earlier case held that there was no state action because the party was not, as in *Condon*, exercising power delegated by the state. *Compare* Smith v. Allwright, 321 U.S. 649 (1944) (holding that Texas had indirectly delegated power to establish voter qualifications, a state function, and that delegation was sufficient to find state action), *with* Grovey v. Townsend, 295 U.S. 45 (1935) (holding that the Democratic Party was not part of the state, so its actions could not be imputed to the state). When the state party then created a private association that held "pre-primaries" for members who then ran in the party primary, and excluded blacks from voting in *that* primary, the Court again invalidated the scheme—despite the fact that, on paper, there was no connection whatever between the "Jaybird Democratic Association" and the state Democratic Party. Terry v. Adams, 345 U.S. 461 (1953).

B. The Public Function Exception

The "white primary" cases provide a segue into the first of the main exceptions to the state action doctrine. The Court has held that a private actor is a state actor if she performs "a quintessential public function" or when the state has delegated a public function to private persons, entities, or organizations. Recent cases, however, have interpreted this rather narrowly, requiring that the function be something we tend to think of as the *exclusive* province of government.

The paradigmatic case here is *Marsh v. Alabama*, 326 U.S. 501 (1946), which involved a "company town." Chickasaw, Alabama, was wholly owned by the Gulf Shipbuilding Co., though it looked like any other town. Marsh was convicted of trespassing after attempting to hand out religious leaflets. He sued, claiming a violation of his First Amendment rights. Rejecting the argument that any suppression of free speech rights was due to private, not state, action, the Court held that "[t]he more an owner, for his advantage, opens up his property for use by the public in general, the more his rights become circumscribed by the statutory and constitutional rights of those who use it." *Marsh*, 326 U.S. at 506. Concurring, Justice Frankfurter added that a "company-owned town is a town. In its community aspects it does not differ from other towns. These community aspects are decisive." *Id.* at 510 (Frankfurter, J., concurring). *See also* Evans v. Newton, 382 U.S. 296 (1966) (holding that city could not operate—even through a private trustee—a park in accordance with a racially restrictive covenant placed on use of the park at time of the devise; "the predominant character and purpose of [the] park are municipal").

But just because property owners invite the public onto their property for their advancement, those owners do not ipso facto become state actors. The Court held that shopping center owners, for example, are not state actors, and could therefore prohibit leafleting and solicitation. Lloyd Corp. v. Tanner, 407 U.S. 551 (1972).

Subsequent cases continued to narrow the public function exception. In *Jackson v. Metropolitan Edison Co.*, 419 U.S. 345 (1974), the Court declined to find state action where a privately owned utility discontinued electrical service for nonpayment, despite the fact that it was a monopoly. The Court began by noting that "[t]he mere fact that a business is subject to state regulation does not by itself convert its action into that of the state for purposes of the Fourteenth Amendment" even where the business is "something of a governmentally protected monopoly." *Jackson*, 419 U.S. at 350, 353. The key was whether "there is a sufficiently close nexus between the State and the challenged action of the regulated entity so that the action of the latter may be fairly treated as that of the State itself." *Id.* at 351.

The plaintiff had three arguments why that nexus existed; the Court rejected each. First the plaintiff cited Metropolitan Edison's monopoly status.

But the Court declined to hold that government-granted monopolies equal state action. The key instead was the degree of connection between the private entity and the state. *Id.* at 352. Then the plaintiff argued that the utility provided an essential public service, which meant that it fulfilled a public function. The Court distinguished the exercise of delegated power "traditionally associated with sovereignty such as eminent domain" from the supply of power. While "the Pennsylvania statute [regulating utilities] imposes an obligation to furnish service on regulated utilities, it imposes no such obligation on the State." *Id.* at 353. Finally, the plaintiff argued that utilities were businesses "affected with the public interest" and, as such, should be considered state actors. The Court thought this proved too much: "We do not believe that such a status converts their every action . . . into that of the State." *Id.* at 354.

The Court found no significance in the fact that the state could have objected to the discontinuance-of-service policy Metropolitan Edison included in the tariff it filed with the state, but didn't. "At most, the Commission's failure to overturn this practice amounted to no more than a determination that a Pennsylvania utility was authorized to employ such a practice if it so desired." *Id.* at 357. It concluded that though Metropolitan Edison was a "heavily regulated" utility that "enjoy[ed] at least a partial monopoly," it was not a state actor.

The Court's cases after *Metropolitan Edison* emphasized both that the public function ought to be something that is ordinarily the *exclusive* province of government, and that the fact that a private organization is almost totally financially dependent on the government does not render its actions state actions. In *Flagg Brothers v. Brooks*, 436 U.S. 149 (1978), the Court held that the threat of sale of stored goods to satisfy a warehouseman's lien was not state action, even though the lien had been created by state law and state law processes were available to force the sale. In *Rendell-Baker v. Kohn*, 457 U.S. 830 (1982), the Court held that education was not an exclusive prerogative of the state; therefore, there was no state action where a private school discharged a teacher even though the school depended on the state for its students and received nearly all of its operating revenue from state funds. Finally, in *Blum v. Yaretsky*, 457 U.S. 991 (1982), the Court held that the decision to discharge Medicaid patients from a private nursing home was not state action.

QUESTION 1. Cover-up. BigMart, a national retail chain, instituted a store policy requiring certain magazines sold at the checkout line that feature cover pictures and content that some customers find objectionable, such as *Cosmopolitan* and *Maxim*, to be covered with opaque screens to shield those covers from customers. Publishers of the affected magazines sue, claiming that the policy violates the First Amendment. A reviewing court would likely:

A. Invalidate the policy, because it is content-based.
B. Uphold the policy, because there is no state action.

C. Invalidate the policy, because the purpose is to suppress ideas.
D. Uphold the policy, because offensive material is not protected by the First Amendment.

ANALYSIS. Did you think this question wandered in from the First Amendment chapter by mistake? As easy as the question is if you think about it, you might be surprised how many people forget that most of the rights in the Constitution are rights against *public actors*, not private ones. The answer to this question, then, is **B**. BigMart is not a state actor and can't violate anyone's First Amendment rights. The other answers are incorrect, because each is premised on the notion that state action is present here.

QUESTION 2. Hired guns. In order to save money, Ames City has decided to privatize its police force. It hires OmniSecurity to do all the policing in Ames City. When, in a case of mistaken identity, Peter is arrested and beaten by OmniSecurity employees, he sues them for violating, among other things, his Fourth Amendment rights against unreasonable searches and seizures. OmniSecurity seeks to dismiss the suit on the grounds that it is not a state actor. A judge would likely rule:

A. For OmniSecurity, because receiving money from government does not make it a state actor.
B. For OmniSecurity, because even monopoly status is not sufficient to impute private actions to the state.
C. For Peter, because Ames City has delegated an essential public function to OmniSecurity.
D. For Peter, because OmniSecurity was hired by the city and is being paid by it.

ANALYSIS. *Metropolitan Edison* teaches us several important things about the public function doctrine, which should help you answer this question. First, receiving money, even to the point where government is your only source of income, is not sufficient to render one a state actor. That means that **D** is incorrect, and that **A** is a possibility. Moreover, being highly regulated by the government, to the point of enjoying monopoly status as a service provider, is also insufficient to confer state actor status. Thus, **B** is a possibility as well. Yet neither is the correct answer. Recall that what the public function *does* cover is the delegation of certain powers normally exercised exclusively by the sovereign. While the Court has not been eager to expand that list, policing would seem to fit the bill. Were the state to delegate the power of arrest to a private organization, that private organization would likely be considered a state actor. **C**, therefore, is the best answer.

C. "Inextricable Entanglement"[2]

Even if the state has not delegated to a private actor some essential public function, the relationship between public and private actors can be so intertwined that it is difficult to tell where one ends and the other begins. Such cases represent a second exception to the state action doctrine.

The classic case of inextricable entanglement is *Burton v. Wilmington Parking Authority*, 365 U.S. 715 (1961). The Wilmington, Delaware Parking Authority built a public parking facility and leased space to private businesses to supplement the revenue from the parking. The stores were built into the exterior walls and faced the street, and were inaccessible from the inside of the garage.

One of the businesses, a coffee shop, refused to serve black customers. A customer who was refused service sued, claiming that the shop's presence in a public parking garage rendered it a state actor. In siding with the plaintiff, the Court considered the following factors: (1) the land and building were publicly owned; (2) the building itself was dedicated to public usage; (3) the commercial areas were part of a plan to fund the construction of the parking facility; and (4) the upkeep of the facility was the responsibility of the state and was paid for out of public funds. *Burton*, 365 U.S. at 723-724. "The State has so far insinuated itself into a position of interdependence with" the coffee shop, the Court wrote, "that it must be recognized as a joint participant in the challenged activity, which . . . cannot be considered to have been so 'purely private' as to fall without the scope of the Fourteenth Amendment." *Id.* at 725. The Court seemed to find it particularly significant that the state could have required nondiscrimination as a condition of the lease, but chose not to.

Four decades later, the Court concluded that a high school athletic association, though putatively a private organization, was also a state actor. The Tennessee Secondary School Athletic Association was composed of representatives from state public and private schools and regulated high school athletics in the state. Brentwood Academy v. Tennessee Secondary School Athletic Association, 531 U.S. 288 (2001). "The nominally private character of the Association," the Court wrote, "is overborne by the pervasive entwinement of public institutions and public officials in its composition and workings, and there is no substantial reason to claim unfairness in applying constitutional standards to it." *Brentwood Academy*, 531 U.S. at 298. Among the factors the Court found significant were the facts that 84 percent of the members were public schools; that the schools were represented by faculty members who in turn selected members from other public employees to form the governing board; public school officials attended meetings in the course of their state employment; state board of education members were ex officio members;

2. I borrow this term from Calvin Massey, American Constitutional Law: Powers and Liberties 1266 (4th ed. 2013).

the TSSAA staff was eligible to participate in the state's retirement plan; and the TSSAA acted as the de facto regulator of high school athletes in the state of Tennessee. *Id.* at 300. The dissenters pointed out that the majority's theory of "entwinement" went beyond the previous requirement that the public and private entities be inextricably entangled and noted that the TSSAA was not performing an exclusive public function here. *Id.* at 314 (Thomas, J., dissenting).

QUESTION 3. Shopping censor. The Plateau is a privately owned, open-air, high-end outdoor shopping area located in Ames City. The Plateau has numerous sidewalks, promenades, and park-like areas where shoppers may sit and rest while visiting the stores. The owners of the Plateau have posted rules forbidding solicitation, leafleting, and other uses of the Plateau's public spaces without express authorization from the owners. Carl attempts to hand out leaflets and give a speech decrying the state of federal finances and is arrested for trespassing, after refusing requests by the owners to leave. He sues the owners of the Plateau for infringing his First Amendment rights. Are the Plateau's owners state actors?

A. Yes, because the owners are carrying out a public function by having sidewalks and park-like areas for speakers.
B. No, because the owners are a private entity and, by definition, not a state actor.
C. Yes, because the Plateau is akin to a company town.
D. No, because the Plateau's owners are not wielding power that is exclusively reserved to the government.

ANALYSIS. Whatever else the Plateau is, it does not fulfill the functions of a town the way that Chickasaw, Alabama, did in *Marsh.* Therefore, **C** is incorrect—however much time we feel we now spend in shopping centers! But even if not a company town, a private entity fulfilling public functions might be a state actor. The Court's cases, however, stress that the public function must be one that is *exclusively* offered by the state. There are private parks and private green spaces, so **A** would not be a reason to hold the owners of the Plateau to be state actors. As for the remaining answers, **B** is incorrect because, as we've seen, private actors *can* be considered state actors despite their lack of a formal public connection. That leaves **D**, which is the best answer, and consistent with the Court's cases that held the owners of shopping centers are not state actors, even though shopping centers resemble in some senses the marketplaces and street corners of days past.

D. Coercion or Encouragement as State Action

Finally, private action can sometimes be considered state action if it has been coerced or encouraged by the state in some extraordinary way. The Court famously held in *Shelley v. Kraemer*, 334 U.S. 1 (1948), that the involvement of the state in the enforcement of racially restrictive real estate covenants between private parties that prohibited the sale of property to African Americans constituted state action. The Court concluded that despite the fact that the agreement was between private parties, its purposes could be secured "only by judicial enforcement by state courts of the restrictive terms of the agreements" and that "but for the active intervention of the state courts, supported by the full panoply of state power, petitioners would have been free to occupy the properties in question without restraint." *Shelley*, 334 U.S. at 13-14, 19.

In later cases, though, the Court seemed to relax its requirement of "active intervention" on the part of the state. By popular vote, Californians amended their constitution to prohibit the state and its political subdivisions from enacting laws prohibiting racial discrimination in housing. The effect of Proposition 14, as it was known, was to override prior laws and prevent new ones from being enacted. Reitman v. Mulkey, 387 U.S. 369 (1967). The California Supreme Court, on whose findings the U.S. Supreme Court relied heavily, concluded that Prop 14's effects would go beyond merely repealing existing law and that it was, in fact, tantamount to an invitation to discriminate. The Court concluded that "the provision would involve the State in private racial discriminations to an unconstitutional degree." *Reitman*, 387 U.S. at 378-379. The Court noted, for example, that in addition to repealing existing antidiscrimination laws, Prop 14 made it impossible for them to be reenacted without first amending the state constitution to repeal Prop 14.

QUESTION 4. **Mama drama.** The University of Ames Fertility Clinic is a privately owned medical practice renting space in a practice group building owned by the University of Ames Hospital, a clinical hospital that supports the research and teaching mission of the University of Ames medical school. The Clinic is a professional corporation whose members are teaching and clinical faculty at the university medical school. While the Clinic rents space from the university and is permitted to use the name "University of Ames" in its practice group name, it has no other affiliation with the university. Patients to the Clinic enter through the practice group building, and not the hospital or the medical school. The physicians, nurses, and other assistants who work for the Clinic are paid out of the revenues of the practice and are not compensated by the state (though the physicians are paid as well by the state for service as faculty members). The Clinic's policy is to provide fertility services to married couples only. Susan, a single woman, sues the clinic for gender discrimination under the Fourteenth Amendment. Is the Clinic a state actor?

A. No, because it is not serving an essential public function, nor is it intertwined with the state.
B. No, because the state has delegated no authority to the Clinic.
C. Yes, because the Clinic and the state university are intertwined.
D. Yes, because the use of the university name might confuse the public.

ANALYSIS. Recall the three exceptions to the state action doctrine: (1) public function, (2) excessive entanglement, and (3) coercion/encouragement. The fact that the public might be confused as to the identity of the actor is not an exception, nor would it, by itself, be sufficient to impute private action to the state. Therefore, **D** can be eliminated. Similarly, **B** can be eliminated because a private actor can be treated as a state actor even if the state has delegated no authority to the former. The State of Delaware, for example, had not delegated authority to the coffee shop in *Burton.* Between the remaining choices, the facts given do not suggest entwinement between the state and the facility. The state is a landlord and has allowed the use of the name; while the doctors are paid by the state in their capacity as clinical faculty members, the state does not support any of the Clinic's operations directly. No other state employees or officers participate in the Clinic's operations. Therefore, **A** is a better answer than **C** on the facts given.

QUESTION 5. Fat fight. Ames City is amending its antidiscrimination ordinance. In addition to prohibiting discrimination on the basis of race, sex, marital status, religion, and ethnicity, the city council has decided to add "sexual orientation." The council briefly considered, but rejected, adding "weight." Humiliated by a local dating service that rejected his application because, according to the owner, the service "didn't accept fatties," Keith sues the city council, alleging that its failure to add "weight" to its ordinance violated his rights under the Equal Protection Clause of the Fourteenth Amendment. Which of the following would be strongest argument in favor of the city?

A. Discrimination by nongovernmental actors is permissible under the Fourteenth Amendment.
B. Failure to outlaw discrimination is not state action.
C. The city is not a state actor.
D. Individuals have not been encouraged to engage in private discrimination.

ANALYSIS. While private discrimination usually won't be considered state action, cases like *Shelley* and *Reitman* demonstrate that there are exceptions. Therefore, **A** is not correct. **C** would not be correct either, because cities *are* considered state actors. **D** is a possibility, but **B** is the better answer. Recall the discussion at the beginning that states are liable for their *actions*, not their omissions or failures to act. Ames City has chosen to protect some classes from discrimination, but not others. **D** is not the best answer because cases like *Reitman* involved alleged encouragement to engage in racial discrimination, a particular concern of the Constitution and the Court. The Court has not extended *Reitman* to cover cases in which the class in question is not a protected one under the Fourteenth Amendment. In any event, the facts here say simply that the city council declined to include weight among the protected classes—not, as in *Reitman*, that it was involved in the repeal of such protections and prohibited their reenactment without some extraordinary steps.

As noted at the outset, this area is a confusing one. Later cases narrowly interpreting the state action doctrine are often hard to square with earlier, more expansive definitions. To sum up, though, a few principles can be kept in mind:

- If a state actor is involved, *failure* to act will not usually furnish grounds to sue. It's the state *action* doctrine, not the state *inaction* doctrine.
- The main exceptions to the state action doctrine have been narrowed over time; many of the earlier expansive cases are bound up with the Court's mission to prevent evasion of its antidiscrimination decisions.
- For state action to be imputed to a private party, (1) the private actors must be exercising delegated authority to perform public functions that are usually the *exclusive* province of government, (2) facts must demonstrate interlocking patterns of private and public involvement that render it difficult to see where government stops and the private entity begins, or (3) the ostensibly private actions must depend in an unusual degree on public power being carried out. Particularly for category (2), you would want to be on the lookout for multiple instances of public involvement, not just one or two, to support a finding of "inextricable entanglement" or "entwinement."

With those rules of thumb in mind, let's take a last look at state action with the following Closer.

E. The Closer

QUESTION 6. Personal foul. In an effort to keep the Ames City Barristas, Ames City's arena football team, from moving to Langdellville, the city council authorized the formation of the Ames City Convention Authority (ACCA), which raised money to construct a new stadium for the Barristas. The ACCA was formed as a public corporation with authority to borrow money in the city's name. It floated a bond issue and oversaw construction. Once completed, the ACCA leased the stadium to the Barristas and contracted with them for its management. The ACCA retains supervisory authority of the stadium management team and is an ex officio member of the management board. Otherwise, it has no involvement with the Ames City Barristas or their management of the stadium. During one of the Barrista's home games, Lyle, a season ticket holder, was thrown out because security guards alleged he was drunk and being disorderly. He was banned from the stadium for the rest of the season, and the cost of his season ticket was not refunded. Lyle sued the Barristas and the private security company with whom they contracted, alleging that they deprived him of his property without due process of law. On the facts stated, would a court find state action?

A. No, because the state has delegated no exclusive public functions.
B. No, because the facts do not demonstrate sufficient entanglement or entwinement.
C. Yes, if the ACCA could have required the management company to observe due process and did not.
D. Yes, because the role of public officials in the management company is sufficient evidence of entwinement.

ANALYSIS. While the state has delegated no exclusive public function, it doesn't have to in order for private actions to be imputed to it. "Inextricable entanglement" and encouragement or coercion are alternative grounds for finding state action. Therefore, **A** is not correct. Further, simply because the state has some ability to require the private actor to observe certain standards and chooses not to do so is not sufficient to find state action. Recall that that same argument was used in *Metropolitan Edison* and was rejected by the Court. Therefore, **C** is also incorrect. The question, then, is whether the facts are sufficient to support a finding of entanglement or entwinement. On the one hand, the team is dependent on the state for financial support of its stadium. Further, state officials are ex officio members of the management board and retain some supervisory authority over the management. However, the Court has held that financial dependency and even heavy regulation are not sufficient to convert private actors into public ones. Further, the board has no public regulatory authority and, aside from ex officio membership on the board, it doesn't appear that there are large numbers of state employees participating in the management or operation of the stadium, unlike the heavy involvement of public school coaches and employees in the *Brentwood Academy* case. Further, the stadium, unlike the parking garage in *Burton*, was not "dedicated to public usage," nor do the facts indicate that the upkeep and maintenance were the responsibility of the state. Taken together, and looking at the Court's recent cases, I think that **B** is a better answer than **D**.

Denning's Picks

1. **B**
2. **C**
3. **D**
4. **A**
5. **B**
6. **B**

10

Congressional Enforcement of Civil Rights

A. Overview

The Thirteenth, Fourteenth, and Fifteenth Amendments to the Constitution (sometimes known collectively as the "Civil War Amendments" or the "Reconstruction Amendments") all contain provisions giving Congress the "power to enforce [the Amendments] by appropriate legislation." The scope of the congressional enforcement power under these Amendments is the topic of this chapter.

The cases in this area address a number of important questions: How far does this power extend? Does the power extend far enough for Congress to remedy constitutional violations the Supreme Court has not recognized? Can the power be used to reverse Court decisions interpreting the Amendments—or, indeed, other parts of the Bill of Rights? These questions—especially those concerning the scope of the Fourteenth Amendment's enforcement power—have occupied the Court since it began to cut back on congressional power to abrogate state sovereign immunity using the Commerce Clause in *Seminole Tribe v. Florida*, 517 U.S. 44 (1996).[1] The following term, the Court established a test by which Congress's exercise of its Fourteenth Amendment, § 5 enforcement power was to be scrutinized. City of Boerne v. Flores, 521 U.S. 507 (1997). Subsequent decisions have confused rather than clarified matters, with relatively recent decisions pointing in opposite directions.

1. The scope of sovereign immunity under the Eleventh Amendment is covered in volume 1, Chapter 2, section C.6. In brief, the Court held that Congress may abrogate state sovereign immunity using only its enforcement powers under § 5 of the Fourteenth Amendment, *Fitzpatrick v. Bitzer*, 427 U.S. 445 (1976), or when Congress legislates using its Article I power to provide uniform rules for bankruptcies. *See, e.g.*, Central Virginia Community College v. Katz, 546 U.S. 354 (2006).

B. Public Versus Private Conduct: State Action Redux

Before we address the scope of congressional power to enforce these Amendments, it is important to review to whom they apply. The Fourteenth and Fifteenth Amendments apply to state action only; the Thirteenth Amendment outlaws both public and private slavery. One of the Supreme Court's first decisions interpreting the Fourteenth Amendment invalidated the Federal Civil Rights Act of 1875, passed under Congress's § 5 enforcement power, which prohibited private discrimination in public accommodations. Civil Rights Cases, 109 U.S. 3 (1883). The Court held that civil rights "guaranteed by the Constitution against State aggression cannot be impaired by the wrongful acts of individuals, unsupported by State authority in the shape of laws, customs, or judicial or executive proceedings. The wrongful act of an individual unsupported by any such authority," the Court wrote, "is simply a private wrong, or a crime of that individual." *Civil Rights Cases,* 109 U.S. at 25-26.

Nearly 125 years later, the Court reaffirmed the state action doctrine when it invalidated the civil suit provision of the Violence Against Women Act, which created a federal cause of action for violence motivated by gender-based animus. United States v. Morrison, 529 U.S. 598 (2000).[2] The Court wrote that the provision was "directed not at any state or state actor, but at individuals who have committed criminal acts motivated by gender bias." *Morrison,* 529 U.S. at 626. Therefore, Congress was without power under the Fourteenth Amendment to provide a remedy against purely private actors.

In contrast to the Fourteenth and Fifteenth Amendments, the Thirteenth Amendment is addressed at both state actors and private individuals. The *Civil Rights Cases* conceded that the Amendment gave Congress the "power to pass all laws necessary and proper for abolishing all badges and incidents of slavery in the United States." But the Court then refused to defer to congressional determinations that discrimination in public accommodations was a badge or incident of slavery. 109 U.S. at 20. The Court reversed that holding in *Jones v. Alfred H. Mayer Co.*, 392 U.S. 409 (1968), and upheld 42 U.S.C. § 1982, which gives all U.S. citizens equal rights to "inherit, purchase, lease, sell, hold, and convey real and personal property." The Court held that congressional determinations of what constituted badges or incidents of slavery were to be evaluated by the Court using a rational basis standard. *Alfred H. Mayer,* 392 U.S. at 412, 418, 422-424.

2. The Court also found that the civil suit provision exceeded Congress's power under the Commerce Clause. For a discussion of that aspect of the *Morrison* decision, see volume 1, Chapter 4, section B.5.

QUESTION 1. Writing rights. Which of the following is not a permissible exercise of congressional power under the Reconstruction Amendments?

A. A federal statute barring state officials from interfering with the right of state citizens to vote in federal elections.
B. A federal statute barring housing discrimination by private parties on the basis of sexual orientation.
C. A federal tort remedy against state officials for intentional violations of federal civil rights.
D. A federal statute prohibiting state laws that incarcerate workers who do not fulfill the terms of personal service contracts.

ANALYSIS. Did you read the introductory material closely? If so, then this question was a piece of cake! Of the three Reconstruction Amendments, only one—the Thirteenth Amendment—reaches non-state actors, and then only to outlaw slavery. The correct answer, then, is **B**: It is aimed at private discrimination based on sexual orientation and is, therefore, outside the scope of the Thirteenth and Fourteenth Amendments. The other distracters are, in fact, actual federal laws passed under Congress's enforcement power and that are still on the books.

QUESTION 2. We don't need no stinkin' badges. A federal statute, 42 U.S.C. § 1981, prohibits discrimination in private contracting. The U.S. government sued several private schools for rejecting students based solely on their race. That is, the schools' policies prevented racial minorities from contracting with the private schools to provide education solely because of the race of the applicants. If the statute is upheld, the reason likely will be:

A. The Fourteenth Amendment requires equal treatment of the races and gives Congress the power to enforce its provisions.
B. Congress could rationally conclude that permitting discrimination in public schools was a violation of the state's responsibility to provide equal protection to persons within its jurisdiction.
C. Congress could rationally have concluded that racial discrimination in contracting is a badge or incident of slavery.
D. The Court will defer to Congress's judgment regarding the need to exercise its enforcement powers under the Reconstruction Amendments.

ANALYSIS. The facts here are based on *Runyon v. McCreary*, 427 U.S. 160 (1976). Even if you are unfamiliar with the case, there are clues that could have led you to the correct answer. First, note that the statute is directed toward *private* discrimination in the making of contracts. That means that any such statute must be based on the enforcement provision of the Thirteenth Amendment. That, in turn, means that Congress must be seeking to outlaw slavery, or at least its "badges and incidents." That eliminates **A** and **B** as answers. **D** is not the best answer because, as we have seen, the Court will *not* always defer to Congress. That leaves **C**, which is the best answer; and it is consistent with the Court's holding in *Alfred H. Mayer.*

Amendment	*Scope*	*Subject Matter*
Thirteenth	Covers state or private actors	Prohibits slavery
Fourteenth	Covers state actors only	Guarantees privileges or immunities of U.S. citizens; protection against state deprivation of life, liberty, or property without due process of law; guarantees equal protection of the laws
Fifteenth	Covers state actors only	Prohibits denial of voting rights on the basis of race

C. Scope of Congressional Enforcement Power

What does it mean for Congress to enforce the Reconstruction Amendments through "appropriate legislation"? The question can be reframed as two separate questions. First, there is the question whether the enforcement power includes the power to define the substance of the Amendments, as opposed to being limited to enforcement of the Court's interpretation of them. A second, related question concerns whether it is appropriate, when seeking to enforce the Amendments, to provide remedies for actions that don't actually violate the Constitution in and of themselves, or that seek to remedy past violations that went unpunished. Or, on the other hand, does Congress's enforcement power extend only to activity that is itself a violation of the Constitution?

Following the Court's invalidation of the Reconstruction-era civil rights acts on state action grounds, the federal government gradually withdrew from the enforcement of civil rights at the end of the nineteenth century, as military occupation of the South ended and "reconciliation" between North and South became national policy. Congress neither passed nor enforced meaningful civil rights legislation until the mid-1960s, when the Civil Rights Act of 1964 and the Voting Rights Act of 1965 became law. The Voting Rights Act, passed under the authority of the Fourteenth and Fifteenth Amendments, produced the first set of cases dealing with congressional enforcement power.

The Voting Rights Act prohibits certain state requirements designed to keep African Americans from voting. In addition, the Act required the Department of Justice to approve certain changes in state and local electoral systems. The Act, however, by its terms applied primarily to states in the South. In *South Carolina v. Katzenbach*, 383 U.S. 301 (1966), the Court upheld the Voting Rights Act, holding that Congress had the power to remedy violations of the Fifteenth Amendment. Congress, the Court held, could have rationally believed that counties with high numbers of racial minorities, but few minority voters, were engaged in violations of the Fifteenth Amendment; and it could provide the remedy it did to address those violations. *Katzenbach*, 383 U.S. at 326-327. In other words, the Court endorsed Congress's power to impose prophylactic measures that would both deter violations and provide a remedy for past violations of rights as well.

The Court later upheld the Voting Rights Act's provisions prohibiting electoral system charges that effectively diluted or reduced minority voting power—even if the changes were not intended to produce that result. Rome v. United States, 446 U.S. 156 (1980); City of Mobile v. Bolden, 446 U.S. 55 (1980). As in *Katzenbach*, the Court endorsed a broad remedial power to protect constitutional rights and to deter officials from violating them. While the Fifteenth Amendment prohibits intentional discrimination, the Court held that Congress had discretion to craft a broader rule applicable to those jurisdictions with a history of purposeful discrimination to ensure that cleverly disguised racial animus wasn't motivating the changes to electoral systems. *Rome*, 446 U.S. at 177, 193.

In 2009, the Court raised questions about the Voting Rights Act's continued applicability to large parts of the South only, but avoided passing on the "covered jurisdictions" question, opting to resolve the specific issue through statutory interpretation. Northwest Austin Municipal Utility District No. 1 v. Holder, 557 U.S. 193 (2009).

Four years later, in *Shelby County v. Holder*, 133 S. Ct. 2612 (2013), the Court declared that the Voting Rights Act's coverage formula and preclearance requirements were unconstitutional. Chief Justice Roberts's opinion began with the observation that widespread denial of voting rights to persons in the covered jurisdictions had justified a departure from the tradition that states were possessed of equal sovereignty in our system. *Shelby Cnty.*, 133 S. Ct. at 2624-2625. "At the time," he wrote, "the coverage formula—the means of linking the exercise of the unprecedented authority with the problem that warranted it—made sense." *Id.* at 2625. Now, it no longer did, he argued.

> In 1965, the States could be divided into two groups: those with a recent history of voting tests and low voter registration and turnout, and those without those characteristics. Congress based its coverage formula on that distinction.

> Today the Nation is no longer divided along those lines, yet the Voting Rights Act continues to treat it as if it were.

Id. at 2628. The Chief Justice held that if Congress is to depart from the principle of equal sovereignty, it "must identify those jurisdictions to be singled out on a basis that makes sense in light of current conditions. It cannot simply rely on the past." *Id.* at 2629.

The dissenters, in turn, criticized the majority for rejecting the deferential review of *South Carolina v. Katzenbach*, and argued that the 2006 reauthorization of the Voting Rights Act easily satisfied *McCulloch v. Maryland*'s standard of "appropriate" and "plainly adapted" to a legitimate constitutional end. *Id.* at 2639 (Ginsburg, J. dissenting). The dissent also sharply criticized the majority for failing to grapple with the legislative record accompanying reauthorization that, it claimed, clearly suggested the continued need for the legislation. *Id.* at 2644 (Ginsburg, J., dissenting).

The Court's retreat from deference to congressional creation of remedies to address recognized constitutional violations repeats a pattern seen in its earlier move to less deferential review of congressional judgments about the extent and severity of violations themselves. In *Lassiter v. Northampton Cnty. Bd. of Elections*, 360 U.S. 45 (1959), the Court held that a New York law requiring voters to be literate in English did not violate the Fourteenth or Fifteenth Amendment. But when Congress passed the Voting Rights Act of 1965, it included a provision, § 4(e), prohibiting the administration of English literacy tests to Spanish-speaking voters who had completed the sixth grade in Puerto Rico.

New York sued, arguing that Congress couldn't use its § 5 powers to "remedy" an alleged violation where the Court had held that the practice did *not* violate the Constitution. Katzenbach v. Morgan, 384 U.S. 641, 643-647 (1966). The Court rejected the challenge, and upheld § 4(e). In doing so, the Court relied on alternative rationales, one much broader than the other.

On the one hand, the Court seemed to reject Court adjudication of a violation as a necessary requirement for remedial action by Congress. The Court, in fact, came close to holding that Congress itself had the power to define, legislatively, the *content* or *meaning* of the Fourteenth Amendment. In the Court's opinion, limiting Congress to enforcing only violations the Court had recognized "would depreciate both congressional resourcefulness and congressional responsibility for implementing the Amendment. It would confine the legislative power . . . to the insignificant role of abrogating only those state laws that the judicial branch was prepared to adjudge unconstitutional." *Morgan*, 348 U.S. at 648-649. The Court was willing to hold that, despite *Lassiter*, Congress could prohibit the literacy tests as "necessary and proper" means of "secur[ing] for the Puerto Rican community residing in New York nondiscriminatory treatment by government. . . ." It is thus "'plainly adapted' to furthering [the] aims of the Equal Protection Clause." *Id.* at 652. "It was well within congressional authority," the Court concluded, "to say that this need of the Puerto Rican minority for the vote warranted federal intrusion upon any state interests served by the English literacy requirement." *Id.* at 653. Congress, moreover, was responsible for "assess[ing] and weigh[ing] the various conflicting considerations.... It is not for [the Court] to review the congressional resolution of these factors. It is enough that we be able to perceive a basis upon which the Congress might resolve the conflict as it did." *Id.* at 653.

But the Court also based its decision on the answer to a more narrow inquiry: whether "§ 4(e) was merely legislation aimed at the elimination of an invidious discrimination in establishing voter qualifications." *Id.* at 653-654. While New York justified the rule as an incentive for its residents to learn English, the Court replied that "Congress might well have questioned, in light of the many exemptions provided, and some evidence suggesting that prejudice played a prominent role in the enactment of the requirement, whether these were actually the interests being served." *Id.* at 654. Congress could have perceived a basis "upon which [it] might predicate a judgment that the application of New York's English literacy requirement to deny the right to vote to a person with a sixth grade education in Puerto Rican schools in which the language of instruction was other than English constituted an invidious discrimination in violation of the Equal Protection Clause." *Id.* at 656. Note that, under this theory, Congress was merely remedying something—invidious race discrimination—that the Court already presumed was unconstitutional. In so doing, Congress was not attempting to define the substantive content of the Amendment.

On the strength of *Katzenbach v. Morgan*, Congress in the early 1990s passed the Religious Freedom Restoration Act (RFRA), which, among other things, replaced the Court's permissive *Smith* test for generally applicable laws that incidentally burdened religious exercise, with the old strict scrutiny test of *Sherbert v. Verner.*[3] Under RFRA, if any federal, state, or local law burdened religious exercise, the government had to prove that the law furthered a compelling governmental interest and that the law or regulation was the least restrictive means of furthering that interest. Otherwise, the law would be invalidated. When the City of Boerne, Texas, refused to issue a building permit to a historic Catholic church to expand, the congregation sued under RFRA. City of Boerne v. Flores, 521 U.S. 507 (1997). The City, meanwhile, claimed that RFRA, at least as applied to state and local laws, exceeded Congress's power under § 5 of the Fourteenth Amendment. The Court agreed.

Contrasting the power to "enforce" the Amendment with "the power to determine what constitutes a constitutional violation," the Court wrote that RFRA attempts to "alter[] the meaning of the Free Exercise Clause," which "cannot be said to be enforcing the Clause." *Boerne*, 521 U.S. at 519. At the

3. Both *Sherbert* and *Smith* are discussed in Chapter 7. In brief, the Court's decision in *Smith* held that generally applicable laws that incidentally burdened religious exercise were evaluated under a rational basis test, not the strict scrutiny of *Sherbert v. Verner.*

outset, then, the Court clearly repudiated the more expansive of *Morgan*'s rationales in favor of a narrower theory of Congress's remedial power.

Not only was Congress's power limited to the fashioning of remedies for constitutional violations recognized by the Court, but "[t]here must be a congruence and proportionality between the injury being prevented or remedied and the means adopted to that end." *Id.* at 520. Otherwise, "legislation may become substantive in operation and effect," enabling "shifting majorities" to "change the Constitution and effectively circumvent the difficult and detailed amendment process contained in Article V." *Id.* at 508, 520, 529. The Court then analyzed RFRA in light of the congruence and proportionality requirements.

Congruence, the Court explained, depended in part on evidence of the prevalence of the alleged violation. "RFRA's legislative record lacks examples of modern instances of generally applicable laws passed because of religious bigotry." *Id.* at 530. Proportionality, on the other hand, required that the scope of the remedy be appropriate in light of the seriousness of the alleged violations. The Court found RFRA to be "so out of proportion to supposed remedial or preventative object that it cannot be understood as responsive to, or even disposed to prevent, unconstitutional behavior. It appears, instead, to attempt a substantive change in constitutional protections." *Id.* at 509.

Remedial measures are warranted only if "there is a reason to believe that many of the laws affected by the congressional enactment here have a significant likelihood of being unconstitutional." *Id.* at 532. "The stringent test RFRA demands of state laws reflects a lack of proportionality or congruence between the means adopted and the legitimate end to be achieved." *Id.* at 533.

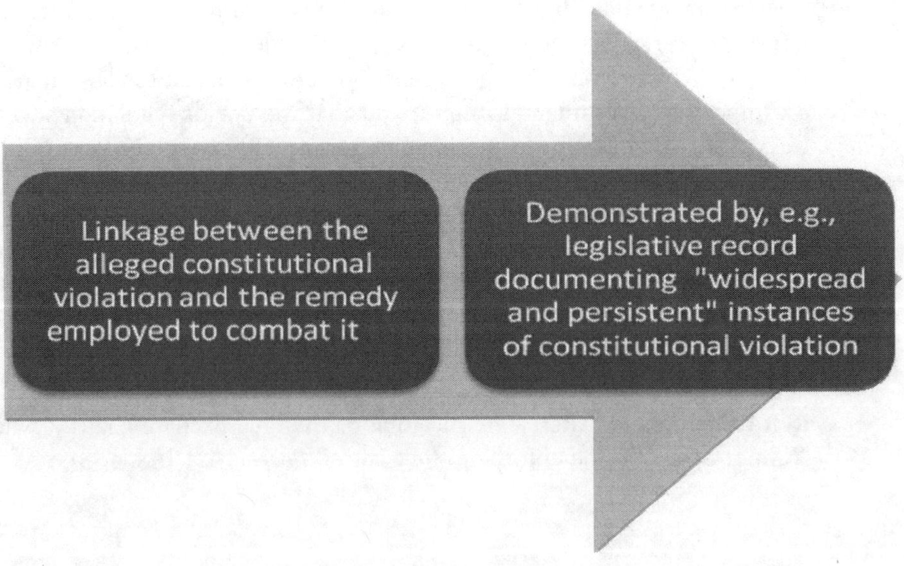

Boerne: **Congruence Requirement**

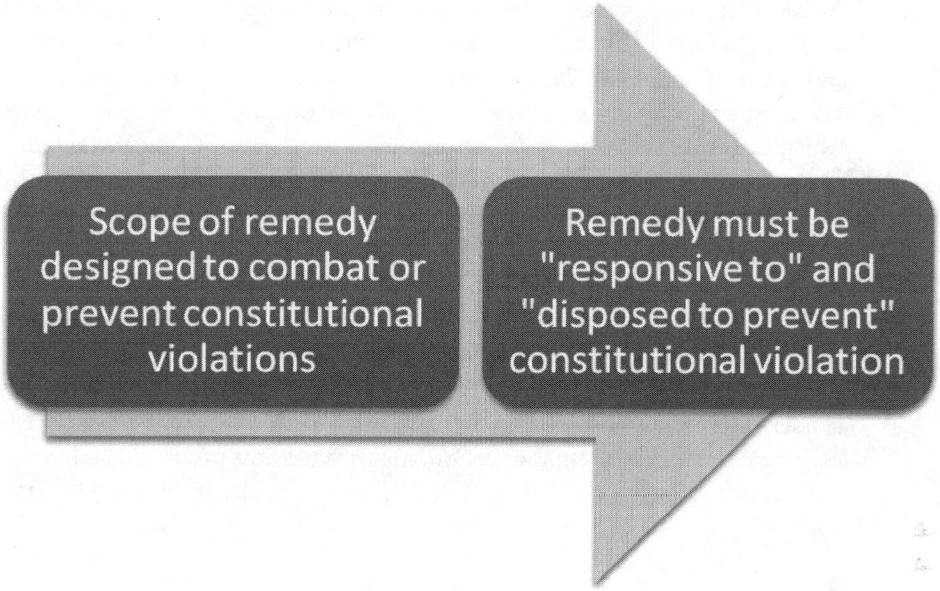

***Boerne:* Proportionality Requirement**

QUESTION 3. *Boerne* free. Consider the following acts passed under Congress's Fourteenth Amendment enforcement authority:

I. A federal law authorizing a private right of action against anyone discriminating in purpose or effect against people who are overweight, based on anecdotal evidence that the overweight are targets of discrimination.

II. A federal law authorizing a private right of action against state and local governments that engage in gender discrimination in employment decisions, where the legislative record demonstrated a record of slow hiring and unexplained pay differentials between men and women in government jobs.

III. A federal law detailing an historic pattern of discrimination in housing and employment against homosexuals and barring all public and private discrimination in housing and employment based on sexual orientation or identification.

Which of the acts are likely constitutional exercises of congressional power under the Fourteenth Amendment?

A. I and III only
B. I and II, but not III
C. II only
D. I, II, and III

ANALYSIS. Remember, when answering questions about congressional enforcement action, to look first at whether the legislation targets state action. If not, then the *Civil Rights Cases* (and later cases such as *Morrison*) hold that Congress has exceeded the power given to it by the Fourteenth Amendment, which is concerned with state action only. (Recall also, however, that private activity might be reached under other congressional powers, such as the Commerce Clause.) Here, though, recalling the state action doctrine would help you answer this question with ease. Both I and III target either private action *only* or both state and private action. Both exceed Congress's authority insofar as they seek to regulate private activity, and thus, neither can be constitutional. That, in turn, means that **A**, **B**, and **D** are incorrect. This leaves **C**, the best answer. In **C**, federal law targets state action only, and then addresses gender discrimination based on evidence that it is occurring in government employment. A private right of action, moreover, seems proportional in relation to the violation or alleged violation on the evidence furnished in the answer.

QUESTION 4. *Boerne* again. Assume that, in the future, the Supreme Court overrules *Plyler v. Doe* and holds that the denial of public education to children brought into the United States illegally by their parents *does not* violate the Equal Protection Clause. Many southwestern states respond by enacting laws denying education to such children. Congress, in turn, responds by outlawing the denial of public education to illegals under § 5 of the Fourteenth Amendment. The states sue, claiming the new law exceeds Congress's power. Congress responds that it perceives the ban to be motivated by racial animus, and that it can point to some evidence in the form of statements by state lawmakers and voters that bears out that charge. If a court upholds the law, it would likely be because:

A. The Court will defer to Congress in the creation of remedies under its Fourteenth Amendment enforcement power.

B. Congress has the power to define the substance of the Fourteenth Amendment's guarantees.

C. The remedy was both congruent and proportional to the alleged constitutional violation.

D. It was rational for Congress to have concluded that a remedy under the Fourteenth Amendment was warranted.

ANALYSIS. The facts are similar to those in *Katzenbach v. Morgan.* If you recognized the similarity, you might have been drawn to **D**, which was the alternative ground for *Morgan*'s holding. But *Boerne* seemed to replace a mere rational basis test with something a bit more searching—and later cases, discussed below, confirm that. Therefore, **D** is not the best answer. Nor is **A**. The Court made clear in *Boerne* that it will *not* defer to Congress's decision to create remedies; it added that Congress may not attempt to define the substance of a constitutional guarantee either, which means **B** isn't correct. That leaves **C**, the best answer. The Court will require a remedy under the Fourteenth (or Fifteenth) Amendment to be both "congruent" with the alleged constitutional violation and "proportional" to its severity. For more about what those requirements mean, read on!

Initially, it wasn't clear that *Boerne* represented a potentially significant limit on Congress's civil rights enforcement power. Two things happened to make *Boerne*'s import apparent to all. First, the Court continued to whittle away Congress's power to abrogate states' sovereign immunity using any authority other than its power to enforce the Fourteenth Amendment. *Compare* Seminole Tribe v. Florida, 517 U.S. 44 (1996) (invalidating, under the Eleventh Amendment, an attempt to abrogate sovereign immunity using the Indian Commerce Clause), *with* Fitzpatrick v. Bitzer, 427 U.S. 445 (1976) (holding that state sovereign immunity protected by the Eleventh Amendment could be abrogated by Congress using its § 5 enforcement power). Second, the Court expanded *Boerne*, making clear that the latter's "congruence and proportionality" requirements had real bite when it came to judicial review of enforcement statutes passed under the authority of the Fourteenth Amendment.

For example, in both *Florida Prepaid Postsecondary Education Expense Board v. College Savings Bank*, 527 U.S. 627 (1999), and *Kimel v. Florida Board of Regents*, 528 U.S. 62 (2000), the Court concluded that Congress had exceeded its authority in authorizing suits for money damages against states for patent infringement and age discrimination, respectively. The Court concluded that Congress had not demonstrated a pattern of patent infringement or age discrimination on the part of states sufficient to warrant the abrogation of sovereign immunity.

In *United States v. Morrison*, 529 U.S. 598 (2000), the Court held that the civil suit provision of the Violence Against Women Act exceeded Congress's powers not only because it outlawed private violence, but also because the remedy lacked congruence and proportionality. Congress could point to only 21 instances of unconstitutional sex discrimination by state and local governments in passing the law. *Morrison*, 529 U.S. at 665.

The high-water mark for limits on Congress came in *Board of Trustees v. Garrett*, 531 U.S. 356 (2001), in which the Court held that employees could not collect money damages from states for violations of Title I of the Americans with Disabilities Act. In doing so, it further clarified what satisfied the congruence and proportionality requirements.

First, the Court said that in assessing congruence and proportionality, one had to begin with the right at issue. In *Garrett*, for example, the Court observed that "States are not required by the Fourteenth Amendment to make special accommodations for the disabled so long as their actions toward such individuals are rational." *Garrett*, 531 U.S. at 367. Once the Court "determined the metes and bounds of the constitutional right," the Court would examine "whether Congress identified a history and pattern of unconstitutional employment discrimination by the States against the disabled." *Id.* at 368. As it had in earlier cases, the Court concluded that the legislative record "failed to show that Congress did in fact identify a pattern of irrational state discrimination in employment against the disabled." *Id.* at 368. General findings and anecdotal evidence were insufficient to establish that pattern.

Further, even assuming a pattern of violation, the remedy furnished by Title I "would raise the same . . . concerns as to congruence and proportionality" raised by *Boerne. Id.* at 372. The Court suggested that the amount of evidence needed to establish congruence bore an inverse relationship to the standard of review employed by a court to review the discrimination. Thus, more deferential the standard of review, the *more* evidence was needed to show congruence. The Court noted the "stark" difference between evidence amassed under the Voting Rights Act of 1965 and that compiled by Congress in connection with the Americans with Disabilities Act. *Id.* at 358.

This relationship between congressional rights and remedies seemed to be confirmed in *Nevada Department of Human Resources v. Hibbs*, 538 U.S. 721 (2003). The question in *Hibbs* was whether Congress exceeded its § 5 power by abrogating states' Eleventh Amendment immunity in suits for money damages by individuals for alleged violations of the Family and Medical Leave Act (FMLA), which requires employers to offer 12 weeks of unpaid leave for workers to care for children or family members. *Hibbs*, 538 U.S. at 724. Despite complaints from the dissenting Justices that the evidence compiled by Congress failed to demonstrate a pervasive pattern of discrimination by state employers, the Court upheld the provision, citing in support of its decision the fact that sex discrimination was subject to intermediate scrutiny by the courts. In contrast to cases like *Kimel* and *Garrett*, the Court observed, "Congress directed its attention to state gender discrimination, which triggers a heightened level of scrutiny." *Id.* at 736. Despite the Court's admonition that gender classifications could not depend on outmoded or archaic stereotypes, Congress mustered evidence suggesting such stereotypes persisted. Specifically, evidence suggested that states had different leave policies based on "the pervasive sex-role stereotype that caring for family members is women's work." *Id.* at 731. Because judicial review was heightened, "it was easier for Congress to show a pattern of state constitutional violations." *Id.* at 736.

The Court then concluded that the FMLA provision was both congruent and proportional because, as noted above, previous legislative attempts to eliminate sex stereotyping failed, resulting in persistent discrimination reflected in state leave policies. This intractability, the Court noted, might result in a relaxation of the proportionality requirement; such problems "may justify added prophylactic measures in response. . . ." *Id.* at 737. "By creating an across-the-board routine employment benefit for all eligible employees, Congress sought to ensure that family-care leave would no longer be stigmatized as an inordinate drain on the workplace caused by female employees, and that employers could not evade leave obligations simply by hiring men." *Id.* at 737.

Garrett and *Hibbs*, then, shed some light on the exact reach of the congruence and proportionality requirements. Congruence, it is clear, is a function of both the protection a particular group or right is given by the Constitution—as interpreted by the Court—and the evidence provided by Congress that rights are being violated and remedial action is required. The more judicial scrutiny to which the regulated activity is already subject, the *less* evidence Congress needs to satisfy the Court's congruence requirement. Conversely, if the regulated activity is subject to minimal scrutiny, then the Court will require more evidence of widespread violation before accepting that a legal remedy is required.

This evidence, moreover, impacts the proportionality requirement as well—especially the extent to which the Court will permit Congress to go beyond remedying the actual constitutional violation and prescribe prophylactic measures that will deter *future* violations or reach hard-to-detect violations. *Hibbs* suggests that proportionality will be relaxed—and thus a more prophylactic remedy permitted—if (1) the Court has applied a heighted standard of review and (2) despite this increased judicial scrutiny, evidence exists that violations persist, that the rights violations are "intractable."

This is all a little confusing. The charts below attempt to express graphically the relationships described above.

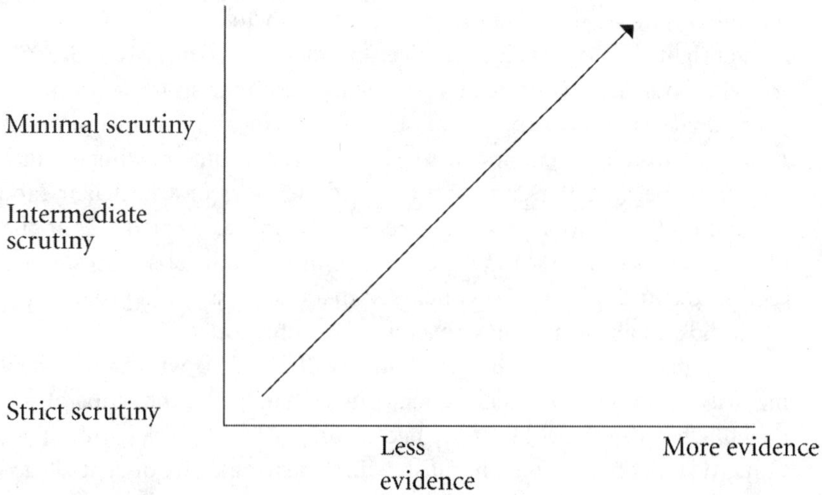

Relationship Between Judicial Standard of Review and Evidence Required to Satisfy Congruence Requirement

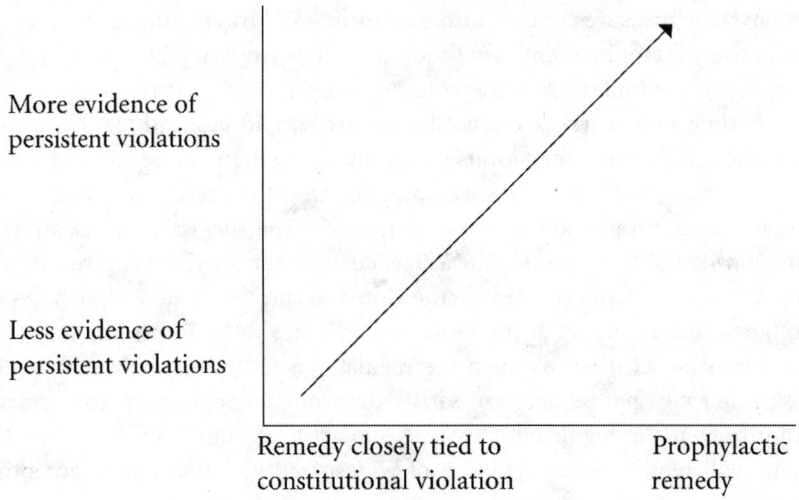

Proportionality and Remedy

The next term, in *Tennessee v. Lane*, 541 U.S. 509 (2004), the Court upheld Title II of the Americans with Disabilities Act, which ensured access to public services and entities and authorized money damages if that access was denied. In upholding the Act's abrogation of sovereign immunity, the Court reasoned that (1) access to courts was a fundamental right previously recognized by the Court and that (2) the Court would, as it did in *Hibbs*, relax the evidentiary standard for Congress to justify its remedial measures. According to the Court,

> Congress had demonstrated "pervasive unequal treatment in the administration of state services and programs," which included deprivation of fundamental rights like voting, jury service, and marriage. *Lane*, 541 U.S. at 524.

The Court then confined its proportionality analysis to "access to courts," as opposed to access to any and all state services or programs. (The plaintiff in *Lane* was a disabled man unable to get to court without crawling on his hands and knees because the courthouse lacked elevators or wheelchair ramps to get him up to the floor on which the courtroom was located.) As applied "to the class of cases implicating the accessibility of judicial services," including "access to courts," the Court concluded that Congress could provide the remedy it did and abrogate states' sovereign immunity. *Id.* at 511.

The dissenters—led by Chief Justice Rehnquist, who wrote the *Hibbs* majority opinion—accused the majority of narrowing the scope of the statutes much more than the Court had in prior cases in order to find proportionality. *Id.* at 550-552 (Rehnquist, C.J., dissenting). The dissent alleged that the evidence in the legislative record provided no support for the proposition that states systematically denied the disabled access to courts; thus Title II swept more broadly than the evidence warranted. That is, the dissenters charged that the cause of action was not proportional. *Id.* at 541 (Rehnquist, C.J., dissenting).

Justice Scalia, though he had joined the Court's earlier cases, wrote separately to announce his rejection of the congruence and proportionality test in toto. *Id.* at 554 (Scalia, J., dissenting). Henceforth, he announced, he would invalidate any statute that sought to remedy conduct that was not *itself* recognized by the Court as a violation of the Fourteenth Amendment. *Id.* at 560 (Scalia, J., dissenting). The only exceptions were those measures "designed to remedy racial discrimination by the States," which he would uphold on stare decisis grounds. *Id.* at 564 (Scalia, J., dissenting).

QUESTION 5. **Keeping it all in proportion.** Based on the descriptions given below, which of the following would likely be upheld by the Court as a valid exercise of congressional enforcement power under the Fourteenth Amendment?

A. A statute authorizing suits by individuals against state educational institutions for failure to offer equivalent athletic opportunities for the two sexes, where Congress had produced evidence that women's sports were often underfunded or the number of sports limited relative to men's sports.

B. A statute authorizing damage suits by gay men and women against states that discriminate against homosexuals by refusing to issue them marriage licenses.

C. A statute authorizing individuals to sue states for money damages for failing to adequately incentivize the construction of low- and middle-income housing, based on evidence that in some areas of the country with high real estate prices, affordable housing was out of reach for many residents.

D. A statute authorizing individuals to sue states for money damages if they infringe an individual's trademark.

ANALYSIS. The place to begin in this problem is with congruence. The Court is most likely to approve of congressional remedies of constitutional violations the Court itself has recognized. Of the four, only gender discrimination warrants heightened judicial scrutiny. As of this writing, there is no Supreme Court-recognized right to marriage for same-sex couples, to affordable housing, or to have one's trademarks protected. Only **A**, moreover, mentions evidence that, despite the recognition of a constitutional right to gender equality, violations of that right by state actors persist. By contrast, the other answers at best reflect anecdotal evidence of violations. According to the Court, the less judicial scrutiny an alleged violation receives, the more evidence the

Court will require—especially if the Court is asked to sustain a remedy, like money damages, that requires abrogation of a state's sovereign immunity. Of the listed answers, then, **A** is the best one. The rest would likely run afoul of the Court's congruence and proportionality requirements.

Hibbs and *Lane* marked such a departure from the approach of earlier cases like *Boerne*, *Kimel*, and *Garrett* that one might have wondered whether the Court was rethinking its approach to congressional enforcement of civil rights altogether. *Coleman v. Court of Appeals of Maryland*, 132 S. Ct. 1327 (2012), however, saw the Court return to form. At issue was the "self-care" provision of the FMLA permitting employees to take unpaid leave to deal with their own "serious health condition" where that condition interfered with the employee's ability to work. In addition, the Act provided for money damages. The question before the Court was whether Congress had the power to abrogate the sovereign immunity of a state to suits for money damages and authorize a private right of action for such damages. The Court said that it did not. *Coleman*, 132 S. Ct. at 1332.

Unlike in *Hibbs*, the Court found unconvincing the three arguments for allowing money damages: (1) the provision itself "addresse[d] sex discrimination and sex stereotyping"; (2) the provision "is a necessary adjunct to" the provision upheld in *Hibbs*; and (3) "the provision eases the burden on single parents." *Id.* at 1334. What the plaintiff was unable to do, according to the majority, was provide "evidence of a pattern of state constitutional violations accompanied by a remedy drawn in narrow terms to address or prevent those violations." *Id.*

First, there was no evidence that "States had facially discriminatory self-care leave policies or that they administered neutral self-care leave policies in a discriminatory way" or that they used "self-care takers" as a proxy for "women." *Id.* Second, there was little evidence beyond "conclusions" and "abstract generalities" to support the abrogation of sovereign immunity and no necessary linkage between the family care and self-care provisions. *Id.* at 1337. Finally, the fact that the self-care provision "helps single parents retain their jobs when they become ill . . . does not explain how the provision remedies or prevents constitutional violations." *Id.*

What is clear from cases beginning with *Garrett* is that congruence and proportionality are interrelated. To the extent Congress is attempting to remedy violations of rights that the Court has not recognized as subject to some form of heightened scrutiny under the Fourteenth Amendment, the evidentiary burden Congress bears to show a pattern of discrimination is greater. But the more evidence shown that the problem is "persistent" or "intractable," to use the Court's language, the more sweeping the remedy may be and the more relaxed the Court's application of the proportionality prong.

D. Closer

QUESTION 6. Ad-mission impossible.

The U.S. Supreme Court has held that race may be taken into account in university admissions processes as part of an individualized, holistic review of candidates. The Court has warned, however, that consideration of race for its own sake and the use of quotas to achieve some kind of racial balance violate the Equal Protection Clause. Assume that, in the years after this decision, Congress compiles evidence from public universities around the country suggesting that schools regularly attempt to circumvent those requirements; for many applicants at competitive public universities, race is *the* factor determining admission. In response, Congress passes a law, modeled on previous state initiatives, that prohibits state universities from considering race at all in admissions decisions and providing a private right of action against those universities that do so under its Fourteenth Amendment enforcement power. Which of the following statements about this hypothetical statute is true?

A. Congress lacks the authority to abrogate the state universities' sovereign immunity.
B. A reviewing court would defer to Congress's decision to exercise its enforcement remedy.
C. Congress would need only establish a rational relationship between the alleged violation and Congress's chosen remedy.
D. The amount of evidence required by a reviewing court to demonstrate proportionality would be reduced, because of congressional evidence of persistent rights violations.

ANALYSIS. In the face of what the Court has called "intractable" violations, Congress has elected to enact a prophylactic remedy against state universities—barring the consideration of race altogether—that goes farther than the constitutional violation acknowledged by the Court (consideration of race as *the* factor in university admissions, the establishment of quotas, etc.). It has also prescribed a private right of action to help enforce that remedy. First, because Congress is attempting to enact it under its Fourteenth Amendment enforcement power, it may abrogate states' sovereign immunity if its remedy is a valid use of its § 5 enforcement power. Therefore, **A** is not correct. Neither is **B**. The power of *Boerne* and its progeny is that the Court will *not* defer; it will, in fact, take a rather hard look at congressional enforcement legislation. While earlier cases like *Morgan* suggested that the review would be minimal, the congruence and proportionality requirements—especially as applied in cases like

Boerne and *Garrett*—represent a non-trivial limitation on that enforcement power. The Court's approach is certainly not the rational basis review articulated in *Morgan.* So **C** is not the best answer either. That leaves **D**. In cases like *Hibbs* and *Lane,* the Court has held that it will reduce the amount of evidence in the record needed to justify a prophylactic remedy under the proportionality requirement if (1) the alleged wrong is based on a classification subject to heightened scrutiny and (2) the evidence suggests that despite that heightened standard of review, violations persist. Here, the Court has held that classifications based on race are subject to strict scrutiny, and the evidence in the question suggests that despite holding that quotas and racial balancing are *not* permitted, public schools are regularly engaging in that activity. If that were true, then the Court would require less evidence, according to its cases, to justify a prophylactic ban on the use of race in any way in university admissions.

Denning's Picks

1. **B**
2. **C**
3. **C**
4. **C**
5. **A**
6. **D**

11

Closing Closers

QUESTION 1. Panning the *kirpan*. A local Sikh youth is expelled from an Ames City public school for wearing a *kirpan,* a small ceremonial dagger, in violation of a city-wide school policy requiring expulsion for students who bring weapons to school. The Ames General Assembly passes a law requiring local school boards to permit students to wear items required by their faith, notwithstanding school policies to the contrary. The legislative history reveals that several members of the General Assembly specifically mentioned a desire to permit the wearing of *kirpans*. A number of school boards in Ames City object, and they challenge the law as a violation of the Establishment Clause. Their suits should:

A. Fail, because the state may exempt the religiously devout from compliance with generally applicable laws.
B. Fail, because no reasonable observer would believe that the exemption meant the state was endorsing a particular religion.
C. Succeed, because there is no valid secular purpose served by the law.
D. Succeed, because the law exempts only religious conduct.

ANALYSIS. Under *Employment Division v. Smith*, there is no free exercise right to be exempt from generally applicable laws or regulations, even if they incidentally affect the religiously devout. The remedy, Justice Scalia wrote, is for the devout to secure relief legislatively. The Court's decisions have adopted a "play in the joints" approach whereby states are permitted to allow things not required by the Free Exercise Clause but not forbidden by the Establishment Clause. Generally speaking, the Court has permitted exemptions from general rules and regulations for the religiously observant. **D**, therefore is incorrect, and **A** is the correct answer. **B** is incorrect, because the "endorsement test" is generally favored by some members of the Court for testing the constitutionality of religious displays or monuments in public spaces. **C** is not correct, because exempting the religiously observant from rules that inhibit their faith could be said to be an act of tolerance for religion that itself could be a secular goal. At the very least, by exempting *kirpans* and other religious items, such as rosaries or yarmulkes, the city is not promoting a religious point of view. **Ch. 7. C. 4.**

QUESTION 2. Taking license. Carl runs a small home decorating business in the State of Ames and advertises himself as an "interior designer" on his marketing materials. The Ames state government neither recognizes nor licenses interior designers or interior decorators, but its legislature is considering a bill that would do just that. Only those persons who either (1) have been in business for 25 years or more or (2) have satisfied a number of educational requirements and completed a two-year internship with a licensed interior designer would be able to advertise as "interior designers" and charge for time spent on clients' projects. Others could advertise themselves only as "interior decorators" and would have to make money by charging mark-ups on items purchased for clients. The legislature describes its licensing bill as an effort to protect consumers from fraudulent design practitioners by ensuring a minimum level of competency in design matters. Carl has been in business for only ten years and has none of the educational requirements specified in the bill. The bill passes, and Carl files suit, alleging that he was denied notice and a hearing on the bill, and that the bill unconstitutionally infringes his liberty interests. A reviewing court should:

A. Reject the procedural due process claim, but invalidate the act on substantive due process grounds.
B. Reject both claims.
C. Invalidate the law on procedural due process grounds only.
D. Find that the law violated both procedural and substantive due process.

ANALYSIS. First things first. Recall that procedural due process distinguishes legislative and adjudicative determinations, or, as described earlier, lawmaking at the wholesale and retail levels. It is not the case that Carl attempted to satisfy the requirements, and then applied for and was denied a license individually. He is simply one of a number of folks who are potentially affected by the Ames legislation. What the Ames legislature has done is make a "legislative determination," for which procedural due process protections do not attach. Therefore, neither **C** nor **D** can be the correct answer. As for his substantive due process claim, it is true that Carl has a "liberty interest" that is adversely affected—his ability to operate as an interior designer despite not meeting the new requirements for licensure. But his liberty interest is not a fundamental one, and thus would garner only rational basis scrutiny. The facts recite that consumer protection is the aim of the statute, surely a legitimate governmental interest; and licensure to ensure compliance with minimum levels of competence at least bears a rational relationship to that end, even if the real reason might be to erect barriers to entry for new interior designers. Under the Court's economic substantive due process cases, Carl loses. **A**, therefore, is not the correct answer, which leaves **B**. Carl loses on both his claims under these facts. **Ch. 2. Ch. 3. B. 2** and **C. 3.**

QUESTION 3. Second verse, same as the first? Assume that Carl, from Question 2, decides instead to file suit claiming that the exemption from licensure for those interior designers with 25 or more years' experience violates the Equal Protection Clause. Carl argues that there is no rational relationship between the length of time one has worked as an interior designer and consumer protection. Carl argues that the real motivation behind the bill was to protect older interior design firms from competition and ensure that they can act as "gatekeepers" (through the apprenticeship requirement) for the profession. Is Carl's equal protection argument likely to prevail in court?

A. Yes, but only if Carl can prove that the actual purpose was not consumer protection, but to protect the livelihoods of the established interior designers.
B. No, because the classification is rationally related to a legitimate governmental interest.
C. Yes, if the state fails to prove that the grandfather clause furthers consumer protection.
D. No, because a statute's legislative "purpose" is never relevant in assessing its constitutionality.

ANALYSIS. The standards of review for the Equal Protection and Due Process Clauses differ only in the addition of intermediate scrutiny for gender and legitimacy classifications in equal protection doctrine. The choice between strict scrutiny and rational basis review turns on whether (under due process) the liberty interest infringed is fundamental or whether a governmental classification is made (under equal protection) according to some fundamental right. Here, Carl is arguing that where the legislature drew the line between those interior designers who would be grandfathered in and those who would not was an unconstitutional classification. But because the classification does not turn on any fundamental right, Carl bears the burden of demonstrating either that there was no legitimate interest here, or that the classification was an irrational one. Because *Carl* bears the burden of proof here, **C** is incorrect because it does not accurately state the law. **D** is also an incorrect statement of the law. Although in cases like *Fritz*, the Court rejected calls to ascertain a law's "actual purpose" and then measure its efficacy in achieving it, purpose is quite relevant in a number of other of the Court's cases. Recall in *Moreno* and *Romer* that the Court's invalidation of legislation was based on what it saw as "animus" toward a disfavored group. Moreover, under *Washington v. Davis* racial discrimination has to be intentional to be actionable; disparate impact is not enough to find a constitutional violation. But purpose is not relevant in all equal protection cases, as the aforementioned *Fritz* illustrated. Therefore, **A** is not correct. At least where there are no fundamental rights at issue, if a legitimate end and a rational relationship can even be *hypothesized*, the legislature will be assumed to have acted on those, even if there is no evidence it actually did—in fact, even if you can prove that it had some *other* end in mind. That leaves **B**, the correct answer: Under existing equal protection doctrine, Carl's equal protection challenge will fare no better than his due process challenges. **Ch. 4. B. 2.**

QUESTION 4. **With interest.** Ames requires lawyers who handle client money to establish separate, interest-bearing trust accounts in which to deposit escrow funds, money from settlements, and the like. Ames also requires that any interest earned on such accounts be turned over to the state bar association to fund indigent defense and to compensate clients whose lawyers have misappropriated their funds. Which of the following statements is true about the Ames law?

A. The law is unconstitutional because it deprives clients of their property without due process of law.
B. The law violates the Equal Protection Clause because only lawyers are subject to the law.
C. The law is vulnerable to a Takings Clause challenge because it takes private property for public use.
D. The law is constitutional because it is narrowly tailored to achieve a compelling state interest.

ANALYSIS. Of the four statements, only one is clearly true. **A** is not the best answer, because the Court no longer invalidates state regulation of private property under the Due Process Clause, unless the law fails the very lenient "rational basis" test—meaning that the state has either failed to pursue a legitimate interest (which funding of indigent defense would be) or that the means used are not rationally related to that end (which the use of interest from client trust accounts would be). **B** is not true for the same reason: Regulating "lawyers" as a class is not regulation according to a suspect or semi-suspect classification and would, therefore, also be subject to rational basis review. **D** misstates the appropriate standard of review; nothing in the facts suggests that the regulation would be subject to strict scrutiny. That leaves **C**, which is the correct answer. The Court has analyzed similar laws under the Takings Clause, which prohibits the taking of private property for public use without just compensation. While the Court held that interest belongs to the owner of the principal, *Phillips v. Washington Legal Foundation*, 524 U.S. 156 (1998), a recent case held that the compensation owed to the owners of that principal was zero, because the interest was so small that owners would never see it once the costs of computing and paying the interest were figured in. Brown v. Legal Foundation of Washington, 538 U.S. 216 (2003). **Ch. 2. C.**

QUESTION 5. Jeepers, creepers, can't I get some peepers? The State of Ames passed a statute prohibiting anyone but a licensed ophthalmologist (an eye doctor with a medical degree) or optometrist (one who has a doctorate in optometry but is not an M.D.) from fitting patients with eyeglasses and from duplicating or replacing lenses in eyeglasses, unless done pursuant to a written prescription from an Ames-licensed ophthalmologist or optometrist. Lee, an optician, sued, claiming that the law violates the Due Process Clause of the Fourteenth Amendment. Before the law passed, he ran a thriving business making and fitting eyeglasses. He argues that the law will put him out of business, or force him to turn his patients over to M.D.'s and O.D.'s. A reviewing court would likely:

A. Rule for Ames, because no liberty interest of Lee is affected.
B. Rule for Lee, if he can prove that opticians can fit and make eyeglasses without a prescription from an ophthalmologist or optometrist.
C. Rule for Lee, because the statute violates Lee's liberty to contract for services with his customers.
D. Rule for Ames, because requiring professional supervision is a rational means of achieving a legitimate legislative end.

ANALYSIS. The facts here are similar to those in *Williamson v. Lee Optical of Oklahoma*, 348 U.S. 483 (1955). Because the statute will bar Lee from engaging in his livelihood, his liberty is very much affected. The state's action here prohibits him from fitting eyeglasses, as he had been doing before the legislation. Therefore, **A** is incorrect. However, when the Court retreated from strict judicial scrutiny of economic regulation, the question became whether the liberty interest being infringed was fundamental or not. If so, then strict scrutiny applies, and the government must demonstrate a compelling governmental interest and narrow tailoring. If not, then the more deferential rational basis standard of review is used. Under rational basis, a regulation is presumed constitutional and will pass muster if it is in pursuance of a legitimate governmental end and the regulation is rationally related to that end. The wisdom or even the efficacy of a particular law is not relevant to that inquiry. So **B** is not correct. For the most part, the fundamental rights recognized by the Court have been either specific provisions of the Bill of Rights or unenumerated rights dealing with some aspects of personal autonomy, such as marriage and procreation. Here, though Lee's liberty—that of him and his customers to contract with one another—is certainly affected, Ames's infringement would not trigger strict scrutiny because that liberty is no longer considered fundamental by the Court. Therefore, **C** is not correct. That leaves **D**, the correct answer. Ensuring patient safety and protecting consumers are legitimate interests; requiring the involvement and oversight of medical professionals in the fitting of medical devices bears a rational relationship to that interest. As Justice Douglas wrote in *Williamson*, "The . . . law may exact a needless, wasteful requirement in many cases. But it is for the legislature, not the courts, to balance the advantages and disadvantages of the new requirement." 348 U.S. at 487. **Ch. 3. C. 3.**

QUESTION 6. **Driver down.** The National Insurance Co. (NIC), a nationwide insurer of drivers and automobiles with agents in the State of Ames, charges men under 25 years of age substantially more for auto insurance than it charges female drivers in the same age bracket. The National Organization for Men (NOM) sues in federal district court, alleging that NIC's pricing practices in Ames violate the Equal Protection Clause of the Fourteenth Amendment. A review court should:

A. Find for NIC, because it is not a state actor.
B. Find for NOM, because the policy is based on archaic and outmoded gender stereotypes.
C. Find for NOM, because statistics can never be the basis for a gender-based classification.
D. Find for NIC, because the policy is rationally related to a legitimate state concern, highway safety.

ANALYSIS. This is tricky! NIC does not appear to be anything other than a private insurance company. Therefore, *as a matter of constitutional law* (as opposed to statutes that regulate private conduct), it is not a state actor. Therefore, the right answer is **A**. The other answers are incorrect because they presume that NIC *is* a state actor. But just for review, remember that gender-based classifications require an important governmental interest and a substantial relationship between the classification and the interest. Therefore, **D** would be incorrect even if there were state action, because it states the wrong standard of review. **B** is correct in that statutory ends can't reflect archaic and outmoded gender stereotypes, but that does not apply here. And **C** is not quite accurate. Though the Court was suspicious of the use of the statistics in *Boren*, it did not say that they would *never* be available to show a substantial relationship between a classification and some appropriate end of government. In *Boren*, the problem was that the Court did not think the statistics were sufficient in that case to restrict men, but not women, from purchasing beer. **Ch. 9.**

QUESTION 7. **Get your gun.** Congress passes the "Second Amendment Restoration Act" (SARA), which requires that any state or local laws that burden an individual's right to keep and bear arms must satisfy strict scrutiny—meaning that the burden is on the government enacting the law to prove both that it served a compelling governmental interest and was narrowly tailored to effectuate that purpose. Outraged, cities and states with strict gun control laws sue, claiming that SARA exceeds congressional power. Congress responds that it is simply using its enforcement powers under the Fourteenth Amendment. It notes that it held weeks of hearings and compiled an extensive factual record of laws used to prevent otherwise law-abiding citizens from possessing firearms for their self-defense.

A reviewing court would likely:

A. Invalidate the legislation, because SARA is an attempt to alter the meaning of the Second Amendment, not to enforce it.
B. Invalidate the legislation, because Congress may not use its § 5 power to pass remedial legislation that does more than enforce the Constitution as interpreted by the Court.
C. Uphold the legislation, as long as Congress had a rational basis for concluding that the use of its enforcement power was warranted.
D. Uphold the legislation, as long there is some evidence to show that state and local governments had been abridging the right to keep and bear arms.

ANALYSIS. Recall that under the Court's case law, the Court's remedial legislation has to be both congruent and proportional; a mere rational basis is not sufficient. Therefore, **C** is not correct. The Court rejected Congress's attempt to "enforce" the Free Exercise Clause through the Religious Freedom Restoration Act because RFRA attempted to substitute Congress's preferred interpretation of the Free Exercise Clause for the one the Court provided in the *Smith* case. That attempt, the Court held in *Boerne*, circumvented the Article V amendment process and usurped the Court's power to, as Chief Justice Marshall put it, "say what the law is." Congress does have some power to provide remedies for the violation of constitutional rights, to the point of providing prophylactic remedies that attempt to head off violations—therefore, **B** is not correct—but it may not attempt to redefine those rights itself. **D** is not correct either, though, because more than "some evidence" is required, depending on the strength of the right Congress is attempting to protect. But here congruence and proportionality are rather beside the point, because Congress is attempting to substitute strict scrutiny for the less rigorous standard of review the Court applied in *Heller* and *McDonald.* Though it wasn't precisely clear what standard the Court did apply, most courts have interpreted it as something close to "intermediate scrutiny." In any event, the Court did not say that all laws regulating arms bearing had to pass strict scrutiny. Therefore, **A** is the best answer. **Ch. 10. C.**

QUESTION 8. Spot check. Consider the following hypothetical statutes:

I. A state statute exempting ceremonial use of peyote from state laws prohibiting its possession or use.
II. A state statute prohibiting private employers from discharging workers who refuse to work on their Sabbath day (either Saturday or Sunday) if their refusal is based on religious grounds.
III. A state statute making scholarships available to needy students who wish to pursue higher education, where one such scholarship is awarded to a student who wishes to attend a private, religious college and study for a career in the ministry.

Which of these would likely be held to violate the Establishment Clause?

A. I only
B. II only
C. I and II only
D. I, II, and III

ANALYSIS. This question again tests your comprehension of the Court's Establishment Clause doctrine. First, the *Smith* Court specifically called on religious groups seeking exemptions from generally applicable laws that burdened free exercise to petition the legislature. Such exemptions, like those granted for the sacramental use of wine during Prohibition, do not violate the Establishment Clause. Because statute I above passes muster, neither **A** nor **C** can be the correct answer. We also know that the indirect governmental support of religious organizations channeled through individuals choosing religious over secular schools also does not generally cause Establishment Clause problems. Therefore, III is likely okay, meaning that **D** is not the correct answer. That leaves II, making **B** the correct answer. The Court held that restrictions on private employers that benefit *only* religions present Establishment Clause problems. The facts of II resemble those in *Estate of Thornton v. Caldor*, 472 U.S. 703 (1985), in which the Court invalidated a Connecticut statute prohibiting employers from forcing employees to work on their Sabbath. **Ch. 7. C. 4.**

QUESTION 9. Misfire. The State of Ames passes a law requiring manufacturers and sellers of firearms to include, in their packaging, studies—disputed by gun manufacturers—that purport to demonstrate that guns in homes are more likely to be used to kill or injure the owner than for self-defense. What is the strongest argument against the Ames statute?

A. The statute is an invalid regulation of commercial speech.
B. The statute furthers Ames's interest in promoting a diversity of viewpoints.

C. The statute is not effective in promoting public safety.
D. The statute forces the manufacturer to engage in speech with which it disagrees.

ANALYSIS. The strongest argument would be **D**, because the manufacturer is being forced to associate itself with a message opposing the use of its product. Such attempts to force manufacturers to advertise opposing views would be subject to strict scrutiny and likely would be invalidated. **A** might look attractive, but it isn't the best answer: Ames isn't regulating the advertisement of guns or preventing the manufacturers from advertising guns as useful for self-defense. **B** is not correct, because Ames is forcing the manufacturer to present only one viewpoint—and one with which it disagrees. **C** is beside the point because the constitutionality of Ames's actions here doesn't depend on the efficacy of the message. **Ch. 6. F. 2.**

QUESTION 10. Brook-ing no disagreement. The City of Mountain Brook, through its Parks Department, oversees the public parks within the city limits. Overton Park is one such park. The Parks Department has issued a set of regulations governing park use. One regulation reads: "Overton Park is designed for the use of Mountain Brook citizens. Those wishing to use the Park must obtain a permit from the head of the Parks Department, who may refuse a permit at his discretion."

Overton Park is best described as:

A. A limited designated public forum.
B. An unlimited designated public forum.
C. A nonpublic forum.
D. A traditional public forum.

ANALYSIS. Because nothing in the facts suggests that the park was created by the city for any specific purpose or set of purposes, the best answer is **D**. Parks and sidewalks have historically been places where citizens congregate to exchange ideas and engage in speech. There is nothing to suggest that the park was created by the city for particular purposes or for all purposes; therefore, it isn't a "designated" public forum (either limited or unlimited) and neither **A** nor **B** is correct. It is obviously open to the public, so **C** is not correct either. **Ch. 6. D. 2.**

QUESTION 11. No Moore. Assume for purposes of this question only that the City of Mountain Brook, discussed in Question 10, passes an ordinance prohibiting the use of Overton Park for campaign rallies. Tom Moore, a candidate for governor, wishes to capitalize on his local roots by holding his rally in Overton Park, not far from where he grew up. Moore challenges the ordinance. The judge should:

A. Uphold the ordinance because it seeks to reserve the park for its intended purpose and is reasonable.
B. Uphold the ordinance because Overton Park is not a public forum.
C. Strike down the ordinance because it is not content-neutral.
D. Strike down the ordinance if Mountain Brook cannot demonstrate a compelling governmental interest and show that the ordinance is narrowly tailored.

ANALYSIS. Because the park is a traditional public forum, any content- or viewpoint-based limitations on speech will be subject to strict scrutiny, although neutral time, place, and manner regulations are permitted. The answer, therefore, is **D**, because the no-campaign-rallies ordinance is a content-based regulation. **A** is incorrect, because it improperly classifies the forum, as does **B**. And **C** is not the *best* answer, because lack of content neutrality does not *automatically* doom the ordinance, though it will be difficult for the City to justify the ban on campaign rallies only. **Ch. 6. D. 2.**

QUESTION 12. Green acres. New Utopia is a newly incorporated city in the State of Ames. Among the first ordinances passed is one that allocates votes to property owners in proportion to the amount of real and personal property owned, with every resident of New Utopia receiving at least one vote. For each additional $10,000 in real or personal property, a resident receives an additional vote. The extra vote(s) are justified on the ground that the more property one has in the city, the greater the stake one has in its governance. Peter, who owns little property and has only one vote, sues, claiming the extra votes awarded on the basis of property violate the Constitution. A reviewing court would likely:

A. Invalidate the ordinance, because it makes wealth a criterion for voting.
B. Invalidate the ordinance because it violates the Fifteenth Amendment.
C. Uphold the ordinance because voting may be restricted to those who have a special interest in the outcome.
D. Uphold the ordinance because the Constitution does not grant voting rights.

ANALYSIS. The Fourteenth Amendment has been interpreted by the Court to protect a fundamental right to vote. **D**, therefore, is incorrect. But **B** is incorrect as well, because the Fifteenth Amendment prohibits abridgement of the right to vote based on *race*, which is not at issue here. And while the Court has recognized withholding or granting votes based on a special interest in the outcome of the election, those decisions are largely limited to situations involving water utility districts where users are charged based on how much water they use or how much land they possess. In general, laws conditioning the franchise on the ownership of property or otherwise linking it with wealth are subject to strict scrutiny and usually invalidated. Therefore, **A**, and not **C**, is the correct answer. **Ch. 5. B. 2.**

QUESTION 13. Tenant troubles. Ames has passed a law prohibiting the summary eviction of tenants for refusal to pay higher rents. Eviction is now a multi-step process that requires a court order, and can take up to three months. A landlord sues, claiming that the new law is a taking for which he is entitled to compensation. A reviewing court would likely:

A. Invalidate the law, because it reduces the value of the landlord's properties.
B. Uphold the law, if it substantially advances legitimate state interests.
C. Invalidate the law, because it is tantamount to government seizure of the landlord's property for the benefit of nonpaying tenants.
D. Uphold the law, because the government regulation has not destroyed the value of the property and has not unreasonably interfered with the landlord's investment-backed expectations.

ANALYSIS. The landlord is making a regulatory takings claim, because the government has not actually or constructively effected a physical occupation of the landlord's property. That means that **C** cannot be the correct answer. Moreover, simply because the regulation may reduce the value of the land is not sufficient to trigger the per se approach of *Lucas*; simply making it more difficult to evict tenants does not destroy all economic value in a landlord's property. So **A** is out as well. **B** is not correct because the Court made clear in *Lingle v. Chevron U.S.A.*, 544 U.S. 528 (2005), that regulatory takings claims are covered either by *Lucas* and *Nollan and Dolan*—for total destruction or land exaction cases—or by *Penn Central*, the balancing test for all other cases. The *Penn Central* test is stated in **D**, which is the best answer. The value of his property has not been destroyed, nor have his investment-backed expectations been unreasonably disrupted. Owners of rental property enter that market aware that legislatures can, and often do, create rights for the benefit of renters. **Ch. 2. C. 5.**

QUESTION 14. Giving props. Ames's state constitution permits voters to amend the constitution through a referendum. Proposition 3 repeals existing laws that include antidiscrimination protections for homosexuals enacted at the state or local level and prohibits them from being reenacted without an amendment to the state constitution. After a bitterly contested campaign during the run-up to the vote, the "Yes on Prop 3" forces prevailed with a bare majority. Thereafter, several gay and lesbian individuals sued in federal district court, alleging that Prop 3 violated their rights under the U.S. Constitution. Which of the following is the strongest argument in favor of the plaintiffs' case?

A. The repeal denies gay men and women equal protection of the laws.
B. The repeal denies gay men and women due process of law.
C. The repeal denies gay men and women the right to further their political aims.
D. The repeal is a denial of gay men's and women's privileges or immunities of United States citizenship.

ANALYSIS. The facts in this question are similar to those in *Romer v. Evans* and Colorado's Amendment 2. The Supreme Court held in that case that the Amendment literally deprived Colorado's gay and lesbian citizens equal protection of the laws because, as interpreted by the state supreme court, Amendment 2 could be construed to, inter alia, prohibit local police departments from setting up special units to investigate bias crimes against gay men and women. **A** would, accordingly, be the strongest argument of the bunch. To hold that failure to add homosexuality as a protected class violates any due process rights would, contrary to *DeShaney*, hold that government has an affirmative obligation to protect individuals under the Due Process Clause. Moreover, though *Lawrence v. Texas* invalidated Texas's criminalization of homosexual conduct, the Court was equivocal on the question whether engaging in homosexual conduct was a fundamental right (*Romer* was similarly reticent). Therefore, **B** would not be the best answer. **D** is easily discarded because, after the *Slaughter-house Cases*, the Privileges or Immunities Clause of the Fourteenth Amendment has not done any significant work in American constitutional law. (Efforts to revive it in the *McDonald* case were rebuffed by eight Justices; the *Slaughter-house Cases* remain firmly in place and the Privileges or Immunities Clause will remain a dead letter for the foreseeable future.) You might have been attracted to **C**, but recall that the cases in which the Court invalidated ballot initiatives and referenda that prohibited certain remedies (like busing) or required special votes to approve laws that guaranteed equal rights in housing were cases involving attempts to combat racial discrimination. The Colorado Supreme Court invoked these cases in its ruling in *Romer*, but the U.S. Supreme Court said those cases were limited to remedies involving race and affirmed on different grounds (i.e., that Amendment 2 literally violated the guarantee of equal protection). Thus, **C** is not the best answer either. **Ch. 4. B. 3.**

QUESTION 15. Which one of these is unconstitutional? Which of the following would, if challenged in federal court, likely be invalidated as a violation of the Establishment Clause?

A. A state law offering financial relief to enable parochial schools in depressed areas to stay open despite declining student enrollment.
B. A state law reimbursing public and private school parents for the cost of after-school programs for academically at-risk students.
C. A federal law providing free textbooks for math, science, history, and economics to all public and private schools.
D. A federal law guaranteeing bonds issued by state governments or private parties to build public or private schools.

ANALYSIS. Much of the Court's jurisprudence in the area of financial assistance to parochial schools turns on the question of neutrality. If the program is neutral, providing aid to both secular and sectarian institutions, it is likely to be upheld. Of the four programs described above, all offer aid to both private and public institutions, except the program described in **A**, which would likely be unconstitutional because it benefits only religious institutions and might be said to advance religion, even if there is a valid secular purpose. **B** would be okay after *Mueller* and *Simmons-Harris*. **C** is constitutional after *Mitchell v. Helms*. Nor would **D** present serious constitutional problems, being rather like the tax exemption upheld in *Walz*. **Ch. 7. C. 2.**

QUESTION 16. Card check. Concerned that the patchwork of state laws governing the issuance of drivers' licenses and other forms of identification was a threat to national security, Congress passed a law requiring each U.S. citizen and resident alien to obtain and carry at all times a national ID card, which must be produced when requested by state, local, or federal law enforcement personnel. A number of people vigorously objected to what was seen as "Big Brotherism" run amok; several burned their IDs publicly, in protest. Federal law prohibits "forging, altering, or knowingly destroying or mutilating" one's ID card. When Alex O'Brien is convicted of violating this provision by burning his card in a protest against Big Government, he appeals, claiming that the law is unconstitutional. Which of the following would be most helpful to his claim?

A. If the destruction provision applied *only* to destruction or mutilation done as a means of protest.
B. If legislative history demonstrated that the purpose behind the destruction and mutilation provision was to deter those who might protest the national ID card from protesting in that manner.

C. Both A and B.
D. Neither A nor B because O'Brien is solely engaged in conduct, which is not protected by the First Amendment.

ANALYSIS. O'Brien *is* engaged in conduct, but it is obvious from the facts that his conduct has an expressive component, namely opposition to the national ID card law. As with flag burning or the burning of one's draft card, the "conduct" here is expressive and is protected by the First Amendment. Therefore, **D** can be eliminated as a possible answer. As long as the statute is content-neutral, however, it will be subject to the less demanding intermediate scrutiny standard of review. *But* if the purpose of the statute is really to suppress ideas, then it will be evaluated according to strict scrutiny. If, for example, the statute prohibited only that destruction intended as a protest, then it would be both content- and viewpoint-based, and thus subject to strict scrutiny. Similarly, if you could prove that—despite its facial neutrality—the purpose was to punish those who burned their cards in protest, that too would garner strict, not intermediate, scrutiny. Because either **A** *or* **B** would be helpful, that means that **C** is the best answer. **Ch. 6. A.**

QUESTION 17. Axe the tax. The State of Ames imposes a 5 percent sales tax on consumer goods, including books and clothing. Ames exempts religious literature, magazines, and items such as church vestments from the sales tax. Does this exemption violate the Establishment Clause?

A. No, because the exemption is required by the Free Exercise Clause.
B. No, as long as there is a valid secular purpose.
C. Yes, because religious items alone are eligible for the tax exemption.
D. Yes, because states may not grant any tax exemptions to religious organizations.

ANALYSIS. Generally applicable laws that indirectly affect religious observance are not infirm under the Free Exercise Clause. Therefore, **A** is not correct. But neither is **D**; the *Walz* decision, for example, upheld the deductibility of contributions to churches, along with other, secular charities. The watchword for the Court has been "neutrality": Is the aid available to secular and sectarian institutions or organizations alike? Under the facts here, which resemble those in *Texas Monthly*, the deduction aids *only* religious materials and thus amounts to government support of religion. Under the Establishment Clause, the exemption would be invalid. Therefore, **C** and not **B** is the correct answer. Benefiting *only* religious materials would tend to demonstrate the lack of a secular purpose. **Ch. 7. C. 4.**

QUESTION 18. Ladies night. Moe decides to increase the traffic at his bar by hosting "Ladies Night" and offering half-price drinks for women. Homer sues, claiming that the discrimination is unconstitutional. A reviewing court should:

A. Declare the classification unconstitutional, because it is not substantially related to an important interest.
B. Dismiss the suit, because beneficial gender classifications are permissible under the Equal Protection Clause.
C. Dismiss the suit, because Moe is not a state actor.
D. Declare the classification unconstitutional because it is based on the archaic and outmoded gender stereotype that unaccompanied women need an incentive to visit bars.

ANALYSIS. Don't you hate these trick questions? Just trying to keep you on your toes. The answer is **C**. Moe is not a state actor; thus, as a matter of *federal constitutional law*, his actions are not subject to review under the Fourteenth Amendment. Note, however, that some state and local laws would prohibit Moe from discriminating against males in this manner. **A**, **B**, and **D** are incorrect because they presume Moe is a state actor. **B** is incorrect also because not all "helpful" gender classifications are upheld. **Ch. 9.**

QUESTION 19. Arise, phoenix! The Phoenix Club is an association of men under 35 dedicated to assisting the Boys and Girls Clubs of Ames City. The Phoenix Club does not admit women as members. The State of Ames (in which Ames City is located) has a human rights statute that prohibits, among other things, gender discrimination in places of "public accommodation." If the Ames Supreme Court concludes that the Phoenix Club is a place of public accommodation, can the Phoenix Club be forced, consistent with the First Amendment, to admit women as members?

A. No, because that would infringe the Phoenix Club's freedom of association.
B. Yes, because the Phoenix Club would not be prevented from communicating its message by admitting women.
C. Yes, if the Phoenix Club is purely commercial in its mission.
D. Yes, because clubs and associations are not protected by the First Amendment.

ANALYSIS. Forced association cases turn on whether a group is engaged in expressive activity and whether the forced association of certain persons would hamper or interfere with the communication of that message. The facts in this question are similar to those in the *Roberts* case, concerning the Jaycees. Clubs are protected by the First Amendment, so **D** is not correct. **A** is not correct, because, as *Roberts* demonstrates, sometimes other social goals can outweigh the associational rights of groups. Justice O'Connor wanted the First Amendment not to apply to groups, like the Jaycees, whose purposes were, in her eyes, "purely commercial," but the Court did not decide the case on those grounds; therefore **C** is incorrect as well. That leaves **B**, which is the best answer. As long as the Phoenix Club is not prevented from communicating its message by the association—especially where the law is in the service of a compelling goal such as nondiscrimination—then the associational rights of its members have to give way to the statute. **Ch. 6. F. 1.**

QUESTION 20. **Life support.** The State of Ames enacts a law prohibiting the use of "do not resuscitate" orders and durable powers of attorney permitting surrogates to request withdrawal of food and hydration from incapacitated patients. Supporters say that in passing the statute the state is embracing a "culture of life." Amy created a durable power of attorney naming her parents as persons capable of requesting withdrawal of food or hydration from her if she became incapacitated in the future. Amy sues, claiming the law is unconstitutional. A reviewing court should:

A. Invalidate the law because it violates her right to refuse consent to unwanted medical treatment.
B. Invalidate the law because it is based on morality.
C. Uphold the law because it is rationally related to a legitimate state interest.
D. Uphold the law because there is no constitutional right to commit suicide.

ANALYSIS. The Ames law infringes on a liberty interest of Amy's; therefore, one must apply the Court's substantive due process jurisprudence. First, however, one can discard **D**, because it doesn't accurately frame the gravamen of Amy's claim. She is not claiming the right to end her life, though the withdrawal of nutrition and hydration would likely result in her death. The law, at any rate, treats the two acts as different. Rather, what she wants is to be able to empower a surrogate to act according to her wishes if she is unable to do so. Recall that in the *Cruzan* case, the Court assumed that individuals have a right to refuse unwanted medical treatment—a right the Court traced back to common law doctrines of informed consent necessary to prevent doctors and others administering care from being held liable for battery. The Court implied that something more than mere rational basis was necessary to infringe that right, though it declined to say whether it was a fundamental one or not. In the case, it held that it was not unconstitutional to require "clear and convincing evidence" of an individual's wishes before permitting surrogates to end life-sustaining treatment; the Court suggested that a "living will" or durable power of attorney would have satisfied the standard. Here, Ames has removed that possibility, thus depriving individuals of their right to refuse medical treatment at the point they need to exercise it most: when they become incapacitated. **A**, therefore, is the correct answer under *Cruzan*. **B** is not correct, because although *Lawrence* disapproved of Texas's invocation of majoritarian morality, the Court did not hold that all laws enacted owing to some moral sentiments were unconstitutional. Ames, for example, could justify the law on consequentialist grounds—that it is better to keep the person alive because death is irreversible, because you can't be sure the person wouldn't have changed her mind, and so on. **C** is not the correct standard of review. While the *Cruzan* Court was a little coy about the nature of the right, it did not simply accept Missouri's reasons for its clear-and-convincing evidence standard at face value. Moreover, Justice O'Connor and the dissenting Justices were clear that they thought the right to exercise the individual right through surrogates was a fundamental one. **Ch. 3. C. 4. (b).**

QUESTION 21. **Permission slips.** Ames State University, a public university, has a policy of requiring all students requesting contraceptives from Student Health Services to furnish parental permission before they can be dispensed. Ben and Carrie, both Ames State students, file suit in federal court, claiming that the policy violates their constitutional rights. A reviewing court would likely:

A. Dismiss the lawsuit because the university is not a state actor.
B. Dismiss the lawsuit because there is no constitutional right to obtain contraceptives.
C. Invalidate the policy because it violates the Equal Protection Clause.
D. Invalidate the policy because it interferes with their individual decision whether or not to have a child.

ANALYSIS. A state university is considered an arm of the state and therefore a state actor, to which the Fourteenth Amendment applies. Therefore, **A** is incorrect. **C** can be discarded as well, because what Ames State seeks to do is limit the liberty interests of *all* students, not just a class of them. After *Griswold* and *Eisenstadt*, we know that the right of privacy includes the right of individuals to decide whether and when to bear children, and that the government cannot duly interfere with that right. Between the remaining answers, then, **D** is correct; **B** is incorrect because the Constitution *does* protect individuals' rights to obtain and use contraceptives. **Ch. 3. C. 4. (b).**

Questions 22 to 24 concern the following facts: The State of Ames has a statute that defines and punishes the crime of "incitement." As defined by state law, "incitement" means "any speech or expressive conduct intended to produce imminent lawless action."

QUESTION 22. **Make a dent.** A group calling itself the Ames Nativists objects to the recent influx of immigrants into Ames's largest city, Tranquility. The leader of the Nativists, Ned Dent, gave a speech recently in which he urged Amesians to "take back our state by any means necessary." The rally at which Dent spoke was attended by several hundred people. In the days that followed, there were several attacks on recent immigrants. While no one was seriously injured, Dent was arrested and charged with violating Ames's incitement statute. Dent alleges that the statute is unconstitutional on its face. His challenge should:

A. Fail, because the statute meets the constitutional standard for punishing incitement.
B. Succeed, because the statue is content-based.
C. Succeed, because the statute does not meet the constitutional standard for punishing incitement.
D. Fail, because Dent's remarks are unprotected by the First Amendment.

ANALYSIS. *Brandenburg*'s standard for incitement requires that the speech be (1) intended to incite (2) imminent, lawless action and (3) be likely to do so. While the Ames statute includes elements (1) and (2), it omits (3). Thus, the answer is **C. D** begs the question. **B** is incorrect, because although the statute *is* content-based, incitement itself is not protected by the First Amendment because of the judgment that whatever expressive value incitement possesses is outweighed by the need to protect the social order. In other words, like other areas of speech outside the protection of the First Amendment, incitement is excluded from protection *precisely because of* its content. **A** is incorrect because the statute does not comply with the *Brandenburg* standard. **Ch. 6. B. 2. (a).**

QUESTION 23. **Incitement insight.** For purposes of this question only, assume that Ames passes a second statute punishing "incitement of racial hatred." This statute prohibits "any speech or expressive conduct intended to produce, and likely to produce, imminent lawless action against a person or group of persons based on their race, religion, citizenship, or country of origin." If challenged, a court would likely hold this statute to be:

A. Constitutional, because incitement is unprotected by the First Amendment.
B. Unconstitutional, because it is not viewpoint-neutral.

C. Constitutional, because a state may constitutionally punish group libel.

D. Unconstitutional, because the statute does not meet the constitutional standard for punishing incitement.

ANALYSIS. In this case, the new statute has been amended to take care of the earlier statute's *Brandenburg* problem by including the "likelihood" requirement. So **D** is not correct. However, the amended statute has another problem. Recall that *R.A.V.* invalidated St. Paul's ordinance for punishing hate speech that targeted certain kinds of hate speech based on the viewpoint expressed in that speech. The Court's conclusion was that the ordinance was viewpoint-based. Similarly, the statute here restricts punishment of incitement of racial hatred. It too, then, is viewpoint-based and unconstitutional under *R.A.V.* Therefore, **B** is the correct answer. **C** is not correct because though the Court has not officially overruled *Beauharnais*, the underpinnings of that case have been superseded by later Court cases. In any event, this is not a group libel statute; it clearly punishes incitement. **A** is incorrect, because although incitement isn't protected by the First Amendment, government cannot punish *only* incitement directed at persons because of their race or ethnicity. **Ch. 6. B. 5.**

QUESTION 24. **Do the (hate) crime, do the time.** Assume, for purposes of this question only, that Ames has a hate crime statute that provides for harsher penalties if one is convicted of the assault and battery of another and it is proven that the victim was chosen on the basis of race, religion, or national origin. One of Ned Dent's Nativist followers, Ted Wilson, was convicted of assaulting another, whom he had (wrongly) identified as an "immigrant." The jury concluded that, in fact, Wilson had selected the victim on the basis of this mistaken belief. The trial judge used that fact to sentence Wilson to additional jail time, as provided for by the Ames hate crime statute. Wilson appeals his conviction, alleging that the hate crimes statute is unconstitutional. The appeals court should:

A. Uphold his sentence, because the statute is constitutional.

B. Reverse his sentence, because the hate crimes statute is viewpoint-based.

C. Reverse his sentence, because the hate crimes statute punishes Wilson for his beliefs.

D. Uphold his sentence, unless Wilson proves that the statute's purpose was to punish ideas.

ANALYSIS. The facts here are reminiscent of those in *Wisconsin v. Mitchell*, in which the Court held that a similar statute did not violate a defendant's First

Amendment rights. If this surprises you, and seems in tension with the *R.A.V.* case, remember what, exactly, is being punished here: not speech of any kind, but a particular kind of assault. Assault and battery are not considered expressive conduct, even if politically motivated. The statute here punishes that conduct more severely if it is proven that the victim was chosen on the basis of race or ethnicity. The answer, then, is **A**. The other answers assume that the conduct at issue falls within the protection of the First Amendment. It is not the defendant's beliefs that are being punished here; rather, it is his acting on those beliefs that furnishes the basis for punishment. **Ch. 6. B. 5.**

QUESTION 25. Plate debate. The State of Ames has passed a law replacing the Ames state motto on its license plates with the phrase "I Support Our Troops." In addition, there is an old statute on the books that prohibits obscuring or altering any part of a license plate. Andy, a Quaker and an avowed pacifist, places a piece of tape over the phrase and is convicted in Ames state court of defacing his license plate. If he appeals his conviction, the reviewing court should:

A. Reverse the conviction, because the law forces the individual to carry the state's message.
B. Reverse the conviction, because the statute is not narrowly tailored to a substantial governmental interest.
C. Uphold the conviction, because the defacement statute is content-neutral.
D. Uphold the conviction, unless there is evidence that the defacement statute was intended to suppress ideas.

ANALYSIS. When, as in *Wooley v. Maynard*, the government attempts to force individuals to speak when they don't wish to, the regulation is subject to strict scrutiny. **B**, **C**, and **D** presuppose that the correct standard of review is intermediate scrutiny associated with content-neutral regulations of speech. Each is incorrect for that reason. That leaves **A** as the best answer, and the one that is in line with the Court's cases, such as *Wooley*. **Ch. 6. F. 2.**

QUESTION 26. Breach of contractors. 18 U.S.C. § 875 makes it illegal to "transmit[] in interstate commerce any communication containing any . . . threat to injure the person of another. . . ." Under binding Supreme Court precedent, this statute must be interpreted to apply only to those communications not protected by the First Amendment.

Easton is head of a group based in the United States that is opposed to American involvement in Afghanistan. He posts a website containing the names and addresses of all civilian contractors and their families who are currently working in Afghanistan, along with statements praising those who are actively engaged in armed opposition to the U.S.-led occupation. The website also contains statements that the information is being published so that the contractors might know the cost of continuing to participate in Afghanistan's occupation. Fearing for their safety as a result of the information posted on the website, several contractors quit their jobs and leave the country. The U.S. government prosecutes Easton under § 875, claiming that the posting of the names and the praise for the insurgents, in light of the violence in Afghanistan directed against those contractors, constituted a "threat." Easton claims his website is protected by the First Amendment. Which of the following would be *least* helpful to Easton's argument?

A. Evidence that many contractors stayed in Afghanistan.
B. Evidence that he did not intend that any violence come to the contractors.
C. Evidence that the message was communicated publicly to the contractors in general.
D. Evidence that nothing other than names and addresses were published on the website.

ANALYSIS. Of the answers, **B** is the best one. For a threat to qualify as a true threat, it is not necessary that the person issuing the threat have no intention to carry it out. What places threats beyond the protection of the First Amendment is the cost it imposes on the person to whom it is directed. **A** suggests that the contractors did not perceive the statements as communicating a real threat of physical violence. **C** would be helpful for similar reasons; the message, being communicated publicly, might be considered "political hyperbole," not a real threat to inflict bodily harm on those contractors. Finally, **D** would be helpful in defeating the claim that there was ever a communicated threat at all. **Ch. 6. B. 2. (b).**

QUESTION 27. Lo down. Bryson, a bookseller, was convicted of violating Overbrook City's ordinance prohibiting the selling of obscene material, because of his selling copies of *Lolita*, by Vladimir Nabokov. The book, which portrays the sexual relationship between an underage girl and a middle-aged man, was found to appeal to the prurient interest in sex, when taken as a whole, according to the contemporary community standards in Overbrook City. Further, the jury was instructed that it was to apply those same standards to decide whether the book had serious literary, artistic, political, or scientific merit; the jury concluded that it did not. On appeal, a reviewing court should:

A. Uphold the verdict, because the standard used follows the *Miller* test.
B. Reverse the verdict, because the judge instructed the jury to use community standards, as opposed to national ones, to evaluate the work as a whole.
C. Uphold the verdict, because obscenity is not protected by the First Amendment.
D. Reverse the verdict, because the jury instructions violated the *Miller* test.

ANALYSIS. According to the *Miller* test, legally obscene material must, taken as a whole, appeal to the prurient interest and portray, in a patently offensive manner, specific sexual acts proscribed by statute. It must also lack any literary, artistic, political, or scientific merit. Juries apply contemporary community standards to determine its offensiveness, but such determinations are subject to judicial review to safeguard against a particularly censorious group of jurors. Literary, artistic, scientific, or political merit, however, is *not* determined according to contemporary community standards. The jury instruction was, thus, in error, and **D** is the correct answer. Note, too, that the facts don't indicate that there was a statute specifying which sexual activities were proscribed. **A** is incorrect, because the *Miller* test isn't followed here. **B** is incorrect, too; LAPS is not determined by national standards. Rather, the presence of serious content is made according to a "reasonable person" standard. **C** is incorrect because the material is not legally obscene on the facts given here. **Ch. 6. B. 6.**

QUESTION 28. Fee simple. Ames State University collects an annual activity fee from each of its full-time students. Part of this money goes to fund student organizations that elect officers and have a faculty member agree to act as an advisor. When word got out that Ames students were forming a student group for gay, lesbian, bisexual, and transgender students, the Ames General Assembly passed a bill prohibiting state colleges from funding student organizations that refused to affirm their support for "traditional marriage," defined as marriage between a man and a woman. Denied funding and official recognition, the student group sues, claiming that the defunding decision violates the First Amendment. A reviewing court would likely:

A. Uphold the defunding, on the ground that no one has a right to have a state-funded student group.

B. Uphold the defunding, because the state is simply choosing not to subsidize groups that do not support traditional marriage.
C. Invalidate the regulation, because it is viewpoint-based.
D. Invalidate the regulation, because government may never use its funding power to discriminate against ideas.

ANALYSIS. Two answers can be rejected outright. First, it is not true that government can *never* use its funding power to "discriminate against ideas." In fact, when it chooses to subsidize some activities but not others, it is doing precisely that. Therefore, **D** is not correct. **A** can be discarded as well. While it is true that no one has a constitutional right to have a state-funded group, the state is nevertheless bound by the Constitution and could not, for example, agree to fund student groups for whites or for females. Between the remaining answers, **B** is not correct because although the government can choose to subsidize some activities over others, it cannot seek to suppress "dangerous ideas" by withholding funding on viewpoint-based criteria. According to the facts, the only groups excluded are those failing to support "traditional marriage"—meaning, of course, those that do support marriage between a man and a woman *will* get state monies. Because the regulation is viewpoint-based, it is likely invalid under the First Amendment; **C**, therefore, is the best answer. **Ch. 6. D. 5.**

QUESTION 29. Pensioned off. Facing an underfunded state pension that will be unable to fulfill pension obligations within the next ten years, the State of Ames enacted a law reducing the benefits both in the future and those owed to recent retirees, i.e., those who have retired within the last five years. Which of the following provisions would likely furnish the *strongest* basis for a constitutional challenge by existing recipients to the reduction in benefits?

A. Takings Clause.
B. Due Process Clause.
C. Contracts Clause.
D. Equal Protection Clause.

ANALYSIS. In fact, any suit filed would likely attack the new law under each of these provisions. Remember, though, that under the Equal Protection and Due Process Clauses of the Fourteenth Amendment, a court would likely apply a rational basis test to this legislation. The legislation neither infringes on a fundamental right nor classifies according to suspect or semi-suspect criteria. Any Takings Clause claim would likely be subject to the relaxed *Penn Central* balancing as opposed to the categorical rule of *Lucas*. That leaves the

Contracts Clause, **C**, which is the best answer. Recall that when a state governments attempts to impair the obligation of *public* contracts (such as those between the state and its pensioners) it is subject to heightened judicial scrutiny more rigorous than when the state impairs the obligation of private contracts. The Contracts Clause, therefore, furnishes the most promising basis for a constitutional challenge to the pension reform here. **Ch. 2. B. 3.**

QUESTION 30. Un-gunned. Under federal law, any person accused of sexual misconduct involving a minor, including possession of child pornography, must surrender all firearms as a condition of being granted bail. Andy was arrested for possession of child pornography. An avid gun collector, Andy sues in federal court, claiming that the provision regarding firearms violates his due process rights. A reviewing court should:

A. Find for Andy, unless it provides for a hearing to enable him to secure the return of his guns.
B. Find for Andy, because the law violates the Second Amendment.
C. Find for the government, because the regulation does not deprive him of liberty or property.
D. Find for the government, because the provision is rationally related to keeping guns out of the hands of criminals.

ANALYSIS. The Due Process Clause of the Fifth Amendment protects persons from deprivation of liberty or property without "due process of law." At a minimum, that requires notice and an opportunity to be heard. Here, the law deprives Andy of his property, his guns, following not conviction but merely accusation of some crime. Andy does not have merely a "unilateral expectation of" property in his guns. After *Heller*, we at least know that individuals have a right to private ownership of firearms in the home for self-defense. That means that **C** is not the best answer here. **B** is not responsive to the question; Andy is not challenging the law itself, he is simply arguing that he ought to have the opportunity to demonstrate that he shouldn't have his guns taken away. For similar reasons, **D** is not the best answer either. First, on the merits of the law, it seems to apply the wrong standard of review. *Heller* has been understood by most lower courts as requiring government to satisfy intermediate scrutiny, not a mere rational basis standard. Second, it is not responsive to the due process concern. That leaves **A** as the best answer. Because his right to possess firearms in his house for self-defense is a constitutional right, Andy at least ought to be afforded a post-deprivation hearing to get those guns back. **Ch. 3. B.**

QUESTION 31. *Casey* at bat. The Ames General Assembly recently passed a statute regulating abortion. Its main provisions are as follows:

I. An absolute ban on post-viability abortions.
II. An informed consent requirement that includes a 72-hour waiting period.
III. A requirement that minors seeking abortions obtain consent from at least one parent, but with a "judicial bypass" enabling a judge to waive the requirement for "mature" minors who cannot obtain parental consent.

Which of these provisions violate the Constitution?

A. I only.
B. I and II.
C. I and III.
D. All provisions are constitutional.

ANALYSIS. According to the *Casey* decision, states may regulate abortion pre-viability as long as they do not impose an "undue burden" on a woman's right to choose to terminate her pregnancy. The Court further held that an undue burden is one whose purpose or effect is to place a "substantial obstacle" in the way of a woman seeking an abortion. Post-viability, however, the state can ban abortions as long as exceptions are in place for the life and health of the mother. We know, then, that provision I runs afoul of *Casey* because the post-viability ban is said to be "absolute" and without any provisions for the life or health of the mother. So **D** can be eliminated. What about II? *Casey* upheld the 24-hour waiting period in Pennsylvania's statute, but the joint opinion suggested that anything in excess of 24 hours might be considered an undue burden. A three-day waiting period would very likely be considered as placing a substantial obstacle in the way of a woman seeking an abortion; therefore it, too, would be unconstitutional, meaning that **A** can be discarded. As for III, *Casey* upheld a provision similar to the one here. Because it would pass muster under *Casey*, **C** is not correct. The answer, therefore, is **B. Ch. 3. C. 4. (b).**

QUESTION 32. Old school ties. In the last year, the Ames General Assembly passed a law prohibiting Ames State University from considering race in the admissions process. Ames State University's admissions department, however, continues to grant admissions preferences to the children of alumni. A group of minority applicants challenged the admissions office's legacy preferences as racially discriminatory because until it was the subject of a court order, Ames State maintained a whites-only admissions policy. The applicants claim that as a result of the discriminatory admissions policy, the legacy preference benefits white students only and puts minority students at a decided disadvantage in admissions. A reviewing judge would likely:

A. Dismiss the applicants' suit, unless they prove that the legacy preference was put into place to intentionally disadvantage minority applicants.
B. Dismiss the applicants' suit because the policy does not discriminate on its face.
C. Invalidate the legacy preference because of the disparate impact it has on minority applicants.
D. Invalidate the legacy preference because preferring alumni is not a compelling governmental interest.

ANALYSIS. To state a claim for racial discrimination under the Equal Protection Clause of the Fourteenth Amendment, you first have to prove discriminatory intent. Although a statute need not be discriminatory on its face, disparate impact is insufficient to establish a racial discrimination claim after *Washington v. Davis.* One may therefore eliminate **B** and **C. D** may also be eliminated; it presumes that strict scrutiny is the applicable standard of review, which would be true only if it were proven that the legacy preference was instituted in order to disadvantage minority applicants. Therefore, **A** is the best answer of the four choices. **Ch. 4. C. 2. (c).**

QUESTION 33. **Combatant ban.** Lucy, a career army officer, sues the government over its continued ban of women in combat, alleging, among other things, that it limits female officers' chances for advancement. If a court upholds the ban, which of the following would be the most likely reason for leaving the ban in place?

A. The government's argument that women, by nature, are psychologically incapable of the violence required for combat.
B. The government's argument that women are physically weaker than men and thus unable to engage in combat.
C. The government's argument that Congress has the authority to "raise and support armies" and that the Court should defer to its judgment on issues such as the combat ban.
D. The government's argument that exposing women to combat would coarsen and "de-feminize" them.

ANALYSIS. Recall that the Court will permit legislators to make gender-based distinctions that are rooted in "real differences" between the sexes, but the classifications may not be made according to archaic or overbroad gender stereotypes or according to outdated notions of the proper societal roles that the sexes may occupy. Further, the "important" governmental interests to which those classifications must be "substantially related" must reflect the real reason for the classification, and not merely be some kind of post hoc justification created after litigation has commenced. **A**, **B**, and **D** all reflect different kinds of stereotypical notions about both the capabilities of women and what are and aren't "suitable" roles for women. None would be acceptable justifications on which to base the combat ban. But recall *Rostker v. Goldberg*, in which the Court upheld Congress's requirement than men age 18 and over, but not women, register for the draft. In part, the Court was careful to stress that it was Congress's responsibility to raise and support armies and that the Court's institutional competence was perhaps lowest when it was evaluating the military's personnel policies. If a court were to uphold the ban on women, the best of the four reasons would be **C. Ch. 4. D. 2.**

QUESTION 34. Driving Dixie down. Ames High School is a public high school in Ames City. The high school's dress code specifies that any student wearing an article of clothing deemed likely to cause a disturbance or hinder the learning environment of others will be asked to change the clothing or be sent home for the day with an unexcused absence. Ronnie, a student at the high school, wore a T-shirt emblazoned with a Confederate battle flag and the words "American by Birth . . . Southern by the Grace of God." Principal Skinner requests that Ronnie turn his shirt inside out; when Ronnie refuses, Principal Skinner sends Ronnie home. (Ames High School had recently been the scene of racial tension between black and white students. Skinner feared that Ronnie's shirt would trigger another round of disturbances.) Ronnie and his parents sue the principal and the school, claiming that Skinner's actions violated Ronnie's First Amendment rights. A judge hearing the case would likely:

A. Rule for Ronnie because there was no proof of disruption.
B. Rule for Ronnie because school officials may not ban speech merely because it is offensive.
C. Rule for the school because Ronnie's T-shirt is not speech.
D. Rule for the school because of Principal Skinner's reasonable fear that the T-shirt would cause a disruption.

ANALYSIS. *Tinker* held that student speech had to be disruptive, but it did not require the school to wait until the disruption had occurred to punish the speech or the speaker. Therefore, **A** is not correct. Further, **B** is not correct either, because the principal wasn't asking Ronnie to remove his T-shirt based on whether it was "offensive" or not, but rather on the principal's fear that it would trigger racial disturbances similar to those that had recently occurred. While *Tinker* said that a vague and undifferentiated fear would not suffice to ban speech, the facts indicate that Principal Skinner is not necessarily being alarmist by worrying about possible disruption. The best answer, therefore, is **D. C** is not the best answer because the T-shirt would be expressive activity, like Cohen's jacket or the *Tinker* children's armbands. **Ch. 6. D. 3.**

QUESTION 35. Carry on. The State of Ames bans the carrying of concealed weapons by anyone other than law enforcement personnel and licensed security guards. Barry owns several coin-operated laundries in Ames City and has to visit each of them to collect the money and service the machines. Several of the laundries are located in high-crime neighborhoods. When Barry is unable to secure a permit to carry a concealed weapon, he sues the state, claiming that the law violates the Second Amendment. A reviewing court would likely:

A. Rule for Barry because the Second Amendment guarantees the right to private firearm possession for self-defense.
B. Rule for Barry because the ban is not narrowly tailored to a compelling governmental interest.
C. Rule for the state because the Second Amendment applies only to the federal government and the District of Columbia.
D. Rule for the state because states may regulate the carrying of firearms outside the home.

ANALYSIS. This question is a little tricky because the Court hasn't provided a clear answer. Nevertheless, like many questions for which there isn't a clear-cut answer, you can back your way into the correct answer. First, recall that *McDonald* incorporated the Second Amendment through the Fourteenth Amendment and applied it to the states. Therefore, **C** can be eliminated at the start. Likewise, you can eliminate **A** because the Court was careful, in both *Heller* and *McDonald*, to stress that the right to private arms ownership is not unlimited. In fact, both decisions mentioned a host of restrictions that the opinion wasn't meant to call into question. **B**, moreover, does not recite the appropriate standard of review; while the Court was not explicit about the standard of review it employed in *Heller*, most lower courts have inferred from the opinion that intermediate scrutiny is the proper standard, not strict scrutiny. That leaves **D**, which is the best answer. The *Heller* Court stressed that the D.C. ordinance prohibited the use of arms in the home for self-defense; moreover, of the laws it didn't intend to call into question, one was the carrying of weapons in sensitive places. Some courts have interpreted this as leaving undisturbed traditional restrictions on the carrying of concealed weapons generally. **Ch. 8.**

QUESTION 36. Under water. The Ames City Waterworks is a privately owned utility that provides water to Ames City and surrounding communities. The Waterworks' policy is to cut off service to any customer whose bill is 30 or more days overdue. After Benny loses his job and falls behind in his payments, the Waterworks cuts off his water. Benny sues the Waterworks, claiming that he was entitled to notice and a hearing before his service was cut off. The summary discontinuance of service, he alleged, violated his due process rights. A reviewing court should:

A. Dismiss Benny's suit because the Waterworks is not a state actor.
B. Dismiss Benny's suit because he has not been deprived of a property interest.
C. Permit Benny's suit to go forward because the Waterworks is a monopoly.
D. Permit Benny's suit to go forward because the Waterworks performs a public function.

ANALYSIS. The question is whether the Waterworks is a state actor or not. Only if it is a state actor is it subject to the requirements of the Fourteenth Amendment. Two of the choices correspond to arguments that the plaintiffs made in *Jackson v. Metropolitan Edison.* In that case, the Court decided that neither the monopoly status of the utility nor the fact that it performed a public function was sufficient to render it a state actor. That means that neither **C** nor **D** is correct. **B** is incorrect because it presumes the matter in question: whether the Waterworks is a state actor. That leaves **A**, which is the best answer and the answer consistent with the *Metropolitan Edison* case. **Ch. 9. B.**

QUESTION 37. Hands jive. Ames City maintains a public park. One portion of the park has been designated "Speaker's Corner," where the public is invited to distribute literature, give speeches, or maintain displays of all types. The Ames City chapter of the National Abortion Action League has erected a giant pair of hands praying the rosary, with a sign explaining that the League is displaying the hands as a symbolic prayer for babies who were aborted in the past year. The city issued a permit for the display; it regularly issues such permits to all displays regardless of content. The Ames chapter of the ACLU challenges the display in the city's park as a violation of the Establishment Clause. In court, the ACLU's challenge would likely:

A. Succeed, because the city's grant of the permit constitutes an establishment of religion.
B. Fail, because the display is purely private in nature.
C. Fail, unless an average observer would think that the display is sponsored or endorsed by the City.
D. Succeed, because the display has no valid secular purpose.

ANALYSIS. The facts here are similar to those in the *Pinette* case, in which a plurality of the Court held that a purely private display in a public forum did not violate the Establishment Clause because it was private, not public, speech. Concurring Justices emphasized the importance of the sign in *Pinette* that made clear who was responsible for the display. The best answer is therefore **B. C** is not correct, because the endorsement test applies only when it is the government itself that is sponsoring the speech. **D** also implies that this is government speech; even if the *Lemon* test did apply, making available public space for private speech could be said to further the free and fair exchange of ideas and views—clearly a valid secular purpose, even if some of the messages or ideas exchanged are sectarian or religious in nature. **A** would not be correct because the permitting itself was done on a neutral basis. **Ch. 7. C. 3. (b).**

QUESTION 38. **Strum und drang.** Mountain Brook City Ordinance 123 provides:

> Section 1. It shall be unlawful for any person to litter a public park.
> Section 2. Violation of this ordinance shall be punished by a fine of not more than $100 or imprisonment for not more than 30 days.

Jean Strum organized a demonstration against corporate bailouts. The rally took place in Overton Park, a city park, and attracted about 100 supporters. During the rally, Strum delivered a speech to the people in attendance. At the conclusion of his speech, Strum said, "I'm sick and tired of the garbage in this administration. Here's what I think about their bailouts of corporate America." At this point Strum walked over to a trash can and dumped its contents on the ground. As the crowd cheered wildly, Strum shouted, "No more bailouts! Let's stop this garbage now!" After littering the park, Strum and his supporters left without picking up the trash. As a matter of constitutional law, may Strum be prosecuted under the aforementioned Mountain Brook city ordinance for littering the public park?

A. No, because littering the park in these circumstances could be construed as symbolic speech, and thus, it is protected from government regulation by the First and Fourteenth Amendments.

B. No, because the facts do not indicate that Strum's actions presented a clear and present danger that was likely to produce or incite imminent lawless action, thereby necessitating an abridgment of his freedom of speech.

C. Yes, because the city ordinance is narrowly tailored to an important and legitimate public interest, is not directed at the suppression of communication, and leaves open ample alternative channels.

D. Yes, because littering the park is conduct, not speech, and therefore it may not be treated by the law as communication.

ANALYSIS. Strum's littering, although conduct, had an expressive component. Therefore, it is misleading to say that it cannot be considered communication, as **D** does. Wearing armbands, burning draft cards or flags—these have been treated by the Court as expressive activity. The question is whether the First Amendment limits the ability to punish this expressive activity. But it is also incorrect to say that simply because the activity may be expressive, the state may not regulate it. So **A** isn't correct either. Looking at the ordinance itself, it is content-neutral and thus the incidental effects on expressive activity—assuming his littering to have some expressive content—must be narrowly tailored to some important public interest, not be directed at the suppression of ideas, and must leave open ample alternative channels of expression. Those conditions are met here. Keeping the park free of litter is undoubtedly an important and legitimate governmental interest; it's hard to see how to advance that interest other than by banning littering. The ordinance does not seem to be any sort of covert effort to squelch the expression of ideas, and it leaves open plenty of ways for Strum to express his opposition to bailouts. Therefore, **C** is the best answer. **B** is not correct, because it suggests the wrong standard of review. Strum is not being charged with inciting anyone to do anything. It is his actions themselves that are being punished. **Ch. 6. C. 3.**

QUESTION 39. **Display(cement).** Which of the following displays would be found most likely to violate the Establishment Clause if challenged in federal court?

A. An original mural in an old courthouse depicting lawgivers from myth and history, including Moses and Solomon.
B. The display of the Ten Commandments in a public school classroom.
C. A Ten Commandments monument donated by a private group to a state and displayed on the grounds of the state capitol, along with numerous other historical and commemorative markers.
D. A Christmas display that included a nativity scene among other, secular symbols of Christmas, including statues of Santa Clause and Frosty the Snowman.

ANALYSIS. The Court's decisions on religious displays on public property are all over the place, with one exception: The Court has consistently restricted the ability of *public schools* to indoctrinate students in religious matters. Therefore, **B** is the best answer. The other answers closely resemble the facts of cases in which the Court has held religious displays *not* to have violated the Establishment Clause. **Ch. 7. C. 3. (b).**

QUESTION 40. No sale. An Ames City ordinance bans the sale of handguns within the city limits. Dan, who lives in a high-crime area in Ames City, files suit in federal court, alleging that the ban violates his Second Amendment rights. A reviewing judge should:

A. Dismiss the suit, because the Second Amendment applies only to federal law or the laws of the District of Columbia.
B. Dismiss the suit, because the Second Amendment does not guarantee the right to buy a gun.
C. Strike down the ordinance, because the ordinance effectively denies Dan the right to own a handgun for self-defense in the home.
D. Strike down the ordinance, unless Ames City can show that its ordinance is narrowly tailored to a compelling governmental interest.

ANALYSIS. This one is a little tricky. The core right in *Heller* (which was incorporated through the Fourteenth Amendment in *McDonald*) is the right to possess a weapon, like a handgun, for self-defense, especially in the home. The city-wide ban on gun sales indirectly strikes at that core right, because a ban effectively forces anyone who wants one to leave the jurisdiction to get that which the Court says one is entitled to have. Therefore, **C** is the best answer. **A** is incorrect after *McDonald*. **B** is likely incorrect as a matter of law, since to exercise the right, one has to have the ability to purchase a handgun. **D** recites the wrong standard of review. **Ch. 8.**

QUESTION 41. Council conclave. The City Council of Ames City begins its public meetings with a prayer. The chair of the city council calls the meeting to order, rises, says "Let us pray," and recites a prayer that asks God for wisdom in the consideration of the city's business. He ends with "In the name of your son, Jesus Christ, Amen." Following the prayer, the first item on the agenda is taken up. Madeline, an atheist who had to appear before the council to request a variance from a city zoning ordinance, filed suit in federal court, claiming that the council's practice violates the Establishment Clause. Her suit will likely:

A. Fail, because prayers opening legislative sessions are constitutional.
B. Fail, because it did not occur in a public school.
C. Succeed, because prayers cannot be sectarian.
D. Succeed, because the facts suggest endorsement by the city council.

ANALYSIS. The Court's recent *Galloway* case upheld a city's practice of inviting clergy to open their meetings, but the Court took pains to note that there were limits. Therefore, neither **A** nor **B** is correct. **C** is not correct either; the Court expressly rejected petitioners' arguments that because the prayers at issue were sectarian, they were not covered by the Court's earlier decision in *Marsh v. Chambers.* That leaves **D**, which is the correct answer. By allowing the chair to lead the prayer himself and to end the prayer the way he did, the council strongly suggests that it is endorsing a particular type of religious observance, which could lead observers to conclude that favorable decisions depend on their adopting the same or similar religious views. **Ch. 7. C. 3. (b).**

QUESTION 42. Yes, Minister. The State of Ames has a Human Rights Act prohibiting discrimination in the workplace against employees based on race, sex, religion, age, sexual orientation, marital status, and parenthood. The state's Human Rights Commission brings suit against a local church for firing a teacher at the school it runs for becoming pregnant out of wedlock, contrary to church policies. The school claims that pastoral duties are within the teacher's job description; indeed, she went through a 12-week program for lay ministers and sometimes presides in chapel. May Ames constitutionally apply its Act to the church for firing the teacher?

A. Yes, because the Act is a generally applicable state law that only incidentally burdens free exercise.
B. Yes, because exempting the church would violate the Establishment Clause.
C. No, the church is constitutionally entitled to govern the conduct of its clergy.
D. No, because the Act is not narrowly tailored.

ANALYSIS. The facts here are similar to the recent *Hosanna-Tabor* case, in which the Court applied the ministerial exception to Title VII. As the Court there indicated, the Free Exercise Clause mandates that churches have power to designate who is and is not a minister, and thus subject to Title VII's statutory exclusion, which is similarly rooted in the belief that churches should be able to control the conduct of their clergy free from state interference. The correct answer, therefore, is **C. A** is incorrect, because the Court has concluded that a congregation's inability to control its clergy is not an incidental burden. **B** is not correct, either. The ministerial exception is not only required by the Free Exercise Clause, according to the Court, any attempt by the state to interfere with ecclesiastical decisions would itself violate the Establishment Clause. **D** misstates the standard of review. **Ch. 7. A.**

QUESTION 43. Weighty matters. In response to news stories that obese men and women were being discriminated against by employers, Congress responds with legislation prohibiting employers (including public employers) from discriminating against overweight job applicants and employees. The Act includes a provision permitting civil suits for money damages against employers who violate the Act. The State of Ames is sued by several job applicants who claim they were denied employment opportunities because of their weight. Evidence produced at trial found that one Ames department supervisor told one of the applicants that her office "didn't hire fatties." Ames argues that the Act is unconstitutional as applied to it. The U.S. government defends the Act as a valid enforcement of the Fourteenth Amendment. Is the Act constitutional, as applied to the State of Ames?

A. Yes, because Congress may abrogate state sovereign immunity by invoking its power to enforce the provisions of the Fourteenth Amendment.
B. Yes, because the Act is generally applicable to private and public employers.
C. No, because states may not be sued for money damages without their consent.
D. No, because the remedy is neither congruent nor proportional to the scope of the discrimination.

ANALYSIS. While Congress *may* abrogate state sovereign immunity—thus exposing the state to liability for money damages—under § 5 of the Fourteenth Amendment, the Court has held that in so doing, Congress needs to prove that its abrogation was "congruent and proportional" to the underlying violation of constitutional right. The more deferential the standard of review, the more evidence Congress needs to present that the problem is pervasive or intractable enough to warrant a federal remedy. Therefore, **A** is a necessary, but not a sufficient condition for abrogating sovereign immunity. **B** is irrelevant to the constitutionality of the abrogation. **C** is incorrect because, as noted, Congress can abrogate states' sovereign immunity in certain cases. That leaves **D**, which is the best answer. The Court has not recognized the obese as a protected class, therefore it would have to demonstrate much more than a single instance of discrimination against the obese by state officials to justify abrogation of state sovereign immunity. **Ch. 10. C.**

QUESTION 44. **Take me to the river.** The State of Ames enacted legislation that legalized gambling in riverboat casinos licensed by the State. Previously, the only form of gambling permitted in the state was at state-licensed dog tracks. Faced with declining revenues, the track owners persuaded the legislature to allow them to install slot machines on track premises. The legislature, however, taxed the revenue from track-based slot machines at a higher rate than casino-based ones. (Casinos, however, did pay other taxes on games of chance not available at the dog tracks.) The track owners sued in federal court, alleging the differential tax rates violated the Equal Protection Clause. A judge should:

A. Find for the State, because the rate is rationally related to a legitimate state purpose.
B. Find for the State, unless the legislature intended to discriminate against the track owners.
C. Find for the track owners, because equal protection principles require that like situations be treated alike.
D. Find for the track owners, because favoring the casino slot machines is not a legitimate state interest.

ANALYSIS. Under the Equal Protection Clause, rational basis review is the default standard of review for all legislative classifications that are not suspect or quasi-suspect. The rate at which gambling revenue would be taxed does not involve either a suspect or a quasi-suspect classification, therefore the challenger would have to demonstrate that there was either no legitimate interest or that there was no rational relationship between the classification and the state's interest. Moreover, if there is any conceivable reason for the classification, it will be upheld, regardless whether there is evidence the legislature relied on that rationale when it made the classification. The correct answer, therefore, is **A**. There could be any number of reasons for taxing the dog track slot revenue at a rate greater than slot revenue from the casino. The facts mention one: that the casinos paid taxes on other games of chance that the dog tracks did not. **B** is not correct because whether the classification was intended to favor one group over another is not relevant to its constitutionality, unless the groups involved members of protected classes. **C** is not so much wrong as it is unhelpful. Slots at dog tracks and those at casinos are arguably *not* "like situations." **D** is incorrect because the state has an obvious interest in collecting taxes from activities like gambling. Whether or not it was "favoring" casino slot machines is, again, not relevant to constitutionality under a rational basis standard. **Ch. 4. B. 2.**

QUESTION 45. Un-bearable. Which of the following laws would a court be *least* likely to uphold if challenged under the Second Amendment?

A. A ban on gun possession by someone convicted of a crime involving domestic violence.
B. A ban on gun possession by an habitual drug user.
C. A ban on sales of guns within the geographical limits of a city.
D. A requirement that guns be registered with local authorities so they could be returned in case of theft.

ANALYSIS. *Heller* recognized the right of law-abiding persons to possess commonly used firearms for self-defense in the home. In the opinion, the Court disclaimed any intent to call into question common prohibitions on gun ownership. These included convicted felons and those who are mentally ill. Based on this "safe harbor," neither **A** nor **B** is correct. Lower courts, in fact, have upheld gun possession bans by both groups. **D** is not a good answer either. A registration requirement would not inhibit the ability of someone to possess arms for self-defense; therefore, it would likely be upheld. That leaves **C**, which is the best answer. The right recognized in *Heller* implies the ability to obtain a gun in the first place. A ban on gun sales within a city's limits would indirectly strike at the core right recognized in *Heller*, and applied to states and municipalities in *McDonald*. **Ch. 8.**

QUESTION 46. Pants on fire. The State of Ames outlaws "false statements" made by candidates for political office about their opponents. If convicted, violators are subject to monetary penalties and even time in jail. A candidate challenging an incumbent for a seat in Congress alleged the incumbent supported "tax increases," which the incumbent denied. The incumbent had voted for a sweeping tax revision that had flattened rates, eliminated loopholes, and ended some deductions. Some fees were raised, however, and the fact that loopholes and deductions were eliminated meant some people's tax bills would rise as a result. The challenger was convicted of violating the statute; on appeal, he claims the statute is an unconstitutional restriction on free speech. A reviewing judge should:

A. Require the challenger to prove the statement is true.
B. Require the state to prove that the law is narrowly tailored to some compelling governmental interest.
C. Require the state to prove that the law is substantially related to an important governmental interest, does not restrict more speech than necessary, and leaves open ample alternatives for speech.
D. Apply the rational basis test because the speech is not protected by the First Amendment.

ANALYSIS. *United States v. Alvarez* refused to categorically exclude false statements about having won military honors from First Amendment protection. Therefore, neither **A** nor **D** is correct. The *Alvarez* Court then applied strict scrutiny because it was a content-based regulation of speech. That means **C** is out, because it recites intermediate scrutiny as the standard to be applied. That leaves **B**, which is the correct answer. **Ch. 6. B. 8.**

QUESTION 47. Preferential treatment. Which of the following statements about the Supreme Court's treatment of racial preferences in college admissions is *false*?

A. The Court will defer to administrators' good faith belief that racial preferences are necessary to obtain a critical mass of minority students.
B. Strict scrutiny applies to race-based preferences in college admissions.
C. Race-neutral means must be considered before adopting race-based preferences.
D. Securing the benefits flowing from a diverse—including racially diverse—student body is a compelling governmental interest.

ANALYSIS. The recent *Fisher* case clarified that uses of racial preferences must be strictly scrutinized by courts to ensure that, in fact, they are narrowly tailored to the government's compelling interest. This includes an inquiry into whether the ends could be achieved with race-neutral means. **B, C,** and **D** are all true statements; that leaves **A**, which incorrectly states the Court's holding in *Fisher*. **Ch. 4. C. 2. (c).**

QUESTION 48. Appraising grace. The State of Ames permits current property owners to pay property taxes based on the value of their homes when purchased. When existing houses are sold, however, the new owner pays property taxes based on the current appraised value of the home. Which of the following would be the best provision under which to challenge the state's property tax arrangement?

A. The Equal Protection Clause of the Fourteenth Amendment.
B. The Due Process Clause of the Fourteenth Amendment.
C. The Takings Clause of the Fifth Amendment, as incorporated through the Fourteenth Amendment.
D. The Privileges or Immunities Clause of the Fourteenth Amendment.

ANALYSIS. Because whether or not one's property is taxed on its current appraised value or not depends on whether one is an existing or a new property owner, the strongest ground for challenging the differential treatment is the Equal Protection Clause. **A** therefore is the best answer. However, the classification here is not a suspect one, and a deferential rational basis test would apply. **Ch. 4. B. 2.**

QUESTION 49. Car wars. Ames City, the capital of the State of Ames, strictly limits the number and type of cars for hire (including taxis and limos) able to operate in the city limits. Ubi is a start-up company relying on drivers using their own cars to pick up people who hail them using a smart-phone app. A city licensing body recently decided that Ubi drivers were subject to the city's licensing regime and ordered them to cease and desist until they comply with the expensive and burdensome regulations governing cars for hire. The owners of Ubi sue the city in federal court, claiming that the regulations violate their due process and equal protection rights under the Fourteenth Amendment. Which of the following statements is *true*?

A. Courts no longer apply economic substantive due process, thus their suit will be dismissed.
B. The court will apply heightened scrutiny if the regulations have no purpose other than to protect the interests of existing cab companies.
C. The court will apply a rational basis test to the regulations.
D. The suit will be dismissed because the right to earn a living is not a liberty interest protected by the Due Process Clause.

ANALYSIS. Though the Court doesn't apply heightened scrutiny to most economic regulations under the Equal Protection and Due Process Clauses, it is not correct to say that it doesn't subject them to *any* review. Therefore, **A** is incorrect. Nor is **B** true. Simply because the legislature chose to protect the interests of an existing group doesn't render its efforts suspect under either equal protection or due process principles. **D** is incorrect as well. The right of Ubi owners to operate their business *is* a liberty interest infringed by the regulations. However, heightened scrutiny is only available if they can prove that the right to run their business free of burdensome regulation is a *fundamental* liberty interest, which it is not. That leaves **C**, which is the correct answer. The burden will be on the business owners to prove that the regulations are not rationally related to any legitimate governmental interest. **Ch. 3. C. 3.** and **Ch. 4. B. 2.**

QUESTION 50. *Tinker,* Tailor. Andi Payne is the Assistant Principal at Ames High School. Which of the following students may she discipline without fear of violating the student's First Amendment rights?

A. The student who advocated legalization of marijuana as part of a persuasive writing and speaking class.
B. The student who wore a T-shirt from a popular local bar that read "Liquor up front, Poker in the rear" and refused to remove it when asked.

> **C.** The student who made comments in opposition to homosexuality and same-sex marriage that a teacher found offensive.
> **D.** The student who make an obscene gesture at a teacher off campus and during the weekend.

ANALYSIS. In holding that a school may punish a student who advocates illegal drug use in *Morse v. Frederick*, the Court noted that the banner-waving student at issue was *not* arguing for marijuana legalization as part of a class, or otherwise engaged in a discussion or debate on legalization. That suggests that **A** is not correct. *Morse* was also careful to reject arguments that schools may punish "offensive" speech, as defined by school administrators. Thus, **C** is incorrect as well. And while schools may punish disruptive or disrespectful behavior on school grounds and at school-sponsored events, the school's disciplinary writ does not run off campus and after school hours. Therefore, **D** is incorrect as well. That leaves **B**, where the student's suggestive T-shirt is rather like the lewd speech given by the student in the *Fraser* case. **Ch. 6. D. 3.**

> **QUESTION 51. Calling the tune.** Congress makes federal funds available to schools for drug education. In light of recent state decriminalization efforts, it has decided to require schools receiving federal funds to adopt, as official school policy, opposition to initiatives aimed at legalizing certain drugs like marijuana. A state school district in a state that is currently debating legalization of marijuana sues, claiming that the requirement violates the First Amendment. A reviewing court should:
>
> **A.** Rule for the United States, because it may condition the receipt of federal funds on compliance with its policies.
> **B.** Rule for the United States because there is no right to receive federal funds in the first place.
> **C.** Rule for the school district, because Congress may not impose speech restriction on the receipt of funds.
> **D.** Rule for the school district because Congress is forcing the district to adopt Congress's message as its own.

ANALYSIS. Congress may place conditions on the receipt of money, but it may not force a recipient to adopt the government's message as the recipient's own and penalize it if it does not. **A** is therefore incorrect because the government has done more than merely condition receipt on compliance with conditions on how the money is spent. **B** is incorrect because the Court has abandoned the right/privilege distinction that it formerly held. **C** is incorrect because the Congress *did* impose speech restrictions in *Rust* on recipients of federal funds, and the Court upheld them. That leaves **D**, which is the correct answer after *Agency for Int'l Development v. Alliance for Open Society Int'l, Inc.* **Ch. 6. F. 2.**

QUESTION 52. Play in the joints. Which of the following would be *required* by the Free Exercise Clause?

- **A.** The inclusion of students studying for the ministry in a state-run program that provided scholarships for academically gifted students.
- **B.** Permitting practicing ministers to serve as members of the legislature.
- **C.** An exemption from a law prohibiting possession of marijuana for members of certain religious sects who view smoking marijuana as a sacrament.
- **D.** An exclusion from gross income of the rental value of homes provided to ministers as part of their compensation.

ANALYSIS. "Play in the joints" is the Court's description of the area in which accommodations of religion can be made without violating the Establishment Clause, but which are not required by the Free Exercise Clause. Of those listed above, only **B** is required. *McDaniel v. Paty* held that Tennessee could not exclude practicing ministers from serving as delegates to a constitutional convention. None of the other choices are *required* by the Free Exercise Clause, but could, as a matter of legislative grace, be given without violating the Establishment Clause. **Ch. 7. B., C. 2., C. 4.**

QUESTION 53. Butt out! Ames City, the capital of the State of Ames, has decided to pass a sweeping smoking ban. Smoking will only be allowed inside private homes. All outdoor smoking is prohibited. Sam sues in federal court, arguing that she ought to be able to smoke outside on her own property. Which of the following would furnish the strongest basis for her claim?

- **A.** The Due Process Clause.
- **B.** The First Amendment.
- **C.** The Takings Clause.
- **D.** The Privileges or Immunities Clause.

ANALYSIS. The smoking ban implicates Sam's liberty interest and the Due Process Clause is the strongest basis for her claim; therefore, **A** is the correct answer. Neither of the other choices would provide much basis for challenging the ban: The ban doesn't implicate her rights to free expression or religious liberty, it doesn't take her property for public use without compensation, nor does it violate any of the privileges or immunities recognized by the Court in the *Slaughter-house Cases.* **Ch. 3. C. 3.**

Denning's Picks

1. **A**
2. **B**
3. **B**
4. **C**
5. **D**
6. **A**
7. **A**
8. **B**
9. **D**
10. **D**
11. **D**
12. **A**
13. **D**
14. **A**
15. **A**
16. **C**
17. **C**
18. **C**
19. **B**
20. **A**
21. **D**
22. **C**
23. **B**
24. **A**
25. **A**
26. **B**
27. **D**
28. **C**
29. **C**
30. **A**
31. **B**
32. **A**
33. **C**
34. **D**
35. **D**
36. **A**
37. **B**
38. **C**
39. **B**
40. **C**
41. **D**
42. **C**

43. **D**
44. **A**
45. **C**
46. **B**
47. **A**
48. **A**
49. **C**
50. **B**
51. **D**
52. **B**
53. **A**

Table of Cases

Index

T